CHOSEN

You have not chosen me but I have chosen you, to go and bear fruit that will remain. John 15:16

CHOSEN

How Christ Sent Twenty-Three Surprised Converts to Replant His Vineyard

EDITED BY DONNA STEICHEN

IGNATIUS PRESS   SAN FRANCISCO

Cover art:
Vincent van Gogh, *The Red Vineyard at Arles*

Photo Credit:
Erich Lessing / Art Resource, N.Y.

Cover design by Riz Boncan Marsella

© 2009 Ignatius Press, San Francisco
All rights reserved
ISBN 978-1-58617-340-1
Library of Congress Control Number 2009923625
Printed in the United States of America ∞

CONTENTS

FOREWORD

George Neumayr

In Gibbonian treatments of the decline and fall of post–Vatican II Catholicism, future historians will no doubt record this remarkable fact: even as the Church's roof collapsed, crushed by winds of change and "progress", converts sought shelter underneath it. Why, these historians will wonder, did anyone join this religion at the moment of its disintegration?

The deepest answer is contained in Donna Steichen's thesis, a thesis the conversion stories that she has collected in this book wonderfully illustrate. That thesis is simply this: Christ, not man, converts, and while His shepherds may flee, He stays, drawing until the end of time the lost and weary to life upon the unbreakable rock of His Church.

For many years, the American bishops' de facto evangelization policy was not to have one. And yet spiritual orphans of the age still crawled to the Church's door. Who was beckoning them to it if not Christ? Who was assisting their movement if not the Holy Spirit? No earthly attraction explains it. After all, the aesthetic glories of the Church, the pomp and power that attracted the superficial and glamorous in previous ages, had for the most part vanished in the drab years following Vatican II.

Thus, the conversions in the midst of the post–Vatican II crisis, compiled here by Steichen, seem particularly pure

and often entertainingly improbable, bearing testimony to
the central truth many of Christ's shepherds had forgotten
during it: that the Church is not a man-made institution
but a divine one—a perpetual repository of truth and grace
so powerful that not even the darkness of scandal can over-
shadow it.

Indeed, were the Church a man-made institution, conversions to it at the height of crisis would make no sense,
perhaps even appear morbid, like people purchasing a pill
after the FDA had declared it ruinous to one's health. But
since God, not fallible man, is responsible for conversions
to His indefectible Church, they can occur in any place
and at any time, even the worst. Christ the Good Shepherd
can take the shards of the broken fence—an emboldened
laity, a courageous bishop or two, a remnant of orthodox
schools and orders—and not only protect His flock but
enlarge it.

In the course of covering the crisis in the Church jour-
nalistically, I have often heard converts say that they entered
Christ's Church not because of His ministers but in spite of
them. A disaffected Anglican student at a secularized Jesuit
college once told me a story along those lines. He said that
upon informing a nun in Campus Ministry of his desire to
enter the Catholic Church, she replied sadly: "Why would
you want to do that?" Having lost interest in the faith herself, she found his eager interest in it baffling.

Such anecdotes are on one level dispiriting but on another
strangely consoling—inadvertent proof of the Church's essential dependence on Christ, who promised never to abandon her to persecution, either by the worldly outside her
or by the Judases inside her. As heresy occasions more lucid
presentations of doctrine, so scandal occasions purification,
a renewed cleaving to Christ and His Magisterium by a

shocked laity, who can then serve as new instruments of His grace.

At the root of the lack of interest in evangelization among many of the clergy is a crisis of faith, a suspicion that the Church is not divine but just a kind of global therapy center people can take a membership in if they happen to like it. And if they do not, who cares? To the extent that fervor exists among these clergy, it appears in the field of ecumenism, as they seek to patch up every religion on earth except their own.

In the meantime, they dismiss the Church's past missionary practices as intolerant, and if they do manage to muster up any enthusiasm for conversions, it is often directed at the wrong kind—converts to heterodox Catholicism. To "fundamentalist" faiths, they even propose what wags have called a prisoner exchange: we will take your liberals, if you take our conservatives.

I was struck by Walter Cardinal Kasper's remark after the Traditional Anglican Communion, a group that represents four hundred thousand people, requested entrance into the Catholic Church. The group's request sounded to me like good news. But not to him.

"We are on good terms with the Archbishop of Canterbury and as much as we can we are helping him to keep the Anglican community together", the head of the Pontifical Council for Christian Unity told the United Kingdom's *Catholic Herald*. "It's not our policy to bring that many Anglicans to Rome."

Never mind that at the very moment he was making this comment, the Vatican, under the leadership of Pope Benedict XVI, had issued a "Doctrinal Note on Some Aspects of Evangelization" reiterating that bishops exist to "lead all humanity to Christ in the Church."

Had the first bishops, the apostles, adopted Cardinal Kasper's ambivalence, they would have shooed crowds away from Jesus as they approached Him to hear His words of salvation. These are, to say the least, mystifying times, in which many of the bishops welcome the worldly hetero-dox with one hand, then halt orthodox searchers with the other; in which they lower the bar of entry for the Tony Blairs even as they elevate it for the traditionalists.

Fortunately, orthodox searchers can still hear Christ's voice through all the ecumenical din and false teaching, and this book is rich in that compelling drama. From witches to the witch doctors of modern medicine, from ferocious skeptics and sinners to ordinary ones, Christ's call to conversion was heard—a call that sounds louder and louder in our age of exhausted hedonism.

Whispering to man in his pleasures, shouting at him (as C. S. Lewis said) in his pains, God speaks to modern man at the terminus of failed secularism, chanting softly: "Come to me, all who labor and are heavy laden, and I will give you rest. Take my yoke upon you, and learn from me; for I am gentle and lowly in heart, and you will find rest for your souls. For my yoke is easy, and my burden is light."

George Neumayr is the editor of Catholic World Report *and a prolific contributor to other journals.*

INTRODUCTION:
A SECOND SPRING, AFTER ALL?

Donna Steichen

Life is hard, we are told, because we have to live it forward but we can only understand it backward. Catholic history, like all history, charts unforeseen crises, days of disrepute unexpectedly succeeding days of glory. The future for which people were prepared was seldom the one they met. In retrospect, we can see how each era sprouted from the one before it, but when they occurred, they seemed to spring from nowhere.

However bad the times were, though, there was always wheat springing up among the thistles. There was always grace enough to inspire heroes to oppose the evils of the day and to nurture the saints Christ sent to rebuild His Church.

During the twentieth century, the Church in America experienced two radically dissimilar eras in a dismaying downward sequence. Now, in the early years of the twenty-first century, she finds herself mired in shame. Predictions about her future seem to depend on the direction one faces.

Look one way, and doom appears inevitable. Forty disappointing years of liturgical degradation, empty catechesis, unchecked theological dissent, clerical desertion, feminist subversion, and general episcopal weakness devastated a thriving Catholic subculture like an interminable pandemic of bubonic plague.

Enabling those disasters were bishops unsuited to revolutionary times. Except for a few radical ideologues and the
rare pathological deviant, midcentury American bishops were
conspicuously ordinary men, better suited to careers as com-
pliant civil servants than as gallant defenders on the barri-
cades of doctrine.

Over four damaging decades, most of the direct liturgical and catechetical wounds were inflicted on the faithful
by agents of the bishops' swelling bureaucracies, but as with
mishandled sexual abuse cases, blame must ultimately rest
on the executive responsible for giving orders and approv-
ing results. The year before he died, Pope John Paul II
revealed his grasp of the problem when he told American
bishops making *ad limina* visits, "The necessary reform of
the Church in the United States calls above all for the interior renewal and conversion of bishops."

At first glance, then, it might seem that the Church's
current crisis is entirely a matter of bad management. But
her rapid decline really began in academia, with theolo-
gians and other scholars who saw themselves as a more
enlightened "second magisterium",[1] free and even obliged
in conscience to dissent from any doctrinal formulae defined
by the "first Magisterium". To accept the traditional definition of theology as "faith seeking understanding" in service to the Church would compromise their professional
integrity, they declared.

They began by demeaning Holy Scripture as the myths
of primitive peoples trying to explain human ills. Soon they
were questioning Church doctrines on the Incarnation, the
Virgin Birth, the Resurrection, the origins of the Catholic

---

[1] Richard McCormick, S.J., "The Relation of Theological Reflection and
Analysis to the Magisterium", *National Catholic Reporter*, August 7, 1968.

Church, and transubstantiation. Challenges were issued to
the exclusively male priesthood and to Catholic teaching
on sexual morality, beginning with contraception and rapidly including homosexuality and priestly celibacy. So swiftly
did those notions spread that, by 1976, at a "Call to Action"
meeting initiated by the National Conference of Catholic
Bishops (NCCB) but dominated by church professionals,
delegates voted to direct the Church to "reevaluate its positions" on homosexuality, birth control, priestly ordination
of women and married men, female altar servers, and democratic decision making on matters of doctrine.

In parishes, numerous priests adopted such views. So did
directors of religious education, mostly women religious and
former religious who had left parochial classrooms to assume
these newly specialized posts in a proliferating ecclesiastical
bureaucracy. Soon they were imposing their new opinions
on the bewildered laity. A great many Catholics were assured,
in confession, in college classes, even in marriage preparation classes, that they were free to attend their children's
invalid weddings lest they alienate them and that decisions
about contraception were theirs to make.

Most of the faithful, however, were first disoriented by
abrupt liturgical innovations. Every Mass seemed to bring
another surprise: hand holding through the Canon, readings from *Time* magazine in place of epistles, noisy inter-
ruptions as worshippers introduced themselves all around,
homilies scoffing at defined dogmas, urgent invitations to
stand in the sanctuary with the celebrant. Even those who
liked the bouncy new hymns found such novelties unsettling.

The NCCB declined to accept the Call to Action report.
But whether because they were daunted by dissenters' academic credentials, overwhelmed by executive responsibilities, or simply unwilling to fight, most bishops kept silent in

their own sees. Instead of disciplining subordinates who openly rejected defined dogma, they shifted their obligation for decisive action to their NCCB colleagues, and beyond them to staff "experts" at the United States Conference of Catholic Bishops, squandering the Church's resources on "renewal" programs that ranged from ineffective to relativist.

At the same time, few showed sympathy for believers who begged for protection from aggressive liturgical, catechetical, and sex education modernizers. The pastoral failures of the period stir up chilling images from the Old Testament book of Ezekiel, written during the Babylonian exile, when the Israelites were being assimilated into the surrounding pagan culture:

> Thus says the Lord GOD: Ho, shepherds of Israel ... you do not feed the sheep. The weak you have not strengthened, the sick you have not healed, the crippled you have not bound up, the strayed you have not brought back, the lost you have not sought, and with force and harshness you have ruled them. So they were scattered, because there was no shepherd; and they became food for all the wild beasts. (Ezekiel 34:2–6)

Presented with such ambiguity and confusion about Catholic dogma, moral doctrine, and the spiritual order, millions of lay Catholics concluded that the Church has no claim to truth and thus no moral authority to command them. Judged by reported contraceptive use; numbers of children; and rates of sterilization, abortion, divorce, and attempted remarriage, Catholic family life became statistically indistinguishable from that of the secular world. Between 1968 and 1998, marriage annulments in the United States rose from 338 to 50,498.[2]

---

[2] Kenneth C. Jones, "Annulments", in *Index of Leading Catholic Indicators: The Church Since Vatican II* (St. Louis, Missouri: Oriens Publishing Company, 2003), 70.

Between 1965 and 2000, regular attendance at Sunday Mass declined from 65 percent to 25 percent.[3]

Then, in 2002, the sex abuse scandals poured over the stunned faithful like a massive sewer break. Not since the fifteenth-century days of Pope Alexander VI and his Borgia offspring has the Church's reputation sunk so low. Scorn for bishops has replaced trust. Across the Catholic spectrum, from the rebel hives of Call to Action and the disdainful precincts of *Commonweal* to such bastions of militant orthodoxy as *New Oxford Review*, voices now warn that the Church has passed the point of feasible restoration. Those who predict her permanent exile to the cultural lunatic fringe point to the 2008 Pew Forum Survey on Religion and Public Life. Based on extensive sampling, its results indicate that the third-largest religious grouping in the populace, 10 percent of all Americans, consists of fallen-away Catholics.

It will be easier to interpret the present trajectory of Catholic affairs when another forty years have passed, but to those who perceive it entirely as a management crisis, the current situation admittedly looks dismal.

Yet, if we look in another direction, it appears that a promising new era has begun in the Church's life. While the old Catholic culture was withering into arid wasteland, a quiet tide of grace was rising out of the dry sand, lapping around the beached keel of Peter's bark, and beginning to lift it.

It is the thesis of this book that we can trust Christ's words to Peter: "Upon this rock I will build my Church, and the gates of hell shall not prevail against it" (Matthew 16:18). He has never abandoned her in her many previous

---

[3] James R. Lothian, "Mass Attendance", in Jones, *Index of Leading Catholic Indicators*, 72–76.

crises, and He will preserve and sustain her again. True to
His promise, the Church never stays dead.

How will restoration come about today, when the means
of evangelization established in healthier times are corrupted, the usual messengers of hope compromised and
shamed? Who, in this grim era, has the authority, credibil-
ity, and sanctity to restore her to health? Only Christ Himself can restore His Church, as Ezekiel foretold when he
wrote, "I myself will pasture my sheep; I myself will give
them rest, says the Lord GOD. The lost I will seek out, the
strayed I will bring back, the injured I will bind up, the
sick I will heal" (Ezekiel 34:15–16, NAB).

He is doing so by pouring out His grace on those He
has chosen to do His work. Even as the shepherds were
failing to protect their flocks, even as their hirelings were
failing to teach the faith, ardent believers among the laity
began taking up the bishops' neglected tasks. Usually without episcopal direction—often even against it—and with
scant help from clergy or religious, they started doing them
out of necessity. But in fact, many were responsibilities properly suited to a well-formed laity, as the fathers of the Second Vatican Council spelled them out in *Lumen Gentium*,
the Dogmatic Constitution on the Church.[4]

In the pro-life movement, for example, the laity proved
bolder, shrewder, and more creative than their bishops, less
anxious about losing political favors, less fearful of media
scorn. Lay activists lobbied lawmakers; addressed any audiences willing to listen; debated abortion advocates; wrote
articles, books, and letters to the editor; published newspapers and journals; and designed pro-life advertisements.
Struggling to be both wise as serpents and gentle as doves,

---

[4] *Lumen Gentium*, chapter 4, "The Laity", 201–6.

they set up telephone hotlines, invented sidewalk counseling, and established a nationwide chain of independent crisis pregnancy programs to link pregnant women and their babies with medical and subsistence care. Working in tandem with evangelical allies, they slowly but effectively helped turn public opinion against unrestricted abortion.

When "new catechetics" taught transient liberal opinion as morally binding while failing to teach even rudimentary Catholic doctrine, concerned parents decided they must assume responsibility for their children's education. Thousands turned to homeschooling. Some developed curricular materials and designed teaching support programs to aid other families seeking the same end. Many parents who themselves had suffered from religious illiteracy learned Catholic doctrine for the first time while teaching it, often from the long-neglected *Baltimore Catechism*. Across the nation, other conscientious Catholics, lay and religious, opened small, independent orthodox Catholic academies.

The pioneer ventures among the new Catholic colleges—Thomas Aquinas College in California, Christendom College in Virginia, Magdalen College and Thomas More College in New Hampshire—were established by laymen to provide orthodox alternatives to long-established institutions grown too secular to hand on the treasures of the faith. Demand for orthodox Catholic education brought a dramatic revival to Franciscan University at Steubenville and led to the launch or rebirth of a growing number of other colleges, among them Ave Maria University in Florida, Belmont Abbey College in North Carolina, Benedictine College in Kansas, John Paul the Great Catholic University in San Diego, the University of Dallas, Southern Catholic College in Georgia, and Wyoming Catholic College.

Lay members formed the backbone of the Catholic charismatic movement, a protective haven for many whose faith
was shaken by the upheaval. Other vital new movements
like Opus Dei, Communion and Liberation, Focolare, and
the Neocatechumenal Way are also largely lay enterprises.

In addition to flourishing new or reborn Catholic publishing enterprises operated by priests and laity together (for
example, Ignatius Press and Scepter Press), publishing houses
launched by laymen include Sophia Institute Press, Emmaus
Road Publishing, and Neumann Press. Recent examples of
lay-initiated journals include *This Rock*, *Lay Witness*, *New
Oxford Review*, *Fidelity*, *Crisis*, *Culture Wars*, and *Latin Mass*,
as well as the long-established *Wanderer*.

Which description is true of the laity, then? Are they
valiant disciples or lax doctrinal illiterates? In fact, both images
are accurate portraits of different constituencies, in different
times and places. If Christ chooses them, and they respond
by immersing themselves in the rivers of His grace, the lax
can become valiant.

We have seen the effects of His grace in the faithful remnant through these decades of crisis. Now that passing years
are shrinking their numbers, we see the same grace at work
in the lives of their children, offspring of the pro-life movement, and products of home schools, private academies, and
the new movements. Graduates of the newly orthodox colleges make up a significant proportion of these assertive young
Catholics, whose mere existence evokes amazement and anxious analysis in liberal academic circles. Some of them wear
T-shirts cheerfully proclaiming "Top Ten Reasons to Stay
Roman Catholic", "Summorum Pontificum: Wake Up and
Smell the Incense", "A Rosary a Day Keeps the Demons
Away", or "I'm the Catholic the Liberal Media Warned
You About". *National Catholic Reporter* columnist John Allen

recently wrote that their brand of "evangelical Catholicism" constitutes "the most powerful current at the policy-
setting level of the church, as well as a dynamic constituency
at the Catholic grassroots." At the Church's "policy-setting
level", it is expressed as what Allen calls Pope Benedict XVI's
"affirmative orthodoxy". Among young "evangelical Catholics", he notes, an identifying characteristic is a voluntary
embrace and public assertion of traditional Catholic belief,
language, and practice.[5]

Promising as they are, however, these children of the remnant remain a minority of their generation and of the whole
Church. Where will Christ find new disciples to help them
rebuild her today? In each of her past crises, she was preserved, sustained, and restored by holy men and women,
called by Christ and infused with the gifts of the Holy Spirit
to defend His Church. Whether or not they were ever can-
onized, those disciples were all prophetic witnesses, so deeply
committed to restoring her beauty and integrity that they
ignored personal cost and bore courageously whatever suffering their mission entailed. They seldom achieved all they
hoped for, but their gallant dedication to the faith moved
others to accept it as true.

Where will recruits be found to join them? In the answer
to that question we see most dramatically the working out of
Christ's promise that the Gates of Hell will not prevail against
His Church. God is still making His grace available today, just
as He did when He showed Ezekiel that He can raise an army
by restoring life to dry bones (Ezekiel 37:1–14). We should
not be surprised to see astonishing acts from the Savior, who
told the Pharisees that if His disciples failed to honor Him,

[5] John L. Allen Jr., "All Things Catholic", *National Catholic Reporter*, March
14, 2008.

the very stones would cry out (Luke 19:37–40); natural
impossibility is no hindrance to Him. No one can predict
whom He will choose: the great-grandson of that most scan-
dalous of popes, Alexander VI, became the great Saint Francis Borgia, second only to Saint Ignatius Loyola himself
in organizing the Society of Jesus and, with Saint Charles
Borromeo, one of the most important figures of the
Counter-Reformation.

We see that same grace acting in the lives of the twenty-
three authors who tell their conversion stories in these pages.
They were not drawn to the Church by sound evangelization programs but by Christ Himself. Despite their marked
differences in origin, education, and field of service, each
one makes it clear that it is Christ who did the choosing.
They testify that Christ touched their hearts and inter-
vened in their lives in unexpected, sometimes even miraculous, ways to call them to become living stones, working
with Him to rebuild His Church from the ruin into which
she has fallen (1 Peter 2:4–9). Some of their accounts are as
astonishing as if they had been drawn from a collection of
medieval miracle stories.

Christ can find converts anywhere, no matter how
unlikely the place or time might seem: in secular leftist
academia, in prison, within a family of atheists, in an occult
company of goddess worshippers, even among yawning
pewsitters nominally within the Catholic Church. Of the
unexpected themes that have emerged in the editing of
this collection, the most striking is God's persistence.
Extraordinary times demand extraordinary means. All the
stories in this book tell of the extraordinary measures He
is currently using to call new disciples into His service
and thus to restore all things in Himself. Over and over,
their stories demonstrate how patiently Christ pursues His

resistant quarry, down the nights and down the days, as long as may be necessary.

The late Pope John Paul II often predicted that the Church would enter a second spring in the new century. Perplexed listeners wondered what signs he could be seeing of such a new Pentecost, of which the rest of us caught no glimpse. Now we begin to see. Even if secular society should fall into ruin, even if all other shepherds should fail, Christ Himself will rescue His Church, just as He promised. As the Lord told Ezekiel, then "you shall know that I, the LORD, have spoken, and I have done it" (Ezekiel 37:14).

Chapter 1

Only the Beginning of the Adventure*

Elizabeth Fox-Genovese

An adult conversion to Catholicism—or indeed to any form of orthodox Christianity—is not an everyday occurrence in the American academy. Most secular academics seem to receive any profession of Christian faith with a vague sense of embarrassment. Adherence to Judaism or Islam is another matter, although why is not immediately self-evident, since both impose stringent demands upon their faithful. Perhaps they meet with greater tolerance because they are less familiar, perhaps because, whatever the reality, they do not carry Christianity's taint of having long figured as the religion of a male European elite that allegedly used its faith to cow others into submission. Nor does it change anything to remind skeptics that, in the United States, Catholics long suffered a discrimination that was, in its way, almost as implacable as that suffered by black Americans. A vague, nondenominational Christianity—or, better yet, Unitarianism—may be acceptable, but Catholicism lies

* This article was originally published in April 1, 2000, in *First Things: A Monthly Journal of Religion and Public Life*. It appears here with the permission of the author.

beyond the pale. Catholicism is not something that people "like us" embrace.

Thus when, in December 1995, I was received into the Catholic Church, my nonbelieving colleagues tactfully refrained from comment, primarily, I suspect, because they literally did not know what to say. More likely than not, many of them assumed that, having lived through some difficult years, I was turning to faith for some form of irrational consolation. Consequently, from their perspective, to acknowledge my conversion would, implicitly, have been to acknowledge my vulnerability. Others, who were less sympathetic, doubtless assumed that my turn to Rome reflected what they viewed as my reactionary politics, notably with respect to abortion. From their perspective, I had exiled myself from acceptable conversation of any kind.

I have no intention of berating my colleagues or other secular academics, but rather to call attention to aspects of the prevailing secular mind-set that make the idea of conversion virtually incomprehensible. For secular academics, the language and practice of faith belong to an alien world. Not understanding faith, they are ill prepared to understand conversion to it. Having long participated in the reigning discourse of secular intellectuals, I understand all too well where they are coming from, and I readily acknowledge that indeed "there but for the grace of God go I."

More important, however, my long apprenticeship in their world allows me to reflect upon their unreflective assumptions, for those assumptions cut a broad swath through our culture as a whole, challenging faith at every turn. So firm is their hold upon our culture that they are imperceptibly permeating the fabric of faith itself, constantly challenging the faithful to justify and rejustify our beliefs.

Believers, in sharp contrast to nonbelievers, welcome conversion stories as heartening evidence of God's grace and the workings of the Holy Spirit. The conversion of a secular intellectual in particular seems to snatch a soul from the very jaws of feminism, Communism, nihilism, atheism, or some other fashionable secular ideology. Given the broad gap between belief and nonbelief that both sides perceive, it is not surprising that both hostile and sympathetic observers expect conversion stories to be dramatic. Like Saint Paul on the road to Damascus, the convert is generally expected to have experienced a moment of blinding illumination followed by a radical change of life. This expectation testifies to a widespread sense that the tenets of faith and those of the world, of Jerusalem and of Athens, are in conflict. While emphatically not disputing the significance of the deep differences between the views and attitudes of believers and those of nonbelievers, I did not myself experience conversion as a radical rupture with my past. This is not to say that I did not experience the journey to belief as what my students call "life-changing": in essential ways, I did. Nonetheless, in other ways I did not. In many respects, my conversion fit neatly—almost seamlessly—into the continuum of my life, and from this perspective, it was a natural stage in the journey rather than a new departure.

For practical purposes, I grew up a nonbelieving Christian. Wait a minute, you may fairly protest, is that not an oxymoron? How can a nonbeliever describe herself as Christian if faith constitutes the essence of Christianity?

Time and again throughout the Gospels, Jesus evokes belief in Himself and the Father, who sent Him as the only test or standard. Think of Martha at the time of Lazarus' death: "Yes, Lord; I believe that you are the Christ, the Son of God, he who is coming into the world" (John 11:27). And

Martha is not alone. Time and again petitioners receive what
they seek because Jesus fulfills their belief. As He tells Martha,
"I am the resurrection and the life; he who believes in me,
though he die, yet shall he live, and whoever lives and believes
in me shall never die" (John 11:25–26). A Christian, by
definition, is one who accepts Jesus Christ as his personal
Savior and, no less important, as Lord. Everything depends
upon belief.

The story of modernity has arguably been one of the
marginalization and discrediting of belief, or, perhaps more
accurately, its relegation to the realm of radical subjectivity.
Modernity, in other words, has systematically divorced faith
from moral and intellectual authority. Until well into the
twentieth century, however, the mounting assaults on faith
did not entirely erase the living legacy of Christianity from
Western culture. If nothing else, the moral teachings of the
Decalogue and the Sermon on the Mount continued to
receive a measure of respect—in exhortation if not uni-
formly in observance. My early years conformed precisely
to this pattern, especially with respect to the Decalogue,
which my parents took with utmost seriousness. In retrospect, it seems to me that my father especially never doubted
the truth of Dostoyevsky's troubling question: "If God is
dead, is not everything permitted?" Yet neither he nor my
mother was a believer, and neither taught us to believe.
Like many other honorable and upright modernists, they
apparently grounded their strong sense of morality in the
integrity of the individual.

Throughout my nonchurchgoing, nonbelieving adult years,
I had always considered myself a Christian in the amorphous cultural sense of the world. Having been reared on
the Bible and Protestant hymns, I was conversant with the
language and basic tenets of Christianity. I had, moreover,

been reared with a deep respect for the great Hebrew prophets, assorted Protestant leaders, and Catholic saints, and even the unique value of Jesus Christ as the preeminent exemplar of loving self-sacrifice. Never, I am grateful to say, did I, like too many secular intellectuals, denigrate or disdain believing Christians, whom I had always been inclined to regard with respect. But for long years, I did not give much thought to joining their number. By the time I had completed college and then graduate school, I had so thoroughly imbibed materialist philosophy that it did not occur to me to look beyond it. My quests, such as they were, focused upon the claims and contours of moral worthiness in a world that took it as a matter of faith that "God is dead."

Over the years, my concerns about morality deepened, and my reflections invariably pointed to the apparently irrefutable conclusion that morality was, by its very nature, authoritarian. Morality, in other words, drew the dividing line between good and bad.

During the years of my reflection, however, the secular world was rapidly promoting the belief that moral conviction, like any other idea, expressed the standpoint of the person who enunciated it. And it was becoming a widely shared belief that there were as many moralities as there were people and that it was inappropriate to impose one's own morality on another whose situation one could not fully understand. Although as predisposed as any to respect the claims of difference, whether of sex, class, or culture, I increasingly found this moral relativism troubling. It seemed difficult to imagine a world in which each person followed his personal moral compass, if only because the morality of some was bound, sooner or later, to clash with the morality of others. And without some semblance of a common standard, those clashes were more than likely to end in one or another form of violence.

My more wrenching concerns, however, lay elsewhere. Thinking and writing about abortion had led me to an ever greater appreciation for the claims of life, which were so often buried beneath impassioned defenses of a woman's right to self-determination, especially her right to sexual freedom. When I began to think seriously about the issue, my commitment to women's right to develop their talents predisposed me to support the legality of abortion, at least up to a certain point. Even then, I found it impossible not to take seriously the life of the fetus that was being so casually cast aside. The emerging discussions of assisted suicide only intensified my discomfort, as I found myself worrying about one human being deciding whether another's life is worth living.

How do we know? I kept asking myself. *How ever can we know?*

Today, it is easy to see that I was instinctively revolting against a utilitarian or instrumentalist understanding of the value of human life. For I did understand that as soon as we admit as a serious consideration whether our obligations to others are inconvenient, the value of any life becomes negotiable. At this point, as you will note, my internal struggles still unfolded within a secular framework, although I fully appreciated that devout Christians and Jews viewed reverence for life in its most vulnerable forms as a divine commandment. Indeed, I was slowly coming to envy the certainty that religious faith afforded, and I began to think seriously about joining a church. At the same time, I knew that no matter how noble and well-intentioned, worldly preoccupations were not an adequate reason for doing so.

As if barring my path to church membership stood the figure of Jesus Christ. The churches I most respected all required that prospective members affirm their personal faith in Christ as Lord and Savior. I did not question the legitimacy of the requirement, but nothing in my previous life seemed to have prepared me to meet it. To the best of my knowledge, I had no personal experience of religious faith and no real grasp of its nature. When I was twenty, Andre Amar, a brilliant professor of philosophy and a devout Jew, had spoken to me of religion as a realm unto itself, irreducible to any other, and his words had lodged in my mind, but I did not fully understand them. To this day, I cannot point to a single moment of conversion, no blinding light that opened my eyes, no arrow that pierced my heart. Almost imperceptibly, the balance between doubt and faith shifted, and, on one ordinary day, it came to me that I had decided to enter the Catholic Church.

It would be easy to think that my decision, however lacking in drama, represented the end of my journey to faith. Instead, it marked only the beginning of what is proving to be an adventure I could not previously have imagined. The Sunday after reaching that decision, quietly and alone, I went to Mass at the Cathedral of Christ the King in Atlanta. Both my Catholic-born but at the time unbelieving husband and my devoutly Catholic friend and graduate student Sheila O'Connor would happily have accompanied me, but I did not tell them where I was going.

I had not attended a Mass since my youth, during visits to France, and then only rarely. I had no clear idea of what to expect, although I knew enough to know that I could not receive Communion. Yet an almost visceral instinct told me that this first direct encounter with the faith I was planning to embrace was something I could not foresee and must undertake alone.

By now, most of my specific memories of that morning have merged with the countless times I have attended Mass at the cathedral since. All that stands out is my response to that first hour, as a Catholic-to-be, of confronting the figure of the crucified Christ that dominates the cathedral. There, directly in front of me, was the Lord I had pledged myself to serve—a Lord whom as yet I barely knew and who nonetheless seemed to hold me fast.

Shortly thereafter, thanks to the help of Sheila's mother, I began to receive instruction from Father Richard Lopez, the remarkable priest who remains the confessor and spiritual director for my husband and me. Father Lopez rapidly determined that I was much more familiar with Catholic theology than he had reason to have expected, and thereafter his instruction focused primarily upon the practice, rituals, and traditions of Catholicism. Between our meetings, I read the *Catechism of the Catholic Church* and other books on the elements of Catholicism, attended Mass, and learned and said prayers.

During the meetings, Father Lopez guided me through the practical meaning of words and rituals. We discussed the significance of the colors priests wear during the different seasons of the liturgical calendar, the role of the Virgin Mary and the saints as intercessors, the structure of the Mass, and more. In retrospect, what astonishes me is how much I learned and how little I truly understood.

For the words we exchanged, valuable as they were, remained mere words. Learning them felt like a privileged initiation, but I used them rather in the way in which one learns to say the beads of the Rosary before one begins to grasp the immediacy of the events they signify.

In deciding to enter the Church, I had decided that I believed in Christ Jesus and accepted Him as my Lord and Savior, but even as my love for and commitment to the Church deepened, I remained unsure of precisely what my faith meant or from whence it derived. Father Lopez reassured me that faith and faithfulness were, above all, matters of the will rather than the emotions, which, he insisted, remain inherently suspect. His words conformed to what I had learned from my own reading in Catholic theology and eased my occasional misgivings about the elusiveness of my own feelings. On the day of my reception, which included the sacraments of baptism, confirmation, penance, marriage, and Communion, a transformative joy consecrated a decision that now seemed to derive as much from the heart as the mind.

That joy, although varying in manifestation and intensity, has persisted since. But my understanding of its meaning has not ceased to change and grow. Today I see more clearly than I could at the time that much of my initial hesitation and diffidence derived from my unconscious persistence in materialist habits of thought. Like any good rationalist, I kept looking for unambiguous explanations for my turn to faith, and although the possible candidates abounded, none clearly stood out as the reason. It took two or three years for me to begin to understand that the decisive action had not been mine but God's. In principle, we all know that faith is a gift or grace, not a personal accomplishment. But if my case is as common as I suspect it is, we find this knowledge surprisingly difficult to believe and make fully ours. Thus, with the best of intentions, we try to earn that which lies beyond the reach of even our most heroic efforts and which exceeds any merit we can conceive.

An important part of what opened me to Catholicism—and to the peerless gift of faith in Christ Jesus—was my growing horror at the pride of too many in the secular academy. The sin is all the more pernicious because it is so rarely experienced as sin. Educated and enjoined to rely upon our reason and cultivate our autonomy, countless perfectly decent and

honorable professors devote their best efforts to making sense
of thorny intellectual problems, which everything in their environment encourages them to believe they can solve. Post-
modernism has challenged the philosophical presuppositions
of the modernists' intellectual hubris, but, with the same stroke,
it has pretended to discredit what it calls "logocentrism",
namely, the centrality of the Word. In the postmodernist universe, all claims of universal certainty must be exposed as delusions, leaving the individual as authoritative arbiter of the
meaning that pertains to his situation. Thus, what originated as a struggle to discredit pretensions to intellectual
authority has ended, at least in the American academy, in a
validation of personal prejudice and desire.

Sad as it may seem, my experience with radical, upscale
feminism only reinforced my growing mistrust of individual pride. The defense of abortion especially troubled me
because of my inability to agree that any one of us should
decide who has the right to live. But my engagement with
faith drew me into more general reflection about the importance of charity and service in the life of the Christian.
Initially, I had shied away from the idea of the imitation of
Christ and even from the entreaty in the Universal Prayer
to "make me holy." Such aspirations struck me as the ultimate presumption: Who was I to pretend to holiness, much
less to the imitation of our Savior?

Gradually, those fears began to dissipate, and I found myself
meditating upon the Gospels' teaching on service, above
all, that "the Son of Man did not come to be served, but to
serve and to offer His life as a ransom for all" (Matthew
20:28). Having been received in the Church on the day
after the Feast of the Immaculate Conception, I also pondered the Holy Mother's response to the Annunciation: "Let
it be done unto me according to Thy Word" (Luke 1:38).

The injunctions to charity and service unmistakably applied to all Christians, but it was difficult to deny that, since the moment of the Virgin Mary's response to the Angel Gabriel, they applied in a special way to women. Her example, as Hans Urs von Balthasar has reminded us, offers the exemplary embodiment of faith. "Faith is the surrender of the entire person: because Mary from the start surrendered everything, her memory was the unsullied tablet on which the Father, through the Spirit, could write His entire Word."[1]

It is incontestable that, throughout most of history, women have suffered injustices and abuse that cry out for redress. It is no less incontestable that the path to justice and dignity for women—the recognition of their equal standing with men as human persons—cannot lead through the repudiation of the most basic tenets of our faith. No amount of past oppression can justify women's oppression of the most vulnerable among us—or even our repudiation of our own specific vocation as women.

Pope John Paul II has written extensively on the special dignity and mission of women, frequently provoking the shrill opposition of feminists, especially Catholic feminists. Above all, feminists deplore his insistence upon the abiding differences between women and men and upon women's exclusion from the priesthood. I would be astonished if, at one point or another, every woman has not tasted some of that anger, the outraged sense of "Why me? Why should I always be the one to give?" And it does not help if men interpret women's yielding as proof of men's superiority.

Not expecting Heaven on earth in the near future, I see little prospect that either of these responses will simply

---

[1] Hans Urs von Balthasar, *Mary for Today*, trans. Robert Nowell (San Francisco: Ignatius Press, 1996, orig. edition 1987), p. 45.

evaporate. Yet both miss the key to the Holy Father's theology of the person, namely, that the essence of our humanity lies in our capacity for "self-gift". This understanding
links our relations with one another to our relation to God,
reminding us of the danger of treating another person as an
object. It also suggests that, whether in relation with others
or in communion with God, our highest realization of self
results from the gift—or loss—of self.

In our time, it is countercultural indeed to see the loss or
effacement of self as an admirable goal. Our culture's obses-
sion with identity and the rights of the individual seems to
suggest precisely the reverse. You will nonetheless recall the
first Beatitude: "Blessed are the poor in spirit, for theirs is
the kingdom of heaven" (Matthew 5:3). For years the passage, when I thought of it, puzzled me. In what way was
poverty of spirit to be seen as desirable, especially in a Christian? And what, precisely, did poverty of spirit mean? I
had left the question, together with others that I hoped
someday to understand, in the back of my mind until I
happened upon Erasmo Leiva-Merikakis' eye-opening explanation in his *Fire of Mercy, Heart of the Word: Meditations on
the Gospel according to St. Matthew.*[2]

Pointing out that this is not merely the first of the
Beatitudes, but the only one in the present tense, Leiva-
Merikakis explains that the poor in spirit are those who
literally "beg for their life's very breath"—those who depend
upon God the way we all depend upon air to breathe. Poverty of spirit is the grace of those who have emptied themselves of everything but the desire for God's presence, "who
offer God a continual sacrifice from the altar of their spirit,
and the sacrifice in question is the very substance of their

[2] Ignatius Press, 1996.

being" (p. 187). And those who achieve poverty of spirit have their reward in the present as well as the future, for to live in poverty of spirit is indeed to live with God.

A decisive moment in my journey in faith came when, one day, seemingly out of nowhere, the thought pierced me that Jesus had died for my sins. And, immediately on its heels, came the devastating recognition that I am not worth his sacrifice. Only gradually have I come truly to understand that the determination of worth belongs not to me but to him. God's love for us forever exceeds our control and challenges our understanding. Like faith, it is His gift, and our task is to do our best to receive it. The knowledge, even when partial and imperfect, that He loves us also opens us to new responsibilities and obligations. For if He loves us all, He also loves each of us. And recognition of that love imposes on us the obligation to love one another, asking no other reason than God's injunction to do so. As fallen human creatures, we are nonetheless likely to continue to search for human reasons that justify our loving service to those in whom we find little or no obvious redeeming value. And the best human reason may be found in the faith that God has freely given us: our nonjudgmental love of the other remains the condition of God's love for us. For, knowing how little we merit His love, our best opening to the faith that He does lies not in the hope of being better than others but in the security that His love encompasses even the least deserving among us.

Elizabeth Fox-Genovese was the founding director of the Institute for Women's Studies at Emory University in Atlanta, where she was the Eléonore Raoul Professor of the Humanities. She stirred astonishment and controversy among her academic peers when she entered the Catholic Church in 1995. She died on January 2, 2007.

Chapter 2

Searching for the Mind of God

Susan Bujnak

The time is October 1982. The place is the Conventual Francis-can residence in Rome. The occasion is the upcoming canonization of Saint Maximilian Kolbe. My husband and I are drinking caffè lattes with a priest friend; against the background of the lush gardens, an Italian television camera crew is interviewing Francis Gajowniczek, the Polish sergeant whom Saint Maximilian replaced in the starvation bunker of Auschwitz.

After breakfast, we meet Mr. Gajowniczek and his wife. He talks about his survival, the fact that he was chosen to live while others died. "Why? Why me?" he asked himself over and over. "I'm so unworthy."

The guilt traumatized him. "Finally," he said, "when I went back to Poland I understood that I had been chosen to be a witness to God's love, the love that enabled Saint Maximilian to lay down his life for me in the horror of Auschwitz."

I think every convert to the Catholic faith at some time or another asks, "Why me? Why did God choose me?" My conversion, so unlikely from the circumstances of my life, has been a gift from God. I've been chosen, like a tugboat in the harbor, to lead others to the shore. This story describes His grace as I saw it, the mercy from Heaven that rains down and covers the whole broken world.

My birth in Ogden, Utah, coincided with the Battle of Britain, and in some ways our mixed-religion household mirrored the war; each side wanted to win. This was not done consciously, but in all my parents' decisions concerning their children's religion, there was tension—and then to ease the tension, benign neglect.

My parents were raised in Christian homes, in a religious culture—they were charitable and generous to a fault. Like parents everywhere, they wanted us to be happy. My brilliant, restless father and my artistic mother loved their three children and surrounded us with every good thing that the post–World War II boom economy offered. That we would be crushed by the tidal wave of a changing America was inconceivable in the forties and fifties. That Almighty God wanted to give us something infinitely more valuable than material goods and culture, they never realized.

We moved from Ogden to Mount Vernon, Washington, when I was three. My childhood was colorful, calamitous, and painful—a portent of my future, an expulsion from the Garden of Eden. My moral formation was driven by the American culture that in the forties was still outwardly Christian but not necessarily religious. My parents went to church, sort of. My father, a lapsed Catholic, usually stayed home and made breakfast for the family. My mother, a Low Church Episcopalian who found herself in a High Church parish, faithfully took me to Sunday worship with her. Religion was acknowledged in our family—we always had a crèche at Christmastime—but it was not well understood. (When God was mentioned, He was used as a prefix.) Not being Protestants, we didn't study the Bible. Not being Catholics, we had no catechism. Christmas meant Santa Claus and Bethlehem. My mother would hand-dip chocolate fondants, bedeck the holiday tables, and make jeweled angels for the

Christmas tree and eggnog for the parties. Easter meant shopping in Seattle—new clothes, complete with spring bonnet and white gloves. And it meant flowers from my father: he always bought fragrant gardenia corsages for my mother, my sister, and me and a white carnation boutonniere for himself and my brother. Easter also meant an egg hunt, baskets overflowing with colored marshmallow bunnies, and white sugar Easter eggs with little farm scenes surrounded by royal icing. We probably went to church, but I never connected Easter with religion.

To be fair, religious symbols for Easter suitable for young children are not naturally attractive. The wounded God-man on the Cross is a far cry from Baby Jesus in the manger. But this childhood satisfaction of my senses remained deep in my psyche; it would later draw me into Judaism and then Catholicism. No Cromwellian confession of faith could ever supplant it; no nihilistic philosophy could ultimately compete.

I don't remember learning anything in Sunday school except how to make a wooly lamb. Children were separated from the adults until after the homily, at which time we marched upstairs to join the congregation for the Episcopalian Creed: "I believe in one holy, catholic, and apostolic church ..." At one point, and this was probably the first time I used my reason, I told my parents that I didn't believe in any of the articles in the Creed, I could no longer claim that I did, and I would like very much to stay home with Dad and make breakfast. They agreed. I was about eight years old.

The government funded Christian practices in the forties. In Washington State, we said both the Pledge of Allegiance and the Our Father prayer every day in grammar school. But I was an adult before I discovered that neither the pilgrims nor Francis Scott Key wrote the Our Father. Nor is God an old man with a long white beard. And the Gospels are not just songs that blacks sing in Southern Baptist churches.

Where did I learn about right and wrong? On reflection, I think it was from western movies. Every Saturday I would sit in a darkened theater and watch the good cowboys (they wore white hats) arrest the bad cowboys (they wore black hats). Roy Rogers, Tom Mix, and the Lone Ranger were my teachers: in these American heroes, courage was everything. It was simple. You helped the little guy; you stood up to the bully. (This praise of courageous action would later influence my fascination with the various subcultures and "heroic" antiestablishment cultures of the sixties and seventies.) Although I dimly realized the law said you could do certain things and you couldn't do other things, I never connected the law to moral actions. So, if it was legal, it was a good thing, it was American, it was right. If it wasn't against the law, then it was allowed. From western movies I learned there are moral judgments to be made, but I had no tools for choosing between them. (Dostoyevsky's character Ivan said, "If there's no God, then everything is permissible.") What was right and what was wrong? About what should I be courageous? What happens when the bad guys start wearing white hats?

Along with movies, my childhood was influenced by the fairy tales I read. These stories are awash with deeds of good and evil. The comings and goings of the invisible world appealed to me—I developed a taste for mystery, a yearning for the unknown kingdom where upright deeds are eventually rewarded. Again, the paths to happiness were the virtues of courage and kindness. The fact that the good princess was always beautiful made a big impression on my young mind; I equated beauty with morality for years afterward. Thus were my strivings, such were my heroes. Armed with western movies, fairy tales, and movie magazines, I faced the culture of the fifties. The social norms were few: you wore gloves and a hat when you went out in public, and you never wore white shoes in San Francisco—that sin was left to the tourists from Los Angeles. Meanwhile, the battle cry of our set was, "If the going gets tough, go to Hawaii."

I did have a personal relationship with Jesus when I was young, although I didn't know He was connected in any way to religion. Where this friendship came from, humanly speaking, I don't know. But when I talked to Him, I knew somebody was there. This lasted until about the age of twelve, and then, well . . .

I don't remember losing Him. It was like when you're gardening late and then you realize that really you can no longer see what you're doing, so you go into the house. The falling away was gradual, "a sleep and a forgetting";[1] day turned into twilight, and twilight into night, until finally in my teens all was dark, and I never noticed. Twenty-three years later, when the light of Christ ultimately overcame my darkness, however, it was a precipitous event.

In the meantime, I was nourished at the table of my culture. By now, we were living in California after a five-year residence in Vancouver, British Columbia. The consequences of my parents' benign neglect opened the door to an increasingly fragmented existence: I was a leader in high school, but my preoccupation with "finding myself" dominated my life, and as a result there was a lot of pain. I tried to do some good by joining the pioneer civil rights movement, the National Association for the Advancement of

---

[1] William Wordsworth, "Ode: Intimations of Immortality".

Colored People (NAACP), but I was quickly pulled out in the belief that it was a Communist-front organization. My churchgoing high school friends intrigued me, and on one Sunday or another I attended every one of their places of worship: Lutheran, Methodist, Presbyterian, Mormon, and Baptist. I even made an altar call at a Billy Graham crusade, but when the emotional rush subsided, I forgot all about it, and they never contacted me. The Mormons attracted me because of their strong families, but I couldn't relate to their virtuous life. It seemed to me that in order to be a Mormon you had to be perfect, which I wasn't—nor did I want to be. Still, I admired them.

Many years later, I discovered that a number of my Protestant friends were actually Jewish. In my mind, they were the warm, interesting ones, which may explain why I liked them so much.

By the end of the fifties, I was living in San Francisco. I worked for an insurance company during the day and sipped a newly arrived drink called "espresso" at Mike's Pool Hall at night. Here I met my first modern subculture, the "beatniks". Here I encountered the lived-out philosophy of the French cult hero and father of existentialism, Jean-Paul Sartre. The Beat Generation fundamentals were simple: spontaneity, open emotion, and visceral engagement in often gritty worldly experiences. Its writers were controversial, arguing that conformity is the greatest evil in society, the world's most spiritually destructive and oppressive force.

Another popular philosophy was embodied in the "nada, nada, nada" prayer of Ernest Hemingway: nihilism argues that the world, especially past and current human existence, is without objective meaning, purpose, comprehensible truth, or essential value. Movie mogul Cecile B. de Mille was more perceptive: he said you don't break the Ten Commandments, you break yourself on them. The intellectual vacuum left by my suburban high school was now filled to the brim with these heady concepts.

The Beat Generation fueled the romantic days of North Beach, burgeoning coffeehouses, the City Lights bookshop, Jack Kerouac, and Indian sitar music. It was all sandals, beads, and beards. Thrown into the mix was the avant-garde Hungry I club, where the Kingston Trio introduced folk music and the comedian Lenny Bruce outraged the sensibilities of "the bourgeoisie" as we huffily called them then, or "decent people" as I would call them now. This small piece of San Francisco real estate, Columbus and Broadway, was the West Coast epicenter of bohemian life. A rebellion was launched against the conservative social norms of the 1950s, like *The Man in the Grey Flannel Suit.*

Imagine my surprise when I discovered that the freedom-loving existentialists were no less oppressive. One evening I was seen dining with a lawyer friend, and the next day, my professedly nonconformist friends excoriated me for abandoning my sandals and wearing a dress and high heels. That was my first philosophical epiphany. Their argument went something like this: "Wearing high heels (as the bourgeois do) means you're conforming, but wearing sandals (as we do) means you're free."

I laughed and said, "You've got to be kidding." I mean, we were rebelling against conformity, right?

A small article of Catholicism intruded into my otherwise pagan life in the form of a large necklace with carved wooden beads about the size of marbles—it was part of an Italian Rosary. Novelist Henry Miller had given two to his secretary, and my friend, who was rooming with her in Big Sur, gave one to me. We figured out what it was. I knew my grandmother prayed the Rosary, but I never connected it to religion. In fact, the word "Rosary" had no meaning for me.

In September 1961, Brownie Hawkeye camera in hand, I was sailing on the *Groote Beer*, a student ship bound for France. We tossed and churned for nine days but eventually made land. Traveling through the French countryside, I was struck by the fact that every town had a church (I could see the tall spires across the landscape). This was a revelation to me. Clearly, I was entering a world unlike my own. It never occurred to me that every American town has a church too. In Spain three months later I actually wandered—out of curiosity—into the astonishing thirteenth-century Palma de Mallorca cathedral. To this day I can feel the interior of that Gothic church, every sense of mine engaged, every thought stilled. It was wholly Other. At the time, I attributed these curious feelings to the fact that the church was foreign—you know, not American, and that's why it was so different from First Presbyterian in Menlo Park. The Real Presence was biding His time.

Without ever identifying it as such, I was immersed in a Catholic culture for the three years I lived in Europe. In Spain I became acquainted with Marxism, socialism, and humanism. My friends were anti-Catholic, and as they were identifiably secular humanist artists and intellectuals, the government watched their activities. It was from them that I heard about the "evils" of the head of state, Franco—and Franco was synonymous with the Catholic Church. They were bitter about the outcome of their civil war; they felt their country had been thrown back to the Middle Ages. (Kissing in public was considered a minor offense. If you didn't stop your car when the Guardia Civil—Franco's police—signaled, they could shoot you, no questions asked.)

My friends were right that it wasn't a democracy. But emotionally, I liked the culture. Under the iron hand of the Catholic dictator, Spain abounded in outward virtue. Your purse was safe. Families were large, happy, and intact; the social life was stable and seamless. Fathers actually played with their children, and women were beautifully dressed. The Spanish people were warm, engaging, and intellectually stimulating. There was an energy in my friends that was driven by a search for truth and a genuine love of their country. The wine from Rioja flowed, the regional food was rich and varied, the bulls ran in Pamplona, and the pageantry of the religious festivals was staggering. Spain (and France) introduced me to the architecture, history, art, and literature, to the beauty and majesty, of the millennia-old Catholic culture. Yet, philistine that I was, the only comment I could make about the Church was that the Franciscan monk at a nearby table had no business being so heavy.

This is probably as good a place as any to mention the puppeteers. Mary Beck, in her book *Expecting Adam*, introduced me to the concept, and I like it. It is a metaphor for the certain knowledge that someone outside of you is moving events, making particular things happen. Beck elaborates: "In Japan I had seen a style of puppet theater called Bunraku, where the puppeteers stand right onstage, moving these elegant dolls around without the slightest pretense of invisibility.... [They] are so skillful that you actually forget they're on the stage, even though there are three of them to each puppet. After a few minutes, you'd swear the puppets were moving themselves" (p. 12).

I think this description fits the angelic world and how they help us. As a gift to me after I withdrew from Him, Jesus sent me a growing awareness of the angels. For a long time, I called them "coincidences". Later, in Europe, when their guidance and protection became so pronounced, I began to think of them as "unseen forces", benevolent "energies" who had my welfare in mind. Not yet transcendent, not yet all-powerful, but at least personal. I'll give you an example. I had purchased a stunning handmade ring in the south of Spain and later lost it at a campground in the coastal town of Valencia. By the time I discovered it was gone, it was too late to go back for it. Six months later, on a small boat that ferried people from the tiny primitive Mediterranean island of Formentera to the only slightly larger island of Ibiza, my ring turned up. A woman from New Zealand was wearing it. She found it by a sink—where I had removed it to wash my hands—and she forgot to turn it in to the somewhat dilapidated entrance booth. She was overjoyed to find its owner. We became friends on the spot. That sort of thing happened to me all the time, and nobody could ever convince me it was just chance. (After I became a Catholic, I called these happenings "grace notes". God makes music with our lives; He's attracting our attention. We're not meant to linger on them. They're not superstitions, but grace notes that make the music richer. They let us know that Somebody's there.)

By now, I was disillusioned with existentialism—its gloomy prognosis and its lack of connection with the real world. *These writers need to get a job where they work with their hands, with normal people, pump gas or something,* I opined as I dropped Louis-Ferdinand Céline's *Journey to the End of Night* overboard in Greece. And whereas I had had no opinion about the Catholic Church before I went to Europe, I now considered it an enemy of mankind. It was time to go home.

I sailed from Europe in 1965 but at the last minute decided to stay in New York City, still searching for some purpose in my life and pretty sure I wouldn't find it in California.

Circumstances of a friendship forged in my high school days landed me in the thick of objectivism. Two of my best friends offered me a place to stay. They were close friends of the founder of objectivism, Ayn Rand, and of her partner, Nathanial Branden. With my friends' help, I joined an objectivist therapy group so I could find myself—perhaps objectivism could explain life. (I had traveled to Europe with a copy of Rand's *The Fountainhead* in my luggage.) Ayn Rand told my friend Patrecia, "You may not like reality, but you *can* focus on it." That suited me right down to the ground. But the essence of her philosophical argument is that "man's highest moral purpose is the pursuit of his own rational self-interest and of his own happiness." Now, that comes pretty close to what Saint Thomas Aquinas wrote about the virtue of temperance—but only if you don't read the rest of what the saint said on the subject. Rand's philosophy is a "bent" interpretation, and in real life Rand's system makes for a lot of self-absorbed people. Group members took themselves way too seriously; one couldn't picture them thumping away on a tambourine, for example. I contrasted my objectivist therapy hours with the happy hours spent in Spain and decided that my sessions were going to have the shelf life of a nectarine. (Branden himself had a good sense of humor, as did my friends. But the others?) So, although the philosophy seemed courageous and self-protective, it didn't work for me. Later, when I discovered Christianity, I realized that what I had observed was the logical extension of Rand's atheist-based philosophy of self-worship.

The next few years brought a flood of philosophies and beliefs to explore: the Asian religions, the Russian Gurdjieff and his New Jersey commune, astrology, tarot, *I-Ching*, psychology and all its tributaries, and the feminist movement. Parallel to this was a growing interest in Judaism.

My heart and soul were being captured by the Jewish culture; I seemed to be a magnet for Jews. All my friends were Jewish. My employers were Jewish. My professors were Jewish. I lived next door to a Reform synagogue. My senses, my intellect, and my whole being gravitated to these people. There was a richness there that I had experienced in Spain, a warmth, a vitality. The Yiddish word is *mench*. (Think *Fiddler on the Roof*.) Unlike my Spanish friends, whose identity was separated in their minds from their cast-off religion, my Jewish friends were simply that—Jewish. Like the turtle that carries its house wherever it goes, their person, their race, and their religion were one. That oneness, that corporate unity that I observed, became such a part of my thinking that later, I could never accept anything else than "One shepherd, one flock."

The Manhattan Jewish culture was also liberal. It was the late sixties; we marched in antiwar parades, we hated Republicans, we loved feminist icon Betty Friedan. I was in therapy, I went to the New School for Social Research, and I worked at Columbia University. It was an iconic sixties life, but my search for meaning remained elusive. I no longer celebrated Christmas, and I never thought about Christianity. This lasted for five years. The schools changed, my curriculum vitae changed, and my therapist worked himself out of a job (as good therapists hope to do). I walked my dog in Central Park; I went to museum exhibit openings. Taken all around, life was good. Painful, but good.

Yet something was still missing. Some thread that I couldn't pick up: a sense of nobility, of purpose that my adventures with the culture weren't bringing forth. I hadn't found what I was looking for.

In 1970 a trip to Israel changed all that. Influenced by my Israeli hosts, I grew to love the Jewish culture and beliefs even more. One incident in particular became the defining moment in my spiritual odyssey. Under the tutelage of the architect of the Israel Museum in Jerusalem, I was shown a huge room entirely devoted to the Hebrew Scriptures—both to the sacred scrolls themselves and to the tabernacles that housed them. I asked him what these exhibits were. He informed me that the tabernacles contained the Hebrew Bible, the Torah: "It is the center of our belief—it is the Word of God, the mind of God."

My heart leaped up. "What an admirable religion this is", I exclaimed. "It worships an *idea* and not *statues!*"

On my return I read Max Dimont's *Jews, God and History*, a book whose main premise is that the survival of the Jews and their monotheist God is unlikely, "unnatural", and unparalleled in history. And yet, here they are—and here He is. Indeed, as Walker Percy had asked, "Who ever mentions the Hittites?" Where are the Amorites, the Assyrians, or even the Visigoths? Gone. Conquered, annihilated, or absorbed. But the Jews, who hadn't even had a homeland for nearly two thousand years, live intact all over the world in spite of the efforts to eradicate them as a people, as a religion. God and the Promise. By the time I was finished investigating Judaism, I had gone from being an "amiable agnostic" to being a theist. Like pagan Abram, plucked from the city of Ur, I encountered the one true God at last.

It made perfect sense to me; it was rational. There has to be a God. The only question now was where to find Him. As I mentioned before, the Eastern religions were out. That left Christianity, Judaism, and Islam. After quickly rejecting Christianity—I didn't even believe in Christ as a historical person—I rejected Islam, because I didn't want to wear a headscarf for the rest of my life. I had known three Saudi princes when I was in college and met many Arabs touring in France. I liked them as individuals, but I didn't like the role of women in their culture.

That left Judaism. Well, it made sense. Everyone I knew was Jewish; I loved them; and the life I had experienced in Israel and seen outlined in Dimont's book convinced me that they were the chosen people. Not only that, I lived next door to a synagogue (or "temple", as the Reform Jews also refer to it). The rabbi at Stephen Wise Free Synagogue met with me. I told him right away that I was against organized religion.

"Don't worry", he said. "We're very disorganized."

I was relieved and consoled—so, you could be religious and have a sense of humor. In September 1972, Assistant Rabbi Sally Priesand, the first ordained woman rabbi in history, admitted me into the Jewish faith. It was Succoth, the Feast of the Tabernacles, and I was her first convert. Happy tears streaming down my face, I took the Hebrew name of Ruth. "[W]here you go I will go, and where you lodge I will lodge; your people shall be my people, and your God my God" (Ruth 1:16–17). Succoth, how appropriate—the gathering in of the harvest, the thanksgiving. I had come out of the desert at last. Slowly I studied Hebrew, learned the *Sh'ma Yisrael* ("Hear, O Israel, the LORD our God, the LORD is One") and the beautiful prayers for the blessing of the bread and wine (remember again *Fiddler on the Roof*), and attended temple services on Friday nights. My liturgical cup was running over. I was at peace.

Eventually, however, a problem surfaced: Judaism had temporarily satisfied my hunger for worship and for the truth about the existence of God. But when I wanted to know how to live, when I needed to get through the day, no code was offered, save that of "freedom". So I stayed with my culture. I'd throw an *I-Ching*, read *Ms. Magazine*, and check my astrological sign. (And let me say right here, your sign might be able to tell you how to get through the day, but it doesn't care if you do. It doesn't love you.) Eventually, the temple services were not proving to be of help either, although the people were wonderful. The fact that I am not ethnically Jewish began to tell. Much later, I realized that the Reform Judaism I had joined doesn't have a theology as I came to understand one; rather, it is cultural, secular humanism with the God of the Old Testament eternally acting as a Savior of the Jews. Unlike the Orthodox Jews, Reform Jews are not waiting for a Messiah—they're waiting for a Messianic Age, an age of peace and enlightenment. I wanted God and Him only. The sermons at my synagogue were somewhat political, Zionist, if you will. The rabbi talked movingly about the country that God saved but not so much about the God who saved it. So I wasn't much closer to knowing about Him than before, and my spirit began to hunger again. I had steeped myself in the Old Testament; I knew there was something more.

Divine Providence soon brought two influences into my life. First, a politically conservative Jewish dean of a college—a friend of conservative scholar Russell Kirk—gradually increased my awareness of objective truth. My mind began to find a home in logic. Actually, his arguments were the first logical ones I remembered hearing. And then I met a thoroughly orthodox Catholic secretary who had only a high school education and was one of the best-read, most intelligent persons I had ever known. We became very good friends.

On January 24 in the Holy Year 1975, I approached my secretary friend with a question that I'd been pondering: "When you Christians pray, do you pray to an old man with a long white beard, or what? I mean, who is your God?"

She answered thoughtfully, "We believe that God is a thinking, feeling, willing Being who is all-powerful, all-knowing, and all-loving—from all eternity. You can think of Him as a mind, if you want to."

I was stunned. God is a mind? And a Catholic is telling me this? "Okay," I said, my feminist heart ready for battle, "but what about Jesus? Who do you say he is?" (I thought He was a fictional figure created by men to keep women in a state of subjection.)

"Well," she replied, "we believe that in a particular point in time and in a particular place on earth, this thinking, feeling, willing Being became incarnate—took on a human form."

"You mean you believe Jesus was God?" I queried incredulously.

"Yes", she replied calmly.

Never in thirty-five years had I heard a claim more astounding—more outrageous, actually, when you think about it—although I wasn't feeling anything but shock. "But why a man? Why not a woman?" (*I've got her now*, I thought, triumphantly.)

She replied that God had only three choices if He wanted to be incarnate: either an animal, a woman, or a man. An animal was out—think about it. A woman was out too. God had something He had to do. In the Hebrew culture, a woman would never have been able to do it; she would not have even been crucified; she would have been considered crazy if she claimed to be the Messiah. He had to come as a man. A light went on in my head.

"Oh, I see. It was a marketing problem. The message was more important than the media."

Having been in advertising, I could relate to this puzzle. Of course, I see now that Jesus' male gender is necessary for other reasons, but the analogy worked for me then; it erased my hostility to the Person of Christ. I went home that night and wrote in my *I-Ching* diary, "Faye says that Jesus is God."

A week later she gave me C. S. Lewis' *Mere Christianity* to read. I wasn't interested in Christianity, but I did want to go to the C. S. Lewis Society meeting for other reasons and thought I should at least read one of his books. I had never heard of him. At the end of my reading, I confidently made an appointment with my rabbi. "I've just read a book," I told her, "and in it the author makes such a compelling case for Christianity—I can't find a flaw. After almost two thousand years in which to work out a rebuttal, there must be a book. Can you give it to me?"

She made a valiant attempt but didn't really address my question. She remarked that Jesus never said anything original, that He merely quoted from the Hebrew Bible. I didn't know whether or not that was true (it isn't), but it wasn't one of Lewis' arguments. Again, she tried to help me by showing me a number of books about Saint Paul. I had no clue who Paul was, but I knew he wasn't the man Lewis was writing about. We parted amiably, and I decided to ask my intellectual mentor, the Jewish dean.

"We haven't written the book because we can't", he told me.

"But if Lewis is right," I protested, "then the Messiah arrived a long time ago, and His name is Jesus. I mean, we have to move on."

His answer bewildered me: "Any thinking Jew today can become only an Orthodox Jew, a Communist, or a Catholic."

The idea that Christianity had any merit whatsoever—intellectually, socially, politically, or even historically—was a complete abomination to me. As a feminist and card-carrying member of the National Organization for Women

(NOW), I blamed Christianity in general, and the Catholic Church in particular, for the sad plight of women—back-alley abortions, unequal pay, and too many children. As a liberal (vestiges remained), I blamed the Church for the horrendous poverty in the world, especially in Mexico. (I did not know that Mexico was Marxist and had been under a socialist regime for nearly fifty years.) As an "intellectual", I had contempt for the charismatic, revival-style expressions of faith, which is how I viewed Christian prayer (whirling dervishes always appealed to me—but then I never had one in my backyard, so they weren't very real). And I blamed the Church for what I called intellectual tyranny, the slow progress of the sciences and culture, the banned books, and the influence of the Catholic Legion of Decency on morality in Hollywood films (oh, would that someone could bring them back today).

Months later, an evening spent with a Catholic bibliography routed my deeply held conviction that Catholics were ignorant and superstitious—think "Western civilization" and you have the Church.

In short, I was confronted with the possibility that what I had always called day was actually night, and what I called night—was day. The Day Star.

For the next few months I read, searched, questioned, and discussed Christian authors: C. S. Lewis, Saint Augustine (*The Confessions*), Thomas Merton, and others. I continued to attend the C. S. Lewis Society meetings long after my original motive for visiting it was forgotten. The group assembled there delighted me as no group had ever done—and I had been involved with a lot of them. Here was intellect, wit, and most of all, charity. Here were many confessions of faith, and no faith—our resident atheist was a perfect Lewis character, logical and honest. Best of all, at the conclusion, after the paper was presented and the discussions were over, we had tea: a real British tea with cakes and sandwiches. Sandwiches with thinly sliced cucumbers and butter layered between white bread, dainty triangles whose crusts had been cut off for the sake of civility. Two bites into this long-forgotten edible, I had another epiphany—like Marcel Proust's *Remembrance of Things Past*—a remembrance of teas I attended in Canada when I was twelve. Long ago, that girl talked with Jesus. *Whatever happened to her? Where did she go?* I asked myself.

Father Walter Hooper, Lewis' friend and editor, was scheduled to be the guest speaker at the July meeting. Here we go, I thought—the acid test. In all my other pursuits, Providence had arranged for me to see, meet, or know my gurus or their immediate disciples. Each time, I had been disillusioned. In 1961 I sat next to Jean-Paul Sartre at the *Deux Magots* café in Paris. For us in North Beach, it had been all sandals, beads, and beards. Here in Paris, Sartre was dressed in a three-piece suit with a gold watch chain, his nails looked manicured, and his pink face was clean-shaven. His eyes blinked behind his gold-rimmed glasses, and his balding head shone in the sun. This is our leader? He looked like a banker.

Most of the cultural icons I had met were amiable, but they weren't people whom I could finally trust. Here, at the C. S. Lewis Society meeting, Father Hooper's intellectual abilities were expected, of course. But I was accustomed to intelligent "celebrities". His humility was another matter. Ashes drifting down his black clerical garb, he smoked one cigarette after another. "I know I should quit," he apologized with a smile, "but I just can't." He was exactly like the heroes in Lewis' books—a little lower than the angels, an ordinary person, an authentic human being who yet was heir to a Kingdom, a child of God. I saw the living Christ embodied in this twinkling, rumpled, earthen vessel; it would have been impossible, I knew from experience, for him to counterfeit his humility.

If that is what Christ does in a person, I thought, *that is what I want to be.*

I tearfully surrendered to that Power, that Love, and confessed that Christ is the Son of the living God. The Messiah had come; the story was completed. The last question to be answered now emerged, however: In which church will I find Jesus? In which church will I find the true image? He promised that He would never leave me an orphan. I believed that, absolutely.

I can't write this story without mentioning the influence of Pastor Don, my Catholic father's Baptist uncle, and Aunt Ruth, his wife, both of whom I first met two weeks before I met Father Hooper. Uncle Don had been a "penniless pastor" for fifty years in Ohio, and meeting his family was my first encounter with people who spoke about Jesus openly, lovingly, and with respect. I was also surprised to learn from Uncle Don that he gave a copy of *Mere Christianity* to people who wanted to know about the faith: "After you read it," he would say, "come back and we'll talk. Lewis explains it much better than I do."

If the faith were just about its embodiment in one couple, I would have become a Baptist on the spot.

After the July meeting with Father Hooper, I set out to search the wide body of Christian doctrine in America—I was a marketing analyst, after all. It didn't take me long to narrow the field. Using Leo Rosten's *Guide to Religions in America*, I eliminated those churches whose doctrines were riddled with secular humanist beliefs that I had already lived by. Other confessions of faith didn't hold to the orthodoxy that Lewis had given me a taste for—their beliefs about Mary, the Mother of God, about sacrifice and mystery were either too anemic or not there at all. As a practical matter, I returned to the Episcopal church, which was down the street from the synagogue.

At the Episcopal church, I met many Catholics who had left the Catholic Church for a variety of reasons, none of which made sense to me, although I believe they were sincere. "They took Saint Christopher off the calendar." "They wouldn't pray the Rosary at my father's funeral." "You'll find that it's much easier being an Episcopalian."

"Easy" I already knew about. What I wanted was truth. Interestingly, no one ever said, "I examined the truths of the Catholic faith and found them to be in error." During this exploration of Christianity, I met a lot of fallen-away Catholics and unchurched Christians of other denominations. Everyone was very kind and supported my spiritual journey. But in the lapsed Catholics I began to be aware of something I didn't see in any other individuals. In our discussions, they had an expression on their faces that was elusive, some angst or vigilance perhaps. No matter how wide their smile, their eyes had a poignant look. I couldn't figure out what it was, but I never saw this in an unchurched Baptist or Lutheran, for example. (They always seemed quite at home in their world without faith.) This led me to wonder why the Catholics had this "look". I could see that they were avoiding Something; there was something concrete that they had left. It spurred me to look closer: *Maybe I won't like it either, but at least there's an entity there, something concrete that I can discover.* (In retrospect, I think it is the effects of their First Holy Communion. How could anyone consume the Body and Blood of the living God and not be irrevocably changed?)

Many weeks passed. One day, after the local Episcopalian bishop said, "You don't have to believe in God to be a good Episcopalian", I realized that I could no longer ignore the Catholic Church. That behemoth had to be reckoned with; I could put it off no longer—I had to find out what the Catholic Church teaches. My friend Faye had always answered my questions in a way that left me satisfied, but she was just one person, after all; perhaps those ideas were limited to her. Besides, she couldn't satisfy me as to the social teachings of the Church, that is, marriage and divorce. At my age, I still had hopes of finding a husband. But to find a man who was not divorced was inconceivable in New York City, so the Church stood in the way of my happiness.

*   *   *

It's September 1975. Faye and I are visiting Saint Patrick's Cathedral—her daily Mass, my first time. Over to the side, some people are sitting in the pews away from the main altar.

"What are they doing?" I query, innocently.

"Visiting the Blessed Sacrament", she replies.

"What's that?" I wonder.

"It's the Eucharist, Holy Communion, you know."

My jaw drops. "You mean they're visiting a piece of bread?" I ask, stupefied. Was there no end to this?

"Well," she continues, "for us, it's not bread; it's Jesus."

That was the second most astounding claim I had ever heard in my life. "Jesus, Himself?"

"Yes."

"Is that what all Catholics believe?"

"Yes."

Well, I tell her, I could never believe that. The thought made me ill. We left the cathedral with me looking askance at my friend.

The next day, I thought about my experience: "Either those Catholics are all demented, or there's something going on that I don't understand—I need to find out who these people are."

It was at that point that I purchased the Catholic bibliography. Name after brilliant name rolled down the pages; the "father" of this and the "father" of that in science, mathematics, and physics; emperors, actors, explorers, statesmen, novelists, physicians, and poets from all over the world. Here was the Church, here was everything I knew and loved about Europe and America. It was impressive.

And yet, I did not believe in the Real Presence.

But that was not to last.

One week later, I was standing in front of Faye's desk, talking about sewing machine sales, when Christ broke in—all in a moment, the grace of the Holy Spirit flooded my soul. I remembered Jerusalem—"If I forget you, O Jerusalem, let my tongue cleave to the roof of my mouth" (Psalm 137:5–6). I remembered the museum, the Jewish tabernacles, the sacred scrolls—the mind of God, the Word. Then I saw the tabernacle at Saint Patrick's Cathedral—"And the Word became flesh" (John 1:14). It was Jesus. And I believed. Anyone who has had this experience knows that you just can't make it up—it comes from outside yourself; it's out of your control.

Not quite sure what to do with this belief, I decided to read about the experiences of other people. Faye introduced me to the great converts of the Oxford Movement in England: Cardinal Newman and Cardinal Manning. I read other English converts: Ronald Knox (*A Spiritual Aeneid*), Arnold Lunn (*Now I See*), Oliver Barres (*One Shepherd, One*

Flock), B. W. Maturin (*Men Who Left the Movement*), and others. Their arguments for the truths of the Church were very persuasive. I didn't like the way my thoughts were turning. My options were running out; the Hound of Heaven was closing in. My world was being upended, and I didn't like it.

One last objection to the Church raised its ugly head. If I become a Catholic, I might never be able to marry. Aha, here's a very practical reason to stay out of the Church. *But*, I reasoned with myself, *if Jesus is in the Catholic Church, in the Real Presence, and you go away, do you think He'll reward you for turning your back on Him? Send you a husband? No, probably not. Well, then you'll have neither a husband nor Jesus. But, on the other hand*, I continued, *if you come into the Church, at least you'll have Jesus*.

My argument made sense to me. *Oh well*, I reminded myself, *if God intends for me to marry, nothing on earth can stop Him. Like the "children of Abraham", He'll raise up a husband out of the very stones if He has to*. (And He did.)

That autumn, in New York, I signed up for six weeks of the "come and see" classes at Saint Patrick's Cathedral, still hoping that somehow I could get out of becoming a Catholic, alarmed at the thought of leaving all that was comfortable and known to me. Four very different priests led the classes. There I saw the faith expressed through a Franciscan missionary (a former New York City fireman); a Jesuit, Father Thorton (a former prisoner of the Chinese Communists); and two diocesan priests. And we had a saint. When the archbishop, Cardinal Cooke, came to see us, the whole class stood up without thinking; it was the natural response to the holiness of this priest. (Indeed, his cause for canonization is already under way.) The newspaper staff at the cathedral invited us to their annual Christmas party festivities. To my delight, I saw holiday-trimmed tables brimming over with roast beef and ham, cheeses, thick breads, and bunches of grapes and other fruits. There were kegs of draft beer and magnums of red wines and white wines along one wall.

Well, I said to myself, *a religion that feels this way about food and wine just can't be all bad.* (God has a way of drawing me to Him through my stomach, I've observed.)

By the end of the classes, with an aching heart and a weary brain, I could no longer ignore my conscience— Rome is right. She is the Church of Christ. She is the completion of the Hebrew story of salvation; she is the "one, holy, Catholic, and apostolic church". My confirmation day would be December 9 in Our Lady's Chapel at Saint Patrick's Cathedral. I sent for my baptismal certificate, according to their requirements, and when it arrived I saw for the first time something I had never known: I was baptized in Saint Joseph's Catholic Church in Ogden, Utah. Was it the grace of my baptism that had led me to this moment? No doubt, and with the prayers of the whole Mystical Body I was brought into the light of Christ, "the light [that] shines in the darkness, and the darkness has not overcome it" (John 1:5).

Although my life afterward would be filled with joy and certainty, I went to my confirmation not with happy tears streaming down my face but "in cold blood". It wasn't romantic; it was a leap of faith—I was entering an unknown world. This would be forever, this decision of mine. Fortunately, I had been forewarned about the "weariness", because it happened to Father B. W. Maturin, another convert whose letters I had read. (This holy priest gave his lifejacket away and perished with the *Lusitania* in 1915.) Some weeks later, my former rabbi took my former pastor out to lunch, to console him. But, as Rabbi Sally related to me later, he graciously ceded the battle with the words "England's loss is Rome's gain." These were the humble people of faith whom God had given to me on my journey!

After my entrance into the Church, God poured out a cornucopia of blessings on my life: my first retreat director was Father Walter Ciszek, S.J., whose cause for canonization has been introduced. Through my work with the Co-Workers of Mother Teresa, my first two spiritual advisors were Father John Hardon, S.J., and Father Benedict Groeschel, C.F.R. The first practicing Catholics I ever lived with were Mother Teresa, Sister Nermila, and five other nuns in the contemplative community Mother had just founded in the South Bronx. (Mother invited me there as a "come and see".) As I said, God made my Catholic honeymoon very rich—I thought everyone in the Church would be like them. But, of course, we aren't—at least not that we can see. And my hat is off to pastors who labor anonymously in unglamorous parishes worldwide; theirs is the story of the first thirty years of Christ on earth. God grant them the glory of the Kingdom.

Eventually, after many twists and turns, I ended up in my old hometown of Menlo Park, California, where I met my husband, "Abraham's rock", as he calls himself. My father came back to the Church. My sister converted. My husband and I made three pilgrimages to Europe and the Holy Land asking God to bless our family with children. (He did.) It was on one of these trips that we met "the chosen" prisoner saved by Saint Maximilian Kolbe, Francis Gajowniczek, in the Franciscan gardens of Rome. Like him, I hope that my life will be a witness to the power and glory of God, whose grace is the one constant in this whole wide world.

Susan Hall Bujnak lives a contemplative life in the Ojai Valley, California, where she cares for her husband, Bernie, a stroke survivor, and is currently writing her memoirs. She homeschooled their two daughters, both of whom are now graduates of Thomas Aquinas College in Santa Paula, California.

Chapter 3

Finding God in China

Steven W. Mosher

> I give you the end of a golden string
>   Only roll it into a ball
> And it will take you to Heaven's Gate
>   Set in Jerusalem's Wall
> William Blake

My first confession is burned into my memory. The year
was 1991, and Easter, the date set for my reception into the
Church, was mere weeks away. I was elated at the prospect
of receiving my Lord and my God in Holy Communion,
but my joy was tempered by the hard prospect of penance.
Before I could commune, I had first to confess. The golden
string that would ultimately take me to Heaven's gate led
through the confessional.

My instructor in the Rite of Christian Initiation of Adults
(RCIA), following the modern and quite misleading convention, referred to my impending encounter as "reconciliation". But the implications of this soothing word with
its pop psychology sound—that God and man have had a
falling out and need to sit down together and work out
their differences—are only half true. The falling out is real,
of course, but it is solely man's doing, and so is solely
man's to confess. The ugly serpent of my ego understood

instinctively that a meeting between God and man is never a meeting between equals but is in the very nature of things an abasement, a humiliation, of the first order, and so coiled up tight in resistance. I could almost hear it hissing in resentment.

The thought of baring my soul in front of a human audience was also foreign to me. I'd never really been held accountable by anyone, after all. Not by my mother, who worked long hours as a nurse. Not by my father, who had his own demons to wrestle with and who in consequence was rarely home on weekends. Aside from a few incidents of the "who broke the window" variety (usually me), I had never been expected to own up to anything.

My proud flesh quailed at the prospect of shaming itself in front of a man who, *alter Christus* though he may be, was sure to be disgusted by both the magnitude and quantity of the sins I had accumulated over the course of forty-three years. Following my confession, I was sure that Father O'Sullivan, the good Irish pastor who led Saint Anthony's parish in Southern California, would avert his eyes whenever I came into view. As for mine, they would be permanently downcast in his presence.

My cradle Catholic wife, who is so understanding in so many ways, was more or less mystified by my hesitations, having gone to confession on a regular basis since she was a child. It was not that she thought nothing of it. It would be more accurate to say that she thought everything of it. It was, in fact, one of the organizing principles of her life. She would no more have gone months without confession than she would have gone months without bathing. For me, on the other hand, the thought of my first "bath" was dreadful. I was afraid that, along with layers and layers of encrusted sin, my very skin would come off in the wash.

My sacramentally sanctified spouse had little idea of the filth in which this prodigal son had wallowed. Mendacious me had been careful to tell her only a small part of my past life. Why, I told myself, should I populate her imagination with the dead images of my past life that were haunting me? Convinced, as always, by my own rationalizations, I kept my secrets to myself.

Finally, the Saturday morning appointed for my first confession arrived. As I staggered out the door under the weight of failings sensible only to me, my wife called out cheerily, "Do you want me to pack you a lunch?"

I can be remarkably dense when distracted. I stopped, half supposing that she was going to enlighten me on some new wrinkle of Catholic practice. "Tell me why I need to take a lunch?"

She delivered her punch line: "Because you're going to be there all day."

I managed something between a grimace and a grin, and turned to go, escorted by the chiming of her laughter.

I had dreaded encountering Father O'Sullivan in the confessional, but Providence had arranged for there to be two priests hearing confessions at Saint Anthony's that day. Besides our pastor, Father O'Sullivan, there was an elderly priest, gaunt with age, by the name of Monsignor Cluny. I knew at once that Monsignor Cluny was my man. For three long decades he had been posted to the Chino Men's Prison, where as the Catholic chaplain he had heard the confessions of countless convicted murderers, rapists, and the like. No evil I had committed would shock this hardened confessor. Besides, after hearing my confession, he would disappear behind the high walls of his prison, while I, for my part, would still be able to make eye contact with Father O'Sullivan.

So I sat down with Monsignor Cluny—Father O'Sullivan occupied the only confessional, so, to my discomfort, we were face-to-face—and nervously told him that it was my first confession. I had some vague notion of going through the Ten Commandments one by one, a process that, including all the subcategories and sub-subcategories of sin, might have made my wife's parting joke a reality. Instead, I blurted out: "I have broken every commandment, Father. I have sinned before God and before man. I have so much on my conscience that I don't know even where to begin."

After a pause, which in such individuals generally indicates that they are praying, this holy man said gently, "Then start by telling the sin that weighs most heavily on your conscience." All hesitation now gone, I spoke my great sin at once.

Monsignor Cluny listened, nodding. Thus I found confessing my sins less stressful than I feared. At the end, for all of my past sins—great, middling, and small—he gave me absolution.

As he made the sign of the cross, I experienced a soaring sense of freedom, all the more exhilarating because it was so unexpected. I had abased myself before God, submitted to His judgment, swore fealty to His laws, and bound myself to punctiliously obey them. And yet, paradoxically, in binding myself to these many strictures, I was set free. God had broken the self-forged fetters of my selfishness and released me from the tiny dungeon of my ego. I would soon enough set about imprisoning myself again, but for the moment I felt an incredible lightness of being and a deep sense of peace that, under the circumstances, made no sense at all.

I found to my surprise that I was weeping and, even more surprising, that I was not in the least embarrassed to be doing so. Thanking Father, I left, still weeping. I wept—quietly, joyfully—all the way home. Tears were still streaming down my face as I walked into the house.

My beloved took one look at my tear-stained face and came running to embrace me. There would be no jokes now. "Oh, honey, was it that bad?" she said, backing up to look at me, her face a picture of sympathy.

I shook my head, grinned through my tears, and said, "No, it was that good."

*   *   *

At some point in each person's life, the way is illuminated by a divine light, perceivable not by the senses but by the soul. He is given the end of a golden string and is given to understand that it leads to Heaven's gate. But whether he holds fast and follows it or whether, after a while, he again wanders off on his own—or, what is the same thing, carelessly lets it fall from his grasp—is up to him. God's "equal opportunity policy" of matriculating souls into Heaven is not intended to enforce equality of results (unlike some of our earthly versions) but only to provide true and perfect equality of opportunity. There is no such thing as the salvation of all, as the universalists would have it, or the salvation of only the "elect", as the Calvinist predeterminists would have it. There is only the salvation of those who elect it.

For my part, I came across my golden string several times when I was a boy. I picked it up trembling when I was eleven, as Brother Jason preached hellfire and damnation in the little Nazarene church that my grandmother attended. But fear soon gave way to more immediate sensations as an early puberty and strong paternal encouragement led me to chase the girls of the working-class neighborhood in which

we lived. It was a case, I later reflected ruefully, of the vice
of the father being visited upon the son. As for the ball of
golden string I was carrying, this proved quite a hindrance
in this particular pursuit, so I put it aside.

I discovered it again when I was nearly sixteen, when I
was drawn to the sight of a large cross newly erected not
far from the high school I attended. I picked the ball of
golden string out of the mud of lust and willfulness and
forgetfulness where I had dropped it and followed it to the
cross, which turned out to belong to a newly built Lutheran
church. This I attended throughout my high school years
with ever less devotion until I scarcely noticed that I had
again lost my way, my marker, my string.

Years later, in college, while studying for an advanced
degree in biological oceanography, I was subjected to a massive dose of Darwinian cant. In reaction, unconvinced by
the unlikely argument that life had arisen, proliferated, and
evolved into beings intelligent enough to wonder about their
own origins solely by chance, I sought the string again. I
wound it up for a while, in a kind of desultory agnostic
fashion, before abandoning it in favor of my former pas-
time, which Pascal so aptly called licking the earth.

I also put aside my pursuit of a Ph.D. in biological oceanography in favor of one in cultural anthropology, not fully
realizing at the time that I had merely exchanged one form
of reductionism for another. I had gone, as it turned out,
from those who believed that everything from amino acids
to altruism could be explained in terms of reproductive
fitness to those who maintained that human societies, even
"human nature"—their quotes, not mine—were nothing
more than cultural constructs. It is as if most people
are unwitting participants in a kind of permanent masquer-
ade, wearing masks not to hide their faces—they have

none—but rather to mold their otherwise formless plasticity into the semblance of a human face, and their group into the semblance of a human community. Intellectually, it was much like fleeing from a tribe of Maori cannibals into the welcoming arms of a band of Borneo headhunters. Either way, it was hard to keep your head on straight.

There were cultural anthropologists, I soon discovered, who were prepared to defend, in the name of cultural relativism, any and all practices, however bizarre or perverted, that any human group, however obscure and insignificant, chose to adopt. They were convinced that even failed cultures, living at the margins of human existence, had important lessons to teach the rest of us. These lessons not uncommonly had to do with free love, feminism, environmentalism, or one of the other ersatz religions that have infected the thinking of moderns. A prime example of this is Margaret Mead, who sought to defend her promiscuity by purporting to find a whole culture devoted to such practices. This hoax, which she perpetrated in *Coming of Age in Samoa*, so perfectly conformed to the sexual attitudes and appetites of her academic peers that it went unchallenged for half a century.[1] Then there was anthropologist Ruth Benedict, Mead's lesbian lover, whose personal

[1] See Derek Freeman, *Margaret Mead and Samoa: The Making and Unmaking of an Anthropological Myth* (Cambridge, Mass.: Harvard University Press, 1983). Freeman himself was subject to incredible vitriol as a result of his debunking of the Mead myth, in part because he had criticized the "founding mother" of American anthropology and in part because his critics were loath to believe that their unrestrained sexual appetites did not represent the "normal" condition of man in nature, or at least in Samoa. In 1999 he published a second volume, responding to the charges of his critics, called *The Fateful Hoaxing of Margaret Mead: A Historical Analysis of Her Samoan Research* (Boulder, Colo.: Westview Press, 1999). He got the better of the arguments but the worse of the press.

predilections led her to become a primary exponent of
the theory of moral relativism, which can be seen as her
effort to render irrelevant, if not expunge entirely, all traditional Western attitudes toward her sexual misbehavior.[2]
Even cannibalism and human sacrifice had their defenders, who maintained that such practices enabled cultures
to live in harmony with the environment by preventing
overpopulation. All were ready to lash out at critics, not
with reasoned arguments, but with accusations of cultural
arrogance and ethnocentricity. Their rebuttal to every
claimed cultural universal from monogamy to monotheism
followed the same form: "Have you not heard of the (insert
name of group, say, the Garondi), among whom (insert
name of practice, say, polygamy) is the norm?" they would
say smugly.

I am abashed to have once wanted to join their ranks, since
I now understand that a proper anthropology seeks not that
which is peculiar and unnatural in the cultures of man but
what is universal and laudatory. In short, it seeks that which
illuminates the natural law bequeathed to us by our Creator. As Saint Augustine notes in his *Confessions*, "Thy law
is written in the hearts of men, which iniquity itself effaces
not." It was much later before I learned this, however.

I was in my thirtieth year before I came across the golden
string again, and in a most unlikely venue. It reappeared,
gold and glimmering before me, in the midst of the suffering and blood that marked the birth of China's one-child

---

[2] Ruth Benedict's "A Defense of Moral Relativism", *Journal of General
Psychology* 10 (1934): 59–82, is one of the most influential and often-
reprinted contemporary defenses of ethical relativism by a leading figure in
twentieth-century anthropology. It is reprinted in numerous anthologies, including *Everyday Life*, ed. Christina Sommers and Fred Sommers, 3rd ed. (San
Diego: Harcourt, Brace and Jovanovich, 1992).

policy, beckoning me onward like a light in a distant window on a dark night.

* * *

The year was 1978, and the diminutive dictator of China, Deng Xiaoping, had just begun to cautiously peek through the bamboo curtain that had long isolated Communist China from the rest of the world. Eager to feed on the abundance of technology, capital, and markets he saw flourishing there, he agreed to an exchange of scholars with the United States.[3] This was a one-sided business from the beginning, and not just in terms of numbers. As the members of the U.S. Committee on Scholarly Communication with the People's Republic of China (PRC) dickered over the tiny roster of fifty American scholars who would on Deng's writ be allowed into China, the first of thousands of Chinese academics and agents—it was often impossible to distinguish one from the other—began flooding into the United States. That Beijing later accused me of espionage is not surprising, since so many of their supposed "scholars" were actually engaged in that line of work.

The committee finally decided that I was to be the first American social scientist allowed to do research in the PRC. I owed this unexpected honor to a certain facility in the Chinese language, which I acquired during a year at the Chinese University of Hong Kong, and also to certain ambitious professors at Stanford University, whose surrogate I was and whose ideas about Chairman Mao's great experiment in socialism I carried, like retroviruses, within me. At

[3] In the years to follow, to maintain himself and his minions in power, Deng Xiaoping was to construct a fascist dictatorship on the ruins of Mao's failed socialist paradise. But all that was in the future.

the time Mao and Maoism remained objects of admiration, if not veneration, in certain circles, mostly academic.

It would be an exaggeration to say that I went to China to join Chairman Mao's Red Guards, as Malcolm Muggeridge went to Moscow intending to offer his services to Stalin to help build socialism.[4] But I was favorably disposed toward Maoism all the same, having been taught by tenured professors, whose grasp on the truth I had no reason to doubt and whose ranks I hoped one day to join, that it had been a great boon for the peasantry. That few of these eminent pedants whose lectures I had attended and whose books lined my shelves had ever visited a Chinese village, or even spoken with a Chinese peasant, should have been, so to speak, a red flag. When I finally had a chance to ask them, San Gen, Ah Ming, and other villagers I spoke with had an entirely different opinion of the commune system. I have recounted this story in detail elsewhere.[5] Suffice to say here that the villagers referred to the Chinese Communist Party itself as the *da dizhu*, or "big landlord". Given that Chairman Mao, in his carefully elaborated demonology of class enemies, reserved a special place in Marxist hell for "big landlords", this was a damning comment.

In March 1979 I took up residence in the village of Xingcha in the Pearl River Delta of Guangdong Province. This also comprised, along with several satellite villages, the eight-thousand-member Xingcha Production Brigade. The brigade belonged to Jun'an Commune and was itself divided into smaller "production teams". As these titles suggest, agricultural production was organized along military lines, with

[4] See Malcolm Muggeridge's moving memoir, *Chronicles of Wasted Time* (Vancouver, B.C.: Regent College Publishing, 2006), especially chapter 5 of chronicle 1, "Who Whom".

[5] See my *Broken Earth: The Rural Chinese* (New York: Free Press, 1983).

peasants expected to labor each day in the collective fields under the orders of commune cadres. Like Muggeridge in Moscow, the squalid reality of communal life, with its multiple privations and omnipresent regimentation, quickly disabused me of the illusions with which I had arrived. Peasants sat down to meager meals of broken rice and salted vegetables, not, as I had read, to heaping platters of pork, beef, and fish, which in fact could be found only at official banquets, but there abundantly.

I was welcomed to Xingcha by Secretary Ho, who, as the senior Party official resident, effectively ran the place. Short and squat, he made up for his lack of height by his extreme breadth, possessing wide shoulders, thick, sinewy arms, and a broad face. Seated, as he was during official meetings, he made an imposing figure, but he was scarcely taller standing. Behind his back the villagers referred to him as "Toad". The first time I heard this nickname I laughed out loud, it so perfectly captured the man. He had a flat, expressionless way of watching you, not unlike a toad eyeing an insect it was about to devour. I have seen that same look of reptilian alertness on the faces of many Chinese officials, bred into them by the necessity of enforcing unpopular policies on an often sullen population.

Secretary Ho and I quickly formed a friendship of convenience, bound together as we were by reciprocal obligations. It was his job to keep watch over the "foreign friend", as I was referred to in officialdom, reporting my comings and goings to higher authority. For my part, he was the key to all the official documents, statistics, and directives I hoped to collect for the Hoover Institution of Stanford University. This was the assignment I had been explicitly given by Professor A at Stanford, whose understudy I was. By providing me with much of what I requested, Secretary Ho was able to report authoritatively on my activities up the chain of command, while I was able to obtain more and better information than I would have been able to manage on my own. So we both benefited.

We became partners in another venture as well. "Xingcha Production Brigade doesn't have a single truck to get our goods to market", he complained to me one day. "Chinese trucks are poorly made and hard to get." Eyeing me thoughtfully, he said: "We would like you to buy a Japanese-made one in Hong Kong and give it to us." He went on to say that he would advance me currency in *renminbi* for the remainder of my research expenses in China. I could then use, he suggested, the remainder of my research funds, held in a U.S.-dollar account in a Hong Kong bank, to buy a truck there and ship it into the country. Because it would ostensibly be for my personal use, the standard import duty, a whopping 100 percent of value, would be waived.

I agreed to this proposition, although it formally violated both the foreign exchange and import laws of the PRC. I cannot say that I lost any sleep over either violation, an insouciance that did not, unlike some of my other private activities, result from the state of moral confusion to which I was then habituated. The black market exchange rate between the *renminbi* and the U.S. dollar, just like that between the *renminbi* and the Hong Kong dollar, was much more widely known and used than the official one. Only American innocents on guided tours, retired schoolteachers from Peoria and the like, would think of going into a People's Bank to exchange money, in effect donating half the value of their currency to the state. And even they would soon be enlightened by their Chinese tour guides, who were only too eager to profit from the *heishi*, or black market, in currency themselves. As far as importing the truck for my personal use, well, I did use it for a short time after my arrival, before handing the keys over to Secretary Ho, so the letter of the law would seem to have been satisfied.[6]

On the evening of March 7, 1980, Secretary Ho came over bearing the Party directive—marked "secret", as all such directives were—that would radically alter the direction of my life. "The Central Committee of the Chinese Communist Party of Guangdong Province has adopted a new policy", he said, in the tone of one sharing a confidence. I scanned "Jun'an Commune Planned Birth Measures", as the directive was called, to learn that the provincial authorities had concluded that the population of the province was growing too rapidly ... and had decided to impose a cap on population growth of 1 percent during 1980.[7]

The last set of characters seemed to jump off the page. *A cap on population growth of 1 percent.* I looked up questioningly at Secretary Ho. "It's very clear *what* you are ordered to do", I said. "But *how* are you going to do it?"

---

[6] The Chinese government later accused me of espionage, citing the matter of the truck and the documents. I had no choice but to deny, with appropriate mental reservations, that any such truck transaction ever occurred. Had I "confessed" to such "crimes against the people", as Beijing referred to them, Secretary Ho might well have gone to prison.

I tell this story now because Secretary Ho some years ago passed beyond the reach of all earthly authorities. Like many Chinese, he was an inveterate smoker, though with more opportunities than most to indulge his habit, since people would leave him packs or even entire cartons of cigarettes in return for the favors he was able to dispense because of his position. He died of throat cancer in the early nineties.

Looking back on this episode, I am still convinced that I did the right thing by accepting Ho's offer. It was, in fact, an act of charity. I did not profit one *fen*—penny—from it, while it made life for the villagers of Xingcha, my neighbors and friends for a year, a little easier.

[7] "Jun'an Commune Planned Birth Measures", directive signed by the Jun'an Commune Revolutionary Committee, dated March 7, 1980 (copy in my possession).

"It's very simple", he said patiently, understanding that I had no experience with the vast persuasive power of one-party dictatorships. "In my brigade there are about eight thousand people. At the end of the year, there can be no more than eight thousand, eighty alive. Read the rest of the directive. Here's what the provincial authorities have told us to do. No women will be allowed to bear a second child within four years of her first. Third children will be strictly forbidden. Finally, all women who have borne three or more children by last November 1 are to be sterilized." He rattled off the new regulations matter-of-factly, not looking in the least abashed. I had begun to have a very bad feeling about what was about to unfold in the village.

"What I mean is," I responded, "it's already March. Nearly all the babies who are going to be born in Xingcha in 1980 have already been conceived—"

"We are launching a planned birth *gaochao*", he broke in. A *gaochao*, or high tide, was a kind of political tsunami that, like its seaborne counterpart, rises up suddenly and sweeps all before it. "We'll go from house to house, identifying all the women who are pregnant with illegal children. These will attend study sessions, where they will be told that, for the good of Jun'an Commune, they must get an abortion."

The *gaochao* struck the following morning. By midday, Toad and his underlings had rounded up several dozen pregnant women, whom he told in no uncertain terms to terminate their pregnancies. While some submitted after a day or two of lengthy "study sessions", others continued to resist his blandishments and threats. On the morning of the fourth day, the eighteen remaining holdouts were suddenly arrested and taken away to an undisclosed location. Their crime, the villagers were told, was that they were pregnant with "illegal" children.

I went after them, finding them locked up in a small room at the commune headquarters. The windows were shuttered, and a guard stood at the door, presumably to thwart any of this sad, disheveled little group who might try to bolt. I thought the idea of escape ludicrous given that all the women were heavy with child and totally dispirited, sprawling listless and dejected on the short plank benches that were their only resting places. As my eyes adjusted to the dim light—a naked 25-watt bulb hanging by its wire from the ceiling provided the only illumination—I noted their grim faces and pained eyes, blood-flecked from lack of sleep and crying. It was like a scene out of Dante's purgatory. Hell would come later.

A commune cadre, Wei by name, stood before these beaten-down creatures, scourging them with his voice. "You are here because you have yet to 'think clear' about birth planning", I heard him saying as I came in. "You will remain here until you do."

The unexpected arrival of the commune's "foreign friend" gave Comrade Wei pause, and when he began speaking again it was in folksy tones about how rich and powerful China would become if only everyone would stop having children. After a couple of minutes of this, however, he seemed to decide that my presence was no threat. Or perhaps he began to worry that, as "a friend of China" (for I had been so described in a communication from Beijing), I might report him for not carrying out the new party line vigorously enough. In any event, as I sat there in the perpetual gloom with my tape recorder running and my notebook open, he went back on the attack.

"None of you has any choice in this matter", he said slowly and deliberately. "You must realize that your pregnancy affects everyone in the commune, and indeed affects everyone in the country." Then, visually calculating how far along the women in the room were, he went on to add, "The two of you who are eight and nine months pregnant will have a cesarean-section abortion; the rest of you will have a shot that will cause you to abort."

Several of the women started crying at this pronouncement, and Comrade Wei, apparently deciding that his words had had the proper effect, sat down for a while. Other officials were soon at work on the women, softening them up further with alternating barrages of promises and threats.

But it was Comrade Wei who, toward the end of this cruel day, dropped the bombshell that would cause the expectant mothers incarcerated here to abandon all hope of resistance. "Do not think", he said, speaking slowly and with great force, "that you can simply stay here, eating the government's rice, until you give birth. We will not allow that. If you should go into labor before you give us permission to perform an abortion, we will simply take you to the clinic for the procedure at that time. You will go home alone." This death sentence was greeted by the women with open gasps and sobbing. The threat and the response burned into my mind like stigmata. *Agree to an abortion, or we will kill your baby at birth*, I numbly wrote down.

My disgust over the mistreatment of these young women was already high, but it was a visit to the commune medical clinic that awoke me to the full horror of the situation. This rather primitive facility, with its seventy beds, had been hastily converted into an abortuary at the beginning of the *gaochao* and now served as the government's killing fields. The doctor in charge told me that nearly all of the women confined there were within a month or two of term and confirmed that, yes, they were terminating the more advanced pregnancies first. Comrade Wei's vow that no child would be born alive was obviously no empty threat.

The actual slaughter of the innocents was done in assembly-line fashion. As soon as a woman was brought in, a powerful poison was injected directly into her uterus. Most babies died within twenty-four hours of receiving this lethal injection and were born dead the day following. Late in pregnancy the drug was proving less effective, however, and some babies did not die as planned, or if they did, labor did not follow. In these cases the doctors would open the woman up surgically and remove the now dead or dying baby. This is what Comrade Wei was referring to when he threatened the women with cesarean-section abortions.

My tour of the clinic ended in the operating room, where all such abortions were done. This room was constructed of the same gray concrete as the rest of the hospital but had large windows in each wall. The low operating table in the center of the room was already occupied. A short, stocky peasant woman in her early twenties lay on her back as a nurse busily painted her exposed, swollen stomach with a yellow antiseptic solution. An occasional curious face appeared surreally at the windows, only to be quickly driven away each time by shouts from the nurse.

The doctor followed, making a series of swift injections into the woman's abdomen. As he waited for the anesthetic to take effect, he explained to me that the woman had been given an injection of poison early the previous day, and that it had been determined that the fetus had died, but that there were still no uterine contractions. Now, he went on, oblivious to the woman lying underneath his gesticulating, gloved hands, the fetus would have to be removed, thus and thus. The woman for her part stared fixedly at the ceiling throughout his verbal dissection, her body immobile. Only her laboring, calloused hands, clenching and unclenching at her sides, gave a hint as to her anguished state of mind.

The doctor made the first incision, drawing a bloody line across her lower belly with a scalpel. I turned to go, but the woman's broken cries drew me back and I watched, horrified, as the doctor soon pulled a tiny, limp body from her torn womb. The light seemed to fade from the room, as if it had suddenly been transformed into an antechamber of hell.

With the studied callousness of young men who are the principal beneficiaries of the sexual revolution, I had up to this point entirely avoided thinking about the abortion question. This cavalier mind-set was mightily reinforced by a Stanford education, during the course of which it was made amply clear to me that abortion was a "women's issue"—indeed, the quintessential women's issue—and was therefore not a fit subject for male cogitation anyway. For the most part, the young women of my acquaintance believed that contraception, sterilization, and, especially, abortion on demand had set them free, a view that I was, I shamefully recall, only too happy to endorse. Even when contraception failed, as it invariably did, these foolish former virgins innocently went in for their abortions believing what they had been taught by barren feminists, namely, that having an abortion was the moral equivalent of clipping one's toenails and, for that matter, no more physically taxing than having a tooth extracted. Then there was the population question. We had all been required to read our Paul Ehrlich and Garrett Hardin, so we *knew*—with sophomoric certainty—that the world had too many people, that the commons was being trampled, and that China, in particular, was already dangerously overpopulated. In sum, I was a doctoral candidate in anthropology at Stanford University, an academic acolyte at one of America's High Temples of Secular Humanism. Along with the other acolytes, I had been taught to

chant all the right credos and espouse all the right causes
by the assorted sages, oracles, and other frauds in residence
there.

Yet now I had witnessed an actual, real-life abortion in all
its gruesome detail. The act I had previously considered to
have no more significance than a tooth extraction had turned
out to be a capital crime, complete with a very dead victim
and a grievously wounded mother. I became pro-life in a flash
of recognition of our common humanity: a tiny son of Adam,
and my brother, perfect in every detail of his anatomy, had
been executed by government fiat.[8] Population bomb or no,
I could not but mutely mourn his passing.

I was led to inquire where his body and, for that matter,
all the hundreds of bodies of his fellow victims, would be
buried. The local gravedigger, I found out, was hard pressed
to keep up with the constant stream of corpses. This har-
ried man arrived at the clinic before dawn each day—he
had been warned to come early to avoid public notice—
pushing a little handcart. Filling the handcart with yesterday's
harvest of sorrow, usually fifteen to twenty corpses in all,
he would set out for the hills in the distance. There, after
making sure that he had not been followed by some griev-
ing family member, he would bury them all in a single
unmarked grave. It occurred to me that these mass graves
may someday be discovered by future archaeologists who,
horrified by this callous disregard of human life, may wonder
what strange and bloodthirsty deity could have compelled

[8] American feminists could not bring themselves to condemn this kind of
abortion on demand, even though the demand for the abortion originated
with the government and went against the wishes of the women themselves.
Many endorsed China's one-child policy, continuing to do so even after it
was clear to outside observers that forced abortion was the order of the day.
This is a story I have told in my talk "The War on People".

child sacrifice on such a scale. Can they possibly comprehend how fear of a late twentieth-century phantasm called
"overpopulation" could lead China's brutal dictatorship, one
of the Baals of our time, to consign tens of millions of its
own helpless subjects to the flames? I think not.

The tragedy of the abortions that the peasant mothers
of Xingcha were forced to endure was given further poignancy by a quiet ritual that I happened to observe during *Qing Ming Jie*, the "bright and clear" festival that falls
in early April. On this festival, on which Chinese remember their ancestors, I happened to visit a neighbor woman
who had gone through a cesarean-section abortion a month
earlier. I found her standing before the high mantle on
which rested the family ancestral tablets, chanting. Eight
sticks of incense were smoldering away in a sand-filled
urn in front of the tablets, one for each of the eight ancestors, male and female, in the previous four generations.
Her chants consisted of prayers for the repose of their souls
in the next world, and petitions for peace and prosperity
for her family and herself in the present one. But instead
of ending the rite at that point as I expected, she instead
lit a final stick of incense. I watched, puzzled, as she bent
down and placed it in a tiny cup decorated with red paper
that stood in the corner of the room. She began chanting
again, but this time her prayers were so broken by sobs
and tears that I could not make out the words. After
she had regained her composure, I asked her about that
final stick of incense. She had been praying for "the
unborn one", she explained to me, the child that she had
lost.

As I took stock of what I had seen—the killing of full-
term, healthy infants at birth; the poisoning of viable unborn
children in the last few weeks of pregnancy; abortions

performed on women against their will at all stages of pregnancy; the enforced contraception and sterilization of women whose fecundity had been declared a danger to the state—the sense that all of this was truly wicked grew. As strange as it seems to me now—and as strange as it certainly must seem to the reader—for a time I resisted this all too obvious conclusion, so stunted were my moral faculties by the toxic idea that "good" and "evil" were merely cultural constructs. In the intellectual shadowland I then inhabited, there were no fixed horizons and compass points, only lighter and darker shades of gray receding off into the indeterminate distance. The concept of cultural relativism cast too dim a light for me to catch even a fleeting glimpse of evil, but out of the gloom ghostly specters from China past emerged unbidden, each claiming to be the precursor of the deeds I had witnessed.

Hearing such justifications issue from the mouths of Stanford professors, however, was another matter. Their pitiful efforts to explain away what I had seen finally awakened me to how corrosive the relativistic world view was, not just to one's moral sensibilities, but to one's common sense as well. Professor B, for example, took the position that "forcing a woman to have an abortion in the third trimester of pregnancy was no worse than the Reagan administration denying poor women federal funding for abortions", displaying an insensitivity to the suffering of Chinese women that left me shaking my head in disbelief. Others failed Ethics 101, arguing that the noble—in their view—end of controlling China's population justified the means, however base and cruel, used to reduce the number of babies born. There were even those who dismissed forced abortion as a modern version of infanticide, which "has long been culturally sanctioned in China", as if this warranted the killing of full-term healthy infants by the state.[9] What I found the most troubling, however, was that this blizzard of chilling rationalizations for an obviously inhumane policy contained not one single, solitary snowflake of sympathy for the Chinese babies who were dying. What kind of people were these?

Well, to begin with, they were exactly the kind of people whose intellectual prowess I had, up to that point, greatly admired and whose world view I had wholeheartedly embraced. It is humbling for me to reflect that it took an evil of truly Herodian proportions, in conjunction with the obvious moral bankruptcy of my mentors, to rouse me from my relativistic slumbers. But for the grace of God, manifested in the bloody witness of hundreds of innocent, unborn Chinese children, I too would surely have gone down the tenure track to perdition.

The discovery that there was Evil loose in the world—the word must be capitalized in this context—was a great shock to me. It was as if I had been sleepwalking through a pleasant dreamscape and opened my eyes to find that I was actually waist-deep in a putrid cesspool. I had been wallowing in immorality most of my adult life, of course, but my senses had been so dulled by relativism that I was largely oblivious to the stain and the stink that pervaded not only my own life but that of humanity in general. Now, brought up short by the state-mandated murder of millions of infants—for the scenes I had witnessed were being repeated all over China—the stench in my nostrils was overpowering. *How could God,* I asked myself, *if He is*

[9] Similarly, there are anthropologists who will defend even human sacrifice and cannibalism in the name of cultural relativism, while bridling at criticism as "ethnocentric".

God—that is, if He is all-good, all-knowing, and all-powerful—permit such wickedness?

My dilemma, to paraphrase G. K. Chesterton, was this: If it be true that a Communist Party official can feel exquisite happiness in forcing a woman pregnant with an illegal child to have an abortion, then I could draw only one of two conclusions: I must either deny the existence of God, as all atheists do, or I must deny the present union between God and man, as all Christians do.[10]

Skeptics, beginning with Epicurus in ancient Greece, have long argued that the existence of evil proves that God does not exist.[11] Saints, among them Saint Augustine of Hippo, maintained that evil results from the misuse of the free will that God has gifted us with and that, in any event, even evil deeds serve God's good purposes in ways beyond our understanding.

At the time, I admit to having been troubled by the recurrent thought that the universe was mad. In my darkest moments during the abortion campaign, it seemed to me that I was simply flotsam in an endless sea of chance and happenstance, being driven about by waves that rose up from nowhere and then subsided without a trace. I could discern

[10] Chesterton, writing in the early years of the twentieth century before the rise of bloodthirsty one-party dictatorships, used as his example of "positive evil" someone who took pleasure in vivisecting cats. Now, I am a friend of felines, and no less opposed to vivisection than he was, but the scale of evil has grown so enormous in our time that this particular diversion seems almost quaint by comparison with, for example, the state-mandated murder of millions of babies.

[11] "Either God wants to abolish evil, and cannot; or he can, but does not want to.... If he wants to, but cannot, he is impotent. If he can, but does not want to, he is wicked.... If, as they say, God can abolish evil, and God really wants to do it, why is there evil in the world?" (Epicurus, as quoted in James A. Haught, *2000 Years of Disbelief: Famous People with the Courage to Doubt* [Amherst, N.Y.: Prometheus Books, 1996]).

no governing intelligence, no larger pattern of meaning, no ultimate purpose to life, only a world of blind brutality and casual viciousness without end. So be it. Nor did it help that I was behaving as though I was already firmly in the camp of the atheists, daily living out the bedlam of their beliefs. Like them, I ate, drank, fornicated, and made merry. It all made it that much harder to avoid the conviction that tomorrow, like the poor naked godless apes that the atheists imagined us to be, we would all fall stone dead.

And yet . . . from the time I was a boy I had felt that tug of something infinitely greater than myself. Now it urged me onward, prompting me to consider whether there did not exist a countervailing good to the evil I had witnessed. I came to imagine this good as a huge counterweight, something like the thousand-ton damper that architects hang on the top floors of a hundred-story skyscraper and that is designed to keep the building stable even when the earth trembles and hurricane-force winds roar. In the end I decided to seek the Good, understanding more by intuition than anything else that it would in due course lead me to God. So I checked myself out of the insane asylum of atheism and picked up the golden string again. This time, finally understanding what was at stake, I took a firmer grip on it than ever before, resolved to follow wherever it might lead.

By 1983, when I returned to the United States from Asia, I would describe myself to others as a pro-life agnostic. By this I meant that, while I was emphatically against abortion, my belief in a Supreme Being remained rather vague, so much so that He and I still had not established a regular channel of communication. My return coincided with the publication of my book about my China experience that I, with apologies to Pearl Buck, called *Broken Earth: The Rural*

Chinese. Broken Earth was widely reviewed and sold well, further infuriating my former colleagues at Stanford University, who were already upset by its graphic depictions of forced abortions and failed Maoist revolutions. As I tussled with Stanford over my doctorate—in the end, the president of the university refused to award it to me on the grounds that he did not "trust" me—several things happened to help me along on my faith journey.

One day I received a call from a Catholic priest who introduced himself as Father Paul Marx. I did not know it at the time, but Father Marx, a Benedictine monk with a doctorate in sociology and a passion for the unborn, was arguably America's greatest living pro-lifer. Speaking in his soft voice, which carried just a hint of a German accent from his Minnesota childhood, Father invited me to speak at his upcoming pro-life conference in Washington, D.C. I am afraid that the words "pro-life" set off alarm bells in my head. I had been taught at Stanford that pro-lifers were all fetus-loving fanatics who were only too ready to burn down abortion clinics, assault abortionists, and engage in other violent acts. Such slanders, all of which I was soon to find out were false, nearly kept me from accepting Father Marx' invitation.

What changed my mind was a visit to that bastion of radical feminism, the National Organization for Women (NOW). Walking through the doors, I had convinced myself that the news that millions of their sisters in China were being forcibly aborted and sterilized would finally be received with the gravity and determination that such outrages deserved. The organization would issue press releases of condemnation, organize demonstrations of protest, and probably light up the night sky over Beijing with their hellish fury. After all, women in China were being denied what

NOW leaders regularly declared was the most sacrosanct right of all women, their *right to choose.*

I met with two of NOW's senior leaders and sought to share with them the horrors I had witnessed. The atmospherics were cool from the outset. The two uttered not one word of sympathy for the women of China as I spoke, and seemed to stare distastefully at the pictures of forced abortions that I had brought as evidence. But I was nonetheless taken aback by the judgment they pronounced after I had finished. For the more senior of the two declared with an ineffable sense of rectitude in her voice that will stay with me forever, "I'm personally opposed to forced abortion. But China does have a population problem."

And that was that. I was dismissed from their presence, just as I was soon to be dismissed from Stanford, driven off like a scapegoat of ancient Israel bearing the sins, in my case, of multiple instances of political incorrectness. I had questioned abortion, population control, and the Maoist revolution, a triptych of leftist causes, and for this I was driven out into the academic wilderness, left there to languish in the hope, apparently, that improvidence would force me into some other profession far away from academe.

I resolved to go to D.C. to speak at Father Marx' conference, pro-life or no. If the movement that claimed to be pro-choice was not willing to live up to its name and defend the *choice* of Chinese women to bear children, I thought, then perhaps the movement that described itself as pro-life would. At the conference, I was pleasantly surprised to find myself in the company of hundreds of truly remarkable human beings. Pro-lifers in the flesh—as opposed to the caricatures propagated by their pro-abortion antagonists—proved to be kind and generous spirits who gave freely of their time and treasure to the cause of unborn children, who, with rare exceptions, would never be able to thank them, at least in this world. And, what was paramount from my point of view, they overflowed with sympathy for the plight of Chinese mothers and babies and offered to help both in various ways. I came to count these gentle and well-balanced people among life's major blessings, their bright, shining presence on earth implying a better life to come. By way of contrast, the rather bizarre personalities I had encountered among the Stanford faculty—fatuous, self-absorbed, grasping at honors and recognition, big-brained but somehow small-minded—cast a very dim and uncertain light indeed. I suppose I stopped regretting my lost Ph.D. at that point, understanding that advanced degrees not only do not confer wisdom but may in fact blind one to very large truths—about the sacredness of all human life from conception through natural death, for example—a realization that brought me one step closer to conversion.

It was around this time that I stumbled upon the work of Saint Thomas Aquinas, which for me personally was something akin to finding the Dead Sea Scrolls. For just as the scrolls demonstrated the authenticity of the Scriptures, so did the *Summa* of Saint Thomas Aquinas teach me the validity of reasoning one's way to the Truth, which is God. Or, as Pope John Paul II was later to write in his 1998 encyclical *Fides et Ratio*, "Faith and reason are like two wings on which the human spirit rises to the contemplation of truth; and God has placed in the human heart a desire to know the truth—in a word, to know himself—so that, by knowing and loving God, men and women may also come to the fullness of truth about themselves (cf. Exodus 33:18; Psalms 27:8–9; 63:2–3; John 14:8; 1 John 3:2)." [12]

The secular humanists at Stanford, by rejecting God, had sheared away the two wings referred to by the Holy Father. This is easy to see in the case of faith, which they openly and scornfully rejected as myth and superstition. But reason, which they claimed to honor, actually fared little better, for they hedged it with such conditions as to render it largely impotent. I had been expected to believe that man's capacity for objective knowledge was limited, that the search for ultimate truth was futile, and that the question of whether a Supreme Being exists had long been answered in the negative. Other dogmas that were beyond reproach included materialistic evolution and socialism. With the large questions—What is man? What is God? What is the state?—foreclosed or predetermined, we were left, in the Department of Anthropology, to think in a minor key. Our theories were mostly inconsequential efforts to explain trivial phenomena in mostly moribund cultures. Most of the time we busied ourselves recording the exotic minutiae of such cultures, many of which will almost certainly cease to exist within a few generations. A dead-end occupation if there ever was one.

Reading Saint Thomas Aquinas, these scales fell from my eyes. For here was a philosophical edifice that not only encompassed all of creation but also reached up to the very heavens, including proofs for the very existence of God. Perhaps it was just intellectual snobbery on my part, but I was tremendously relieved not to have to make a blind leap

---

[12] *Fides et Ratio*, opening paragraph, http://www.vatican.va/holy_father/ john_paul_ii/encyclicals/documents/hf_jp-ii_enc_15101998_fides-et-ratio_ en.html (accessed February 1, 2007).

of faith of the kind popularized by that apostate monk Martin Luther and his *sola fide*. I doubted that my still wobbly legs of faith were strong enough to carry me over the vast chasm between me and God. On the other hand, if I could construct a bridge to Heaven out of solid blocks of reason, then perhaps, just perhaps, I stood a chance of making it to the top. And it was Saint Thomas Aquinas of blessed memory who revealed this possibility to me, teaching me from across the centuries that God spoke to man through his reason, as well as through his faith, and that one could therefore read, think, and study one's way into the Catholic Church. This I proceeded to do.

In the economy of grace that helped to win my salvation, my wife, Vera, played a major, providential role. Taking to heart Saint Paul's admonition that the sanctified spouse should sanctify the unsanctified one, she was everything that love should be: patient and kind, selfless and self-giving, and—necessarily given my character—long-suffering. I believe that she intuitively recognized in these early days that preaching at me would be counterproductive, so she did something far more powerful: she prayed for me. I was insensible to these prayers floating heavenward and would probably have objected had I known, but of course she had the good sense not to tell me.

Then came the day we were walking across the plaza in front of the old Spanish mission church in San Luis Obispo, California. Suddenly the bells in the bell tower began to peal, summoning one and all to Mass. It turned out that they were pealing for me as well, for Vera suggested, in that gentle, loving way of hers, that we go to services together. I agreed to attend my first Mass—rather readily as I now recall—but my attitude when I entered the church was scarcely that of the typical pew sitter. I felt more like a visiting anthropologist there to observe an ancient religious rite than a participant in the sacred mysteries of the living God. But I found myself unexpectedly uplifted by the Liturgy of the Word, while the Liturgy of the Eucharist created in me an eagerness, which I was unable to satisfy in a concrete way for several years yet, for communion with Christ. The final blessing came too soon. It was as if a song once sung but long forgotten had found its way back to my lips, or a profound truth once known but long veiled had made its way back into my consciousness. I began attending Mass on a regular basis, though it was some years later before I actually joined the Church.

As I learned more about the Catholic faith, no doctrine touched me more deeply than the communion of saints. The idea that we wayfarers should be aided in our pilgrimage by those who have gone before us links our world to the next in a marvelous and positive symmetry. Once I recognized this truth, it seemed especially applicable to my own circumstances, in which the great cloud of witnesses that Saint Paul speaks of in Hebrews (12:2) bore mostly the visages of Chinese babies. I had spoken out on behalf of these millions of innocent victims of China's inhuman one-child policy in books, articles, and interviews, in congressional testimony and at pro-life conferences, in season and out of season. Not to be outdone in generosity, this vast multitude of heavenly intercessors had implored the Father on my behalf for a decade, or so I came to believe. I had interceded for them in a weak human way, while they had interceded for me in a powerful supernatural way, an arrangement much to my benefit.

By 1988 I was eager to cross the Tiber—if that is the proper expression to describe a onetime Lutheran, sometime atheist's journey home to the Catholic Church. But a midyear move to Washington, D.C., delayed my entry into the Church for two more years. Each Sunday at Mass I could only watch longingly as hundreds of parishioners, including Vera, received Our Lord in Holy Communion while I remained rooted in the pew like an impenitent sinner. I was a sinner, of course, but by that time a decidedly repentant one.

It was not until the fall of 1990, after we had resettled in Southern California, that I was finally able to embark upon the nine-month course that would lead to my entry into the Church. Along with the fourteen other confirmandi in my RCIA class, I was told by our pastor that we would be received into the Church the following Easter—provided that we learned the essentials of the Catholic faith in the intervening months. But a few sessions with our RCIA instructor, a lay volunteer, convinced me that this would not be easy, because the faith was simply *not* being taught. It was as if I had signed up for a course in calculus and found that the professor was actually lecturing on numerology. There were certain superficial similarities between what we were being taught and the Catholic faith, but these masked profound underlying differences.

Almost every class period produced examples of this confusion, but two in particular stand out in my memory. One class period early in the term our instructor began by laboriously drawing a triangle and a circle upon the blackboard. Pointing at the triangle, he explained that it represented the old notion of the Catholic Church as a rigid hierarchy. At the apex was the pope, followed by the cardinals, archbishops, bishops, monsignors, and priests in descending order, with we, the laity, occupying the very bottom rung. This view of the Church, he told us authoritatively, had been consigned to the dustbin of history at the Second Vatican Council. The post–Vatican II view of the Church, he went on, is one in which we are all fundamentally equal in our practice and understanding of the faith and is represented by the circle. He went on to suggest that there was no fundamental difference between priests and laypeople and that we must all give primacy to conscience.

I sat there in near shock. My instructor in the Catholic faith, selected by my priest and approved by my bishop, was rejecting one of the teachings that had drawn me to the Catholic Church in the first place, namely, a divinely instituted ecclesiastical hierarchy that, guided by the Holy Spirit, can and does pronounce infallibly on the moral questions of our time. Without hierarchy, there can be no firm grounds for rejecting any reading of the Bible, however errant or idiosyncratic, as long as it is sincerely held by a baptized Christian. To me it all sounded suspiciously like "the priesthood of all believers", the notion advanced by Martin Luther that all the faithful are divinely authorized to teach.

I am not joining the Church to sit around the campfire in a circle and sing "kumbaya", making new "advances" in Christian faith and morals as the Spirit moves me, I thought to myself. I was through with making up my own moral code as I went along, bending it to each new situation in ways advantageous to me. What I wanted was what our instructor had so casually dismissed as archaic and outmoded—the Magisterium. Hierarchy meant authority, and authority meant protection from error. I kept silent, however, more out of politeness than anything else.

Then came the showing of *Shuah*, a thirty-five-minute film about the life of Christ. In the film, Our Lord went by the nickname of "Shuah", a cute contraction derived from the Aramaic *Yeshuah*, or Jesus. The towering fault of the film was that it portrayed Our Lord not as the strong, commanding figure that He in reality was but *as a lame, lisping weakling.* I groaned inwardly as I watched the actor sibilate and stumble about. How could Jesus Christ have mesmerized crowds of thousands, as Scripture records, if He had had a severe speech impediment? How could He have traversed the stony paths of ancient Israel, walking many hours each day, if he was barely able to hobble around on a clubbed foot?

This time I could not restrain myself. As soon as the closing credits began scrolling down the screen, I turned to the instructor. "Why did you show us this?" I said.

"Well," he said slowly, "because we want to emphasize the humanity of Jesus."

"No one here doubts there was a historical figure named Jesus", I responded, perhaps a little more sharply than I had intended. "What we are all here to find out is whether He is the Christ, the Son of the living God. It's His divinity that you need to be convincing us of, not His humanity."

The final straw was the textbook required for the RCIA class, which was called simply *The Way.* The author bore down relentlessly, for page after numbing page, on social justice issues such as poverty. Having been in the People's Republic of China, I did not share his obvious conviction that governments, as opposed to faith, charity, and strong families, could readily solve these problems. At the same time, when it came to questions of personal morality, he seemed completely out of his depth. His treatment of the Ten Commandments was brief and unsatisfactory. The pressing culture-of-life issues of our day—abortion, contraception, sterilization, divorce, euthanasia, homosexuality, and so forth—received scarcely a mention.

I called Father Marx. "Father, my RCIA class is using a book that is more suitable for a social worker than a Catholic convert", I told him. "I need to find out what Catholics really believe, or I'm not going to go through with this." In the back of my mind was the vague idea of casting my lot with the fundamentalist church a couple of miles up the road. Although the pastor did not have the fullness of the truth, I understood that he opposed abortion and divorce and fearlessly preached the Ten Commandments, not the pap that I was being force-fed.

"Don't do anything hasty", Father Marx responded. "I'll send you a real catechism."

Father's "real catechism", which arrived the very next day, turned out to be none other than Father John Hardon's classic *Catholic Catechism*.[13] Although it was some years before I realized it, Father Marx had sent me what was arguably, in those days before the *Catechism of the Catholic Church*, the best contemporary summary of the teachings of the Catholic faith. I opened it immediately, and there, on the overleaf, Father Marx had written that he would be praying for me. Over the next two days, I read it from cover to cover. Next to the Gospels, it is the book that has had the most profound effect on my life, for from it I learned much, not only about the faith I profess, but about the conduct that it demands. *Not everybody in Catholicism has lost their senses*, I recall thinking as I read it.

In my words I was more charitable, of course. I did not correct what our instructor had to say, even when he got things wrong. Nor did I quote from Father Hardon's *Catholic Catechism*, even though I had it with me and often had to suppress the urge to pull it out and say, "Now look here ..." Instead, I just asked questions—lots of questions—about the

---

[13] John A. Hardon, S.J., *The Catholic Catechism* (New York: Doubleday, 1974).

faith. And I also "amplified" certain of the instructor's answers when they were sketchy or, not infrequently, wrong. I was learning that there was a lot more room inside the Catholic Church than there appeared to be from the outside and that in some dioceses error was even permitted to coexist with the truth. With Father Hardon at my side, and Father Marx praying for me, I did my best to combat error diplomatically within my small circle of confirmandi.

On Easter Sunday 1991 I came into full communion with the Roman Catholic Church. It was a glorious spring day, as I recall, but there was no less glory in the tabernacle of my heart, for I received the great grace of Holy Communion with Our Lord for the first time. But, as I was soon to learn, one never receives great graces without a compensating cross. The economy of salvation cannot long run at a deficit. The name of this particular cross was Andrew Christian Mosher, my fifth child, who was born on April 8, 1991, eight days after I entered the Church.

All of our children up to that point had been instruments used by God for our purification and sanctification. They provided early and ample opportunities to practice the corporal works of mercy: they came into the world naked, and we clothed them. They came into the world hungry, and we fed them. They came into the world thirsty, and Vera, who always breast-fed her babies, gave them drink. All the things that we are instructed by Our Lord to do for the least of these our brothers, Vera and I did for our own children, as all parents do. Our children also led us to practice the spiritual works of mercy, including praying for the sick, as any parent of an ill child can testify. But Andrew would teach us the most important lessons of all.

All of our children have been born by cesarian section, and Andrew was no exception. So that Vera could avoid labor, which would have been dangerous for her, he was delivered two weeks early. Still, he came into the world at seven and a half pounds, and our pediatrician, after giving him a quick examination, pronounced him healthy and then disappeared. A nurse put him into an isolette and, with his proud father in tow, wheeled him down the corridor toward the nursery. By the time we arrived, Andrew had turned blue and stopped breathing.

Thereupon began a month-long nightmare. Or perhaps it is better called a trial of faith. Andrew, who was to all outward appearances normal, turned out to have immature lungs that were unable to absorb oxygen. Even more serious, he had a condition called patent ductus arteriosus, which in plain English means that his blood was going in a blind loop from his heart down what was left of his umbilical cord and back. The umbilical cord, for eight and a half months his lifeline for oxygen and nourishment, now ended at his belly button. Unable to get oxygen from his lungs *or* his umbilical cord, he was suffocating.

An oxygen mask was strapped to his tiny face, but this helped only marginally. Then a tube was quickly placed into his lungs, and pure oxygen was pumped in, but as the hours passed he grew still worse. The only hope of saving his life, the neonatologist finally informed me, was to transfer him to the Children's Hospital of Orange County, where he could receive extracorporeal membrane oxygenation, or ECMO for short.

At the time, this was a fairly novel and decidedly dangerous procedure, but we had no choice but to agree. The surgery involved cutting open the right side of Andrew's neck, exposing the carotid artery and the jugular vein. These blood vessels were then cut, and canullae—small tubes—were inserted into his heart. Venous blood was pumped out through the jugular vein, oxygenated through a membrane, and then pumped back into his heart through the carotid artery. He was now getting enough oxygen to survive, and his lungs were being given a chance to mature. And the clock was ticking.

The chief risk of ECMO, aside from the sacrifice of two of the three main vessels carrying blood to and from the brain, is blood clots, which can lead to strokes and heart attacks. So as soon as Andrew went on ECMO, he started receiving massive doses of an anticoagulant drug called heparin. This reduced the risk of clots but carried with it serious risks of its own, primarily that of internal hemorrhaging. In Andrew's case, the bleeding began almost immediately, seeping from his belly button and darkening the bandage over the incision on his neck. Although we could not see it, there was internal bleeding as well. Because of the risk of serious hemorrhages, babies could stay on ECMO for only ten days. After that, we were told, they had to come off, whether or not their lungs were ready. Otherwise, the hemorrhaging itself would kill them. Andrew had ten days to recover. Or perhaps only ten days to live.

My wife and I began praying for Andrew's recovery. We prayed separately at first—we had never up to that point prayed together—but Andrew's survival drew us together in a common cause. We overcame our initial awkwardness about praying in each other's presence and were soon reciting a daily Rosary together, a practice that we have continued in the years since. Not that our prayer life was limited to a single daily Rosary. Rather, as Andrew's life hung in the balance, we prayed without ceasing, as Saint Paul instructs us to do. We were even praying in our sleep, dreaming about saying Rosary after Rosary. This was the first lesson that Andrew, just by being there, taught us: he taught us to pray.

Yet the days kept going by with no improvement. I was going to the hospital, which was an hour away, three times a day, once in the morning, once at noon, and once in the evening. My wife, who was recovering from a cesarian section, was not physically able to make the journey, but she went with me in spirit. Each time that I would go up to his tiny bed and look questioningly at the nurse who was monitoring his progress, she would shake her head. "His lungs still aren't able to help exchange oxygen. They are still immature. We're still having to bypass them using ECMO."

A week had passed, perhaps the longest week of my life. I was painfully aware that there were only three days left before Andrew would have to come off ECMO—and die. I was utterly exhausted—physically, mentally, and emotionally. That was the hour that I put my trust completely in God. In my mind I was Abraham, leading his son Isaac up the slope of Mount Moriah, laying my innocent son down on the stone altar, preparing to sacrifice his life for love of God.

Standing outside the entrance to the neonatal intensive care unit (NICU), I prayed the prayer that I had been unwilling to pray up to that point. I said to God, "He was Yours before he was mine. And if You want to take him, I give him freely back to You."

I cannot tell you what it cost me to say those words. It was an admission that I, Andrew's father and supposed protector, was powerless to protect my son. It was an admission of utter helplessness and dependence upon God, our common Father. Here was another lesson taught me by my tiny son, a lesson of total submission to God's holy will.

God, as we say, is never outdone in generosity. From the moment I prayed that prayer, Andrew began getting better.

At least, when I walked through the doors into the NICU, the nurse greeted me with, "We're turning down the ECMO bypass. And Andrew's patent ductus arteriosus has closed." One might say that Andrew's turnaround was remarkable, but that would be an understatement. It was miraculous. I gave my son to God when he was sick and dying, and God gave him back to me whole.

There were other lessons as well. Andrew helped me understand the meaning of suffering. He helped me to understand the great sacrifice of Our Lord on the Cross that purchased for us our redemption. And I think he helped me understand the meaning of suffering in our own lives, where we complete what is lacking in the great sacrifice.

Andrew's birth, near death, and recovery did not mark the end of my spiritual journey, nor even the beginning of the end. There were many more children yet to come, each with their own lessons for Vera and me. And there were years of pro-life work with Father Marx that would take us to countless countries on six continents. But this time— the time of my First Communion and my first cross as a Catholic—did perhaps mark the end of the beginning, a beginning that dated back to March 1980, when I firmly grasped Blake's golden string for the first time. In the meantime, I journey on, determined to keep rolling it up into a ball until I arrive safely at Heaven's gate set in the wall of the heavenly Jerusalem. Home at last.

Steven W. Mosher, president of the nonprofit Population Research Institute since 1996, is widely recognized as one of the world's leading authorities on the population question. His writings demonstrate that overpopulation is a myth and that the efforts of population controllers to reduce human numbers have led to massive human rights abuses. Steve came face-to-face with the nightmare of population control when he was the first American social scientist to live in rural China in 1979–1980. What he witnessed in China shocked him deeply: pregnant women hunted down by population control police and subjected to forced abortion for violating China's one-child-per-family law.

Steve returned to his studies at Stanford University and wrote about the population control horrors he witnessed in China. Bowing to demands of the Chinese government, Stanford expelled Steve Mosher rather than grant him the Ph.D. he had earned.

Steve Mosher's books include the best-selling A Mother's Ordeal: One Woman's Fight Against China's One-Child Policy; Hegemon: China's Plan to Dominate Asia and the World; China Attacks; China Misperceived: American Illusions and Chinese Reality; Journey to the Forbidden China; *and* Broken Earth: The Rural Chinese.

Articles by Steve have appeared in the Wall Street Journal, Reader's Digest, *the* New Republic, National Review, Reason, *the* Asian Wall Street Journal, Freedom Review, *and numerous other publications.*

Steve Mosher and his wife, Vera, live in Virginia with their nine children.

Chapter 4

Better than a Thousand Good Days in the World

Catherine Schneir

I don't know how to write about my conversion. Like any miracle, it makes little sense, it defies reason, but in spite of the odds, here I sit, a Roman Catholic, living a life I never even knew was possible.

I think it would be accurate to call the family in which I was raised "average". We certainly appeared to be—my parents, my sister, and I lived a relatively normal life. Liberal Jews from the liberal South Side of Chicago, my father was a staunch Zionist, my mother a committed feminist. Though neither had a firm faith in God, they were members of a local synagogue, celebrated holidays, and sent their daughters to Hebrew school. What my family possessed, largely, was a strong cultural identity: we saw ourselves as part of a historical people, but what should have been faith in God had been replaced with secular ideas. Secular ideas bring little happiness and much angst, and my parents' marriage was always teetering on demise. Boundaries, fidelities, were constantly in question, standards in flux. What was true one day could be disproven and rejected the next. It was an unpredictable, dangerous world in which to grow, and we were anything but happy.

My faith story began when I was about ten years old. Every
year, during the Christmas holiday, my family would escape
the frigid Chicago winter and spread beach towels in the Florida sand. One winter, my mother decided to forgo Florida
and set her sights on Mexico, taking her little troop on the
usual gringo tour south of the border. That tour happened
to include the shrine of Our Lady of Guadalupe. I'll never
forget our first view of the steeples of that beautiful shrine,
but even more impressive was the courtyard. There, men and
women, elderly people holding crutches, and children my own
age crawled on abraded knees across the uneven pavers of the
courtyard into that huge doorway of the church, praying, begging for miracles. For Jewish urbanites, this was unsettling
behavior, a horrible sight that reeked of mindless superstition. Yet I found myself moving toward that dark doorway,
drawn by interest and curiosity. What I saw there, for the first
time in my life, was faith, and it was irresistible. The face of
Our Lady of Guadalupe was love, and that day, I fell in love.

Returning home to the imposed routine of normal life,
I continued my secret love affair. Several blocks from our
home stood an imposing church, Saint Thomas the Apostle.
I began "sneaking in". A natural mimic, I learned to make
the sign of the cross and to genuflect, but mostly, I wanted
to find the beautiful lady whom I'd met in Mexico. She
was in the back of the church, surrounded by candles, and
I would kneel beside her, telling her my childhood woes
while she would patiently listen.[1]

In that church, I would feel a Presence. Unable to explain
it any other way, I told my parents that when our synagogue

[1] I learned later that the statue in the back of Chicago's Saint Thomas the
Apostle Church is not Our Lady but Saint Thérèse of Lisieux. We are, then,
recipients of her petals. Thank you, Little Flower.

was empty, it felt like an echo-filled hall, while the church, when empty, didn't feel empty at all. Could a Jewish child sense the presence of Christ in the Eucharist?

One day, as I began to feel more and more at home at Saint Thomas, I decided to explore. There were doors, many of them, and overcome by curiosity, I decided to open one. Lo and behold, inside that first door sat a huge, fat man, almost wedged in to what I thought must have been a closet. I screamed, he screamed, and the next thing I knew, he was leading me out of the church by the shoulder. Up to his office we went, where he asked many questions. Being sure I'd met my doom, I told him anything I thought would appease him. Was I Catholic? Oh yes, of course! Why then was I not in his Catholic school? We were too poor to pay the tuition, I told him. He asked my phone number and called my home. As he spoke to my father, his face softened and he started to laugh. Learning that I was an innocent interloper, he dismissed me from his office and told me to go home. It wasn't until years later that I realized I'd walked into this poor priest's confessional. Still, it took a long while for me to have the courage to meander once again into a Catholic church.

Time passed, college commenced, and the sixties ensued. What I retained from my early encounter was a sense of a good God and a deep desire to live for more than just myself. A die-hard do-gooder, I became a meditating hippie, believing rightly that love would change the world, but believing wrongly that it would be my love that would do the trick. Throughout that confusing decade, there remained for me and for many who accompanied me an honest desire to find Truth, and an uneasiness with the values promoted by the culture. If nothing else, we were wide open to change. Being wide open can be a very good thing, but it can also be dangerous and can produce much misery.

It wasn't misery that led me to Christ, however; it was joy. After difficult college years and tumultuous relationships, I met a wonderful man named Harvey. From what I'd experienced of life thus far, I didn't believe in marriage because I'd never seen a good one. And so it was a long, slow process learning to trust this kind man. But I did learn to trust, and we became true and fast friends. Then something I thought impossible happened. We were married.

Tumult, divorce, and infidelity were all around us, but we simply loved one another. To experience an ordered life, a reliable love, filled my heart with such gratitude that I began to long for God. All I wanted was to say "thank you". So I began again, looking for Him, letting everybody in. Mormons, Jehovah's Witnesses, evangelicals—all found a ready listener in my living room. I believed in God, but I had no idea who He was or where to find Him.

Ultimately, it was not a stranger but a friend, a neighbor, who set me on the right path.

When we moved into our new house, the neighbors to our right groused about the neighbors to our left. They had six children—three times the national average and at least twice as many as anybody else in the neighborhood. It would be noisy, we lamented.

We feared the children would be unsupervised, the family permissive, a bad influence on our sons. But the opposite proved true. Sue's children were mild mannered, polite, and happy. Our boys became fast friends, and we adults did too. That she was a Catholic interested me, and since I was letting everyone else give me an earful, I figured she deserved a shot too.

It was providential; she was willing. At first, we considered reading Scripture, but for reasons unexplained, I suggested we study Vatican II instead. A third friend joined us, and for months, we three tore through documents, dissecting, explaining.

I'd had a long-standing interest in things Christian; I was acquainted with evangelical Christianity and was fairly familiar with the Gospels, but this Catholic Church was different. I had never encountered anything like it: deeply sane and thoroughly reasoned, there were simply no questions to which the Church lacked good answers. My heart was already disposed to Christ, but my head was somewhere else entirely. Resistant, stubborn, and afraid, I had to begin the process again of learning to trust—this time, to trust in an institution. But continuous positive encounters build trust, and using my intellect, using my reason, I encountered Truth. Catholicism is a profoundly intelligent faith.

After a year of studying Vatican II, we embarked upon the lives of the saints, and I was hooked—a fish caught. Terrified, I realized that without ever intending it, I'd changed in a way that was now unchangeable. I'd encountered a relational God, Jesus Christ, and had been transformed by the encounter. But there I was, in my astonishingly happy marriage, partnered with a Jewish man. What would happen? How would the family survive?

I'll tell you the frank and honest truth—it was very tough. I am forever grateful to the people who helped me find my way into the Church, but, of course, they could not erase my previous existence. It was nearly impossible for family and friends not to perceive conversion as an offense, a rejection of who they are and what they'd shared. Almost till the day she died, my mother carried a grudge, but by the grace of God, she managed to put it aside before her last breath. There are friends who to this day won't break bread with us, people whom we still love. This is a cross I accept. It's worth it, every bit of it, and God's promise to return a

hundredfold everything we've lost is a promise to take to
the bank.

My husband knows me well and was not surprised when
I told him I wanted to take the leap and become a card-
carrying Roman Catholic. He wasn't happy—he was afraid—
but he was characteristically supportive and never tried to
obstruct me. Yes, we had sent our children to Hebrew school,
but we were only loosely affiliated with our temple. He
was what could be described as a contented agnostic, and
he was willing to let me plunge into a new life of faith as
long as I didn't expect him to dive in after me. For twenty
long months, I was in a Rite of Christian Initiation of Adults
(RCIA) program, plenty of time for us both to become
accustomed to a new routine and a new life.

One thing I've failed to mention is that my husband is
a physician and I'm a nurse. What helped him accept my
decision was his profound respect for the Church's moral
teachings, particularly on life issues that pertained to our
professions. Both of us, even before we had the Church
to help us, were already convinced of the immorality of
abortion and euthanasia, but we were particularly interested in documents that connected abortion to contraception. For us, these were new ideas that absolutely made
sense. They were patently correct, we knew it, and we
were grateful to find an institution brave enough to teach
unpopular Truth.

Though he lacked faith, my husband recognized that the
Church enriched our lives and provided us with protection
from error. And so it was, after I was baptized, that he
brought our three children into the living room one morning, unannounced, and explained to them that he had
thought carefully about their upbringing and had decided
that it would be best if they were baptized too. Faith was a

great gift, he explained, one he was lacking, but with which I'd been blessed. And so, he said to them, follow your mother. Go with her.

Nine months after my baptism, our three children became Catholic, with my husband and our friends present to support us. Our youngest, being too small to lean over the baptismal font, was lifted up by her Jewish father. It was breathtaking.

Though Harvey went with us to Mass every Sunday, faithfully, there was still the painful reality of his absence at the Table. But how he tried! He attended RCIA classes briefly, he met privately with a priest, he prayed, but he never felt comfortable taking the leap. So he remained always with us, yet outside the Church.

Then, one day, the unspeakable happened. It was Mother's Day, and Harv was doing some cleaning for me, working with harsh chemicals. The fumes, it seems, triggered an asthma attack. Being a physician and a lifelong asthmatic, he had an arsenal of medicines that were his usual remedies, but this day, nothing helped. We got in the car and sped to the emergency room. By the time we arrived, he was pale, and the ER physician was alarmed. He administered treatments, injections, but Harv was shutting down, almost unable to move air. Finally, in desperation, the doctor decided to intubate him and put him on a respirator. We both knew this was a last-ditch, desperate measure and that Harv might die.

From the minute we'd arrived at the ER, I'd tried to get in touch with a priest but had failed. No one was available. In this dire moment, I asked Harvey if he'd like to be baptized. He nodded weakly. I poured a cup of tap water and baptized him in the name of the Father, the Son, and the Holy Spirit as any layman may in an emergency. Harv laid back, rested, and began to improve. Within a couple of hours, he was unobstructed, the tubes were removed, and the whole nightmare was behind us. As terrible as the night had been, we knew that simultaneously, a great miracle had occurred, and right there, in the busy intensive care unit, I crawled into his hospital bed, into his arms, and we wept for joy.

A friend asked me how it is that we can be happy as Catholics when there are so many difficulties, so many scandals in the Church. I've concluded that we have an advantage. Having lived a godless life has given us the edge. Once, we felt entirely alone. Now we know we're never alone. Once, we couldn't discern between good and evil. Now we are able to make life-affirming choices. Once, we didn't recognize that our lives had eternal value. Now we know that we're made in the image and likeness of God. Once, we didn't know that we were loved. Now we know that we're so deeply loved that the Creator of the universe gave His life for us. The rest seems small. I told my friend, "A bad day in the Church is better than a thousand good days in the world." This is the truth, and knowing it makes happiness easy.

And thus Harv and I began the whole process of adjustment all over again, this time with him as head, as it should be, as God intended. It was sixteen years ago that I entered the Church, and nine years ago that Harv was baptized, and we grow stronger in our marriage and in our faith with each new day. The Church on earth isn't perfect, but she's the very Church established by Christ, with Peter as head, and we're forever grateful to be here.

It is, for sure, an adventure, something two Jewish kids from Chicago's South Side never thought possible, an adventure that will continue for all eternity.

Catherine Schneir lives in Santa Paula, California, with her husband, Harvey, and their daughter, the youngest of their three children. Their married sons live nearby, with their growing families.

Chapter 5

Meeting Jesus

Roy Schoeman

I grew up Jewish in a middle-class suburb of New York City, the son of Jewish refugees who had fled Germany in the early days of Hitler's reign. My parents were active in the local "conservative" congregation, and by American standards, I had a fairly religious Jewish upbringing. I went for after-school religious instruction twice a week all the way through from first grade until college, was Bar Mitzvahed, and frequently—although not always!—attended services on the Sabbath, in addition to, of course, the Jewish holidays. I grew close to the extraordinary rabbis whom God graced me with for my religious formation and even wrestled with the issue of a religious vocation for myself. The summer between high school and college I spent traveling throughout Israel with a charismatic, "mystic" Hasidic rabbi, Rabbi Shlomo Carlebach, who each night gave a "concert", which was, in reality, an ecstatic Hasidic worship and praise service. I briefly considered staying in Israel to study at one of the many ultraorthodox yeshivas there—the closest thing Judaism has to "religious life"—but returned to begin my studies at Massachusetts Institute of Technology (MIT) in mathematics and computer science. In college I initially tried to maintain my religious fervor and was active in a local counterculture neo-Hasidic congregation-*cum*-seminary but soon fell into both the mores and the mind-set more typical of MIT. There is a close relationship between the maintenance of purity, both in mind and in behavior, and intimacy with God; although He might initially relax His rules as a sort of "loss leader" to draw one into a relationship with Him, sooner or later one can no longer expect the consolation of experienced intimacy with God if one does not play by His rules. As I abandoned the rules, I lost the intimacy. By the end of college, the joy of prayer had become an abstract memory, and I was almost entirely ensconced in the ways of the world. After a few years of working on the design of new computer systems, I went on to Harvard Business School for an M.B.A. and, as a result of an exceptional performance there, was invited to join the faculty to teach and pursue studies toward a doctorate, in preparation for a tenure-track career.

While all this was going on, there was, however, another and deeper dimension to my life. In losing touch with God, I also lost the sense of intrinsic purpose and direction to my life; at each juncture, I chose the path of least resistance, the path that, in the eyes of the world, constituted success—which being on the faculty of Harvard Business School at the age of thirty most certainly did—yet as I achieved each milestone, I was met with an ever deeper sense of emptiness, of meaninglessness, to the victory. By this time—about four years into my Harvard "tenure-track" career—I was inwardly overwhelmed with a sense of pointlessness bordering on despair. This was by no means unique to me. A colleague on the faculty, a chaired professor and department head, once revealed to me that the day after he was finally granted tenure, the culmination of

over a decade of effort, he almost quit, overwhelmed with
the sense of emptiness and pointlessness in everything for
which he had strived so hard. Although I had long since
left behind a conscious religious life and prayer, my primary solace during this period was found in long solitary
walks in nature. It was on one of these that I received the
most singular grace of my life.

It was early one morning in early June, during a mid-
week break I had given myself, two or three days on Cape
Cod before the crowds arrived. I was walking in the dunes
between Provincetown and Truro, alone with the singing
birds before the world woke up, when I, for lack of better
words, "fell into Heaven". That is, I found myself most
consciously and tangibly in the presence of God. I saw my
life to date laid out before me, seeing it as though I were
reviewing it in the presence of God after death. I saw everything that I would be pleased about and everything I would
regret. I also knew, from one instant to the next, that the
meaning and purpose of my life was to love and serve my
Lord and God; I saw how His love enveloped and sustained
me every moment of my existence; I saw how everything I
did had a moral content, for good or for ill, and which
mattered far more than I would ever know; I saw how everything that had ever happened in my life was the most perfect thing that could be arranged for my own good by an
all-good, all-loving God, *especially* those things that caused
me the most suffering at the time; I saw that my two greatest regrets at the moment of death would be all of the time
and energy I had wasted worrying about not being loved,
when every moment of my existence I was held in the sea
of God's unimaginably great love, and every hour I had
wasted not doing anything of value in the eyes of God.
The answer to any question I mentally posed was instantly

presented to me; in fact, I could not hold a question in my mind without already being shown the answer, with one, all-important exception—the name of this God who was revealing Himself to me as the meaning and purpose of my life. I did not think of Him as the God of the Old Testament whom I held in my imagination from my childhood. I prayed to know His name, to know what religion to follow to serve and worship Him properly. I remember praying, "Let me know your name—I don't mind if you are Buddha, and I have to become a Buddhist; I don't mind if you are Apollo, and I have to become a Roman pagan; I don't mind if you are Krishna, and I have to become a Hindu; as long as you are not Christ and I have to become a Christian!" This deep-seated resistance to Christianity was based on the sense I had of Christianity as the "enemy", the perversion of Judaism that had been the cause of two millennia of Jewish suffering. As a result, although this God who revealed Himself to me on the beach had heard my prayer to know His name, He also heard, and respected, my refusal to know it too, and so gave no answer at the time to the question.

I returned to my home in Cambridge and to my ordinary life, yet everything was changed. I spent all of my free time in seeking after this God, through quiet time in nature, reading, and asking people whom I thought might know more than I did about such "mystical" experiences. Since this was Cambridge in the 1980s, it inevitably led in some New Age directions, and I ended up reading primarily Hindu- and Buddhist-based spiritual writings. Yet one day, walking through Harvard Square, the cover illustration of a book in a store window caught my eye, and without knowing anything at all about the book or its author, I went in and bought Saint Teresa of Avila's *The Interior Castle*. I devoured it, finding great spiritual nourishment within, but still gave no credence to the particular claims of Christianity.

I continued in this undiscriminating, eclectic path for exactly one year. One year to the day after the experience on the beach, I received the second-greatest extraordinary grace of my life. I frankly admit that, in all external aspects, what took place was a dream. Yet when I went to sleep I knew little about, and had no special sympathy for, Christianity or any of its aspects; when I awoke I was hopelessly in love with the Blessed Virgin Mary and wanted nothing more than to become as totally Christian as I could. In the "dream", I was taken to a room and granted an audience with the most beautiful young woman I could have ever imagined; without it being spoken, I knew that it was the Blessed Virgin Mary. She agreed to answer any questions I might ask her; I clearly remember standing there, weighing a number of possible questions in my mind, and asking her four or five of them. She answered them, then spoke to me for several more minutes, and then the audience was ended. My experience of the event, and my memory of it, are as of something that took place in full wakefulness. I remember all of the details, including of course the questions and the answers, but all pales beside the greatest aspect by far of the experience: the ecstasy of simply being in her presence, in the purity and intensity of her love.

When I awoke, as I said, I was hopelessly in love with the Blessed Virgin Mary and knew that the God who had revealed Himself to me on the beach had been Christ. Yet I still knew almost nothing about Christianity, including having no idea of the difference between Protestants and Catholics. My initial foray into Christianity was into a Protestant church, but when I brought up the topic of Mary with the pastor, his thinly veiled contempt made me say to myself, "I'm outta here!" Meanwhile, my love for Mary inspired me to spend time at Marian shrines, especially those of Our Lady of La Salette— both the one in Ipswich, Massachusetts, and the one at the site of the original apparition, high in the French Alps.[1] So I found myself, willy-nilly, frequently present at Masses, and although I still had no belief in the Catholic Church, I was filled with an intense desire to receive Communion. In fact, the first time I approached a priest and asked to be baptized, I still held no Catholic beliefs. When he asked me, "Why do you want to be baptized?" I angrily blurted out the truth, "Because I want to receive Communion and you guys won't let me unless I am baptized!" I thought he would throw me out on my ear; instead, he nodded sagely and said, "Aha. That's the Holy Spirit at work."

I still had to wait several years and mature in my faith before baptism, but throughout the process my love of Mary and my thirst for the Eucharist guided me, like a compass, toward the goal. I am infinitely grateful to God for my conversion; I am infinitely grateful to God for the people He gave me to lead me on my path, and I am particularly grateful to God for the opportunity to have written this story, and to you, dear reader, for having read it.

Roy Schoeman grew up in New York City. Before his extraordinary mystical experiences, he served on the faculty of Harvard

[1] The Blessed Virgin Mary appeared to two young shepherd children high in the French Alps in 1846, giving them a message of prayer and repentence; this apparition, named after the nearest village, is known as "Our Lady of La Salette". For a description, see, for instance, Jean Jouen, M.S., *A Grace Called La Salette* (Attleboro, Mass.: La Salette Publications, 1991), or Br. Francis Mary Kalvelage, F.I., *Marian Shrines of France* (New Bedford, Mass.: Academy of the Immaculate, 1998).

Business School. Since his conversion, he has pursued theological studies, appeared on Eternal Word Television Network (EWTN), and written and spoken widely about the Catholic faith as the fulfillment of God's messianic promise to the Jews. His books include Salvation Is from the Jews, *and* Honey from the Rock, *both published by Ignatius Press. The author can be contacted by email at schoeman@catholic.org or via his Web site www.salvationisfrom thejews.com.*

Chapter 6

Race with the Devil:
From the Hell of Hate to the
Well of Mercy*

Joseph Pearce

"A sound atheist cannot be too careful of the books that he reads." So said C. S. Lewis in his autobiographical apologia, *Surprised by Joy*. These words continue to resonate across the abyss of years that separates me from the abysmal bitterness of my past.

What is true of the atheist is as true of the racist. Looking back into the piteous pits of the hell of hatred that consumed my youth, I can see the role that great Christian writers played in lighting my path out of the darkened depths. Eventually, with their light to guide me, I stumbled out into the dazzling brilliance of Christian day. Looking back along that path, I can see, in my memory's eye, the literary candles that lit the way. There are dozens of candles bearing the name of G. K. Chesterton, of which *Orthodoxy*, *The Everlasting Man*, *The Well and the Shallows*, and *The Outline*

---

*An earlier version of this essay was published in *This Rock* magazine. It appears here with the permission of the author.

of Sanity shine forth particularly brightly. Almost as many candles bear the name of Chesterton's great friend, Hilaire Belloc, and several bear the name of John Henry Newman. And, of course, there are the flickering presences of Lewis and Tolkien. These and countless others light the path by which I have traveled.

Long before any of these candles were lit, I found myself groping in the unlit tunnel of racial hatred, the angst and anger of which had all but obliterated the blissful memories of a relatively carefree childhood. Guilty of ignorance, I left my innocence behind and advanced into adolescence with the arrogance of pride and prejudice—boyhood bliss blistered by bitterness.

I grew up in a relatively poor neighborhood in London's East End at a time when major-scale immigration was causing major demographic changes. The influx of large numbers of Indians and Pakistanis was quite literally changing the face of England, darkening the complexion and adding to the complexity of English life. Perhaps inevitably, the arrival of these immigrants caused a great deal of resentment among the indigenous population. Racial tensions were high, and violence between white and Asian youths was becoming commonplace. It was in this highly charged atmosphere that I emerged into angry adolescence.

At the age of fifteen I joined the National Front, a new force in British politics that demanded the compulsory repatriation of all nonwhite immigrants. As a political activist, my life revolved around street demonstrations, many of which became violent. I filled my empty head and inflamed my impassioned heart with racist ideology and elitist philosophy. It was at this time that I made what I now consider to be my Faustian pact, my pact with the Devil (not that I had heard of Faust nor, as an agnostic, had any particular belief in the Devil).

Nonetheless, I recall making a conscious "wish" that I would give everything if I could work full time for the National Front. My "wish" was granted, and I abandoned my education to devote myself wholeheartedly to becoming a full-time "racial revolutionary".

I never looked back. At the age of sixteen I became editor of *Bulldog*, the newspaper of the Young National Front, and, three years later, editor of *Nationalism Today*, a "higher-brow" ideological journal. At eighteen I became the youngest member of the party's governing body. Whether I believed in him or not, the Devil had certainly been diligent in answering my "wish".

Apart from the racism, the sphere of my bitterness also included a disdain for Catholicism, partly because the terrorists of the Irish Republican Army (IRA) were Catholics and partly because I had absorbed with the anti-Catholic prejudice of many Englishmen a conviction that Catholicism is a "foreign" religion. Such prejudice is deeply rooted in the national psyche, stretching back to the anti-Catholicism of Henry VIII and his English Reformation, to Elizabeth I and the Spanish Armada, to James I and the Gunpowder Plot, to William of Orange and the so-called Glorious Revolution. I knew enough of English history—or at least enough of the prejudiced Protestant view of it that I had imbibed in my ignorance—to see Catholicism as an enemy to the Nationhood that, as a racial nationalist, I now espoused with a quasi-religious fervor.

It was, however, in the context of "the Troubles" in Northern Ireland that my anti-Catholicism would reveal itself in its full ugliness. The IRA's bombing campaign was at its height during the 1970s, and my hatred of Republican terrorism led to my becoming involved in the volatile politics of Ulster. I joined the Orange Order, a pseudomasonic secret society whose sole purpose of existence is to oppose "popery", that is, Catholicism. Technically, although only Protestants were allowed to join the Orange Order, no actual belief in God appeared necessary. As a "Protestant" agnostic I was allowed to join, and a friend, an avowed atheist, was also accepted without qualms. Ultimately, the essential qualification was not a love for Christ but a hatred of the Church.

In October 1978, still only seventeen, I flew to Derry in Northern Ireland to assist in the organization of a National Front march. Tensions were high in the city, and toward the end of the day, riots broke out between the Protestant demonstrators and the police. For the duration of the evening and well into the night, gasoline bombs were thrown at the police, Catholic homes were attacked, and Catholic-owned shops were looted and destroyed. I had encountered political violence on the streets of England but nothing on the scale of sheer anger and violence that I experienced in Northern Ireland.

My appetite whetted, I became further embroiled in the politics of Ulster, forging friendships and political alliances with the leaders of Protestant paramilitary groups, the Ulster Volunteer Force (UVF) and the Ulster Defense Association (UDA). During a secret meeting with the UVF army council, it was suggested that I use my connections with extremist groups in other parts of the world to open channels for arms smuggling. On another occasion an "active service unit" of the UVF, that is, a terrorist cell, offered me their "services", assuring me of their willingness to assassinate any "targets" that I would like "taken out" and expressing eagerness to show me their arsenal of weaponry as a mark of their "good faith". I declined their offer as politely as possible—one does not wish to offend "friends" such as these. The times were dangerous. Within a few years, two of my friends in Northern Ireland had been murdered by the IRA.

Back in England, violence continued to erupt at National Front demonstrations. In 1979, in an Indian area of London, outside an election meeting at which I was one of the speakers, a riot ensued in which one demonstrator was killed. A few years later, a friend, an elderly man, was killed at another election meeting, though one at which I was not present.

It was only a matter of time before my extremist politics brought me into conflict with the law. Predictably, in 1982, as editor of *Bulldog*, I was convicted under the Race Relations Act for publishing material "likely to incite racial hatred" and was sentenced to six months in prison. The trial made national headlines. As a result, prison authorities were fearful that my presence might provoke trouble between black and white inmates, so I spent much of my sentence in isolation and in solitary confinement. Ironically, one of the other prisoners in the top-security wing was an IRA sympathizer, imprisoned for slashing a portrait of Princess Diana with a knife. He and I saw ourselves as "political prisoners", not as mere "common criminals", like the murderers who were serving life sentences, who constituted the majority of prisoners in the top-security wing.

Unrepentant, I continued to edit *Bulldog* following my release and was duly charged once again with offenses under the Race Relations Act. On the second occasion, I was sentenced to twelve months' imprisonment. Thus I spent both my twenty-first and twenty-fifth birthdays behind bars.

During the first of my prison sentences, Auberon Waugh, a well-known writer and a son of the great Catholic novelist Evelyn Waugh, had referred to me as a "wretched youth". How right he was! Wretched and wrecked upon the rock of my own hardness of heart. Years later, when asked by the priest who was instructing me in the Catholic faith to write an essay on my conversion, I began it with the opening lines of John Newton's famous hymn extolling the "amazing grace ... that saved a wretch like me". Even today, when forced to look candidly into the blackness of my past, I am astonished to consider how truly amazing was the grace that somehow managed to take root in the desert of my soul.

How did that cactus of grace, growing at first unheeded in the desert of my just deserts, become the cataract of life-giving waters washing my sins away in the sacramental grace of confession? How, to put the matter more bluntly, was I freed from the prison of my sinful convictions? How was I brought from the locked door of my prison cell to the open arms of Mother Church?

With the wisdom of hindsight, I perceive that the seeds of my future conversion were planted as early as 1980, when I was still only nineteen years old. In what barren soil they were planted! At the time I was at the very depth of my political fanaticism and was indulging the worst excesses of my anti-Catholic prejudices in the dirty waters of Ulster Protestantism. Few could have been further from Saint Peter's gate than I.

The seeds were planted in a genuine desire to seek a political and economic alternative to both the sins of Communism and the cynicism of consumerism. During street confrontations with my Marxist opponents, I was incensed by their accusation that, as an anti-Communist, I was, ipso facto, a "storm trooper of capitalism". Convinced that Communism was a red herring and that it was possible to have a socially just society without socialism, I refused to believe that the only alternative to Mammon was Marx. In the course of my quest to discover such an alternative, someone suggested that I read more about the distributist ideas of Belloc and Chesterton. At this juncture one hears echoes once again of Lewis' stricture that "a sound atheist cannot be too careful of the books that he reads", not least because the book to which he was specifically referring was Chesterton's *The Everlasting Man*, a book that precipitated Lewis' first tentative steps to conversion. In this, at least, I can claim a real parallel between C. S. Lewis and myself: for me, as for him, a book by Chesterton would lead toward conversion. In my case, however, the book that was destined to have such a profound influence was a lesser-known book of Chesterton's.

The friend who suggested that I study the distributist ideas of Chesterton informed me that I should buy Chesterton's book *The Outline of Sanity* but that I should also read an invaluable essay on the subject entitled "Reflections on a Rotten Apple", which was to be found in a collection of Chesterton's essays entitled *The Well and the Shallows*. As he suggested, I purchased the two books and sat down expectantly to read the volume of essays. Imagine my surprise and consternation to discover that the latter book was, for the most part, a defense of the Catholic faith against various modern attacks upon it. And imagine my confusion when I discovered that I could not fault Chesterton's logic.

The wit and wisdom of Chesterton had pulled the rug out from under my smug prejudices against the Catholic Church. From that moment, I began to discover the Church as she is, and not as her enemies allege her to be. I had begun the journey from the canard that she is the Whore of Babylon to the realization that she is in fact the Bride of Christ.

It was, however, destined to be a long journey. I was lost in Dante's dark wood, so deeply lost that I had perhaps already strayed into the Inferno. It is a long and arduous climb from there to the foot of Mount Purgatory. However, I was in good company; if Dante had Virgil, I had Chesterton. He would accompany me faithfully every inch of the way, present always through the pages of his books. I began to devour everything that I could get my hands on by Chesterton, consuming his words with ravenous delight. Through Chesterton I came to know Belloc; then Lewis; then Newman. During my second prison sentence, I first read *The Lord of the Rings*, and though I did not at that time fathom the full mystical depths of the Catholicism in Tolkien's myth, I was aware of the myth's goodness, its objective morality, and the well of virtue from which it drew. And, of course, I was aware that Tolkien, like Chesterton, Belloc, and Newman, was a Catholic. Why was it that most of my favorite writers were Catholics?

It was during the second prison sentence that I first started to consider myself a Catholic. When, as is standard procedure, the prison authorities asked my religion at the beginning of my sentence, I announced that I was a Catholic. I was not, of course, at least not technically, but it was my first affirmation of faith, even to myself. A significant landmark had been reached. Another landmark, during the second prison sentence, was my first fumbling effort at prayer. I am not aware of ever having prayed prior to my arrival at Wormwood Scrubs prison in December 1985, at least not if one discounts schoolboy prayers recited parrot-fashion to an unknown and unsought God during drab and lukewarm school services many years earlier. Now, in the desolation of my cell, I fumbled my fingers over the beads of a Rosary that someone had sent me. I had no idea how to say it. I did not know the Hail Mary or the Glory Be, and I could not remember the Lord's Prayer. Nonetheless, I ad-libbed my way from bead to bead uttering prayers of my own devising, pleading from the depths of my piteous predicament for the faith, hope, and love that my mind and heart desired. It was a small but significant start.

My release from prison in 1986 heralded the beginning of the end of my life as a political extremist. Increasingly disillusioned, I extricated myself from the organization which, for more than a decade, had been my life, and which had delineated my very raison d'être. As a fifteen-year-old, I had "wished" to give my life to the "cause"; now, in my mid-twenties, I desired only to give my life to Christ. If the Devil had taken my earlier "wish" and granted it infernally, Christ would take my newfound desire and grant it purgatorially.

Having spent the whole of the 1980s in a spiritual arm-wrestle, in which I fought within my heart and my head between the hell of hatred within myself and the well of love promised and poured out by Christ, I finally "came home" to the loving embrace of Holy Mother Church on the Feast of Saint Joseph 1989. Today, twenty years on, I still find myself utterly amazed at the grace that saved a wretch like me.

Joseph Pearce is the author of critically acclaimed, best-selling biographies of great nineteenth- and twentieth-century Christian authors, among them Wisdom and Innocence: A Life of G. K. Chesterton; Literary Converts: Spiritual Inspiration in an Age of Unbelief; Tolkien: Man and Myth; The Unmasking of Oscar Wilde; *and* C. S. Lewis and the Catholic Church *(all from Ignatius Press). He is also writer-in-residence and associate professor of literature at Ave Maria University in Florida and coeditor of the* St. Austin Review *(StAR), an international magazine dedicated to reclaiming Catholic culture.*

Chapter 7

Ye Must Be Born Again

Kristine Franklin

I was watching cartoons when I decided to ask Jesus to be my personal Savior. At the commercial break, I ducked into the kitchen and said the prayer. "Jesus, come into my heart." I was four years old. I wanted Jesus to take away my sins. I wanted to go to Heaven. My mother wept for joy when I told her that I was a born-again Christian.

I understood that the world was divided into Christians and non-Christians, and I wanted to be a Christian. Our church sent missionaries to preach the Good News to non-Christians around the world. The missionary from Sudan drove a car painted to look like a tiger. The missionaries from Japan dressed up in kimonos and sang in Japanese. I loved the missionaries and their stories. I wanted everyone to know about Jesus.

Our church also sent missionaries to preach the gospel message of salvation in Catholic countries. Catholics were as lost as the cannibals of New Guinea. In a way, they were worse off than the cannibals. Catholics *thought* they were Christians. We believed that there were very few Christians in places like Italy, Spain, and Brazil. Catholics needed to be saved.

I was taught that to be a missionary was to answer God's highest calling—to take the message of salvation to those who were perishing. When I was six years old, my older brother drove from Seattle to El Salvador to be a missionary. Over the years, he served in Spain and Mexico as well. His love for the people was sincere, his conviction that Catholicism was a religion of Satan, unshakable. My brother was the hero of the family.

We had relatives and neighbors who were Catholics. My mother often explained the difference between our biblical Christianity and Catholicism. Catholic worship was ritualistic, like pagan worship. Our worship was straight out of the New Testament. Catholics repeated empty, memorized prayers like the heathens; we prayed from our hearts. Catholics had adopted ancient female deities and turned them into a new false goddess, Mary. We knew Mary was a sinner like everyone else. She was nothing more than the womb God used to carry Jesus. Catholics worshipped Mary and bowed down to statues and crucifixes.

Catholics thought they could earn their way to Heaven, through good works. We knew that salvation was a free gift. Catholics added rules and doctrines that were not in the Bible; we used the Bible alone. I was taught that Catholics were not allowed to read the Bible, that they were slaves to their evil priests, and that they were commanded to have large families so that the cult could grow.

We believed that during the Great Tribulation, the Antichrist would rise up and rule the earth by the power of Satan. Any day, Jesus would take the true believers up to Heaven in the Rapture. When I asked my mother who the Antichrist might be, she said, "Probably a Catholic pope."

My mother loved Jesus with all her heart. She was kind, generous, even-tempered, and compassionate. She read the

Bible daily. My mother prayed for the salvation of family members, starting first with my father and all of our unsaved relatives. Mom prayed for neighbors, public officials, and strangers in far-away lands. When President Kennedy was shot, she wept because he was Catholic and had died without salvation. Over the years, I absorbed all of the beliefs that my good mother taught me. I had no reason to doubt her.

*   *   *

When I was eight, our pastor gave a fiery sermon on the need to be baptized. He said that baptism did not save us but that if a Christian refused to be baptized, it meant he was ashamed of Jesus. I asked to be baptized.

Our pastor was skeptical about baptizing someone so young. I had to meet with him to discuss my theology. He wanted to make sure that I understood that baptism did not save me or make me a Christian, that it was nothing but a testimony. I understood, and he allowed me to be baptized.

The pastor was waiting for me as I walked down the steps into the baptismal pool. The pastor put his hand on my head, asked me if I had asked Jesus to be my personal Lord and Savior, and when I said yes, he tipped me backward into the water and baptized me in the name of the Father, and the Son, and the Holy Ghost. When I came up out of the water, I felt a thrill of joy. Now Jesus knew for sure that I was not ashamed of Him.

Most of my school friends went to church, but they didn't talk like the Christians I knew. I didn't know how to categorize these people. I didn't know where they fit. My mom called them churchgoers.

My mom told me that most other churches got the Bible wrong. Lutherans baptized babies, Pentecostals spoke in tongues, and Presbyterians didn't believe in the Rapture. Methodists believed a person could lose his salvation through sin. Any belief that was unlike our own was unbiblical.

A lot of churchgoers were not Christians. They needed to be saved. And once they were saved, they needed to join a Bible-believing church and read the Bible for themselves. Most importantly, real Christians needed to learn from preachers who taught sound doctrine, which meant doctrine like ours.

The war in Vietnam raged, students protested, hippies dropped out and dropped acid. I began to have questions that the faith of my little church could not answer— questions about the meaning of existence, the purpose of suffering, the definition of morality.

During junior high I attended a Christian coffeehouse run by ex-hippies who had accepted Christ and were "getting high on Jesus" instead of drugs. The nineteen-year-old lay preacher who was in charge of Bible study taught us about the Five Points of Calvinism.[1] He said that Jesus had not died for the whole world but only for those who were predestined for salvation, that some people could never be saved.

When I asked my mother why we should evangelize if everyone is predestined to either salvation or damnation, she grew concerned. "Kristine," she said, "I worry about you. Just believe, that's all. *Believe*."

I *did* believe, but I wanted to know. Was the war in Vietnam part of God's will? Why would God predestine people

---

[1] For a full explanation of the Five Points of Calvinism from a Catholic point of view, please see James Akin's article "A Tiptoe through TULIP", *This Rock* 4, no. 8 (September 1993), http://www.catholic.com/thisrock/1993/9309fea1.asp.

to Hell? Was I predestined to salvation or not? I persisted
with my questions but found the answers I received to be
simplistic and unsatisfying, and I said so. I earned labels at
home and at church: Rebellious. Has a problem with authority. Worldly.

I lost two friends in a car accident. My parents separated.
My mother was diagnosed with fatal cancer and died within
two years. My family was broken, my questions unanswered,
my mother gone. I decided that the faith I'd been raised
with was phony and shallow, so I stopped going to church.

At college I made a lot of friends who had been raised in
one religion or another but had laid their religious beliefs
aside in pursuit of pleasure and autonomy. I tried to convince myself that my childhood religion had been a sham
and decided it was more important to have fun than to be
good. My desire for God was extinguished, and my heart
grew dark.

My sister and her husband were serving as missionaries
in western New Guinea, Indonesia, and one afternoon I
received a cable message from my brother-in-law. Would I
be interested in working as his secretary for six months?
The mission would pay my way to Indonesia, and I could
live with my sister and her family. I was longing for a connection to family, and I replied within the hour. *Yes! Now
what?* Soon I was on a plane flying across the Pacific. I felt
hopeful for the first time in years.

*   *   *

Out of courtesy, I attended church and Bible studies with
my sister and her missionary friends, but at first, none of it
penetrated my heart. I was immune to the things of God.

Like everyone who lives abroad, I soon began to experience culture shock. I was frequently ill with one tropical disease after another. I grew depressed and anxious and felt like I was trapped in a third-world hellhole. How could these missionaries stand this life?

I already knew the answer. Their lives had meaning, their sacrifices made a difference, while my life was shallow and self-focused. They lived for Christ. I lived for Kris. My miserable state was my own fault, but I knew the remedy.

I cried long and hard. I begged for God's forgiveness. "I'll do things Your way." I prayed as I had never prayed before, and I knew God heard me.

From that day I read the Bible faithfully. I memorized Bible verses. I prayed. I went to Bible studies and church services and tried hard to listen and apply what I heard. The selflessness of the missionaries was infectious, their courage inspiring. I deeply appreciated the way they seemed to cooperate across doctrinal lines. I naïvely assumed that it didn't matter if one was a Baptist or a Quaker; all that mattered was the gospel. I asked the Lord to make me worthy of the highest calling.

I finished my college degree at Biola University in La Mirada, California. During a theology class on the end times, our professor pointed out that most Christians did not hold to our dispensationalist[2] doctrines, that our belief in the

---

[2] Biola University holds to a system of evangelical theology called "dispensationalism". Dispensationalism was created by an Englishman named John Nelson Darby in the mid-nineteenth century. His teachings were accepted and promoted in the United States by a lay preacher named Cyrus Ingerson Scofield, who, together with wealthy financier A. C. Gaebelein, published a Bible with dispensationalist study notes in 1917. The Scofield Bible was a hit, coinciding with the newborn fundamentalist movement. Many people accepted Darby's system and Scofield's notes as a correct interpretation of Scripture, left their mainline denominations, and formed congregations with

Rapture was almost exclusively limited to "our" kind of Christians. This was news to me! Wasn't the Rapture in the Bible? Wasn't it plain to everyone?

The professor explained what various other Christians believed and showed how each doctrine in turn could be proved from Scripture. Then he said, "Don't live or die for the Rapture. Choose a view and be able to back it up from Scripture." I was stunned at the thought of choosing my own doctrinal position. I'd been told all my life what to believe. After thinking about it, I voted with the majority and rejected the doctrine of the Rapture. Being "left behind" had been a common scare tactic for getting people to accept Christ. I wanted nothing to do with it, so I threw it out.

After graduation I met my husband, Marty. He had no formal Bible training and had not even heard of dispensationalism. To Marty, specific doctrines were unimportant. A personal relationship with Christ was all that mattered. He had had a born-again experience as a teen and had been nurtured at non-denominational Young Life meetings. I hated doctrinal fighting and had seen plenty of it while I was growing up.

We were newly married and decided to choose a church together, from scratch, so we did what many people do—we went church shopping. We tried a Plymouth Brethren church, but women there were required to wear a veil. We tried a Free Methodist church but disliked how they taught that salvation could be lost through sin. One Lutheran church had no young people at all. We decided it was "dead". First Christian

doctrinal statements based on a dispensationalist interpretation of Scripture. Moody Bible Institute, Dallas Theological Seminary, Bob Jones University, and Wheaton College are examples of dispensationalist-influenced institutions; *The Ryrie Study Bible* and the *Left Behind* books are examples of dispensationalist-influenced publications.

Church was too big. Finally, we settled on a Baptist church that offered interesting sermons, music we liked, and best of all, an instant set of friends who were just like us.

Over the next eight years, we made every sacrifice necessary in order to become missionaries. Marty renewed his teaching license and took Bible courses from Moody Bible Institute. In 1989 we were accepted as candidates with a well-known evangelical mission agency. Our mission had personnel in Guatemala whose children attended the Christian Academy of Guatemala. Would we be willing to go there?

It was common knowledge that Guatemalans, being uneducated and Catholic, were very easy to bring out of darkness and into the light of salvation. We were thrilled to be part of that great harvest.

After two years of training and fundraising, we were sent to language school. The language institute in Costa Rica existed for the sole purpose of training evangelicals to be missionaries in Spanish-speaking countries. We were a diverse bunch, but we all had the same purpose: to take the gospel to the lost, which meant the Catholics.

One day in a conversation class the teacher brought in a pamphlet for us to read and discuss published by the Catholic bishop of San Jose. I was startled by two things: first, that many Catholic beliefs were the same as mine; and second, that I had never before read anything about the Catholic Church, her doctrines, beliefs, or practices, not even an anti-Catholic book.

Everything I believed about the Catholic Church had been absorbed since childhood and never questioned. Clearly, Catholics believed some things that were biblical. How like the Devil, I thought, to mix in some truth with the error.

We arrived in Guatemala in the spring of 1992. I was eager to make a home for my family in our new country.

After we had settled in, we did what evangelicals do in a new town. We went church shopping again.

We settled on a small neighborhood church that had been founded by dispensationalist missionaries. It was as familiar as my childhood church except for the exuberant music. We sang and clapped and felt very Latin American. This is what we'd longed for—to be part of the big family of God where it didn't matter whether we were American or Guatemalan.

We were surprised to find that a number of our new friends at El Camino Church were divorced and remarried. "I went on a Cursillo retreat", said Pablito, a successful businessman. "The priest told me to stop sleeping with my wife and seek an annulment from my first marriage. So we became evangelicals."

We met other couples that had joined El Camino Church for reasons that surprised us. "This church is closer to my house", said one person. "The music is better", said another. "Now I can prescribe the Pill", said a young doctor. While some described a definite conversion experience, it was not always the first reason they gave. Certainly, I was glad these people had left the Catholic Church. At least now they heard the truth preached every week.

One Sunday the American missionary in charge of the church announced the publication of a new hymnal. Each family was required to purchase one since the church itself could not afford the expense of hymnals. I wondered at the wisdom of asking Guatemalans to spend a good chunk of money when the overhead projector worked just fine. Still, when the hymnals went on sale, we bought one.

A few weeks later Pablito mentioned to us privately that a number of members were complaining about having to buy hymnals.

"You know why we are really getting hymnals?" said Pablito. "I'm on the elder board—I can tell you. If you're holding a book, you can't clap. The missionaries don't want anyone to think we're Pentecostals."

When I was twelve, our pastor had been fired for speaking in tongues during a Bible study at his home. Half the congregation had followed him to create a new church.

In college I'd had a professor—a former Catholic—who believed that speaking in tongues could lead to demon possession. He not only believed that speaking in tongues was a useless practice, he believed it was sinful and diabolical.

In Guatemala the Pentecostals and the Non-Pentecostals were in a heated competition for members. A Non-Pentecostal missionary could work years to establish a little congregation, only to have the well-funded Assemblies of God or Foursquare Gospel missionaries move into the neighborhood, blast rock music into the streets, hold healing meetings, and lure the faithful away from the truth.

I felt tainted by unknowingly taking part in the conflict. Marty and I made constant jokes about the hymnbooks, if only to cover up our disgust and disappointment at this pettiness on the mission field.

One afternoon I attended a women's Bible study, led by a veteran missionary. Right away I realized that one woman, Anna Maria, was clearly a Catholic. She spoke of her relationship with Jesus in a mature and insightful way. She knew the Bible. And, though she was a woman in her forties, she was pregnant with her fifth child.

I knew Catholics were not supposed to use birth control, and I admired Anna Maria for living what her church taught. I was curious to meet a Catholic who loved Jesus! For the first time it occurred to me that maybe all Catholics didn't need to be rescued from their church. Maybe what they needed was more information about salvation. Maybe if there were more true Christians in the Catholic Church, they wouldn't need evangelizing.

Anna Maria left early, and I shook her hand and kissed her cheek, Guatemalan style. I told her I hoped we could get to know each other better. As soon as the door closed behind her, a debate ensued.

"She might be saved already", said one woman.

"No, she's still committed to Catholicism", said the leader. "She never has made a decision for Christ, but I think she's close."

"And if she becomes a Christian," said another woman, "her whole family might follow."

"And she could get her tubes tied", said someone, and the other ladies laughed. When the laughter died down, we bowed our heads and prayed for Anna Maria.

I felt sick. I wanted to know Anna Maria, to be her friend, maybe even ask her about her church. She was a person, not a project! Anna Maria already loved Jesus. What more did she really need?

We'd spent years getting ready to save souls, but when faced with my first potential convert, my fervor evaporated. I didn't want to be *this* kind of missionary. I was ashamed of those ladies and the way they had talked behind Anna Maria's back. I didn't return to the Bible study, and I never saw Anna Maria again.

*　*　*

It was Easter Sunday, but there were no decorations, no flowers. The service began with a hymn, but it wasn't an Easter hymn. The pastor preached for an hour but mentioned the Resurrection only at the end. Finally, we sang an Easter hymn, and then it was over.

When I got home, I burst into tears. "It's *Easter*, for Heaven's sake!" I told Marty. "No flowers? No sunrise service? *Nothing*. And the pastor didn't even mention the Crucifixion!"

"I'm sure it's a reaction to the Catholics", said Marty. "They make such a big deal over Holy Week."

"Then the Catholics have something right", I said. "It *is* a big deal. First we get hymnbooks so we won't be like Pentecostals. Now we skip Easter so we won't be like Catholics. It's insane!"

Over the next couple of months, we began to realize that the hymnbooks and muted Easter service were just the tip of the iceberg. "We don't want to do that because —— group does it", was often the explanation for decisions, and it disturbed us tremendously. We did what all evangelicals do when they don't like something at their church. We looked for another church.

We visited a couple of megachurches, one Pentecostal and the other Non-Pentecostal. The Pentecostal pastor whipped the people into a frenzy of moaning and speaking in tongues while the TV cameras rolled. People fainted. People yelled. We didn't go back.

At the Non-Pentecostal megachurch, the pastor spent an hour convincing people to come forward and pray for salvation. He worked the crowd like a pro, pleading, condemning, offering the free love of Jesus and certain Heaven. This was familiar territory for me. I'd grown up with altar calls. Hearing it in my second language forced me to evaluate it as though I were an outsider looking in. Was this really how God operated? Come forward, say this prayer, and you're in?

We accused the Catholics of believing that baptism saved them. Did a prayer save us? When I was a child, I'd been thrilled to see the hundreds of people who went forward at a Billy Graham crusade. Now the whole thing made me squirm.

We attended for a few more Sundays, but every week it was the same. Long, pleading sermon, syrupy music, altar call. We looked elsewhere.

We began to attend the Union Church, an American church established to serve the needs of English-speaking Protestants. Marty and I joined an adult Sunday school class, only to stop going when we realized it was a battleground for differing theological opinions. We wanted no part in debate.

Why did we need to go to a building? I wondered. Jesus had said that when two or more gathered in His name, He would be with them, and certainly both Marty and I had been instructed well enough to instruct others! Why should we have to listen to someone else's sermon?

Our kids were tired of church shopping, and so were we. Many Sundays, we stayed home, read the Bible, sang songs, and prayed. We called it "home church", and our kids loved it. Surprisingly, no one criticized us for it. Lots of missionary families did "home church".

It wasn't long after arriving in Guatemala that we were faced with the disintegration of our hope of working in Christian harmony with our own mission team. Our meetings began with prayer but usually ended in dispute and disagreement. Each of the men and women on our team had a substantial prayer life and knowledge of the Bible, and not one of them had any obvious vices or emotional issues. But when conflict arose, suddenly the big happy family I had dreamed of, the gospel team with one goal, one vision, one unbreakable bond in Jesus Christ, became a bickering, dysfunctional disaster, incapable of solving its own problems or arriving at consensus. We were not the only ones experiencing disharmony. It was the norm among all mission groups.

I attended another ladies' Bible study, exclusively for missionary wives. Most missionaries rented modest homes and lived on a tight budget, but the home where this Bible study was held was spacious and elegant, surrounded by a security gate and electrical lock system. The roof sported an enormous satellite dish. A luxury car was parked in the carport.

A maid answered the gate and let me in. In the house, another maid worked in the kitchen. A gardener labored in the parklike back yard. I spotted my friend Lani Bogart and sat beside her on the elegant sofa. The hostess welcomed us, the maid served coffee, and we began the meeting with a prayer.

The lesson was on the Rapture. The teacher spent a lot of energy trying to convince us that the doctrine of the Rapture was essential to a proper view of the Bible and Christian life. I remained silent throughout the meeting.

Afterward, Lani and I met for coffee at our favorite café. "You were quiet during Bible study", she said. "Was it the car, or the Rapture?"

"It's me", I said. It felt good to be honest with this gentle, accepting friend. I didn't dare breathe a word of dissatisfaction to any of our own team members. "I'm just not comfortable with this missionary thing", I whispered.

"It takes time to adjust", said Lani.

"Doing Bible gymnastics to prove something as stupid as the Rapture is a shameful waste of time", I said. "And a missionary in a country as poor as this one should not drive a BMW!"

"Some people are called to minister to the upper class", said Lani.

"Fine", I said. "But who ministers to the really poor people in this country?" I'd been working in conjunction with a photographer on a writing project with children who lived at the city garbage dump. Their stories shocked and saddened me.

"I don't know anyone who would live there", said Lani. "It wouldn't be safe."

"Nuns live at the dump", I said. "Catholic nuns."

"Wow", said Lani.

I sipped my coffee and watched the afternoon rain pour down the windows in a solid sheet of water. I wanted to see the good in the work of the Evanglical missionaries and not be critical. I wanted Guatemalans to come to Christ with their whole hearts and minds and souls, but my heart was in turmoil.

"Pray for me", I said, and Lani assured me that she would.

* * *

One day, just after I'd finished my morning Bible reading, I glanced out of my window and saw a poor construction worker relieving himself in the field next to our house. *How could a man like that ever have a personal relationship with Jesus?* I wondered. *He probably can't read.*

I sat back down on the bed, my Bible in my lap. This book wasn't just words; it was the Word of God. What did Billy Graham always say? After accepting Christ, start reading the Bible every day. *But what if a person couldn't read?*

It wasn't just owning and being able to read a Bible that made Scripture accessible to me. I had a lifetime of education to go with my literacy, and a lifetime of sermons, Bible studies, and books that explained the Bible, not to mention university-level theology courses.

When I picked up the Bible to read, I came at it with everything I knew about the culture and history of the peoples mentioned in its pages, all I had picked up over the years regarding the original languages, the settings, the politics, Judaism, ancient literature, Greek philosophy, the Roman Empire. I didn't "just read the Bible", I read the Bible from within a vast and educated context.

I had been taught that the Bible, and the Bible alone, was the Word of God. The Bible, and the Bible alone, told us everything we needed to know to get to Heaven. But now I realized that a person needed a whole lot more than a Bible and the ability to read in order to understand Christianity. All of my life I had listened to pastors and teachers explain what the Bible meant. The Bible was never given to us "alone"; instead, it was doled out with meticulous, *authoritative* explanations.

Fifty percent of Guatemalans were illiterate. *Fifty percent.* I had learned to read when I was five! For the first time I realized that my literacy made me one of the world's elite. I could read. That meant I could access the Word of God. My Christianity was a religion of the literate elite.

Still, just being able to read was not enough. I'd been taught that the Holy Spirit helped the individual Christian come to right conclusions about the meaning of Scripture. How did the Holy Spirit illuminate the Scriptures for those who could not read?

And why, if we all had the same Holy Spirit, didn't our doctrines agree? Why did no preacher on earth simply stand up, read the Bible from the pulpit, and allow the Holy Spirit to illuminate it for us? *Because it didn't work!* We could never be sure that anyone had it right. One man's doctrine was another man's heresy.

I was very shaken by this line of thinking, and for a change of pace, I decided to read some Christian history. I borrowed *The History of Christianity* by Paul Johnson from a fellow missionary and began to read. I read about Clement, Ignatius, Polycarp, and Leo, men whose names I'd never heard before. I did not know about the Arians, Donatists, Montanists, Manicheans, or Gnostics either. I didn't know that Catholic bishops had made the final decision on what books made up the New Testament and that Catholic popes had ratified the decision. I didn't know that the Catholics had given us our New Testament and that Martin Luther had actually removed books from the Old Testament on his own authority.

Johnson's book was not a panegyric. His descriptions of turmoil and corruption only reinforced my prejudices against Catholicism. It did, however, open my eyes to several things: that I was ignorant about the early Church and completely ignorant of the Catholic Church, corrupt or not; and that for most of history, most people had been illiterate. Reading history also revealed something else to me. Doctrine had *always* been a big deal.

I tried to explain it to Lani. "Doctrine is about what's true and what's not true. We have to get it right in order to have any kind of relationship with God and to know how to live the Christian life." For once the Pentecostal–Non-Pentecostal debate proved useful.

"You believe speaking in tongues is allowed," I said, "and you can prove it from Scripture." Lani nodded in agreement. "Well, I was taught that speaking in tongues is sinful!"

"That's ridiculous!" said Lani.

"The same people who say that speaking in tongues is sinful can prove their position from the Bible, just like you can prove that speaking in tongues is okay!" I said.

"Sometimes we have to agree to disagree", said Lani.

"What about this?" I said. "Baptist missionaries say that once you are saved you can sin a hundred times a day and still go to Heaven. Free Methodist missionaries say that if you commit big sins you can lose your salvation and go to Hell. Which is it? *How can we know for sure?*" I didn't let her answer but kept on talking.

"Church of Christ missionaries teach that baptism is necessary for salvation. Pentecostals say it is only a testimony. Quakers don't baptize at all. They can't all be right!"

"We can't know everything", said Lani. "I've always thought that the diversity among Christians was healthy."

"One group of people likes rock music, the other likes hymns, that's one thing", I said. "But doctrinal diversity is not healthy. There's something wrong with it. Doctrine is about truth, life-and-death *truth!*"

"It's unrealistic to think that sinful humans could all agree on doctrine", said Lani.

I countered, "You know that verse in Ephesians where Paul says we are supposed to maintain the unity of the Spirit in a bond of peace?"[3] Lani nodded. "Paul says that there is one body, one Spirit, one hope, one faith, one baptism. He doesn't say there *should* be, but that there *is*. Was that just wishful thinking on his part, or is it true?"

"Is it possible it's just your personality that needs it to be so sure?" asked Lani. I knew she meant the question kindly.

"Of course it's possible", I said. "But I can't help thinking it's important for all of us. Two opposite doctrines can't both be true. It's one or the other. We missionaries could be giving people a gospel message that is tainted by errors."

[3] Ephesians 4:1–6.

"God will sort it out", said Lani. "We just have to be faithful."

*   *   *

Marty had been raised Episcopalian, leaving that church after a born-again experience in his teens. For the first time in our marriage he expressed a desire to return to the liturgy of his childhood. His birthday fell on a Sunday that year, and after breakfast he said, "Let's visit an Anglican church for my birthday." We looked in the phone book and found the only Anglican church in Guatemala.

The first thing I noticed when we walked into the Cathedral of Saint James was that no one was talking. How unlike an evangelical church, I thought, where people joked and visited while waiting for the service to begin. These people knelt and prayed. The music began, and the minister processed up the aisle. He was decked out in bright green. I wondered if green was the standard color or if he could choose whatever color he wanted. There were readings and psalms and a prayer. No bulletin instructed us in the procedure; no one announced what came next.

We recited the Creed. Marty knew it by heart. We recited the Lord's Prayer. Marty also knew this by heart, but I did not. Stand up, sit down, kneel. It was confusing, and I felt stupid.

The visiting American minister was shockingly liberal and effeminate. His sermon was pathetic, but I knew we hadn't come for the sermon, so I made a conscious decision not to stew. I knew from my reading that liturgical worship was all about communion.

In the church of my youth, communion was tacked on to the end of a Sunday service once a month. Communion was only a remembrance, a symbol. When I was about ten, as the plate of tiny crackers and thimble-sized cups of grape juice was passed down our row, my mother whispered to me, "You can take communion now." I felt grown-up but never understood why I needed crackers and grape juice in order to remember that Jesus had died for my sins. I always tried to have the right frame of mind—to *remember*—but truthfully, communion was always a strange event to me.

Now I was in a church where not only did they take communion each week; they went forward to receive it. Anyone who was baptized was welcome. I followed Marty's lead, though I felt awkward and self-conscious. We filed up and knelt in front of a rail. The moment my knees hit the velvet cushion, I felt a tremendous jolt in my heart.

Suddenly my eyes filled with tears, and I had to choke back a sob. *Dear God!* I thought. *I am on my knees! Why have I never knelt before?*

Afterward Marty asked if I'd like to come back, and I said yes. I wanted to know more about this liturgy and eucharist stuff, and I wanted to worship God on my knees.

When I told Lani, she was cautious. "They're so much like Catholics," she said, "so into ritual ... don't you think it's kind of empty?"

"It's different", I admitted. "But I want to learn. Before the Reformation, this is what church was like."

"Before the Reformation, the Catholics were in charge. You can't go back to that."

"Don't worry", I said. "I'm mostly just observing."

"Be careful", said Lani.

We attended the Episcopal church for several months, skipping the English services and attending the Spanish services, over which the bishop presided. His sermons were informative and biblical, but the main event was always the eucharist. I ceased feeling self-conscious and looked forward to kneeling for communion.

One Sunday there was a baptism. I had never witnessed an infant baptism before. The bishop, along with the parents and godparents, stood at the font with the baby in his arms. He called all the children in the congregation to come gather round. He bent down and let the children see and touch the baby.

"Do you remember the story in the Gospel where Jesus welcomed the children?" Several little heads nodded. "Jesus welcomes this baby into His family today, through the waters of baptism, just like He welcomed each of you. After he is baptized, this baby will be a Christian baby, and he will be part of God's family and our family."

I was profoundly moved as the bishop poured water on the baby's head and said the words of baptism. Before the Anabaptists, who were the distant founders of my childhood faith, *all* babies were baptized. I'd been taught that infant baptism was wrong, but how was this wrong? Hadn't whole households been baptized in the book of Acts?

I read a book by historian Randall Balmer entitled *Mine Eyes Have Seen the Glory: The Evangelical Subculture in America*. The book described the roots and development of evangelicalism, a historically new, homegrown American social phenomenon, foreign to the practice and beliefs of Christianity in most of the world. The author wasn't negative or critical. He simply described American evangelicalism from a historian's point of view. I saw it from an evangelical missionary's point of view and was stunned.

We could eat at Wendy's, McDonald's, or Pizza Hut, shop at Ace Hardware or Sears. We could buy Whirlpool washers, Apple computers, or Barbies. What did American missionaries bring to Guatemala? Churches. There were over two hundred different kinds of evangelical missionaries in the country!

We weren't bringing "the simple gospel". We were bringing chaos. I had no doubt that lives had been changed, hearts converted, marriages healed. Jesus saves! I believed it with all my heart. I wanted everyone in the world to know Jesus Christ, but this huge, complicated missionary subculture, this vast jumble of churches and belief systems, and the myriad of gospels was American first, Christian second.

With all of these thoughts stirring up my soul, I ordered a book called *Evangelical Is Not Enough* by Thomas Howard. I knew that Tom Howard was the brother of Elisabeth Eliot, one of the most influential evangelical writers in America and a personal hero of mine. I had no idea what the book was about. The title made me curious.

I hadn't read two chapters when I began to weep. Every word resonated in the depths of my soul, and I realized with a shock that I wasn't an evangelical anymore. I wanted the liturgy, and I wanted the eucharist. I wanted to be part of the Christian family that went all the way back to the apostles. I too longed for real worship with Christ at the center instead of a pastor with a polished, persuasive lecture.

Marty read the book and underlined half of it. We discussed it for days. We realized that, as missionaries, we were in a troubling position. All of our supporting churches were evangelical. Attending an Episcopalian church could get us in serious trouble.

One day we received the news that our biggest supporting church had split and the pastor had taken half the congregation with him. The church no longer had a mission budget, and suddenly our monthly donations were short by several hundred dollars. We needed to return to the States in order to seek increased donations to make up for the loss.

We had a private meeting with the team leader and were granted permission for a short leave. Our team leader said that he had heard we were going to the Episcopal church. He then informed us that he had the authority to forbid us to attend there because "it doesn't look good for the team."

"I'm not sure you have that authority", said Marty, very evenly.

"I do have the authority to recommend that you not be allowed to come back to Guatemala." The threat was clear, and we took it to heart.

We kept that conversation to ourselves and, without telling anyone, made plans to leave for good. We wanted people to come to Christ, but we didn't support the proliferation of churches or the Americanization of Guatemalan Christianity. Something was wrong with the picture. It was hard to put a finger on it, but we knew we didn't want to be part of it, nor did we want our friends donating their hard-earned money to support it.

We had seen other missionaries come and go—turnover was very high. Now it was our turn, and we were filled with sorrow. We'd spent most of our married life preparing for mission life. Now we were returning as failures. I knew my family would be deeply disappointed. As the plane rose into the sky above Guatemala City, I leaned my head against the window and cried. My dream of being a missionary had evaporated.

When we got to the States, we resigned from our mission board. Mission life was not for us. The leaders at the home office embraced us and prayed for God's blessing. Our hearts were dark and deeply grieved.

Marty was offered his old job back at Hibbing High School, so we moved there and set up household. In Hibbing we had a ready supply of evangelical friends who expected us to return to the Christian and Missionary Alliance Church, where we'd been members before. They were surprised and puzzled when we didn't show up for church.

They were even more shocked when we enrolled our children at Assumption Catholic School. Had we lost our minds? No matter how hard we tried to explain it, even our closest friends could not grasp the titanic changes our Guatemalan experience had worked in our hearts. They politely changed the subject when we described our observations about the mission community or the discoveries we had made by reading history. The best we could do was to explain that we desired historic Christianity and that we could no longer be part of a community that was constantly experimenting with its form of worship or had been founded by a group that had split from another group, like so many churches we had attended.

We began to attend Saint James Episcopal Church. We thought the Episcopalian church was historical. And no one cared that our children were in Catholic school.

I had ceased believing that the whole of Christianity had gone apostate after the death of the apostles. I continued to read, study, and ponder the history of the Christian faith. One day I came across the following quote:

> And at the hour when the cock crows they shall first [of all] pray over the water. (When they come to the water, let the water be pure and flowing.) And they shall put off their clothes. And they shall baptize the little children first. And if they can answer for themselves, let them answer. But if they cannot, let their parents answer or someone from their family.[4]

---

[4] *The Treatise on the Apostolic Tradition of St. Hippolytus of Rome.*

There was no mention of individuals asking Jesus to be their "personal Savior" or praying the "Sinner's Prayer". There was no suggestion that baptism was only a testimony. Baptism was the normal, historical way to be saved!

There was no Christianity apart from the Church, and baptism was the way in. Children were as welcome as adults. Even children who could not "answer for themselves".

Jody, at six years old, was not baptized. We explained to her that baptism would make her a Christian for sure, and she replied that her teacher, Sister Jane, often prayed for the poor, unbaptized babies of the world. Jody was eager to be baptized.

By this time we were on the Episcopalian diocesan mailing list. One afternoon I opened the quarterly newsletter and read about how recent church donations had been distributed to a recycling center, gay ministries, and an abortion provider. I threw the newsletter in the trash. This is what they were doing with our tithe money!

I knew from my incessant reading that Henry VIII had had no justification to break with Rome—that the Anglican church had been founded on one man's obsessive desire to get rid of his proper wife. At least the other churches we'd attended had been founded for doctrinal reasons! Marty and I decided we couldn't continue at a church that was committed to immoral causes and founded on divorce.

We stayed home the next Sunday and sang songs with the kids, read from the Bible, and did "home church" all over again.

*   *   *

By now I'd had ample opportunities to observe the Wednesday school Mass at Blessed Sacrament Church. It wasn't much different than the Episcopalian liturgy. There were Latin words in big gold letters around the inside of the ceiling. I recognized some of the words because of my Spanish: "flesh" and "blood" and "Father". Episcopalians believed in a spiritual communion, but I knew that Catholics believed that their Eucharist was truly the flesh and blood of Jesus. I decided to learn more about it.

I bought a copy of the *Catechism of the Catholic Church*. I was astounded at the reasonable and biblical explanation for every belief, including transubstantiation. Could it be true? I read John, chapter 6, over and over again. It was so clear, so plain, so straightforward! I had always believed that the Bible should be interpreted at face value, but in this instance, I had never taken Jesus at His word! How had I missed it before?

I joined some online discussion groups and ordered a set of tapes from Catholic Answers, a debate between a Catholic and a fundamentalist on the topic of *sola scriptura*. When the tapes arrived, I popped them into the player.

I'd stopped believing in *sola scriptura* more than a year before. Now I realized that when it came to the "Bible alone", I was fully on the Catholic side. Everyone added to the Bible, that much I had figured out. It made sense that God put the Church in place to be the interpreter of Scripture. It was reasonable, and it was biblical. It also solved the problem of the doctrinal smorgasbord.

No individual had the ability or the mandate to interpret Scripture for himself, to figure it all out on his own, or to teach others his own private views and call it Truth. Christ established the Church, and from the Church came the Bible. If we wanted to know what the Bible meant, we could turn to the Church, its author. It made perfect sense.

One Saturday afternoon in January, I suggested that we go to Mass. We were lonely and hoped someone would reach out to us. No one spoke to us; no one stopped to talk. The church was nearly empty by the end of the last hymn. We sneaked past the priest and drove home. We had no desire to go back.

For the next month, we did not attend church. Marty and I were both depressed and discouraged. Our love for Jesus was still there, but where was His Church? We read the Bible, we prayed, we discussed everything we'd been through. In theory, there were a lot of good things about the Catholic Church, but the thought of becoming Catholic was unappealing. We didn't know where we belonged, but we knew we didn't belong in an evangelical church.

One day Marty was at home in bed with the flu. I heard him yell something from the bedroom. I ran to see what he needed. He was sitting up with the open *Catechism* in his lap.

"It's incredible", he said. "It's *more* Christian than anything I've ever read." He let out a huge sigh. "I was starting to think we would never find the Truth, and here it is. We have to know more about Catholicism, from the source."

I ordered more tapes and books. We read everything we could about the Catholic Church. We discussed theology at meals, in the car, and in bed. I read apologetics and the Church Fathers. Marty studied the *Catechism*.

One day Marty said, "We're going to have to become Catholics." We had talked Catholic theology for a whole month, but we had not talked about *becoming* Catholic. Despite being intellectually convinced that Catholic teaching was more biblical and more completely Christian than anything else I'd ever been taught, I had not taken the emotional step of imagining myself as a Catholic. I hadn't told anyone that we were reading Catholic books and listening to Catholic tapes. I hadn't even told my family that our kids were in Catholic school!

"I don't know", I said.

"Do you want to call the priest, or should I?" asked Marty.

"You do it", I said.

*   *   *

The big statue of Mary made me nervous. The little Irish priest made me nervous. Father O'Donnell smiled and said, "Now, what can I do for you?"

Marty and I told him about our background, our families, our missionary work, our questions and studies. He listened and asked a few questions. Finally Marty said, "I think we need to be Catholic."

"Only the Holy Spirit could have led two people like you to the Church", said Father O'Donnell. "Welcome home."

Home. I let the word sink in. I had never felt at home in any church, not really. I'd always assumed it was I who didn't fit, never the other way around. I wanted the truth, and by God's grace I'd found it. I was on my way home.

"You could be confirmed at Easter", said Father O'Donnell. "Or you could wait another year. It's up to you."

Marty turned to me. "Do you want to wait? I can wait if you aren't ready." The thought of waiting was worse than the thought of getting on with it!

"I want to be a Catholic", I said.

"You can meet with the associate pastor every week between now and Easter", said Father O'Donnell. "Ask all of your questions, and please know that there is no obligation. You can always change your mind."

We met with Father Timothy Deutsch, and at our first session he announced in a deep, serious tone, "We will begin with the natural law." Our formal Catholic education had begun.

Learning more about Catholic theology was pure joy. We read and studied and looked forward to our meetings with Father Deutsch. Entering the Catholic community was another thing altogether. It was like being foreigners all over again.

After a lifetime in friendly Baptist and Methodist churches, where newcomers were regularly invited to dinner or to join a Bible study or to sing in the choir, we were amazed at how we could go to Mass week after week without being greeted except for a handshake and "Peace be with you." No one was particularly interested in the fact that we were preparing to become Catholic. No one reached out to us in friendship.

We were lonely, strangers in a new land. We were discovering the treasure of the Catholic faith, and we wanted to talk about it! Spiritual fellowship was something we had come to expect as a given of Christian life, but during this time the only fellowship we experienced was via e-mail, with converts and cradle Catholics we had never met.

We realized that the weeks of loneliness and the lack of emotional connections to the people in our parish was a blessing in disguise. We were becoming Catholic for one reason only: we had come to believe that the Catholic Church is the Church that Christ founded and that she speaks with the voice of Christ on earth. Other churches had some of the truth, but we wanted it all. We wanted the fullness of the faith. We wanted Truth with a capital *T*, and by God's grace we would have it, whether cozy friendships and spiritual fellowship were part of the package or not.

*   *   *

The date was April 15, 1995, and Marty and I had just been confirmed. The powerful, moving events of our first

Holy Week were fresh in my mind. Easter was indeed the greatest feast of the year! Finally we were in the one place where Easter was celebrated with the joyous solemnity it deserved! In a few moments we would receive *real* Communion for the first time. I squeezed Marty's hand and pulled Jody close.

I had tried hard to love God. Now I would enter into a physical union with Him through Jesus, His eternal and incarnate Son. The Marriage Feast of the Lamb was not some mysterious future event—it was here and now, and forever. Communion was not juice and crackers and trying hard to remember—it was the real Jesus, Body and Blood, soul and divinity.

The church was packed. Did these people know what they had? I hoped so. I had lived thirty-five years without the Eucharist. It was hard to wait even a few minutes more.

I looked up at the Latin words painted in big gold letters around the inside of the Church. I knew now what they said. *My flesh is food indeed, and my blood is drink indeed. He who eats my flesh and drinks my blood abides in me, and I in him. As the living Father sent me, and I live because of the Father, so he who eats me will live because of me* (John 6:55-57).

Marty, Kelly, and I were invited forward to receive Communion before the rest of the congregation. First, Jody received a blessing. I was next in line. Father O'Donnell held up my dearly beloved Lord Jesus, present under the humble appearance of bread, and whispered, "Kris, you've waited for this all of your life." Then he said, "The Body of Christ."

"I believe", I replied. "Amen."

As I knelt after Communion, I thought: *Now I know why the martyrs were willing to die. I would die too, rather than give this up.*

*   *   *

My family members were utterly devastated by our becoming Catholic. My older brother didn't communicate with me for over a year. In his words, we "walked straight into the jaws of Satan." It was a long time before we settled into a strained, polite relationship.

All but a handful of our evangelical friends wrote us off completely. A few people were curious enough to ask to read some Catholic books. Doug and Lani Bogart, our good friends from Guatemala, wanted a thorough explanation. We sent them books and tapes. A few years later they were also received into the Church, and Doug has since been ordained a deacon.

It took a couple of years to make friends, much longer than it had ever taken when we were Protestants. We were foreigners to the culture, and our expectations for spiritual friendship did not match the reality of life in our own parish. Even so, we never ceased to praise God for allowing us to become Catholics, to share in the Feast at every Mass, to experience certitude about doctrine and morality, and to know the definitive answer to life's most important question: *What must I do to be saved?*

Receiving Jesus in Holy Communion for the first time was the happiest day of my life. Nothing else has ever come close. That joy and the knowledge that I was home at last consoled me as I passed through the struggles and heartaches that were also part of our conversion.

*   *   *

By the mercy and grace of God, both of our children are devout young adults, faithful to the Church and convinced of her Truth. The sweet spiritual fellowship we experience as a family is an indescribable joy. The task before each of us Catholic Franklins both now and for the rest of our earthly days is to *be* fully Catholic: to know the truth about ourselves, to know the truth about God as given to us infallibly by the Catholic Church, and to live in imitation of Jesus Christ. Through the divine power of the sacraments and the trustworthy teachings of our Church, we have all the tools we need to become the saints God created us to be. At least once a week, if not more often, one of my family members will say, "It is so *great* to be Catholic!" It is great. It is also a miracle for which I thank God with all of my being.

I am absolutely convinced that everything the Catholic Church proclaims and teaches is true. My mind is satisfied, my heart is filled to the brim, and my soul is continually filled with joy. I am home! What a gift after so many years of wandering! I no longer have to ask, *"How can we know for sure?"* because the answer is as close as the Catholic Church, my Church, the Church of Jesus Christ Our Lord.

Kristine Franklin and her husband, Martin, live in Hibbing, Minnesota, where she writes prize-winning Catholic-compatible novels for children and teens, leads Scripture study classes for adults, and takes memorable photographs. Martin teaches at Hibbing High School. At present, their two children are college students.

Chapter 8

Through the Ministerium
to the Magisterium

Paul Quist

On the last Sunday of March 2004, I stood before my congregation at Calvary Lutheran Church of Edmonton, Alberta, and read my letter of resignation to the shocked assembly. I had been their pastor for nearly twelve years. I assured these 230 beloved parishioners that this was not a rash decision but the result of a protracted period of prayer, reading, suffering, conversation, and fasting.

Almost exactly a year later, on the last Saturday of March 2005, my wife, Carol, and I, together with our children, stood before 2,500 people at the Easter Vigil Mass in Saint Patrick's Cathedral, Melbourne, Australia, to be received into full communion with the Roman Catholic Church. At that time, Jonathan was seventeen, Kari fifteen, and Kirsten eleven. We all still marvel at God's gracious goodness in leading us toward such an unexpected and blessed turn.

* * *

Carol and I are of Scandinavian Lutheran stock. We were both about as Lutheran as you can get. I figure there had not been a Catholic in the family since the Reformation, with the exception of my wife's father's cousin, who married a Catholic after his first wife's death and subsequently became a Catholic. I grew up in a Swedish Lutheran family in Wisconsin. My maternal grandfather was a Lutheran pastor, as were both my maternal uncles. Among my cousins and in-laws I have numerous pastors. Carol grew up in a Norwegian Lutheran family in Canada. We both attended Lutheran Bible schools and colleges. Her oldest brother and his wife are both Lutheran pastors, one sister is married to a Lutheran pastor, another sister is married to a onetime Lutheran youth director, and her youngest brother was also a Lutheran pastor—until he was received into the Catholic Church in August 2006.

Carol and I got to know each other while serving on a traveling music–public relations team from the Lutheran Bible Institute in Seattle, Washington. We were married in 1982. Carol, a communications major from Concordia College in Moorhead, Minnesota, had completed her B.A. in 1980, so she worked to get me through school. In 1983 I received a bachelor's degree in biblical studies from Trinity Lutheran College, near Seattle. Subsequently, I earned a Christian studies graduate diploma at Regent College, Vancouver, British Columbia, and a master of divinity degree at Luther Seminary in Saint Paul, Minnesota.

After my ordination in 1988, we moved to Calgary, Alberta, for my first call as a pastor. Sixteen years of fruitful parish ministry ensued—four years in Calgary and twelve in Edmonton. Our family was growing: Jonathan was born in 1987, Kari in 1989, and Kirsten in 1994. Our faith in Christ was growing; my preaching was touching people; we were content in Lutheranism, perhaps even proud to be Lutheran. (Having our kids enrolled in a Catholic elementary school only confirmed my resolve that I would die a Lutheran, as the depth of catechesis they received there was less than inspiring.)

Yet certain events in our lives and in North American Lutheranism raised some niggling doubts. In June 1990 I traveled from Calgary to Saint Olaf College in Minnesota to attend a conference called "A Call to Faithfulness". This meeting, sponsored by three independent Lutheran journals, addressed the problem of "liberal Protestant drift" that seemed to be infecting the sister communions of the Evangelical Lutheran Church in America (ELCA) and Evangelical Lutheran Church in Canada (ELCIC). Even back in the early eighties, the biggest challenge facing faithful Lutherans was the push from many leaders to normalize homosexuality. At "A Call to Faithfulness" I met many devout, faithful, well-educated Lutherans who worried as we did about the state of the ELCA and ELCIC. We strategized together about how to bring the ship back on course, how to steer it toward theological and confessional integrity.

One of the more prominent among those faithful Lutheran leaders was Richard John Neuhaus. Just months after that conference, Neuhaus announced that he was becoming a Catholic. His defection (as we viewed it then) really rocked the boat. What some Lutherans were realizing was that, without the moorings of the Church's Magisterium and faith in sacred Tradition, Lutheranism would inevitably drift toward moral and theological relativism.

Nonetheless, my colleagues and I were convinced that Rome was not the direction to go. Crossing the Tiber, we thought, could only muddy the clear waters of the gospel of justification by faith. We were certain that God's grace, as revealed through the Word of God (both Scripture and Christ Himself) and explained in the Lutheran Confessions, is enough to keep people firm in faith and discipleship. We felt sure that we did not need Rome's hierarchy, and we eschewed the rules that seemed to hem in freedom and dampen faith.

Now of course, Lutheranism is not monolithic. There are many varieties of Lutheran, running the gamut from Low Church, evangelical types who do not wear clericals and, with the exception of infant baptism, look and worship much like Baptists, all the way to "evangelical Catholics", who look and worship in a manner that appears more Catholic than the liturgy one finds in many Roman Catholic parishes. The version of Lutheranism that I was formed in was somewhere in the middle of that range. However, in the midnineties, I felt drawn to a group that was more evangelical Catholic in worship style and ecclesiology.

In 1997 a pan-Lutheran ministerium called the Society of the Holy Trinity (STS) was organized to work for "the confessional and spiritual renewal of the Lutheran churches".[1] This society calls its members to obedience to Jesus, to praying the daily Office, and to the practice of personal confession and absolution and to providing the same for their parishes. Furthermore, this ministerium expressly states that the Lutheran movement's ecumenical destiny is reconciliation with the bishop and Church of Rome. Joining this society brought significant and positive changes to my personal piety and practice of ministry. As I attended annual general retreats of the society and semiannual regional retreats, I began to look more Catholic, and I wanted to take my parish in that direction. I started to ask the question put to every Lutheran by the German theologian Peter Brunner: "Why am I not a Catholic?" It was not long after I joined

[1] See http://www.societyholytrinity.org.

the STS that my Lutheran bishop (Joseph Robert Jacobson), who had retired early from ministry, announced that he was becoming a Catholic. Another defection?

*   *   *

Around the same time, things were stirring for Carol, as well. In October of 2002 she went with her father to a Lutheran conference on Christian sexuality in Kansas City, Missouri. She heard inspiring lectures by prominent and faithful Lutheran scholars. However, the speaker who touched her the most deeply was the lone Roman Catholic, Father Jay Scott Newman, pastor of Saint Mary's Catholic Church, Greenville, South Carolina. Having heard the best of the Lutherans, Carol was surprised to feel so moved by Father Newman. There was beauty, unity, and a cogent logic to Catholic teaching on sexuality. There was also something attractive, even compelling, about the authority with which Father Newman spoke. After his lecture, Carol told him, "You make me want to be Catholic."

Father Newman simply smiled. The next morning (Reformation Sunday!) Father Newman was the guest homilist in the Lutheran church that hosted the conference. He spoke with great sorrow of the divorce that occurred between Catholics and Lutherans in the sixteenth century. Carol shed tears as she went forward to receive communion while Father Newman sat, present but unable to receive. Never before had she felt the ache of separation between the Lutheran communion and the Catholic Church so keenly.

When Carol got home from the conference and told me about Father Newman, I knew that I had to get to know him. Soon I was sending him e-mails, asking the typical questions about Mary, the saints, the pope, purgatory, etc.

Father Newman gave me good answers, but more importantly, he suggested authors who got me to thinking: John Henry Newman, Scott Hahn, George Weigel, Thomas Howard, and so on. The stack of Catholic books on both sides of our bed grew higher and higher. Of course, all of these books pointed in one direction: to Rome. Carol took courses at a local Catholic college and was introduced to John Paul II's encyclical *Veritatis Splendor*. When she learned that the title means "The Splendor of Truth", she was moved to tears because deep down she knew, despite what postmodern culture asserts, that there is such a thing as truth and that it is splendid.

God also used a significant degree of suffering to help shake us loose. After all, I was not anxious to leave a parish that was appreciative of my ministry and that paid me well by ecclesial standards; on my salary alone we managed to pay the mortgage on our three-bedroom bungalow and to maintain a modest but comfortable lifestyle. I used to joke with my colleagues that if I ever left the ministry I had no idea what I would do, since I had no marketable skills. As my longing to become Catholic grew, that little quip ceased to strike me as funny.

* * *

The year 2003 turned out to be the most difficult of our lives. Not only was I feeling less and less sure that I could remain a Lutheran, we also underwent great stress in the areas of health, finances, and relationships. In July of that year, I started to manifest symptoms of what would turn out to be chronic pelvic pain, a spasmodic condition affecting the muscles of the pelvic floor. For quite a while I feared that I had cancer. In October we put a good deal of borrowed money into an investment that went bad. For a while it looked disastrous. Meanwhile, Carol had a severe falling out with someone close to her. All of these stresses, along with the lack of confidence we felt in our Lutheran leadership, brought us to one of the darkest times of our lives. Yet, in the midst of it all, we had a sense that God was with us.

The moment of clarity came during a bitterly cold November weekend in 2003, when we attended a weekend conference organized by Catholic Family Ministries in Edmonton. Christopher West presented a two-day seminar on John Paul II's *Theology of the Body*. During that very dark period of our lives, the pope's teaching appeared as a beacon of light and hope. John Paul's catechesis about the nature of human love and the meaning of marriage and sexuality astounded us with its evident truth, beauty, and goodness. Orthodox Lutherans believe that there is nothing good left in fallen human nature, that we are totally corrupted and incapacitated by sin. Catholic theological anthropology recognizes the grievous wound of sin resulting from the Fall but teaches that man is still good—indeed, glorious—in that he images God. This was a far cry from the pessimistic anthropology we had believed as Lutherans. We were persuaded that this doctrine is true and biblical.

During the Saturday lunch break, we introduced ourselves to Christopher West and told him that I was a Lutheran pastor and that we were both feeling drawn to Rome. He encouraged us to trust and obey like Mary, to keep saying yes to God's call.

When the conference was over that Saturday night, we lay in bed and wept. We wept because we had been exposed to such beautiful teaching and felt touched by the Lord. We wept because we knew that we had to become Catholic and that this was going to cause great turmoil in our lives. And we wept tears of contrition because we came to realize that we had been duped by our culture about contraception. We grieved because, ten years prior, I had undergone a vasectomy. Also, that night Carol sensed a strong call to study the *Theology of the Body*. Over the weeks that same sense of call grew in me.

The ensuing months were a blur of activity, as we exchanged e-mails with Father Newman, Christopher West, and others who helped us on the journey; read Catholic teaching with renewed vigor; made visits to the doctor; and tried to figure out how we could study and what we could do for a living. I was particularly drawn to pray before the Blessed Sacrament in a chapel devoted to twenty-four-hour adoration (sometimes at three or four in the morning). For Christmas we bought each other Rosaries and started praying to Our Lady. In January it became clear that I did not have cancer. Instead, I suffered from a chronic pain condition, but it was not something that was going to kill me. In March we got our investment money back with only minor losses and paid back our loan. But even before that, a plan and a hope was taking shape within us, to study at the John Paul II Institute for Marriage and Family.

Shortly after hearing the *Theology of the Body* explained at Christopher West's seminar, we presented a video series on it at our Lutheran church. However, it was not long before we realized that we could not smuggle Catholic teaching into a Lutheran congregation, nor could we remain Lutheran. So on Sunday, March 28, I read my letter of resignation to my parish and revealed our plans for the future. In it, I said:

Early in July we plan to fly to Melbourne, Australia, where we will both study for master of theology degrees in marriage and family at the John Paul II Institute for Marriage and Family. When Carol and I first heard the Theology of the Body (last November), our hearts burned within us. We knew that we had to share this good news with the congregation. But more than this, we knew that we must study more. We long to be in the forefront of the battle for marriage and families. We are convinced that this beautiful Theology of the Body is the remedy for the confusion and wounds of our culture of death. We hope to return to the Edmonton area in two years, well equipped and eager to teach.

Within three and a half months of reading this letter, we had sold our house (in which we had half equity), paid off some debts, received our student visas, moved to Australia, and started studying. We did not know anyone in Melbourne, did not know if we would have work when we got back to Canada, and were not entirely positive that we had enough money to make it through two years. But we did have a strong sense that this was God's call.

Going to Melbourne to study at the John Paul II Institute was the best and the hardest thing we have ever done. We were nourished and stimulated by our classes and will always cherish the wonderful friends we made in Australia. There were many times we were brought to tears during Mass by the virtually palpable presence of Christ in the Eucharist or by the cogent preaching of our pastor, Monsignor Peter Elliott (who was also the director of the John Paul II Institute and has since been ordained a bishop). Many faithful priests graced our dinner table, sharing their wit and wisdom. We got to know and love faculty and staff, our wonderful sponsors and their families, Dominican and Capuchin brothers and priests, friends we met through Catholic movements and through special graces of God, and fellow students, most of them half our ages. We enjoyed the Aussie warmth and sunshine, a nice respite from the long, bitter winters of Alberta. It was fun to see a bit of the countryside and to spot an occasional kangaroo, koala, possum, or rainbow lorikeet.

But it was also tough. I struggled with chronic pain, and we both were pushed to the limit to complete our course assignments. Carol earned a master of theology degree in marriage and family, while I worked toward a pontifical master's degree in the same field. By God's grace, our kids did amazingly well, but keeping up with them and their schooling (part of the time homeschooling) was a significant challenge. Money was tight and would have run out early if it were not for the help of Providence, incarnated in the generosity of a few people. God knew how much we could be tested, and always in the nick of time He came through with the grace, strength, or finances that we needed.

The highlight and greatest joy of our trip was being received into full communion at Saint Patrick's Cathedral, Easter 2005. Becoming Catholic required that I write to my former Lutheran bishop. Here is an excerpt from the letter that I e-mailed to him three days before we were received into the Church:

> On more than one occasion, you used the metaphor of a campfire for the ELCIC and urged us to stay put—that we need to hear from all the voices around the campfire. I think that is an apt metaphor. We and all the other Protestant denominations have been huddled around our respective campfires out in the wilderness, having left or been driven out of the city on a hill. Around our campfire I have found warmth and comfort. I have found love and friendship. I have learned to pray. I have enjoyed a rich tradition of hymnody and liturgy. My fellow campers have introduced me to Jesus and taught me to think theologically. Indeed, as a pastor I have had my turn at song leading and telling the

Story around the fire (a great joy and privilege for which I
will always be grateful). But a campfire is not home, and
camping is only provisional—it is not to be a permanent
condition. Eventually, campfires go out, and everybody goes
home. And I have heard the voice of Mother calling me.
At least for me, it is time to go home.

One week after our reception into the Catholic Church,
our beloved pope, John Paul II, died. We were very grateful to have him as our Holy Father "officially", even if it
was only for a week. We cried with the rest of the world at
the passing of John Paul the Great, but we also rejoiced
when Cardinal Ratzinger was elected pope and took the
name of Benedict XVI.

We are so thankful that we have been able to make this
journey together. To be able to move together as husband
and wife, and to have our children freely and joyfully join
with us, was a tremendous blessing. In addition to intentional catechesis at home and theological discussion between
Carol and me and visitors, each of our children received
individual graces or calls from God. Jonathan experienced
a mystical call from Mary in 2003 while vacationing on the
Spanish island of Mallorca, on a three-month foreign
exchange program in Europe, when he joined a throng in
an Easter procession to the cathedral. Kari was stirred by
the Catholic Church's teaching on abortion (particularly in
light of Lutheran equivocation on the matter). Kirsten, who
at eleven we figured would move most easily to Catholicism, actually found it the hardest but was finally moved by
the teaching our family received on the sacrament of
reconciliation.

While still in Australia, on the Feast of Our Lady of Guadalupe, I was able to undergo a successful surgery to have
my vasectomy reversed. While we are thankful for a good

result, still the repair lacks the elegance of God's original design. I continue to live with pain, not as a result of the surgery but related to my chronic condition. I offer up that pain for the salvation of souls and in reparation for the sin of vasectomy.

We returned to Edmonton in August 2006, and I started work as the director of the Office of Marriage and Family Life for the Catholic Archdiocese of Edmonton a month later. I will soon complete my thesis, and then I hope to defend it in Rome. The blessings continue. Two of Carol's five siblings have become Catholic, and a few of our dear friends (former parishioners) have also been received into the Catholic Church. It was my joy last Easter to be the sponsor for a young man who was received into the Catholic Church (along with his older brother and parents) whom I had baptized as an infant when I was his pastor.

*   *   *

When our two-year sojourn in Australia ended, we were exhausted and broke, but we had tremendous joy and gratitude. The value of real estate doubled in Edmonton while we were gone, so we do not own a house anymore. But we have no debt, and God continues to provide generously for us. Every day we are thankful for the many undeserved graces that we continually receive through Mother Church. She is a bottomless well of refreshment, an endless, unfathomable source of living water. Her sacraments, her papal encyclicals, her catechism, her canon law, her social teaching, her saints, her religious orders and lay movements all bring us into deeper relationship with Christ and call us to holiness. There was some sacrifice in our move to the Catholic Church, but it pales in significance to the treasure that is ours. We have discovered the pearl of great price: the fullness of Christ's Church and the deposit of faith.

After being received into the Catholic Church and completing their studies at the John Paul II Institute for Marriage and Family in Melbourne, Australia, the Quists returned to Edmonton, where Paul now directs the Office of Marriage and Family Life for the Catholic archdiocese. Carol is developing curricula to help parents teach theological anthropology and a Catholic vision of sexuality to their children. Jonathan and Kari are attending college at Our Lady Seat of Wisdom Academy in Ontario, and Kirsten is in high school.

Chapter 9

Now I See: Finding the Faith in a Small-Town Public High School

Steven Hayden

The essential cause of my conversion to the Catholic faith was of course Christ's call. But the proximate causes were examples, both bad and good, especially the ugliness of the bad and the beauty of the good.

Drinking, drugs, promiscuity, pornography—those baneful influences of the contemporary world were unavoidable in the small public high school I attended in the early 1990s. In fact, those evils did not wait until high school; they were introduced as early as fifth grade, and four or five years later had become commonplace. Television, music, and movies all helped to support the feeling that nothing was amiss and even implied that failure to participate in a hedonistic lifestyle was somehow wrong. What formal warnings there had been about the dangers of drugs and alcohol came with an undertone indicating that we were expected to ignore them.

Despite such provocations, it is impossible to completely silence the natural law that is written in creation itself, so I cannot imagine that any of us were actually happy. Even though our intellects would not cry out against the sin around us, we could see the pain and unhappiness that it brought. The students who liked to drink became less and less able to do an adequate job in class, and those doing drugs were even worse off. Many students who had graduated in previous years were still hanging around town, doing odd jobs and getting into trouble, giving no sign that they would ever be able to change what they were doing. I saw young men growing arrogant as they boasted of their sexual exploits with young women, and young women who had once seemed wholesome looking used and broken after being discarded by young men. Even among my friends, who did not seem so despicable as some, I could not avoid noticing how fornication and broken relationships eroded much of their joy. The ugliness and unhappiness of sin cried out that something was not right.

I was fortunate in having the contrast of good people and healthy relationships to indicate the right path. My parents loved each other and their children. They did not provide us with the formation to know that promiscuity and other immoral activities were invariably wrong, but they did instill in us a strong sense of accountability. My grandparents too provided an excellent example of what the relationship between a man and a woman ought to be and also showed how important it is to act charitably toward others.

As I looked around me, I began to see that there was division everywhere, though not necessarily opposition. I thought that proved I was becoming skilled at seeing both sides of arguments, and so I took some pride in being able to ride the fence without getting committed to either side. My inability—or unwillingness—to choose one side no doubt reflected my lack of clear formation, as well as the emphatically indoctrinated public school code that all opinions must be equally respected. Thus I became increasingly interested in hearing and trying to understand the arguments for various positions.

One of the strongest such antagonisms, yet one I was barely aware of, was between the life of faith and the daily life I was leading. The example of my tolerant family surely contributed to my lack of clarity about this clash, but the example of my Lutheran pastor was another factor. I was a member of the Evangelical Lutheran Church of America (ELCA). My parents and my father's family were members of this church, and our pastor, Reverend Jeff Blaine, and I had become good friends. He was an example of what we expected our pastor to be: he performed all the duties required of a pastor, gave very good sermons, and was an excellent singer. In addition to a common faith, Pastor Blaine and I shared an interest in science fiction and fantasy novels. I also liked his fondness for early rock music. As I considered future career plans, I began to think that becoming a minister in the ELCA might be a fine choice. I didn't see that I would have to change any of my views or my behavior, and I thought that my abilities, in general, would be well suited for the ministry. I liked to speak in front of groups of people; I also liked to sing and even participated in school musicals.

By the beginning of my junior year in high school, I was quite sure that I had a calling to become a pastor in the ELCA. In addition to attending public high school in Gays Mills, Wisconsin, I was also studying the Bible and beginning to look at ELCA schools where I could go to study theology. When it became known to those around me that I was considering becoming a pastor, the response I received encouraged me. Teachers and adult friends of the family generally seemed impressed, addressing me as though I were more mature than they had realized in the past.

My schoolmates viewed my interest as a curiosity, but from as early as first grade I had never been content to be a follower of my peers. If I was not one of the best at an activity, I lost interest in it. My new vocation was partly fueled by this appetite for distinctive status. Not many of my classmates held the same views I did, and those few who had similar views did not wish to pursue them as I did. My interest in the ministry was sincere, but it did also serve to set me apart from—and, I thought, above—my peers.

Soon I became openly outspoken about my concern for the faith. That attitude was probably what led a Catholic classmate to invite me to join a group that would speak to junior high students about abstinence from premarital sex. Up to that time, I hadn't even thought that such abstinence was desirable. Certainly I had not been exposed to the idea through the media or in my high school "health" class. From my surroundings and the example of my family, I had learned that sexual intercourse was something exclusive, reserved for someone you truly loved, something you would share with the person you intended to marry. But marriage was not required for the act itself, in my estimation; rather, it was something that would become necessary should birth control prove ineffective.

Yet the invitation to be part of this speaking group appealed to me immediately. I relished the prospect of a chance to evangelize. Quickly, I agreed to participate in the abstinence group.

The project began with several preparatory meetings at my classmate's home. Her parents gave me materials to read and explained that the Catholic Church taught not only that abstinence was a moral imperative but also that it was prudent and practical. Barbara Johnson, my classmate's mother, made persuasive arguments and talked specifically about how damaging premarital sexual relationships were to the people involved. I embraced that position and promptly became vocal about it at school and home, a development that took most of my classmates and even my parents by surprise and contributed to my sense of moral superiority.

Participation in the abstinence group gave me mounting confidence. As I found myself associating with college students and recent college graduates, I was pleased to think of myself as a leader and a model for the junior high students. In a sense, I had joined an exclusive club, and I found that very satisfying.

It was during a car trip to one of these classes that I took the next step in my journey of faith. For some time, I had been attending my church service every Sunday. Attendance was not obligatory, but as a general rule I wanted to participate in the worship service. My family had always attended regularly, but there had never been any feeling of guilt when something else came up and we missed the service.

On a Sunday when one of the abstinence classes was scheduled, my parents went away, leaving my brother and me to ourselves. I don't remember why I didn't go to the Sunday service, but I do know that I had no adequate reason for missing. That evening, while riding with my classmate's father, Barney Johnson, on my way to speak to junior high students, we talked about the similarities between the ELCA liturgies and the Catholic Mass. Barney asked about the day's Gospel, to see whether the readings had been the same. I confessed that I did not know, because I had not attended the church service that day. Barney seemed surprised, but he did not reprimand me. My pride would not allow me to escape without reprimand, however. After all, I was mature, I was interested in my faith. Why had I allowed myself to neglect what I claimed was the most important thing for me?

A student athlete, I had just completed a winless season of football and was in the midst of a losing basketball season. On the long bus ride home after a particularly difficult loss, I brooded about losing. Why wasn't I more successful? I was trying to live life the way God would want me to live it, but my efforts weren't reaping immediate, obvious rewards. If God wouldn't help me in these matters, I thought, then perhaps I needed to try things a different way. Even to my adolescent mind, this reasoning was not persuasive. I knew that the real problem was me.

No longer smug about my moral superiority, I said no more than a handful of words to anyone the following day. The closest thing I have felt to that emotional experience since that day is my wretchedness when reviewing my sins in preparation for confession. But in that long-ago instance, I did not know how to change my situation, and there were no glorious words of absolution to wipe away the sin at the end. While I did not despair of salvation, I certainly did feel like Luther's snow-covered dung heap. I was lost, and I yearned for something better, though I did not yet know what it was.

As my junior year was coming to a close, my religious focus turned toward the intellectual. First, I spent time investigating my Lutheran religion. In a book that my Lutheran pastor gave me, I was saddened to learn about the last years of Luther's life. He had done many good things, I thought, yet he seemed bitter and angry at the end. I had hoped that a man who loved God would be happy and fulfilled in the twilight of his life. But in spite of this disappointment, I wanted to know more about his Augustinian origins. That curiosity would later lead me to read Saint Augustine.

Next, my pastor and I discussed *how* Christ was present in the communion bread and wine and how Catholic and

Lutheran doctrine differed in this matter. The Catholic view seemed to make more sense to me even at that time, but I felt that either way, it was certainly the Body and Blood of Christ I was receiving. Surely God would not forsake an entire church of people who were trying to follow Him.

I spent more time studying salvation by faith alone. This led my pastor and me to do a Bible study of Saint Paul's Letter to the Romans. As we two Lutherans studied the book, I was certain that Luther must have been correct about this principle and my Catholic friends wrong. However, my pastor was honorably unwilling to give me a partial view of the question of faith and works. After we completed Romans, he directed me to the Letter of James. Reading Saint James' epistle shattered my certainty about salvation by faith: it was clear that works play an important role in salvation. When I learned that Luther had tried to remove the Letter of James from the Bible, my uncertainty about Luther increased. After all, how could you remove a book from the Bible when the Bible was our only source of knowledge on which to base our faith?

Faith and works came together for me in my friend's mother, Barbara, in whom I encountered an outstanding example of charity. Never had I seen anything artificial in her. She seemed genuinely interested in things that I thought were important, and she was able to be simultaneously honest and kind. When I spent evenings at their house and the day grew late, she would tell me that it was time to leave, and I would go. I was never insulted that she should ask me to leave, and I never worried about overstaying my welcome, because I knew that she would tell me if the time came for me to leave.

* * *

During that summer, Barbara was dying of ovarian cancer. Just as she had presented a noble example of how to live through the preceding year, so during the last months of her life she demonstrated by heroic example how to die. She was in agonizing physical pain. She knew she was leaving her husband and six children behind. She knew what was approaching, yet she seemed at peace, even happy and content. A day or so before she died, I went to visit her. She was in excruciating pain, her legs enormously swollen. She could eat only ice chips. I was not very comforting; I did not know what I could say, or should say. As I sat in awkward silence, Barbara began to ask me about what I was doing. Although she was the one suffering, still it was she who comforted me, not the reverse.

Earlier in the year I had signed up for a Catholic retreat for young adults. Before then, I went to Mississippi with some of the people who would be going on the retreat, to work at repairing houses for people who were unable to do so themselves. In my group were two practicing Catholics and two fallen-away Catholics. This was the first long trip I had made away from home since becoming more interested in my faith. I was struck by the fact that the Catholics were easily able to find a church where the service was the same, or nearly the same, as the one they participated in at home, while I couldn't find an ELCA Lutheran service that at all resembled the one I experienced at home.

About a week after Barbara died, my friends and I attended the Catholic retreat. Its focus was on the Body of Christ, both the Mystical Body of Christ and the Eucharist. For the first time, my attention was centered completely on the Eucharist. I had always thought I was receiving the Body and Blood of Christ when I attended the Lutheran services, and I still felt that I was receiving Christ through

those services. I could see that these Catholics truly treasured the Eucharist. It was isolating and extremely painful
to be forming ties with them but not be able to receive the
Eucharist with them, even when I believed the same things
they did. Still, I admired the fact that they would not let
anyone receive their greatest treasure without first joining
himself to the Church.

I also saw that the Eucharist created a more universal
communion in the Catholic Church. My failed attempts to
find a church in Mississippi had given me a new awareness
of the importance of church universality. I saw the Mass as
a single event in which all of the Catholics of the world
were participating; not only the Catholics of today but everyone who had ever attended Mass since its institution by
Christ was brought together in the Mass. It was this appreciation of the Mass, and my growing desire for the Eucharist, that really moved me to consider conversion.

Another event that summer raised further questions in
my mind about the ELCA: I was asked to be a delegate
from my church to the synod convention. Initially I was
pleased to be participating in my church in such an important way, but my feelings of importance soon disappeared.
As a delegate to the synod convention, I attended discussions that led to votes about what the church would pro-
claim as truth. Furthermore, I would be participating in
the election of a bishop. I knew I did not have the knowledge necessary to make a wise decision in any of those matters, yet my vote had the same weight as my pastor's. Was
this really the way to choose the best leaders or to make
sure that what the church said was true?

As the summer passed, my Lutheran pastor, who had
become an even closer friend, announced that he was moving to a different church across the state. This took away

my strongest supporter of the Lutheran church and led to
my being named to the committee to find a new pastor
for my church. Pastor Blaine must have seen that I was
being drawn to the Catholic Church. Before he left he
strongly encouraged me to wait until I was older before
deciding about conversion. But the fire had already been lit
inside me. Although I was not yet certain that I would convert, I felt that if my search finally brought me to that conclusion, I would not be able to wait as long as Pastor Blaine
would have liked. I knew that there were still many questions that needed to be answered, but I was anxious to continue the search for those answers.

As my senior year began, I found myself discussing the
faith with a couple of my high school teachers. I was still
involved in many activities after classes, and in between, I
would often find myself in the art room, talking about the
faith with my art instructor, Joni, and Kathy, a third-grade
teacher who was a friend's mother. It wasn't long before I
started attending a Saturday morning Mass with these two
friends. After Mass, we would go out to breakfast with the
priest, Father Leon Rausch, S.J., and continue talking about
the faith. Soon, in addition to the Saturday morning Mass,
I was going to both my Lutheran church service and Sunday Mass each week.

At school I was confronted more and more often by students who were behaving badly. None of them ridiculed
me, at least not to my knowledge, but they would deliberately taunt me with their behavior. This presented a new
challenge. It had always been easy to say how wicked the
activities were, but now I struggled to handle these situations with charity. I fear that I failed often. I could not be
sympathetic with the promiscuity of the young men and
was less than charitable with them. The pathetic girls who

were not doing what they should saddened me, because they seemed to be throwing away their chance for happiness in a frantic hunger to be loved.

Next, I began to examine what were typically issues of conflict between Catholics and Lutherans, and I repeatedly found that I did not share the Lutheran objections. I looked more into apostolic succession, and it made perfect sense to me. Lutherans professed that the transformation of the bread and wine was based upon the faith of the persons receiving them and took place within them. Yet my Lutheran church did not have communion unless the pastor was there, so I had always viewed the pastor's role as an essential part of this service. When I understood that the priest was a successor to the apostles, who offered the sacrifice for the people, and that because of his priesthood he could bring about the transformation of the bread and wine into the Body, Blood, soul, and divinity of Christ, it seemed perfectly reasonable to me. The democratic approach of the ELCA both at the synod convention and during the selection of a new pastor convinced me that the claim that the Holy Father spoke infallibly on matters of faith and morals was necessary to maintain the Church, even if it were a ruse. This practical argument quickly led me to believe that God would not leave the Church to muddle through on her own but would be there to constantly guide her in a real way. I believed that the Catholic Church was the Church Christ instituted and that the Lutheran church had separated itself from her. It had not been, as I had earlier believed, a matter of a split of two true churches.

Further, I could not understand why anyone should object to prayer directed to holy men and women who had died. Lutherans all asked other people to pray for them, so why wouldn't we ask the people who were already with God to

help us? Mary was the best example of this. If you were
going to ask anyone to pray for you to Christ, wouldn't
you ask His Mother, if you could?

During the fall of my senior year, my application was
accepted by Thomas Aquinas College in Santa Paula, California. Before her death, Barbara had urged me to apply
there, telling me that this would be the perfect college for
me. She had one daughter who had graduated from the
college a year earlier, and one of her sons was then a junior
there. The Great Books program and discussion method of
the college were very appealing, but the most enticing aspect
was the idea of seeking Truth. The application process
required the student to write about a book he had recently
read. The previous summer I had read the *Confessions* of
Saint Augustine, and I chose that book for my essay, in
large part because Luther had originally been a monk in an
Augustinian monastery. I felt a sense of kinship with Saint
Augustine in moving from a sinful life to a better kind of
life. I admired the way he sought the truth and was not
satisfied with the lies of the world, even when his own
sinfulness obscured the truth of the Catholic Church.

Certain now that I wanted to be a Catholic, I continued
investigating the faith and, as Easter of my senior year
approached, made plans with my parish priest, Father Rausch,
to go to confession and receive First Communion and confirmation. Because he was a solitary pastor with two parishes to cover, we agreed to do this the week after Easter,
which is now celebrated as Divine Mercy Sunday. When I
informed my family of my decision, they were not certain
why I wanted to make the change, but they did not oppose
my decision.

On the Sunday after Easter, I made my public profession
of faith. My sponsor was Kathy, the third-grade teacher

whom Father Rausch had invited to speak about my preparedness to enter the Church. She and Joni, my art teacher, had spent many after-school hours talking with me about the faith. Then I received First Communion and was confirmed Steven Ignatius Augustine Elden. Hayden.

My conversion has always seemed to me to be at once something fantastic and something completely natural and ordinary. I was not knocked off a horse; I did not receive a direct vision from God. However, as He usually does, God worked through everyone around me to bring about my conversion. The series of events that led me from the pervasive bad influences of my high school environment to the Church was too perfect to be chance and could have been accomplished only by Divine Providence. To bring me out of darkness into the light of the Catholic faith, God used the love of my family; the truthfulness of my Lutheran pastor; the magnificent example and teaching of Barbara and Barney Johnson and their daughter, my classmate Marguerite; and the friendship of Kathy, Joni, and Father Rausch. Above all, I credit the prayers of my future wife, Maggie, who had been praying since early childhood for the salvation of her future husband.

Steven Ignatius Augustine Elden Hayden lives in Southern California with his wife and children. He is licensed in the state of California as a civil engineer and is currently working in a completely unrelated job as business director of Mother of Divine Grace School.

Chapter 10

O for a Thousand Tongues to Sing

Carolyn Rae Lemon

As the Sunday school teacher lined up her class for each of the students to give a Bible recitation in front of everybody, the last thing she needed was me—a new girl, a shy girl, a pagan girl who knew nothing about religion. But the teacher was kind. She whispered that I should follow the others, stand at the back, and be very quiet. Obediently, I did so.

Although I was nine years old, I knew nothing about God except as a word my grandfather said, a word that my grandmother told me "ladies do not say". My mother had become ill when I was a baby, so my grandparents were raising me. Someone, probably Mother, had decided I should be sent to Sunday school. This introduction to the basic concepts of Christianity was intended, I suspect, as an exercise in cultural literacy, lest ignorance lead me to ask embarrassing questions in public.

Before I went home that day, the teacher told me that, if I came to Sunday school four times in a row and memorized John 3:16 or the Twenty-third Psalm, I too could have one of the books that the other children had received. Within a month, I had accomplished the tasks and was reading passages from the Psalms and the New Testament in the King James Version. I loved that little book. A whole new world opened up for me as I read stories about Jesus and the strange happenings in Revelation (although I shed tears over the sentence "without are dogs and sorcerers, and . . . whosoever loveth and maketh a lie" because I thought that my dear Boston terrier, Mitzi, could not go to Heaven).

At the First Baptist Church, I learned about salvation. "The Wordless Book" showed me by its colored pages that I was marred by sin (black), but Jesus had shed His Blood (red) to make me pure (white) so I could go to Heaven (gold). I began writing "Jesus Saves" in odd places so that other people would learn this wonderful truth too. Before I was ten, I answered an altar call and was baptized by immersion. I knew baptism was important and that it changed me. I was confused, however, about why plates of bread squares and tiny glasses of grape juice were sometimes passed out at the adult church service. I loved singing "The Old Rugged Cross". At home I would often pray, kneeling, by a prune tree whose branches formed a cross.

When my beloved Great-Aunt Lizzie came for a visit, I showed her my book and wanted to read her the Twenty-third Psalm. A devout though misinformed Catholic, she declined, saying that she heard the Bible only at church. However, she invited me to come to Mass with her on the Sunday during her visit. Although I understood almost nothing, I was fascinated by the mysterious atmosphere, and I loved the stained glass windows, the statues, and the holy water font. I tried to follow my aunt's gestures and posture, and I admired her for knowing what to do. When we came home, I made a cardboard model of the Baptist church and one of the Catholic church, with tiny kneelers that my doll-house dolls could use when they "went to church". Baptist and Catholic: I liked both churches because they were places to worship God, whom I had begun to love. Aunt Lizzie began sending me holy cards, and I pasted them into my scrapbook.

Shortly afterward, the rides to Sunday school stopped, and going to church was no longer mentioned. I continued to read the New Testament and the Psalms, and I learned more through a Lutheran Sunday-school-by-mail program. My mother subscribed to this program for me, and a leaflet arrived each week. These illustrated leaflets recounted Bible stories, and I memorized the Ten Commandments, in the Protestant enumeration, and some simple prayers. I remember wondering why God let people sin, so I wrote my question on my lesson paper, and it was sent back to the "teacher by mail". The query was answered with an explanation of free will, a reply that I did not quite understand but mentally filed away to think about when I got older. Eventually, the Lutheran program ended, and my religious education was put on hold for some years.

Later, I met new neighbors who were Catholics. Sometimes they took me with them to church on Saturdays when they went to confession. No one explained what confession was, but I got to sit in the quiet church as I waited for them. I would look at the windows and statues and think about God. Sometimes the parents then took us for ice cream. Margo, the oldest daughter, who was near my age, loaned me some of her books about saints. I was a voracious reader, and I enjoyed these "Vision Books", as the publisher called them—until I came to the one on Saint Thérèse of Lisieux. When I read that Thérèse got sick during the night but did not tell anyone about it, I decided that she was really stupid, so I returned the book with the rest unread. Margo's family moved away soon, and again all organized religion was dropped from my life. But by then my mother had bought me a complete King James Bible, which I read on my own, though still without understanding very much. When I prayed, it was usually on my knees; that seemed "right" to me if I was going to speak with God.

During my high school years, I joined the Methodist Youth Fellowship. My initial motive was to follow my best friend, who went to the meetings mainly because her family was Methodist and it was expected of her. It was a well-balanced program, and I enjoyed all the aspects of it, from the worship services to the fellowship. In this group I overcame my innate shyness and learned to speak in public without shaking like an aspen leaf. I learned to organize activities and to take responsibility. I studied about Christian history, the Apostles' Creed, and Christian morality, and of course I learned many fine Methodist hymns, one of which provides the title for this reflection. I admired the whole-hearted social outreach of the Methodists. We visited migrant camps, hospitals, detox centers, Indian reservations— wherever there were people in need whom we could somehow assist.

On my own I discovered such devotional (and Catholic) classics as the *Imitation of Christ* and Brother Lawrence's *Practice of the Presence of God*. The whole experience was good, and it contributed a lot to my development as a Christian. Even then, however, something seemed fragile; the Methodists seemed somehow dependent upon the energy and personalities of the ministers and youth group leaders. Also, I had questions that were not being answered.

In my youthful zeal, I pondered about what was most important to do in life. It seemed to me that this was simple:

Do God's will. I should always act as perfectly as possible to try to do what God wanted. The youth minister told me that at his ordination he had refused to answer one of the questions asked ("Are you going on to perfection?") because he did not think perfection was possible. Another teacher said that I was being idealistic and that this was immature. Someone else told me it was dangerous and neurotic to try to aim for perfection. In the face of this discouragement from adults, and after reading Saint Paul's lament (Romans 7:15) and recognizing how often I fell short of my good intentions and high aims, I finally gave up on my quest. I wish I had known more about the saints at that time—they were the examples I was unconsciously seeking. But Margo's good Catholic family had moved away too soon.

My second unanswered question had to do with faith itself. Both in the Baptist and in the Methodist churches, and surely in the Lutheran Sunday school lessons as well, we were told to have faith: "Believe in the Lord Jesus Christ, and you will be saved." "We are saved by faith." But to me, "faith" was not a clear concept. I believed; I wanted to believe, but how much faith was required? If one had any doubts—and my liberal, secular, science-oriented education in high school was certainly working to plant some—could one be sure one had "faith"? No one seemed to understand this worry of mine, and so no one offered me a solution to my question.

When I went off to college, I fully expected to major in religion, a plan for which my family had little enthusiasm. My aspiration was to be a missionary, or perhaps a minister's wife. However, when I registered for classes, the religion courses open to freshmen did not fit my schedule. Ultimately, I graduated without having taken a single philosophy or religion class there. Later, I realized that this omission had served to protect my frail and vulnerable faith from an enormous dose of liberal thinking. My guardian angel had been guiding my slow path toward the Church.

The first Sunday of my college experience, I went to the local Methodist church and found it vastly different from the Community Methodist Church I had been attending: the preaching, the music, the people—everything seemed foreign to me.

I was at a Quaker college, so next I went to the Quaker church. It was huge, and everything about it seemed remote. But eventually, having worked my way through the various other Protestant denominations available without finding a church I wanted to attend more than once or twice, I settled on the Quaker meeting, which met in the campus administration building. This meeting was mainly comprised of kind, unpretentious, older people, and I liked them. The members seemed respectful of each other.

In the beginning, I also appreciated the silence. People spoke now and then, when the Spirit enlightened them, and what they said was often deep and thought provoking. However, soon I concluded that something important was lacking. I had probably never heard the word "liturgy", but here, in the silence of this Quaker meeting, I realized that, in order to worship God in a group, it was important to have a structured communal formula. Ritual was essential lest one's mind just wander and perhaps even close in on itself. I could not think of that as worship. After a time, I stopped attending.

Besides the good Quaker people at the meeting, however, something exterior had impressed me profoundly. Over the fireplace, in the room where we met, there was inscribed a passage from one of John Greenleaf Whittier's poems:

> Early hath life's mighty question
> Thrilled within the heart of youth
> With a deep and strong beseeching:
> What and where is Truth?

During meetings I had plenty of time to ponder those words, and indeed this mighty question thrilled me: I wanted Truth. Beseeching God for Truth became a prayer. It was one that God would grant in time. His time.

For the present, there was my freshman class on Western civilization. The professor who taught this was legendary for his lectures—and for his examinations. The textbook was not actually a textbook. *The Making of the Modern Mind: A Survey of the Intellectual Background of the Present Age* was an overview of Western history written by John Herman Randall Jr. of Colombia University, one of the signers of the 1933 *Humanist Manifesto*. The book was challenging, even intimidating, for an eighteen-year-old mind, and it had its own slant, as I discovered later. However, book and lectures together presented Western civilization, and that meant that we studied Greek thought, Roman law, and the Roman Catholic Church, including the contributions of the monasteries and numerous Catholic thinkers and scientists.

This class involved a "history lab" that we all disliked intensely. It was located in an airless room in the basement of a lecture hall. We had to go there on our own time and pore over packets of "original sources". Actually, these very poor copies of translations of original sources were some-times almost illegible. Still, if I wanted an A, it behooved me to spend some time in that "lab", as the material would come up in exam questions. This reluctant exposure to orig-inal sources was invaluable to my spiritual life. It counter-acted the biases both of the professor and of Randall, the author. In the first semester, there were writings of Greek Fathers, Augustine, Aquinas, Bonaventure, and other Catholics. The professor had chosen them as pivotal to the course of Western civilization. The historicity, goodness, truth, and beauty of the Church shone through the miserable copies I was reading. In that very lab room, I had my freshman "epiphany": If one is going to be Christian, then one must be a Roman Catholic. The Catholic Church is the true Christian Church.

This was an insight I did not welcome. Despite Aunt Lizzie and Margo and some other Catholic friends, I thought Catholics were a little strange. In fact, I was a bit afraid of them. During high school, when I worked at a nearby orchard cutting apricots for drying, a priest came to bless the harvest, and I ducked under the cutting tray so none of the holy water would land on me. In short, I was prejudiced. In our area, Catholics were more apt to be at the migrant camps than at scholars' desks, and by the time I reached college age, I wanted very much to be a scholar.

At that point, I had already stopped attending the Quaker meeting or looking for a church. I tried to put Christianity aside. The second semester's readings, from the Renaissance and the Enlightenment periods, aided me in this. I studied psychology, with an emphasis on behaviorism and other theories of learning. By sophomore year I was working for a professor whose specialty was perception. As I helped conduct experiments involving the brain's interpretation of visual stimuli, my view of man became very mechanistic. I dabbled in individualism, "objectivism", and existentialism—all without the least study of sound philosophy to guide my thinking. Though my grades were good and my ambition established—I wanted to be a professor—a lot was lacking in my qualifications. Although I wanted to be an "intellectual", I did not have the personality for that. Besides, the answers I was now being given by social science and modern philosophy did not completely satisfy me. In high school, I had looked into the cloud chamber in our physics lab and been filled with wonder. There was the same wonder when I saw Saturn or Andromeda through a telescope or a paramecium through a microscope. Learning about the physical universe or biology or the intricacies of the human body had delighted me and made me grateful to the Creator of all. I could not easily put that wonder aside.

Late in my junior year I met Leslie. She was a very intelligent young woman who had been a student at Vassar. While there, she had converted to Catholicism. Her Protestant parents pulled her out of that prestigious school because she would not recant. As a sort of compromise, I guess, she was allowed to continue college, but at our small Quaker institution. I met her soon after her arrival, and when I learned her story, I was amazed.

"You gave up an education at Vassar to be a Catholic?" I asked. There was no question but that she had been willing to pay a high price for her faith. The example of this "latter-day martyr" fascinated me. I decided to examine her faith, the Catholic faith I had fled from two years earlier.

Leslie arrived with a lot of Catholic books that had somehow escaped her parents' wrath. Soon I was borrowing this one and that one. In addition to my course work, I read a great deal about the Catholic Church that semester, and Leslie answered many questions. She was very knowledgeable, and her books answered other questions, so I learned a lot. At one point I borrowed Thomas Merton's *More Seeds of Contemplation*. Here I found the answer to my questions, *How do I find God? How do I know I have faith?*

Merton's answer struck a chord: "The only One Who can teach me to find God is God, Himself, Alone." These words helped me realize that faith is God's gift, offered by Him to each soul. This was not Merton's unique insight—the same answer is found in the writings of many saints. Indeed, it is even in Scripture, though I had missed it before. However, it was while reading the Merton book that I came upon this concept, closed the book, and said to myself, *Of course, that is the answer. If I want to find God, I should ask Him to teach me how to do that. If I am not sure I have faith, what I need to do is ask God for this gift.* I did so. It would be almost a year before I was received into the Roman Catholic Church, but the "seeds" of my conversion were planted in that moment.

During the summer before my senior year, I continued to ask Catholics about their faith, including the young man who would later become my husband. I am sure I was a source of exasperation to some because what the Church believed, and why, interested me more than almost anything else. I wanted to know "everything" before I made a commitment. I realized that I was still very ignorant about Catholic culture and worship even if the doctrines were becoming clearer to me.

That summer I participated in a work-study program run by the state to recruit students to the field of mental health. Working in a state hospital that served both the mentally ill and the mentally retarded was an important experience for me. The neat mechanistic concepts of man that had been part of my education collided with the realities of the human person in distress, and those concepts crumbled.

When I returned to college I knew that I did not want to work in the field of mental health. I was no longer very sure about the theories of learning that we had been studying and that I had hoped to teach and explore in research.

In fact, I had begun to doubt that I wanted to be part of the world of science or social science. Still, I pursued my studies and prepared for graduate school at a university with a good reputation for research.

At the local parish, I also began instruction with a Redemptorist priest. I looked forward to our meetings, which were supplemented by Leslie's books and knowledge. There was a whole new vocabulary to learn, and a new "culture". I was amazed to find that everything I was learning made perfect sense—in fact, it was extraordinarily *wise*. I was also happy to find out how comfortable I was with the Catholic faith. The doctrines, the architecture, the art, the music, the Latin, the moral teachings—none of it now seemed foreign to me. I felt a sense that I had come "home", in fact, that "man was made for the Church."

One Saturday, when I had a list of questions that the parish priest could not answer, I went to Loyola Marymount. An obviously intelligent and apparently holy Jesuit there took the time to answer all my questions, both the good ones and those I later realized were a little silly. He was so persuasive that he demolished my last remaining intellectual doubts. I left there thinking that yes, I had indeed found the Truth I had been seeking most of my life.

By now I was going to daily Mass, and I was longing to receive the Eucharist, the Body of Christ. It was very difficult to wait until the priest decided I could be received into the Church. At one point, Leslie asked the pastor about the delay, and he explained that I would be received at the Easter Vigil, because the Church was returning to that practice. That made waiting more endurable, and I tried to be patient.

Meanwhile, my academic goals changed radically. For a number of reasons, several of them external to my own changing path, I was not sure I wanted to continue in the field of psychology. During several summers, I had taken university classes in subjects not offered at my college, so I had almost enough units for graduation. My final semester of college, I sought a full-time job and took a few night classes to complete my B.A. The job I found was in the business office of the public library. From the start, I loved the work and the library environment. Soon the librarians urged me to consider their field, and it seemed to me much more compatible with Catholicism than the research psychology I had been studying. By then I had been awarded a Woodrow Wilson Fellowship, which I had to give up in order to pursue a new profession, but acceptance into the School of Librarianship at the University of California at Berkeley pointed me definitively in a new direction.

More important, I had made the best decision of my life: I was going to become Roman Catholic. The priest gave me a last admonition: "If you are going to be a Catholic, be a good one." These were words that I did not forget, even when I was not living up to that standard.

On Holy Saturday of my senior year, I made my first confession. Reception of converts was not yet part of the service itself, so late on Easter Eve, after the Vigil service, I was conditionally baptized and received into the Holy Roman Catholic Church. I made my First Communion the following morning, on Easter Sunday. I could not have been happier than I was that day when, for the first time, I received Our Lord—the Way, the Truth, and the Life.

*   *   *

In due time, I married, was confirmed (with Saint Monica as my patron saint), and had children, who were baptized.

Each celebration of a sacrament was rich with meaning. I finished my master's degree in librarianship and began working full time. But in those hectic days, so crowded with important changes, it was hard to focus on the spiritual life.

Life at Berkeley brought with it an assault of ideas, values, and societal expectations that strained or directly clashed with our faith. My husband and I did not have the support of Catholic friends or of my family. After a few years, while trying to balance family, work, and my faith, I discovered that I had pushed prayer aside. Soon my beliefs weakened and my behavior eroded. Around the time of the Second Vatican Council, the media had built false expectations of change and much of the response to *Humanae Vitae* was very negative. Some priests just dismissed the encyclical, so it was a very confusing time for a young married couple who lacked a good formation in the faith. And once sin is allowed in one's life, other sins crowd in like the seven demons in the clean house (Matthew 12:43–45).

Still, my good priest's admonition haunted me. I knew that the Catholic Church was the true Church, and I had embraced this faith with open eyes. It was definitely not the fault of the Church that I was failing to be a good Catholic. At one point I went to confession, but scruples kept me from Communion. I knew this was wrong, but it would take more time until I could accept God's graces and return to the sacraments.

It was then that I began to feel the sweet, hot breath of the Hound of Heaven on my heels again. We moved to San Francisco, and I sought employment there, which led me to become a librarian in a Catholic school. I felt a certain degree of dissonance because I was not practicing the faith, but I was respectful of the Church and I decided I could still do an acceptable job. Meanwhile, there was a good influence on me from many of the faculty, both religious and lay. Still, it would be five years more until my "reconversion".

One night my husband was away, the children were asleep, and I was ready to relax, when—somewhat like Augustine (whose *Confessions* I had not yet read)—I felt a compulsion to "take and read". The book in question was a Catholic Bible, dusty from neglect on the bookshelf. That night I read Mark's Gospel in its entirety. I had the thought, which I later learned was not uncommon, *Jesus was either insane or He was truly God!*

By the time my husband returned home, I had begun going to Mass regularly again. Later I learned that on his trip, he had visited Mike, an old college friend who was our older daughter's godfather. Mike and his wife sensed that all was not well, and they had been praying for us both— exactly at the time when I had that compulsion to return to spiritual reading.

After a few months, I asked to meet with one of the priests associated with the school where I worked. I meant only to ask him a few questions; I was not thinking in terms of asking for confession. However, as soon as I entered the office where we were to meet, I blurted out that I wanted to go to confession. Thus I returned to the sacraments and to full life as a Catholic, knowing that I never wanted to be separated from Our Lord again, no matter what the cost.

That priest was involved with the charismatic movement, so, with a fellow teacher, a religious, I began attending prayer meetings, held at a nearby monastery. Although I did not have a charismatic temperament, I appreciated being with a Catholic community that was full of faith and extremely prayerful. It was a time of growth and of solidifying my faith. My love of Mary and all the saints began to grow stronger. For a second time, I read the life of Saint Thérèse, but this time I was struck with admiration.

After several years, one of the nuns at the monastery suggested that if one is serious about the spiritual life, it is good to find a regular confessor. When I asked one of the priests at school whether he would assume that role, he explained that he had received word that very day that he was being transferred to a new assignment in a different location. He suggested one of his associates, and then we spoke of the spiritual life in general. He introduced me to the Liturgy of the Hours and even gave me an outdated breviary to use in praying the Office.

Just as I was leaving he said, "Oh, you live near the University of San Francisco. Here is the number of a priest there." I supposed he was suggesting a priest friend he knew well; later I learned that the two had met only once, on an airplane flight. His spontaneous recommendation seemed like an inspiration from the Holy Spirit, so I called the priest from USF. His name was Father Joseph Fessio, S.J.

Father Fessio said he would be glad to meet with me, but first he was going to the park to pray. That encouraged me; I thought: *Ah, he has good priorities!*

Good priorities he had indeed. Soon I was helping with the clerical work involved in getting important European theology books translated and published. In the heady days of the 1970s, Catholic publishing companies were closing, or they were making available only what the latest trends dictated. To get the works of Henri de Lubac, Joseph Ratzinger, Hans Urs von Balthasar, and Adrienne von Speyr published, Father Fessio soon realized the best thing to do was to found a new press—Ignatius Press—whose mission would be different from that of the other Catholic publishing houses. Frank Sheed encouraged us, although he warned that the first ten years would be the hardest.

Four years later, Ignatius Press had indeed been founded and its first two books had been printed. By then I had made Saint Ignatius' Spiritual Exercises, which changed my whole attitude toward life. Now, I think, I was more open to what God wanted, instead of trying to work out my own agenda. I was seriously seeking to do God's will, even when circumstances were unexpected. In those years, there came many changes—some painful, some challenging—and many blessings as well.

Thus, with the children already almost grown, I gave up my very secure library job and became the first full-time employee of Ignatius Press. (I was soon followed by an accountant who contributed much by setting up its business aspects.) Looking back I can see how my education as a librarian fitted me very well for publishing work. Training I had almost forgotten, even languages I had studied in high school and college, were restored to useful life. Organizational skills gained at my school and library jobs all proved helpful. Previously, my course had been a meandering one, but God has found uses for much of my experience in my work as a production editor.

Also, I am very blessed in my family, my friends, and my co-workers. The good books we work on; our talented authors; the liturgical life; our retreats and pilgrimages; the yearly cycles of fasts and feasts given to us by Holy Mother Church—all have helped to keep my spiritual life in balance and to make me more faithful. I know that my path was circuitous and that I was sometimes guilty of infidelity to God, but He nevertheless called me again and again. From this knowledge comes a certain humility, and I am ever aware that my faith is a gift from God, not to be taken lightly. The Catholic faith is the Truth, the same Truth for which I sought so long, which God gave me as a gift and which has been such an unfailing source of joy and peace. *Deo gratias!*

> O for a thousand tongues to sing
> My great Redeemer's praise,
>   The glories of my God and King,
> The triumphs of His grace!

Carolyn Rae Lemon lives in San Francisco, where she has worked for Ignatius Press since its founding. She has two daughters and three grandchildren.

Chapter 11

Reclaimed by the Divine Mercy

Father Augustine Hoa Trung Tran

In every conversion, there is a conversion of the head and a conversion of the heart. For many years, I was not open to conversion because both my head and my heart were blocked by pride. I was sure I knew more about "the real world" than believers did, though I later came to realize how truly ignorant I was. God, who loves us in spite of our foolishness, met me where I was, but He did not allow me to stay there. In an amazing chain of events, He used my ignorance to draw me closer to Himself until, finally, He led me out of my darkness into His wonderful light.

I was born in Saigon, Vietnam, in 1967. Both my mother and my maternal grandmother were Catholics, but my father's side of the family was and still is Buddhist. Although I was baptized five days after I was born, my parents did not raise me in the faith. In fact, after baptism, my sister, Hao, and I did not receive any other sacraments as children. Years later, at a Catholic high school in the United States, my sister chose to be confirmed in the faith and received her First Holy Communion. I, on the other hand, did not fully come into the Church until I was an adult in graduate school at the Georgia Institute of Technology—and when I did, it was something so unplanned that for a long time I did not realize it was happening.

My mother, my sister, and I came to America when I was six years old. By the grace of God, we were spared the travails and dangers of escaping on a boat. My parents were separated by that time, and my father had left Vietnam a year earlier for Canada, where he still lives today. My mother had studied English, so she was able to translate for some American reporters who were in Vietnam covering the war. At the end of 1974, just months before South Vietnam fell to the Communists, one of these reporters brought us with him to Chicago. After a year in Chicago, we finally settled in Springfield, Illinois, where I lived until going away to college.

While I was growing up, my family did not practice the faith. I recall going to Mass on Christmas and Easter; but we did not go to Sunday Mass, we never prayed at home, and I was not catechized in Catholic doctrine. God was simply absent from our home.

In Springfield, I first attended public school, where I was not well accepted by my schoolmates. Young children tend to reject peers who are different from them. Being Asian made me quite different, so I had very few friends; but all that changed when I entered high school.

My mother married again, to an American, when I was in eighth grade. Although he too was lapsed from the faith, he had been raised in a Catholic home. Due to financial constraints, he had not been able to go to a Catholic high school. Nevertheless, he did not want me to miss the opportunity to have a Catholic education, so when he saw the difficulties I was having with my peers, he took me out of the public school system and placed me into Griffin Catholic High School, the only all-boys Catholic high school in Springfield. Those were four of the happiest and most formative years of my life. Finally, I felt accepted by my peers. I played football and I had friends. In elementary school, I had not applied myself to my schoolwork, but now I began to excel academically.

However, though we were all required to take a religion course every year, I did not pay much attention to what was taught in it, just as I did not pay much attention to my fine arts courses. In fact, though I was at a Catholic school, the only two things that I really cared about were girls and math. As I was not very successful with the girls, I spent most of my time thinking about math.

In many ways, I considered myself an atheist. Religion was bunk for the ignorant masses, I told myself. In my adolescent arrogance, I thought that true knowledge came only from the sciences. If I could not see, smell, feel, taste, hear, or measure a thing, it did not really exist. It was not until many years later that I realized what ignorance of the scientific method that attitude demonstrated.

Still, if one goes to a Catholic school anywhere in the United States, one cannot help but hear about the University of Notre Dame. When it was time for me to decide on a college, I applied to Notre Dame and I was accepted. My decision had nothing to do with the fact that it was a Catholic university. I thought it was a good school academically and a place where I could have a true "college experience". It had a good football team and was far enough away from home to be "away" but still close enough for me to get home easily.

While I was at Notre Dame, my interests were not very different than they had been in high school: now all I really cared about were girls and aerospace engineering, which was my major. Though I loved what I was studying, thinking about numbers and equations all the time began to give me a perpetual headache. Eventually the headache became an inescapable fact.

Six credit hours of theology were required of all students, so I was exposed at least to the vocabulary of Catholicism; but my intellectual pride had swelled even beyond what it had been in high school. I thought I was smarter and more realistic than my peers, and I was sure that science could answer all life's persistent questions. I put all my faith in science, although at the time I did not know that it was faith.

Catholicism at Notre Dame is very much a part of everyday student life. Each dormitory has its own chapel, its own chaplain, its own daily Mass, and its own Sunday Mass. While I was there, the most popular Sunday Mass in Alumni Hall was at 11:00 P.M. Students would bring along friends who were visiting in the dorm or studying with them. I recall them going to Mass in whatever they happened to be wearing at the time. Most Sundays one of my friends would invite me to go with him to Mass, but I always said no. I never told them why not. They probably thought I was a nonbeliever or a lapsed Catholic. In fact, the reason I did not go was out of respect for my friends. I knew the Mass was important to Catholics, that it was where they went to pray and to worship their God. But if I had gone with them, I would have gone only for fellowship, not to pray to God, because I did not think God was necessary in my life. I did not even believe that He existed.

I still considered myself an atheist. It seemed to me that God was simply a figure people made up to ease their consciences or to give them hope; but though I did not believe in God, I did not want to be disrespectful of my friends' beliefs. I thought that if I went to Mass without the right intentions, that is, not to pray but just to be there socially with my friends, I would somehow taint the Mass for them.

When I graduated from Notre Dame, I was accepted into graduate school at the Georgia Institute of Technology in Atlanta to earn a master's degree in aerospace engineering. Afterward, I hoped to earn a doctorate and go on to teach and do research at a university. I arrived at Georgia Tech in August 1990 not knowing where I would live or what I would do for money. From a bulletin board notice at the student union, I found some guys who were looking for a roommate. Then I procured a student loan and started work on my specialization in flight dynamics and control systems.

Atlanta is in the heart of the Bible Belt, and I was taken aback at being asked routinely what religion I was and where I went to church. I thought, *Well, I was baptized Catholic and I spent the last eight years of my life in Catholic schools, so I guess in some sense of the word, I'm a Catholic.* So I answered, "I'm Catholic", not really believing any of it or even really knowing what it meant.

The standard reaction to my remark surprised me even more. As soon as I said I was Catholic, people would pounce on me, asking, "Why do you worship Mary? Why do you pray to saints? Why do you think that the pope is better than everyone else? Why don't you believe in Jesus and the Bible?"

When they started attacking me, and attacking Catholicism, I thought, *Whoa. Whoa. Whoa! I don't believe any of this Catholic stuff. I don't even believe in God. What's going on here?*

But at the same time, in the back of my mind, I had a sense that what they were saying about Roman Catholicism was not quite right. I was not sure why, but it did seem to me that those were not things Catholicism taught.

Purely out of intellectual curiosity, then, I began to look into Catholicism. I was still sure that it was not true, but it did seem that many intelligent people professed it, including my friends from high school and college. So I decided

I should learn something about it, if only to be intellectually honest. If I was going to reject something, I should at
least know what I was rejecting.

What happened, however, was that as I researched Roman
Catholicism, I began to see that in many ways it was very
logical. If one accepted certain premises that I was not ready
to accept—the existence of God, the truth of the Bible,
the Church, and supernatural realities—then Catholicism
moved logically from one teaching to the next. It was an
internally consistent system of thought, that is, if one were
willing to accept its axiomatic principles. I found that very
appealing.

What I came to realize in my research was that the Mass
is at the heart of Catholicism. If I wanted to understand
Catholicism, I had to understand the Mass. Although I still
did not believe, I thought that my presence would not defile
the Mass for the other people present because at least I
would be there to try to understand what was happening.
So, on the first Sunday after Easter, I decided of my own
volition to go to Mass. That day had not yet been established as Divine Mercy Sunday, but even if it had, I would
not have known about it. I simply chose it at random.

I sat in the back of the Church, which turned out to be
the place of choice even for practicing Catholics. When I
had gone to Mass in the past, with my family, I had never
really paid attention, so I did not know any of the prayers,
nor did I know when to stand, sit, or kneel. I just followed
what everyone around me was doing.

During that Mass, though, I felt an incredible peace.
Through all the six years that I studied aerospace engineering, I had had a constant headache. Walking around campus, I would not notice people saying hello to me because
I was absorbed with trying to solve problems in my head.

My roommates used to tell me that I spouted equations in my sleep; but during the hour of Mass, I was not thinking about numbers or equations, and my head was not hurting. The serenity I felt was like nothing I had experienced before, so I decided to come back the next Sunday—and the next. Every week I was learning a little bit more, and as I kept reading and studying, it made more and more sense.

At one Sunday Mass in the Catholic Center, Father Mario, the Georgia Tech chaplain, invited the congregation to come to weekday Mass. He assured everyone that weekday Mass would only last seventeen or eighteen minutes.

My first thought was, *Who goes to Mass during the week? Isn't going to church once a week enough?* My second thought was, *How can he possibly squeeze everything that we do at Mass into seventeen minutes? That's physically impossible.* So on Monday, once again purely out of intellectual curiosity, I went to see what this daily Mass thing was all about.

True to his word, Father offered Mass in seventeen minutes, including a homily. Even though the Mass was so short, I experienced the same peace and serenity during those minutes that I had experienced during the hour of Sunday Mass. I was not thinking about equations or numbers, and I did not have a headache. I decided to go to weekday Mass whenever I had enough free time during the week. After a few weeks, I started to arrange my schedule around the weekday Mass time, because it brought so much joy and peace of mind to my day.

During that time, I did not receive Holy Communion. I knew from Catholic school and from my research that I was not eligible because I had not been to confession or First Communion. I also knew, intellectually, that Catholics believed the Eucharist was truly the Body, Blood, soul, and divinity of Jesus Christ; that in receiving the Eucharist, one was professing all that to be true; and I was not ready to profess those beliefs. I only knew that at Mass I experienced a peace that I did not feel anywhere else.

As I said, in every conversion there is a conversion of the head and a conversion of the heart. Studying and research were accomplishing my conversion of head, and the peace I felt at Mass was beginning my conversion of heart. But what happened next was what truly led me into my Father's arms.

Christina, a Tech undergraduate who lived across the street from me, had become a close friend of mine. One day, she invited me to her apartment to tell me something very important. When I got there, she confided that she was pregnant. She had decided not to tell her boyfriend, her parents, or his parents. The only person she was telling about this pregnancy was me, and the reason she was telling me was that she had decided to get an abortion and she wanted someone to know in case anything went wrong. She had gone to a clinic near campus, and they told her to get some counseling before the abortion to prepare for it psychologically. They also suggested that she bring her support group along to the counseling sessions.

"Well, you're my support group," she said, "so will you go with me?"

At that point, I was twenty-three years old and did not have an opinion on the issue of abortion. I am not sure how this could have been, but I had never discussed it seriously with any of my friends or anyone in my family. It was a topic that had never come up, so I had never thought about it; but as soon as she said that she was going to get an abortion, I felt that it was the wrong decision. I could not explain it; I could not explain why it was wrong or why I thought it was wrong, but my first instinct was that it was in fact wrong. I did not say that to her because I did not want to make her feel bad or think that I had abandoned her. I wanted to help my friend, but I did not want to condone her decision, so I was in a quandary. I said yes, I would go to the counseling sessions with her, but I did not tell her that I thought it would help me to deal with the situation as much as it would help her.

After I left her apartment, all I could think about was her abortion. I had a difficult time concentrating on my studies, because I felt as if I were doing something seriously wrong by helping her with the abortion, yet I could not figure out how to help her without condoning her actions. Without realizing it, I began to pray and ask assistance from God. After a few days of nonstop praying, it dawned on me that I *was* praying; that is, I was talking to and asking assistance from God.

But wait, I don't believe in God. Why am I talking to a Being I don't believe exists? I asked myself. *Am I crazy? Or do I really believe? Do I think that He does exist?* I was not sure about the answers to these questions, but I continued to pray because I found comfort in it.

The next day, I asked myself why I was struggling with this issue so much. Obviously, my friend did not think that abortion was wrong. I knew that the two guys I was living with had no qualms about abortion. So what was my issue? I realized that I was not really struggling with the abortion itself, because although I could not explain why, I was certain that it was the wrong thing to do. My deepest struggle was with the fact that I was helping someone do something that I considered to be wrong. That is, I was willfully choosing to do something immoral, something that would destroy my relationship with God. I was trying to justify my actions to Him, not to myself. I wanted Him to know that I was just trying to help a friend and that I did not want Him to be disappointed in me for doing so, even though it entailed doing something immoral.

When I realized this, I was shocked. For most of my life, I had felt that God was not present, not necessary. Then, just a few days earlier, I had begun to see Him as a powerful Being far away from me, whom I was asking for help. Now, I realized, I was seeing Him as a personal God who was living in my heart, with whom I wanted to have an intimate relationship. That was why I was trying to justify my actions to Him.

On later reflection, I realized that I was able to take that spiritual journey only because I had opened my mind and heart to His grace. Now that I was no longer willfully fighting against Him, the graces flowed through. So I continued to pray.

A few days before we were supposed to go to our first counseling session, I called my friend to ask her if we were still going on Wednesday.

"Oh, I'm sorry", she said. "I meant to call you. We don't have to go now because I had a miscarriage. I went to the doctor and he confirmed that I had a miscarriage, so we don't have to worry about it anymore."

As I hung up the phone, I felt an enormous sense of relief. I got in my car and drove to the Georgia Tech Catholic Center. I fell on my knees, thanking and praising God. I felt as if God had heard and answered all my prayers, because what happened to my friend was entirely natural. She did not have to have the abortion that I had seen was wrong; and she did not have to have the child, which she did not want. Since she lost the child naturally, no one was at fault. It seemed as if God had taken the whole situation into His hands and dealt with it directly, in His own way, so I thanked Him for listening to me. It was only much later that I learned the effects of the birth control pill and realized that the miscarriage may have been caused by years of being on the Pill.

After I had thanked God for answering all my prayers, I sat back in the chair. Suddenly, He flashed before my mind's eye all the times in my life that He had offered me this gift of faith, but I had simply kept rejecting it. He showed me all the Christ figures He had put in my life through Catholic high school and Catholic college. I had not consciously listened to them, nor had I practiced my faith, but all those Christ figures had helped to form my conscience on some subconscious level. It was because of their influence that I had some inkling that what people were saying was wrong when they started attacking the Catholic faith. When my friend told me that she was going to have an abortion, it was because of their influence that I had a sense that it was wrong. At that point, I realized my atheism had been a product of my will and not of my intellect. I had rejected God because I did not want Him to exist.

I believe that is true of most atheists. To paraphrase Saint Augustine, those who do not believe that God exists have some reason why they do not want Him to exist. I had never studied the arguments for the existence of God, yet I had concluded that all the arguments were invalid, so, obviously, God does not exist. The reality was that I enjoyed living a life of sin, and I did not want to change it.

At least I was intellectually honest enough to admit that if God exists, I would have to change my life. I might have to start giving money to charities. I might have to start praying, maybe even going to church regularly. If God really exists, and He is the Creator of the universe, then I have to start obeying Him. In fact, I have to turn my life over to Him. It was obvious that some of the things I had been doing were condemned by Him, but I enjoyed doing them; so my atheism had been a problem of the will, of my wanting to do my will and not His. That was why I had rejected Him. That and my intellectual pride, telling me that only silly, ignorant people believed in a supernatural Being, while intelligent people realize that science is the one true god.

Hence, it was on that day, sitting in the chapel at the Catholic Center at Georgia Tech, that the scales fell from my eyes and all the arguments came together. Everything I had been reading made sense. The logic and reason had all been there in front of me as I was reading, and that was why I could see the internal consistency; but now I was ready to accept the premises that made it a coherent whole.

I realized that I had put all my faith in science, though science could not possibly answer all the questions. Science can tell us that planets move in an elliptical orbit around a sun at one of the foci, but it cannot tell us why there are planets in the first place. Why is there something instead of nothing? Science does not ask those fundamental questions, so how can it answer them? I had put all my faith in science, and I did not know why. These are philosophical, theological questions, and it turns out that they are far more important and interesting questions than the ones that science asks. This is not to say that science is not fun or useful, only that it has limits.

It was then that I was ready to fully accept the Catholic faith. I started looking for a Rite of Christian Initiation of Adults (RCIA) class so that I could be confirmed and begin receiving Holy Communion. I joined an off-season RCIA class at Holy Spirit Catholic Church in Atlanta. Instead of the usual procedure of starting in the fall and going on until Easter, it started in the summer and the catechumens were confirmed at the beginning of December.

Having decided to be confirmed, I thought that I should start to learn some Catholic prayers. This idea occurred to me as I was sitting in the Blessed Sacrament chapel at Georgia Tech. I did not know what prayers might be uniquely Catholic, but I looked down at the pew. Lying there were some Rosary beads on top of a pamphlet entitled "How to Pray the Rosary". *Oh, I think that's a Catholic prayer*, I thought to myself. *Maybe I should learn how to pray that.* I did not know any of the prayers, nor did I know any of the mysteries, but it was all explained in the pamphlet, so I followed along and found it to be a wonderful meditation on the life of Our Lord and Our Lady. I started to pray the Rosary every day, and after a few months, I began to pray it as my after-Mass thanksgiving.

About a month before I was to be confirmed, some strange thoughts started to pop into my head during my prayers of thanksgiving after Mass. One day, as I was praying the Rosary, I looked up at the pulpit and began to think that if I had been behind it, I would have given a different homily on the day's reading. I readily admit that it was immodest of me to think that I could say the prayers or preach the homily better than the priest who was up there—but thus began my call to the priesthood.

When I realized that what I was thinking about was becoming a priest, I immediately pushed the idea out of my mind. *Even to think about it is absurd*, I told myself. *I could never do that.* I was not yet a confirmed Catholic. I knew nothing of philosophy or theology. I abhorred public speaking; and, God knows, I was not holy enough to be a priest. Besides, all I had wanted for as far back as I could remember was to be Joe Average—to be married; have 2.1 children, 1.7 cars in the garage, and a dog; and live in the suburbs in a house with a white picket fence. That was definitely not a priestly life.

Yet, over the next few months, thoughts of the priest-hood kept coming into my head. At first, they were spo-radic, but then they started to be more frequent, usually popping up while I was praying the Rosary. One Sunday morning a few months after I had been confirmed, I woke up, and immediately the thought of priesthood came into my head. I tried to ignore it, but it would not go away all day. Finally, I decided that I should go to Mass early that evening and pray about it. Up to then, I had not men-tioned my thoughts of priesthood to anyone, because I thought they were crazy; but when I walked into the church that evening, my RCIA instructor happened to be there, and he called me over to where he was standing. Unexpect-edly, he asked me if I had ever thought about becoming a priest.

I did not know how to respond. I told him that it had passed through my mind a few times, but I had not given it any serious consideration. Like many young men and women who are called to the priesthood or religious life, I thought I should keep this to myself. I was not yet ready or willing to admit that I was starting to hear the call. I was afraid if I told people, they would think I was strange and would treat me differently.

I asked my RCIA instructor why he was asking me this. He said that the vocations director for the Archdiocese of Atlanta, Father Don Kenny, was offering the Mass for us that evening. He had thought that it might be a good idea for us to talk. I quickly tried to change the subject, and then I went into the church to pray a Rosary before Mass. As I was praying, Father Kenny came up to me, introduced himself, and asked me if I would like to exchange phone numbers. I gave him my number, and a few days later he called and asked me out to dinner.

I went to meet with Father Kenny thinking that I could finally put these thoughts of priesthood to rest. *Once he hears my story,* I thought, *he will see that I do not have a vocation to the priesthood and I can forget about all this nonsense.*

To my surprise, after I told him everything that had happened to me to bring me to this point, he said, "I think you have a vocation to the priesthood. And I think you have a vocation to the diocesan priesthood here in Atlanta. And if you were to join us here in Atlanta, I'd like to send you to Rome for seminary."

Of course, I thought he was crazy. I assumed he had not heard a word I had said, but I was wrong. Father Kenny convinced me to keep discerning my vocation. He invited me to join the monthly holy hour and the monthly Mass for vocations, so that I could meet other people who were also considering the priesthood or religious life. I did so, still unsure whether or not God was really calling me to the priesthood.

A priest of the Archdiocese of Atlanta once wrote that there are five stages to discerning a religious vocation. They are the same as the stages of grieving that we are all familiar with: denial, bargaining, anger, depression, and acceptance. When discerning a vocation, one can go through these stages daily, or repeatedly every day.

I kept telling myself that God could not possibly be calling me to the priesthood because I was not worthy, which is true, but everyone He calls is unworthy of standing *in persona Christi.* Then I would start to bargain with Him, telling Him that if I got married I could have a dozen children and they would all be priests and nuns. He could have so many more priests and religious if He would just let me have the family that I wanted. Next I would shake my fist at God, yelling at Him for calling me to the priesthood when there were so many other men to choose from, men much better qualified than me. When I felt that I could not run away from this call, I would start to feel depressed that I would never have all those things I had dreamed about from my childhood. Finally, I realized that God does not want me to be unhappy; in fact, He knows best what will make me happy because He made me. Following my own will for so much of my life had not brought me lasting happiness. It was not until I had started to follow His will that I began to feel true peace and joy in my life. So I knew I needed to continue to trust Him.

Finally, I decided to tell Father Kenny that I was ready to apply to the Archdiocese of Atlanta. We had already planned to have dinner that evening, and, once again, I had not told anyone about my decision. I had not told my parents or my friends from Notre Dame even that I was seriously thinking about the priesthood. During dessert, I told Father Kenny that I was ready to apply to the Archdiocese of Atlanta. He said that he had an application in the car that he would give to me after dinner. Since he was the director of vocations, I assumed that he kept a stack of applications in his briefcase. When we got to the car, however, he had only one application, sitting on the passenger's seat, and it had my name already typed on it.

I could not believe that Father Kenny could know so well what I was thinking and where I was in my discernment. What made Father such a great vocations director was that he had a wonderful intuitive sense of when someone had a vocation to the priesthood or religious life. He was not afraid to approach a young man and ask him if he ever thought about becoming a priest, as he had approached me in the church that Sunday evening. He brought our vocations program from seven men to over seventy men in just a few years. He was a wonderful model of faithfulness in the priesthood for his seminarians. We all loved him and had a great deal of respect for him.

In April 1992 I applied to the Archdiocese of Atlanta, and I was accepted as a seminarian a few months later. In January 1993, Father Kenny sent me to Mount Saint Mary's Seminary in Emmitsburg, Maryland, to study philosophy, Greek, and Latin for one semester. My theological studies at the North American College in Rome were to begin in the fall of 1993, so I had to take intensive philosophy and language courses to satisfy the entrance requirements. I finished my philosophy studies at Saint Meinrad Seminary in southern Indiana and then went to Rome, where I studied theology at the Pontifical University of Saint Thomas Aquinas, known as the Angelicum. And, *Deo gratias*, on the Feast of Our Lady of Guadalupe, December 12, 1998, I was ordained to the priesthood of Jesus Christ for service in the Archdiocese of Atlanta, where I happily live and serve today.

Since my ordination, my mother and stepfather have come back to the faith. It was something for which I had offered many Masses, but it happened in God's time and not in mine. Our Lord is infinitely patient. He will always come down to us, no matter where we are, to save us from ourselves. I ignored Him for many years, yet He stood beside me, patiently waiting for me to acknowledge Him. I rejected Him many times, yet He continued to offer me His gift of faith, patiently waiting for me to accept it. When I finally accepted that gift, I found a true and lasting happiness in the arms of my loving Father and Lord.

Father Augustine Tran is a priest of the Archdiocese of Atlanta. Ordained in 1998, he is currently serving as a theology teacher at Blessed Trinity Catholic High School in Roswell, Georgia.

Chapter 12

Waking Up to Truth

Kevin Lents

"Daddy, can we go to church tonight?" Years after my five-year-old daughter spoke those words, they still echo in my heart. It was January 4, 1998, a snowy Saturday, at about four o'clock in the afternoon. I had just come home from work, to find my wife, Sheila, and our two daughters sledding in our backyard.

Keriann, the oldest, came running around to the front of the house in her pink snowsuit and her oversized white snow boots. Since I am six feet three inches tall, she was looking almost straight up from her white fur-lined hood, and tufts of long dark hair were peeking out around her face. She looked like a little Eskimo girl to me—just as beautiful as she could be.

That moment occurred over ten years ago. At the time I was as nominal a Catholic as anyone could be, having been casually baptized as an infant and having converted without conviction before my marriage fifteen years earlier, after which I stopped attending Mass almost immediately. I can't say exactly why I decided to be "unchurched". It just seemed to happen.

My wife, Sheila, was trying to give our daughters some semblance of faith in God. She found it very hard to take them to the Holy Sacrifice of the Mass alone. As for me, I just wanted to stay home on Sunday morning, eat dough-nuts, and watch the latest news from the world of sports on television. The Hound of Heaven had been follow-ing me for years, but I had managed to shrug off His bay-ing. Now, pagan, agnostic, or lapsed Catholic though I was, I said, in essence, "Okay, Lord, You win. I'm coming home."

To Keriann, I simply said, "Yes, we can." This little girl—or the Lord acting through her—had broken through the hardened shell around her daddy's heart.

So we went to the vigil Mass at Saint John's parish in my hometown of Loogootee, Indiana. We haven't stopped attending since then, and we never will. It was the begin-ning of a complete transformation in my life. I found the faith and fell in love with it.

*   *   *

I never claimed to be anything but a very ordinary guy, just another Joe Six-Pack. But back then, what that had meant was worshipping sports and pleasure as my personal gods. I was completely ignorant of Catholic doctrine, but I really can't blame anyone else for my ignorance. It probably wouldn't have mattered who had been trying to teach me the faith or how good a job he was doing. I wasn't inter-ested, so I wasn't listening.

The oldest of four children, I was baptized a Catholic in 1961, but I don't recall ever going to Holy Mass as a child. At that time, Loogootee was 65 to 75 percent Irish Cath-olic, and Saint John's parish even had its own school sys-tem, with grades 1 through 12, though the town's total population was only around three thousand people.

My parents were young, and their marriage was foundering. They had a mixed religious background: Dad's side of the family was Catholic, while Mom's was of various Protestant traditions, but mostly United Methodist. When I was eight years old, my parents divorced, and after that Mom tried to prod her children toward the United Methodist church. To be fair, I admit she gave my sister Kim and me the option of returning to Saint John's Catholic grade school. But I didn't want anything more to do with those rigid Sisters of Providence. I had had a couple of run-ins with my first-grade teacher, Sister Anna Immacula, leading to more than one trip to the principal's office, and I didn't want ever to do that again. So we were off to the Methodist church across town.

We attended services there from time to time. I was even an occasional acolyte. But mostly Mom just made sure we got to Sunday school, which I did not want to attend at all. Despite the fact that I had no clue what it meant to be a Christian, I was even confirmed in that denomination, and my sister Kim was confirmed at the same time.

The confirmation service was held on a Saturday, with the pastor of the church officiating. He gave us grape juice and cubes of wheat bread, and we knelt in front of the pulpit while he preached. I don't remember what his sermon was about, but no doubt it had to do with being an adult Christian. I do remember that my clowning with the boy beside me very much tried the good pastor's patience. This got me into trouble with my mom.

When the service was over, Mom looked at me incredulously and asked, "Kevin, what's wrong with you?"

"Oh, Mom, I really didn't want to be there", I replied. "And I really don't want to go to Sunday school or church anymore."

Soon after that, my mother decided that she would raise her kids to know that there is a God, and that Jesus is God, but she would let us decide for ourselves which church to attend once we were out of her hands.

As a result, throughout my teen years, God wasn't even on my radar screen. I attended weddings and funerals of friends and relatives but rarely went to any kind of Sunday service. Before long I fell hard into the "ways of the world"—that is, into sin—and all I really wanted was to have a "good time", all the time. Life was all focused on me. By my late teens, my thoughts usually centered on girls first, then beer.

As a high schooler, I let some of the girls I was dating talk me into attending a Catholic retreat weekend called "Search". I genuinely enjoyed the experience, but it was primarily focused on "feelings" and "fellowship" rather than on doctrinal truth. Afterward, I attended a couple of the reunions, but they were just more of the same. Soon, my Search experience faded from my memory, much like my friendships with the Catholic girls I had known in high school.

Then, when I was around twenty years old, I started dating my future wife, Sheila. She was a lovely girl of eighteen, with Irish Catholic roots on both sides of her family. Sometime in 1982, it looked like we were heading toward marriage, so I decided to join her in the Catholic Church. Though my intentions were benign, I was joining the Church for the wrong reasons. I was not sincerely seeking to discover Christ's love or to learn the Truths the Church teaches. For that matter, I wasn't even trying to learn what it meant to be a Christian. I guess I was just trying to share what was important in Sheila's life.

For better or worse, there was no Rite of Christian Initiation of Adults (RCIA) program then, as there is in most parishes today. To prepare for my reception into the Church,

I met five times with a priest at a little parish in a neighboring town. I wasn't really catechized in the faith at all. During the fifth session, I went to confession and was confirmed. I'm ashamed to admit that I received both sacraments sacrilegiously, and it was the last time I received the sacrament of penance for more than fifteen years. Whatever the priest's shortcomings as an instructor, I know it was ultimately my own responsibility to uncover the deposit of faith. But I suppose I thought I could pick up whatever was needed by attending Mass with Sheila. I just was not interested in all that "Catholic stuff".

For a short time I went to Mass with Sheila and her family, though I hadn't a clue what was happening. Catholic worship seemed to me like Sunday morning calisthenics: kneel, sit, stand, and genuflect. I thought the "signs" the worshippers made with their hands were like a third-base coach signaling to a batter in a baseball game. I didn't know what to make of it all. Certainly, I didn't realize the great importance of the Mass. No one had ever explained to me that the sacrifice at Mass is the one same sacrifice as that which happened on Calvary outside of Jerusalem in A.D. 33 (Hebrews 10:10; 7:27).

I did not understand what a spiritual life was, so I was not praying outside of Mass either. I had no understanding of basic Catholic doctrines on the papacy, Mary, or the saints; purgatory or indulgences; sacraments or sacramentals—not to mention the Most Holy Sacrament of the Altar, the Eucharist. I knew virtually nothing about the faith. Because I was not genuinely seeking God, or seeking to learn what it meant to be a follower of Jesus, I stopped attending Mass with Sheila even before we were married.

My heart and mind—and my unusual, nearly obsessive, gift of memory—were all concentrated on such things as Notre

Dame football, NASCAR racing, playing softball, lifting weights, and collecting comic books. I had all the sports statistics at my fingertips and all the comic collectors' lore. Actually, football, racing, softball, and the like are not inherently evil but are good in themselves, or at least neutral, but I made them into my god. There were also other, inherently sinful, things in my life, but I won't describe them here.

Making these secular interests my idols reinforced my worldly mentality. I became a confirmed relativist. In an attempt to foster tolerance, we had been taught at public school that "your truth is your truth; my truth is my truth." If everything is relative, then of course there can be no absolutes. What this meant in effect was that if someone wanted an abortion, she had a right to make that choice. What is a family? Whatever you make of it. At least that was what the purple dinosaur told us on PBS. What is your "preference" about sexuality? I didn't care. My thinking was that you could do whatever you wanted, with whomever you liked, as long as it didn't affect my family. Each of us is free to do whatever he wants. After all, this is America. Right?

Of course, I was a "compromiser". "Situational ethics" and "consequentialism" shaped my ethics. To my thinking, there was nothing wrong with "bending the rules" a little—no matter whose rules they were. *Everybody else does it*, I thought, *so why shouldn't I?* If I was "following my conscience", then anything that went wrong couldn't possibly be my fault. Nobody said I had to have a "properly informed conscience", as, I eventually learned, the Church tells us we must.

Outwardly I behaved as if the things of the world would make me happy. After all, isn't being happy what we all want? But inwardly, I wasn't happy. I admired heroes, and I saw in them that heroism was possible. My father subscribed to a Notre Dame football newspaper. One day I read an article there about a recruit who was six foot eight and 320 pounds, an Academic All-State offensive lineman. He had near-perfect SAT and ACT scores. However, at the end of the article, this young man described how he kept all of that in proper perspective. He said that his relationship with the Lord was his highest priority in life. I remember hanging my head in shame and asking why couldn't I have the same kind of faith this talented young man had. I didn't think I had what it took.

I remember looking up at the ceiling and saying, *I know, Lord. I know.* I admired my friends who worked "right-to-life" paper drives and based their choices on moral principles, and others whom I knew had undergone a spiritual change. I wanted to be a man of honor, of virtue, and especially of truth. But I couldn't figure out how to become such a man, thinking it was something I would have to do on my own. And, of course, such a longing could never be squared with my relativist outlook. I could never become a man of integrity while my conscience was so elastic that I could rationalize any action I wanted, including sin.

* * *

Often, in those years before I came to the Lord, He sent me little nudges to call me to Him. Driving past the local Catholic church and parish center during Holy Mass or evening catechism class, I remember how I would turn my head and look at the cars and get a sense that I was supposed to be there too.

Also, I vividly remember encountering a fellow at work who had a "Bible Christian" conversion experience in one of the Baptist churches. He clearly was moved by the Lord to become a Christian. He even choked up and wept about

it while he "witnessed" to me. This made me uncomfortable, and my discomfort got worse when he asked me if I
too had a relationship with the Lord.

Stretching the truth, I told him sheepishly that yes, I was
Catholic, but I didn't practice the faith. When he launched
into an anti-Catholic tirade, I got so angry that the hair on
the back of my neck stood up. Then I asked myself why I cared
what he said when I didn't go to church at all, much less a
Catholic church. Who was I to argue with an anti-Catholic?

*   *   *

In 1997, during October, the month of Our Lady, my wife,
my mother-in-law, and I went up to South Bend to a Notre
Dame football game. On other visits, I had toured most of
the Notre Dame campus, but although I had heard a lot
about "the Grotto", I had never seen it and really didn't
know what it was. While walking around the campus on
that day in 1997, we came upon the famous grotto.

I had not realized that "the Grotto" was an exact replica
of the Grotto of Lourdes in France, where the Blessed
Mother appeared to Saint Bernadette. There is a rock that
came from the original Lourdes grotto built into the bluff-
rock facing of the Notre Dame grotto. Many Catholics were
kneeling there, under the huge trees in their fall colors,
with the Golden Dome in the background, praying their
Rosaries in front of the flickering candles and the statues of
Saint Bernadette and Our Lady. Witnessing this was too
much for me. Tears filled my eyes. To compose myself, I
walked down toward the lake. Suddenly I wanted to share
what these faith-filled, praying Catholics had. I wanted to
be convicted in the way they were. But I still didn't think
I had what it took.

Those things of the world that I was caught up in were supposed to make me feel good, but in all honesty, I knew there had to be something more to existence. I was trying to fill the void in my heart that could be filled only by God's love. That is what Saint Augustine meant when he said, "Our hearts are restless, O God, until they rest in Thee."

I was profoundly moved by that experience at the Grotto, when Our Lady reached out to me and touched my heart. It remains the zenith of my journey home to the Catholic faith. Yet even after that episode with Our Lady, it was still about three months before I entered the door of the local church. The day when I finally did so was that Saturday, January 4, 1998—the day my daughter asked if our family could go to Mass.

* * *

At that first Mass, I did not receive Holy Communion because I wanted to go to confession first, though I had no idea that was one of the precepts of the Church. I only knew that what the priest was holding was somehow supposed to be Jesus. Because I knew I was a sinner, I would not receive. Though I went back to Holy Mass later, I still did not understand what was going on. For that matter, I still did not understand the faith in general, but at least I understood that there was a lot I needed to learn.

About six weeks after I returned to Holy Mass, our parish hosted a weekend retreat called "Christ Renews His Parish" (CRHP). Our pastor prodded me a couple of times to come, and finally I relented. The weekend consisted of prayer, testimonies, the sacraments, and fellowship. The stories I heard from the men putting on the retreat were intensely touching. They were testimonies of how God had actually worked in their lives. Some of their stories were nothing short of miraculous.

The CRHP retreat turned out to be just the spiritual jolt I needed to awaken my desire to learn what it means to be a Catholic Christian. Now that I was ready to listen, the retreat taught me how to pray. I learned that the Second Vatican Council document on Holy Scripture, *Dei Verbum*, quotes Saint Jerome as saying, "Ignorance of Scripture is ignorance of Christ!" (*Dei Verbum* 25). I also discovered that I could crack open a Bible and read it.

Before the retreat ended, I made a general confession, and at last I received Holy Communion in a state of grace. I became a practicing Catholic.

But I was still doctrinally illiterate.

* * *

Where does an adult Catholic in my situation turn to learn the truth about the teaching of the Church? Being a "cradle Catholic" by baptism but not by instruction or practice, I was not quite a convert, but I was as ignorant of Catholic doctrine as any savage in a primitive mission land.

So I started my own study of the Catholic faith. I prayed and I searched and I dug. I wanted to know God and His Son Jesus Christ; I wanted to know what it meant to have a relationship with Him. I wanted to know the truth, not just something that would make me feel good (John 18:37; 14:6; 8:31–32; 1 Timothy 3:15). That first year back in the Church I prayed to the Lord on my knees a lot, asking Him to show me His Truth.

Some of the answers were surprising, and they came from unexpected places. For example, I remember asking a friend, "Jerry, who founded the Catholic Church?"

"Well, Jesus did, of course", he said. "In A.D. 33, in Jerusalem."

I had thought that Christianity sprang up from Jesus Christ, but in the many forms of different Christian denominations. That Jesus Christ Himself founded the Catholic Church was something I had not learned in world history at Loogootee High School. For that matter, neither had my friends, though most of them were Catholics themselves.

*   *   *

An acquaintance from the CRHP weekend gave me a boxed set of audiotapes called simply *The Bible*. Since sports-crazed pagans normally don't have televangelists at the top of their interest lists, I had never before heard anyone talk about where the Bible came from and how to read it. This evangelist said that in the early years of Christianity, the Bible was kept chained up so it wasn't readily available to the "common Christian". That puzzled me, so I asked my well-informed friend Jerry about it. He said he wouldn't recommend that set of tapes, because they included anti-Catholic sentiments. Then he explained that Bibles were chained to the altar in medieval times because they were rare and precious, and Church officials did not want them stolen. They wanted to keep them available for the common Christians.

In place of the first tapes, Jerry gave me another set, titled *How to Explain and Defend the Catholic Faith*, by former Presbyterian minister Scott Hahn. Within five minutes of switching on the first tape of the Hahn set, I felt as if a light had been switched on inside my head. Dr. Hahn, a convert to the faith who had once been very anti-Catholic, was explaining Protestant misconceptions about Catholicism, and he was using the Bible to do it. He explained Scripture passages to the listener and made them easy to understand. The tapes were a godsend.

Soon I began studying the faith in earnest, and I discovered that there is a wealth of instruction available for adults who are searching, much of it superior in quality and magisterial authenticity to the general run of RCIA materials and to a great deal of the religious education materials produced by major catechetical publishers. By arriving at work an hour before "start" time so I could have the computer to myself, I would log on to sound Catholic Web sites like the Eternal Word Television Network (EWTN), Catholic Answers, and Catholics United for the Faith, and study there. After work, I read solid Catholic books and magazines, including Karl Keating's *Catholicism and Fundamentalism*, Patrick Madrid's *Surprised by Truth* series, and *This Rock*, *Envoy*, and *Lay Witness* magazines.

I went to parish missions, and to Catholic conferences organized by Saint Joseph Communications. I attended a Teens Encounter Christ weekend retreat and a Cursillo renewal weekend. I listened to audiotapes by great Catholic apologists like Scott Hahn, Tim Staples, and Father John Corapi. Their talks fed my intellectual hunger, as did those by other speakers like Karl Keating, Patrick Madrid, Steve Ray, Marcus Grodi, Jesse Romero, Michael Cumbie, Rosalind Moss, and Johnnette Benkovic. At the same time, other great Catholic speakers, especially Father John Hardon, Father Benedict Groeschel, EWTN's own Mother Angelica, Bishop Fabian Bruskewitz, Archbishop Raymond Burke, and Father Bill Casey of the Fathers of Mercy, fed my spiritual hunger.

Applying the passion I had been spending on sports statistics and comic book collectors' lore to my search for Catholic truth, I found that I could use the same native talents I had used in those matters to acquire knowledge and retain source citations in Holy Scripture, the *Catechism of the Catholic Church*, papal encyclicals, and conciliar documents.

One enormous blessing has been coming to a better understanding of Christ's Real Presence in the Eucharist. The Eucharist is the "heart and summit of the Church's life" (Second Vatican Council, *Lumen Gentium* 11). I read other wonderful documents on the Eucharist and Eucharistic adoration like *Mysterium Fidei, Ecclesia de Eucharistia, Dominicae Cenae, Inaestimabile Donum, Mane Nobiscum Domine, Sacrosanctum Concilium*, and, in the *Catechism of the Catholic Church*, the entire section on the Eucharist.

Never, ever in my life had I thought I could read such things and begin to understand them. I can't even pronounce the Latin correctly. That puts me in a position to reassure any reader who wants to know what the Church teaches but thinks such official theological works are "too much" for him. If you want to know the Truth—with a capital *T*—this is where you will find it. Read the *Catechism*, the writings of the saints, papal encyclicals, or even Church council documents. I'm still just a "Joe Six-Pack" who sits in the pew like every other Catholic assisting at Holy Mass. Believe me, if I could learn this stuff, *anybody* can learn it! Remember that the men Jesus chose as His first apostles were just working fishermen.

Shortly after "coming home", I began stopping in my parish church on my way home from work to visit with Jesus: just me, Jesus, the angels, and the saints. Ten years later, I still do it. Outside the Mass, this is my favorite form of prayer. Pope John Paul II called adoration of the Blessed Sacrament "strictly linked to the celebration of the Eucharistic Sacrifice" (*Ecclesia de Eucharistia* 25). At first I would sit there choking with grateful and sorrowful tears: grateful for the Lord's Divine Mercy in calling me home, and sorrowful for having waited so long to answer Him. Like Saint Augustine I can say, "How late have I loved Thee, O Lord, how late have I loved Thee."

Suddenly I was on fire for the faith. I wanted to be *fully* Catholic, not 50 percent or 75 percent or 99 percent Catholic. I wanted it all because it made no sense to me to be committed to Jesus Christ part of the way. He asks us to love Him with *all* our heart, *all* our soul, and *all* our mind (Matthew 22:37). He wants our total commitment, and that doesn't leave a whole lot of wiggle room.

* * *

High among the many wonderful blessings conversion brought us are our sons. One day, I was reading Judie Brown's pro-life forum on the EWTN Web site when I saw the words that changed our family forever: *contraception is a mortal sin.* Unnerved by what she had said, I located a copy of Archbishop Chaput's pastoral letter "Of Human Life" and gave it to Sheila to read. After prayerfully studying what the Church teaches on being open to life within the sacrament of marriage, we threw out our contraceptives. Since then, we have been given three beautiful boys to go along with our two girls. Sheila has quit her outside job, and now she homeschools our five children.

God brought our family into a glorious whirlwind, and I wouldn't trade it for anything else. Just writing about it reminds me how unlikely it all was. From time to time I ask myself why God chose me—an ignorant, secular, sinful man, barely a believer in any real sense—to witness for Him and His Holy Catholic Church. Why would our good Lord give me these gifts? Not because I deserved them. It can only be because He who is Mercy and Goodness heard me when I asked Him to let me know the truth. He fulfilled the promise He makes in Matthew 7:7: "Ask, and it will be given you; seek, and you will find; knock, and it will be opened to you. For every one who asks receives, and he who seeks finds, and to him who knocks it will be opened." And now, led and strengthened by His continuing grace through the sacraments and prayer, I want to share the truth with everyone I meet. As a late starter, I feel I have to hurry to catch up.

Hoping to prevent Catholic youngsters from growing up as ignorant as I was at their age, I started teaching catechism. Currently I teach three classes, two to high school students and one to eighth graders. With friends, I have been involved in spearheading conferences to enable those in our area to hear speakers like Marcus Grodi, Tim Staples, Michael Cumbie, Bruce Sullivan, and John Martignoni, all of them converts or reverts who are tremendously effective evangelizers. One recent conference we organized at Saint Joseph Church in Jasper, Indiana, drew more than three hundred people. Sometimes I am even invited to speak at various parishes and conferences in this diocese and others around the Midwest.

Ultimately, my conversion story is about God's awesome goodness, love, and mercy, which I have been privileged to experience firsthand.

Kevin Lents lives in Loogootee, Indiana. He teaches religious education classes and speaks about the faith at conferences around the Midwest. He wrote about his conversion from laxity to fervent faith in This Rock *magazine. He has also been a guest on Marcus Grodi's EWTN program* The Journey Home.

In the near future, Lents expects to publish a book of corrective catechesis, The Language of Dissent.

Chapter 13

Finding Eyes to See With

Sarah Christmyer

Dedicated to Tom and Lovelace Howard, whose unflagging support and love have encouraged me more than they can know.

The rug in Grandma's living room stretched from wall to wall, a soft blanket of gold that gathered up the California sun and shook it back into the room. I loved that rug. It was warm and soft to play on, but mostly it was the place we gathered as a family—aunts and uncles and cousins, three and sometimes four generations of us—to sing, to pray, and best of all, to listen to "jungle stories".

These were stories of surviving in the jungles of Sumatra, where my mother's parents, aunt, and uncle had taken their families so they could tell the tribespeople about Jesus. Stories of people healed of leprosy and other diseases. Stories of enemies reconciled to one another and brought to God. The story of the nail in the can of mandarin oranges, which had found its way into newspapers and magazines: the nail had appeared miraculously in my great-uncle's lunch the very day he'd stopped telling the Indians the story of Jesus' love for them because there were no nails in the jungles, and he couldn't find the words or images to explain how much Jesus had suffered for them.

These were stories every bit as exciting as Daniel in the lion's den, or David and Goliath. Not all the stories were set in the jungles, but they all told of God's great love and care and miraculous intervention in a way that made it impossible to doubt. These were real stories that happened to real people who still lived: to my grandparents and parents and aunts and uncles and cousins. And our stories were woven together and taken up into the fabric of the Story that began in the Garden of Eden. God is the same today as He ever was. It did not surprise me to see the same sorts of things happening in the present that were described in the Bible.

I rolled across the carpet and stretched out under the grand piano. Grandpa Morken was a fine pianist with a fine voice. "Great Is Thy Faithfulness" rolled out of him and shook the floor beneath me. I closed my eyes and let the great hymn carry me away.

*   *   *

I suppose I am the last person one would have expected to become Catholic. I have a rich Protestant heritage, going back for generations and spreading out on both sides. It is a heritage of strong people who love God and who have devoted their lives to Jesus and to sharing the Good News of the gospel. They are missionaries, evangelists, pastors, and Sunday school teachers. They started churches and helped begin some of the great evangelical outreach organizations that continue today.

I owe an enormous debt to my parents and grandparents. By word and example, they not only taught me to know God through the Bible, but they showed me what it means to have a living, personal relationship with Him. The strength and vibrancy of their faith was and is contagious. When I came to a point in my life as a teenager where I needed to choose between going my own way and following God, it was the witness of their lives that convinced me that I wanted to go God's way.

As I reflect on that faith and on my family's "brand" of Protestantism, it occurs to me that it is not rooted in any particular denomination. It did not really come from church at all. It came from living in the Bible and from countless hours of prayer. It came from abiding in Jesus and following Him, from obeying His Word. The church to us was found in the worldwide network of believers in Christ, of whatever stripe or calling. Denominations were man-made constructs that served a useful function but could just as easily lead people astray. The Catholic Church in particular was a crusty, outmoded vehicle that had seen its day, seemingly swept aside in the rush of new life inspired by the Holy Spirit at the Reformation. We were Christians, pure and simple.

*　　*　　*

Given my strong evangelical heritage, how *did* I become Catholic? It's a good question. I would have felt comfortable worshipping in nearly any Protestant church, though it would have been hard to take on the label of Methodist or Baptist or some other denomination. I didn't think any church was 100 percent right doctrinally—they are run by humans, after all—but I also didn't want to be pigeonholed. Ultimately, though, any of them would have been okay, if I had had to choose. What would not have been okay was to be Catholic.

At the time, I believed that what made someone a Christian was his personal relationship with God and whether he had asked Christ into his life. I didn't understand why Catholics seemed to think that just because they were Catholic, they were Christian, regardless of the strength of their faith and whether they practiced it. I assumed that there were true Christians in the Catholic Church, but I thought that was *in spite of* the misguided teaching they had received. After all, I had relatives in Catholic countries who worked hard to convert Catholics and "bring them to Jesus." My grandparents went to Belgium because at the time, the Catholic Church didn't allow people to read the Bible and persecuted them if they did. Maybe in America Catholics were allowed to read the Bible, but I hadn't met any who actually did. I also had it firsthand from a lot of ex-Catholics that they had known nothing of the love of God, only the judgment. They had no idea whether they were saved. They were motivated to go to church by fear that they'd end up in Hell if they missed a Sunday. Some were so afraid of God that they prayed to Mary instead. And they had this idea, which I thought was the height of arrogance, that they were the one true Church. If you had told me back then that I'd end up Catholic someday, I'd have said you were out of your mind.

Life is never as simple as we'd like it to be. When I fell in love, it was not with a nice WASP (white Anglo-Saxon Protestant) preacher or missionary but with a lapsed Irish Catholic. Mark rarely mentioned his Catholic roots, and he soon began going to church with me. Little did I know how strong those roots would prove to be!

* * *

In time we were married. My grandfather performed the ceremony at a friend's estate, outdoors next to a lake. So remote did Mark's Catholic background seem that no priest was present.

From time to time I worried about Mark's faith. He was not at home at Tenth Presbyterian, and he seemed like a fish out of water among my family. Like most "cradle" Catholics, he kept his beliefs quiet. He appeared not to know any Scripture because he didn't know his Bible the way we did; and to someone like me, for whom the Bible was the one and only source of revelation about salvation, that didn't look good. I knew he loved God. He said he was a Christian. He acted like a Christian. He just didn't *talk* like any Christian I knew. And as we thought about having children, I started to worry. How in the world would I raise them in the faith with someone so different from me? What if we faced problems differently? What if (God forbid) he started teaching them different things? I began to have moments of deep dread and even panic. What had I gotten myself into?

We moved to the suburbs and began looking for another church. Very soon we came to a standstill. I thought I could find a good Episcopal church like Christ Church, the one I'd attended in college, and recapture what I still remembered as the best church experience I'd had, but I didn't get the chance. Any church but that one, Mark said. No way would he go to some church that came about because a king wanted to get a divorce. Not only that, he asked, why didn't we visit a Catholic church? He had patiently followed me around to all sorts of Protestant churches and even the local Quaker meeting, and now he was tired of it. The least I could do was to give a Catholic church a try.

I was horrified, scornful even. But turnabout was fair play, and I agreed to go. The first place we tried was not the ideal choice for a visiting evangelical. No music to speak

of. People came in late and left early. Babies cried. Unintel-
ligible sermon, if you could even call it that. I couldn't
wait to leave and gloat over the mistake. Mark, on the other
hand, came out at peace. He may not have liked the atmosphere any more than I did, but he felt he'd been to church
for the first time in many years.

Words are inadequate to explain the abyss I felt opening
before us. Apart from the figurative slap in my face (how
could he feel he hadn't been to church before this?), I
couldn't fathom what Mark found in that service. My choice
of words here is instructive: it was a *service* to me, something that could be judged on how well it was performed.
I had no concept of the importance of the Eucharist, and
Mark either didn't or couldn't explain it. But whatever Mark
had been outwardly for the last fifteen years, he was Catholic on the inside, and those old roots were stirring back to
life.

Soon after that, we learned I was pregnant. My brother's
wife was expecting their second child, and we had deep
discussions over whether we should baptize the babies as
infants or wait until they could decide for themselves. This
is one of the issues that Protestants agree to disagree about,
and there are scripturally based arguments on all sides of it.
I had been baptized as an infant, but my brothers were dedicated to God, and then all of us were baptized (me for the
second time) when we were ready as teenagers to make a
public declaration of our faith. This approach made sense
to me, but still I wasn't sure.

When Abby was several months old, my grandfather dedicated her along with several others of his great-grandchildren,
at a family reunion.

I did not realize that Mark sat through that service wondering why we stopped short of baptizing the babies. Why

not go all the way? And why such an individual thing—why not involve the whole community, which would be involved in bringing the child up in the faith? He started to think that I had done my thing, from my tradition, and now we should do what was right according to his tradition.

One day he startled me with a question: "Don't you think we should baptize the baby Catholic?"

"Oh, right", I scoffed. "Are you *kidding?*"

He was not. And from that time on, I felt that I was being sucked into a dark hole. So anguished was I over the whole matter that, when I agreed for his sake to have Abby baptized, I didn't invite anyone. I didn't celebrate. I felt like crying. Yet in the end I was surprised by the beauty of the liturgy. The words expressed just what I wanted for my daughter, though I was uncomfortable that they were said in the context of a Catholic service.

I'm not sure what I would have done if we hadn't found Daylesford Abbey, a nearby Norbertine community where we went to hear a Christmas concert. The music was fabulous, and as we walked out, Mark noticed a schedule of Sunday Masses. I agreed to try one, and we went the following Sunday. Something in the liturgy spoke to my soul. It was much simpler than what I remembered from Christ Church, yet much the same. Beautiful music. A good homily. People who obviously wanted to be there. You could feel God's Spirit. And best of all—no statues of Mary cluttering up the front. No incense. No enormous crucifix to distract me. Nothing to make me feel that it had to be Catholic. It was, I thought, the perfect compromise.

Well, maybe not perfect. Mark was very happy. I was moderately so. But there was one nagging issue that came up every week: the Eucharist. I knew that as long as I wasn't a Catholic, I couldn't partake. I didn't mind going and not receiving; I'd been to plenty of churches that rarely had communion. But it was a continual reminder of a division between us that was growing, not closing. I shut out those thoughts and prayed for help.

* * *

By this time, I was filled with fear at what was happening; with anger at God that I was in this position at all; and with a load of pent-up, unanswered questions.

One Sunday, the priest announced the start of an RCIA class.[1] Armed with a list of objections, I marched off to join. Here was my chance to put together a solid case against the Catholic Church, so we could go back where we belonged.

I will never forget that first class, or the second. I expected to hear papist propaganda but just sat there, stunned, as I was hit between the eyes with "Who is God?" and then "Who is Jesus Christ?" "Who is the Holy Spirit?" "Who are you, and where do you stand before God?" *Whatever happened to "Who is Mary?"* I wondered. *What about "Who is the pope, and why should we worship him?"* I couldn't get them to go off on tangents. Instead, week after week they unfolded the fundamentals of the Christian faith in simple clarity. I had to admit: here was a *Christian* church.

Now that we had a second child, the issue of baptism was back at the forefront, and I couldn't wait to hear what they had to say about it. I remember sitting on the edge of my seat as I listened to a straightforward, uncomplicated

[1] RCIA, the Rite of Christian Initiation of Adults, is the usual process by which adults are instructed in the Catholic faith and are received into the Church.

explanation. Here's what baptism is. Here's what confirmation is. Here's how they fit into the scheme of salvation. And it made sense!

I wanted to jump up and shout, "That's what I've always believed! How did you *know*?" That explanation tied together a lot of loose ends and niggling questions that plagued me. And I thought, *We have spent so much time searching and praying and arguing over what these things mean, and it's already been done!*

This was a watershed for me. I had come face-to-face with the Church: a physical, recognizable entity, established by God on earth for a purpose, to safeguard His deposit of faith. To guide His people. To spread the news of His love. Maybe here was the one to arbitrate between the Baptists and the Presbyterians, to say "wait a minute—THIS IS THE TRUTH."

It had always bothered me to be in the position of judging people and denominations and deciding for myself what was true. I know it is a popular thing to think that truth is what you decide is true, but I don't buy it. If God is who He says He is, then certain things are true regardless of our opinions, regardless of whether or not we understand. There must be Truth with a capital *T* behind questions like "Who is God?" and "Why am I here?" and "What must I do to be saved?"

All my life I had believed that if we just studied the Bible and prayed for guidance, the Holy Spirit would guide those who loved and obeyed God into knowledge of His Truth. But then, how can different earnest, God-fearing, praying Christians seek Truth from the Holy Spirit and come up with different interpretations of Scripture? How can they find different answers to the big questions?

The classic Protestant resolution is to agree on the basics and let the rest slide. One church I used to attend has this posted on its Web site under "What We Believe": "In essential beliefs—we have unity. . . . In nonessential beliefs—we have liberty. . . . In all our beliefs—we show charity."

That sounds attractive. It's an easy way to allow everyone to coexist. But who gets to pick what the basics are, those "essential beliefs" in which we are to have unity? Baptism seems pretty basic to me. Salvation's a big one. And how do we know who is right? I could no longer let the question alone.

* * *

This launched me on the most painful part of my journey. The thought of having a real doctrinal and moral authority was attractive to me, but there was a problem. If I were to accept the authority of the Catholic Church, I would have to buy the whole package. Infallibility. Apostolic succession. The Marian doctrines. Those were tough. I wasn't quite sure I was ready to make the step. And after what happened next, I almost didn't.

The parish set up a panel discussion to answer our questions. I had mine ready but thought I'd wait and see first what others had to ask. I was completely taken off guard as the questions exploded, one after the other, about the Church's teaching on birth control. Most of the others in the class were engaged to be married, and this was a hot topic. One of the priests explained the teaching of *Humanae Vitae*.[2] After more questions, another priest stated quite clearly that here in America, we do things differently.

---

[2] *Humanae Vitae* (*On the Regulation of Birth*; 1968) is an encyclical by Pope Paul VI that affirms the Catholic Church's teaching on abortion, contraception, and other issues regarding human life. *Humanae Vitae* is Latin for "of human life".

Contraception is a matter of individual conscience, and the decision must be made prayerfully between the two spouses. I couldn't believe what I was hearing. Did he think he was a *Protestant*? There I was, wondering whether I could accept that there was an authority to be reckoned with, and he's telling me that an official pronouncement from the pope *doesn't matter*. That blew my mind. I stood up, made my protest, and walked out. RCIA had decided nothing for me.

I was beside myself, nearly despairing, when out of the blue, someone sent me a tape to listen to. It was a conversion testimony by Kimberly Hahn, who had recently entered the Church. That tape spoke straight to my heart. Here was someone, finally, from a background similar to mine, who had walked where I was walking. She must have explained some theological issues, but what spoke to me most powerfully was her pain. I got in touch with her, and she very graciously listened and talked me through some of my concerns. One thing she asked stood out:

"Did you have everything settled before you started on this journey, or did you have questions? When do you think they will all be answered?"

I realized then that I will always have questions and that I cannot expect, in a short time, to solve complicated theological issues that better minds than mine have worked on for centuries. After all, I wasn't looking into Buddhism or Islam. If the Catholic Church was truly Christian, as I was beginning to understand her to be, then becoming Catholic shouldn't be so much different from finally deciding to join one of the Protestant Christian denominations.

I had come to a place where I thought perhaps I should become Catholic. The division between Mark and me was too great to bear. We were at a standstill. If we were both heading in the same direction, maybe God could lead us where He wanted us to go. I didn't know, though, if I could make the sacrifice. It would mean jumping off the solid and familiar platform on which my life was built. It would mean becoming what I had viewed in the past as a kind of second-class Christian. It would mean hurting and maybe alienating friends and family members, who would not understand. ("Remember—we are *Reformationist* Christians!" my great-aunt once told me.) The pain of separation I was feeling from my husband, through not being able to share together in the Eucharist, would become a separation from the rest of my family in the very area that held us together. I could hardly bear it. I had never felt such a depth of pain and isolation.

One night, I dreamed God came to me. "Who brought you here?" He asked. I began to protest that it was certainly not my choice when I realized that *He* had brought me. He stretched out His hand toward me: "Are you going to follow, or not?"

I knew then in my heart what I had to do. Deciding between churches had paralyzed me. There were too many issues, too many pros and cons, too many unknowns. But faced with this question—"Will you follow me?"—I had to go on. I was terrified. But it was better to leap from a cliff in the dark following God than to continue on familiar ground by myself. We had moved across the country by this time. I joined another RCIA class to become Catholic.

One of the first things we had to do was get remarried in the Church. I would have preferred telling no one, but my parents knew, and it hurt my mother deeply. The situation was so painful for her and for me that we didn't discuss it. My father, though, would sit and talk and pray with me. He wanted to make sure I knew what the issues were and had thought them through, but he assured me that whatever decision I came to, he was behind me. That support meant a great deal.

There was little joy for me in the Easter Vigil Mass the night I was received into the Church. For my confirmation name I chose Helen, after my grandmother. Saint Helena is known as the "seeker of the true Cross", and I thought that applied to Grandma as well. I felt her presence with me that night. "Remember, honey," I could almost hear her saying, "without a death, there can be no resurrection."

I felt like I was at a funeral. But what then seemed like a death turned out to be a new beginning. Without this death to my old idea of what Christian faith should be, my resurrection to a fuller understanding of that faith would have been impossible.

*　　*　　*

It is an old adage that you can't know a man until you've walked a mile in his shoes. I found that I couldn't know what it meant to be Catholic until I'd been one a while. At first it was very lonely. Catholics weren't unfriendly, but they seemed like people from a different country, speaking a different language. I was used to connecting with other Christians around the Bible, but there were no Bible studies. I was used to fellowship groups where we sang praise songs and prayed together; here hardly anyone sang, and the only prayer meetings I knew about involved the Rosary, with which I wasn't comfortable. I would go to Mass and focus on the Liturgy of the Word, drinking in the beauty of the Scripture while the people around me seemed distracted or bored. Then I'd start drifting off as we headed into the Eucharist, just as everyone else perked up and got into it.

I developed an intense need to understand. Until I heard Kimberly Hahn's testimony, I had found no one who understood my questions, let alone answered them. Now, beginning with Scott Hahn and David Currie, there seemed to be a wave of Protestant ministers becoming Catholic and writing about the scriptural roots of the Catholic faith, explaining what they had discovered on their journeys in language I could understand. I devoured every book I could get my hands on, dug out the sermons of John Henry Newman, studied Frank Sheed's *Theology and Sanity*. I bought a copy of the new Catholic *Catechism* and pored over it. I read Church documents and encyclicals and began reading the Church Fathers. I was consumed. And little by little, the lights started to turn on. There were times when the flashes of realization grew so intense I could hardly bear it. It was an amazing season of growth.

All this time I had been active in Community Bible Study, a fine Protestant organization that draws people from all denominations into serious study of the Bible. They make a point of avoiding points of division, but it became increasingly obvious to me that there is a chasm between the way Catholics and Protestants perceive the Bible. It began to bother me that we never took the Catholic view of a particular passage or issue into consideration. And I began to long to study the Bible with other Catholics.

There were several reasons for this. To begin with, I didn't know how to be a Christian without Bible study. I couldn't imagine why so few Catholics studied or even read the Bible on their own. My experience of the Mass was limited, and the only ways I knew to draw close to God were through prayer, by meditating on the Word and putting it into practice. I longed to share the riches I found in Scripture with my new Catholic family. But there was another reason. As

I grew in understanding and became more Catholic in my thinking, an astonishing thing happened. The closest comparison to it is the day I got my first prescription glasses. I walked outside and stopped still to stare around me.

"The trees—they have leaves!" I said to Mark. Not that I hadn't seen leaves before, but on the trees they always seemed a mass of green. That had never seemed to me anything but normal. It was the same with the Bible. I assumed my vision would improve as I learned more and grew, but I never imagined there was a whole new way of seeing. When I started reading the Bible through the lens of the Church, it was as if someone had handed me 3-D glasses. The familiar landscape took on new clarity and brilliance.

I had often thought of Bible study as the cutting and polishing that brings out the clarity and brilliance of a diamond. To carry that a Catholic step further, just as a diamond is held secure and shown to best advantage by the proper setting, so the Church's Tradition and Magisterium[3] safeguard and illuminate Sacred Scripture. They are the proper setting within which it should be read. I had read that in the *Catechism* and assented to it in my mind, but I was stunned by the difference it made in practice.

It has been a relief to give up my struggle to decide doctrine for myself and instead learn from the Church. The Magisterium is not always popular in a day when relativism rules and each individual is his own god. But especially today, with increasing challenges to morality and truth in our society and in the world, I am grateful that the Church

[3] In the Catholic Church, the Magisterium is the teaching office of the pope and the bishops in communion with him; to them has been entrusted the task of authentically interpreting the Word of God (cf. *Catechism of the Catholic Church*, no. 100).

under Peter is founded on a Rock and that God promised that the gates of Hell will not prevail against her.

* * *

I have been a Catholic now for fifteen years. That I *am* Catholic is old news. Yes, I am at home in a strong parish and have wonderful Catholic friends. And I have found a niche for myself writing Catholic Bible study material. Yet even so, the fact that I remain Catholic is puzzling to some of the people in my life. How can I be happy, they wonder, in a Church whose hierarchy has been rocked by scandal? How can I be at home in a Church whose representatives have made so many mistakes? How can I be happy in a Church where, often as not, liturgy is "done" badly, meaning you can't count on hearing good music or a good homily?

It took me a while to get to this place, but I can finally say that in the eternal view, those failings *don't matter.* When the liturgy is celebrated reverently and when the hierarchy gives a good example, it is like icing on the cake, which may sound unlikely from one who used to judge a church based on the quality of the music or the pastor's preaching. But week after week, year after year of going to Mass has reshaped the way I think about worship. We mortals need a way to approach God, and that way is Christ. It is true that Christ is present with me when I pray, or when I gather with two or three friends in His name, and it is true that I can call on Him and reach out to God anytime I want or need to, which as a Protestant I felt was sufficient. But in the Mass, Christ is present in a unique and powerful way equaled nowhere else outside of Heaven: He is there in the Word; He is there in the person of the priest; He is there in His Body the Church; and He is there, most especially, on the altar.

The Catholic Mass spells out how to approach and worship God and, at the same time, leads us through the steps we need to take. Every Eucharistic gathering in the world, however clumsily done, gathers us into Christ's Body and presents us before the throne of glory, where we offer ourselves with Him and then receive His very life. In Catholic worship, it's not all about me. It's about all of us, as the Body of Christ, presenting ourselves to God as a living sacrifice, which is "our spiritual worship" (see Romans 12:1). Only there can true unity be achieved, because there we are most fully united with Christ.

Today I understand why Mark felt he'd finally been to church that first time we went to Mass together. I understand why countless Catholics can go Sunday after Sunday, even to a poorly conducted "service". They're not blind fools who don't know any better or who fear they'll go to Hell if they don't go to church. They're not going for the pretty words and beautiful music, even if they would prefer that. They're going for something far more important: to be part of the Body of Christ, and to receive it. The absence of world-class choirs and homilies doesn't change the reality of the Mass.

Convert Rosalind Moss tells how, before she became Catholic, she used to sit in the parking lot watching people come out from Mass. There didn't seem to be much friendly fellowship going on outside, and few gathered out front to chat. They just came quietly and left at the end. What could be drawing them? She saw right away what it took me years to see: they were drawn by the presence of Christ. Her conclusion? "Now, that's what I call a personal relationship with God!"

All it took were eyes to see with. I will forever thank God that He opened mine.

Sarah Christmyer is a member of Saint Norbert Parish outside Philadelphia, where she lives with her husband and four children. She comes from a long line of evangelical missionaries and now writes Bible studies for Ascension Press and edits of The Great Adventure Bible Timeline *program. She also is coauthor with Gayle Somers of two studies on Genesis (Emmaus Road Publishing).*

Chapter 14

Looking for Something Bigger than the Universe

Stephanie Block

I was aware very early that there was an *Other*, while lying in my crib, watching the light play off the walls and along the polka-dotted quilt. Looking out from my eyes was *me*. Soon my mother or father would come into the room to start the morning business—and they were *others*. Yet there was this *Other* in the light and air of my room, unseen but present.

Later, when there were more words, my father and I had conversations about infinity that began with learning how to count, first my ten fingers and then up to a hundred. No matter how many numbers I knew, I could never come to the end of them. My father always found another number to trump the last one.

Impatient, I wanted him to give me the number at the utter end of everything.

There was no last number. Numbers just went on and on ... forever, infinitely.

We walked out in the summer night to count stars. No matter how many I could see, he told me, there were stars beyond them.

But what was beyond the stars? My mind envisioned a glass globe, filled with planets and stars. But outside all that, where it ended, what came next? Something, surely, was bigger than the universe.

As best I can recall, I was formally introduced to God around the age of three. My father had a Presbyterian friend who invited us to come and hear the minister at his church. We all went—Mom, Dad, and me. The pew cushions were scratchy and I had to sit still for a long time.

My father made it clear that he didn't believe in all the "nonsense", but his friend—and, as it turned out, my mother—did. The minister's sermons were very good, they said, and my father agreed to attend services regularly for a while. I would be baptized in a pink and white dress that my mother made and, as soon as I turned four, put into the children's choir, run by a woman who sang in the Metropolitan Opera House chorus.

I can see myself being baptized, standing on a plush, red carpet in a circle of adults at the front of the congregation. The black robes of the minister moved in front of me while water rolled down my forehead in the name of the Father, and the Son, and the Holy Spirit. I'd been strictly forbidden to wipe it off, so while great things were said over my head, I agonized at the rivulet slowly running along my nose. God, it turned out, was the name for that *Other*, though it was beyond me what He had to do with this place.

It was about this time my mother taught me the Our Father. It took several days of practice in the dark, after I had kissed my dad goodnight and was tucked into bed. Once I had learned it by heart, she told me that some people say prayers before they go to sleep, so I might like to say the Our Father and ask God to bless my family. She had me learn a little litany: God bless Daddy; God bless Mommy.

Who else should we ask God to bless? Once I understood the way it might be done, we never mentioned the matter again, and the saying of night prayers came to an end.

No sooner was I baptized and happily singing in the choir than the minister changed congregations, releasing my father from attending any more services. However, as it was educational for a child to learn music, there were no objections to driving me to church and dropping me off or even to helping with choir-related projects.

The next year, I started school and learned that there were very few Presbyterians in the world. Most of my classmates were Jewish, and my neighborhood playmates were Irish Catholic. Religion was a perennial topic. My Catholic friends made novenas and ate fish on Fridays; my Jewish friends turned up their noses at ham sandwiches and went to Hebrew school all day Saturday to prepare for their bar mitzvahs and bat mitzvahs. I had choir practice on Wednesday afternoons and wore a white cotta with a big red bow around the neck on Sunday mornings.

Boy troubles began in first grade. I think his name was Richard, and he was a pest. He made me really, really mad, and I lay in bed at night stewing over Richard. I made up stories about Richard behaving badly and then getting his just deserts. Richard would get hit by a car and die because he was so naughty. Richard would be caught by a policeman and sent to jail the rest of his life. Richard tied me to a tree, but I smacked Richard over the head with a rock, sending Richard rolling down the hill and out of the universe. Good for me! There was great comfort to be found in imaginary solutions.

After a few months of Richard stories, it occurred to me, while lying in my bed staring into the darkness, that the *Other*—God—could hardly be pleased. The Richard of

my stories was a lot worse than the Richard in my class.
Thinking about bad things to do to Richard, who wasn't
really all *that* bad, wasn't fair or kind. I was uncomfortable
knowing that God knew what I was thinking and realized
that I didn't want to keep butchering Richard with God
watching. It came down to God or Richard.

I wondered if I could *pretend* that God didn't see. Of
course, He *did* ... but if He didn't, I could think about
beating up Richard all I wanted.

But ... if He didn't see, He didn't exist. Now there was
a thought. What if God *didn't* exist?

I pretended there was no God, and the thought opened
into a waking nightmare. I saw the gaping abyss of noth-
ingness in which I, who had been and had known that I
was, ceased.

There is no way to write the terror of this experience.

I had never been afraid of the dark before. I had never considered what it was to be alone before. It was indescribable.

It would be too charitable to say that I had become an
atheist or even agnostic. This was a cold-blooded, deliberate act of self-mutilation. I had gouged out my spiritual
eyes but not the memory of what they had seen. The trick
was to remember less and less.

*   *   *

My father was editor for a historical quarterly, an accomplished pianist, a poet, and a humanist who had done doctoral work in aesthetics at Columbia University. He held
passionate opinions about the capacity of man to achieve a
sort of immortality through art and science. As far as I could
tell, this was not a respectable sort of immortality because,
say what he would, it ended when the world ended. The

immortality that impressed me was related to infinity; that is, if anything was *really* immortal, it needed to go on forever.

His father had been an equally passionate socialist, inventor, and biology professor with an evangelical zeal for evolution and eugenics, traveling the Wild West with charts that explained the facts of good human breeding to hapless frontiersmen. He called himself Unitarian, but his actual religion was a confusing mélange of atomic consciousness and practical ethics. He also peddled "Baker's Elixir", but that's another story.

With these two gentlemen in my stock, and being totally immune to Presbyterianism, by high school I was eating a philosophical diet of Camus, Sartre, and Nieztsche, understanding only so much of their work to know that if truth were relative and God was dead, even great art had nothing to offer that struck me as worth a lifelong struggle.

To make matters worse, I had joined the church youth ministry, led by an enthusiastic and thoroughly modern Scottish seminarian who had us reading, among other things, Paul Tillich's *The Courage to Be*, which exhorted men to keep up hope in the face of godless possibilities; *Secular City*, by Harvey Cox; and *The Passover Plot* (a sixties version of the *Da Vinci Code*). I suspect the point of reading this material was simply to provide fodder for good discussion, but I took the nihilistic arguments to heart: educated people believe mankind exists by accident. We're here on our own, and nothing is fixed or reliable, so we may as well make the best of it.

I had no intention of making the best of it. I was consumed with a longing that caused physical pain in my stomach and heart. If life had no meaning other than what I subjectively projected onto it, consciousness was unbearable. I often walked over to the neighborhood Catholic church, whose doors were always open, and sat in the stillness, aching.

I began to hoard sleeping pills and ditched school for theater rehearsals or afternoons in the library. I thought I might find something to make taking an overdose of those pills unnecessary, but always came up empty. Faust's pact with Mephistopheles haunted me, in which he offers his soul to Satan, only to be able to "once say to the fleeting moment: Stay, thou art lovely!—Then let me die and let Hell swallow me up!" I would have been willing to make such a pact, had I believed in the Devil.

In the winter of my senior year, there came a morning too gray and too sad to get out of bed. My parents had gone to work and I stared at the ceiling, contemplating its grimness and mine. A nasty inner voice urged me toward the stash of pills. There is freedom, it promised. I held the first handful in my palm.

*   *   *

It was not the *Other*, but a presence nevertheless, that entered the room. It was nothing I could see or hear, and yet it was as if it said: "You are still very young, and there are many things you don't know. Wait a while, and if you're still unhappy, death will still be here."

I stayed in bed for the rest of the week and gave what I decided was a voice of self-preservation one year to show me something I didn't know.

*   *   *

Presbyterians have created a democratic church. The congregation elects a board of elders, whose members are ordained into service and then commissioned to hire a minister, negotiate the minister's salary, and plan the programs for congregational needs.

One elder and the minister from every congregation in a given area attend the regional presbytery each month to vote on matters of broader concern. Public policy, presbytery political positions, and disciplinary matters are determined by a majority vote.

Once upon a time, the elder was just that—older and presumably wiser. But this was 1969, and the reigning minister, a very bright, social-gospel sort, considered how much more he could accomplish if the board of elders had people on it who thought as he did. A young, passionate, articulate, liberal person whom he could take to presbytery meetings and who would vote the way he did would be invaluable. I was free-thinking, an outspoken pacifist, and very active in the congregation. He nominated me.

I went to his office. "Look," I said, "let's be honest. I don't know if I even believe in God."

He laughed. "I don't know if I do either."

That was quite a shock.

"I can't take the oath for being an elder—the 'I believe' Creed stuff . . ."

"No problem. Let's figure out what you *can* promise."

So, before the Presbyterian congregation of my childhood church, I knelt and swore to keep searching for God and to serve my congregation. These weren't the traditional oaths, but I was told that I was the youngest Presbyterian up to date ordained an "elder".

* * *

I didn't want to go to college. It seemed an awful waste of time, as I assumed I would find there only increasingly subtle arguments for the hollowness of life. My mother's tears prevailed, however, and I entered Hunter College, a part of the New York City public university system.

Talk about depressing! The entire campus of Hunter College is contained in a single building the size of a city block. In those days, its walls were several shades of industrial gray, washed in the unremitting glare of fluorescence. The bathrooms and halls were dirty and covered with graffiti. Worst of all, the first students I met hated Shakespeare and grooved on pop music. Here was a new cause for despair.

I did, however, look forward to the Introduction to Philosophy class.

My memory of that first philosophy class is very intense. It was in a room many stories up, and if one looked over his left shoulder, out the windows, he saw the play of light in the sky and the lengthening afternoon shadows of autumn creep over the city. I sat toward the back of the room, where I would be unnoticed if the class proved dull.

Professor Alice Jourdain entered. She was tall and slender and moved with a striking dignity that contrasted to typical New York brusqueness. The reason became apparent— Professor Jourdain's accent betrayed that she had been raised in Europe.

She greeted the class graciously, and I was charmed. Daughter of generations of feminists, I was pleased that my philosophy professor was a woman. My expectations soared.

Professor Jourdain did not disappoint. She opened that first class with a wonderful question, "What is truth?" Here was someone who understood the important issues, perhaps the only issue that mattered ultimately. Without any bourgeois fencing, she had simply launched it. My arm shot up, waving wildly. I knew that I was philosophically precocious and was desperately anxious to make a strong first impression on this woman, in the same way I had impressed and sometimes intimidated my high school teachers. It was very important to me that she understand right off the bat that I was, though rather young, every bit her intellectual equal.

She snapped at the bait. Catching my eye and giving a barely perceptible nod, Professor Jourdain indicated that I might speak. "Truth is subjective, of course", I said. "You have your perceptions and I have mine, and ultimately that is all we can say."

I smiled as modestly as I could at Professor Jourdain, confident of our shared understanding and half-expecting that she would take me aside after class and suggest that I was really too advanced for an introductory philosophy course and should go directly into a graduate study of existentialism.

She returned the smile and said in her rich, cultivated tone, "Oh, my dear, I am so glad you gave that answer. That is *precisely* what I had hoped you would say!"

My chest swelled at those words, which I inferred as praise.

The following hour and a half, however, were the most fantastic of my life. Professor Jourdain was a preposterous woman. She shredded that statement about truth and refused to let me voice my thousand objections, which she confidently assured me would be answered later in the course.

I was ready to tear my clothing with frustration. Who did she think she was? Where did she come from? I pulled out the college catalog, looking for some academic credentials. Professor Jourdain had a Ph.D. after her name, but she clearly had obtained a teaching position fraudulently, for no institution of higher learning, not even Hunter College, could support such ignorance. Well, I would expose her before the semester was over!

I spent that weekend talking to myself. She had said thus; well, I would answer *this*. I covered my kitchen table with books. How had Sartre expressed it? I wouldn't be unprepared at the next class. In the end, however, every objection of mine was systematically overturned. I learned to speak less frequently because I so often spoke stupidly. I learned to listen more closely because I discovered, to my horror, how little I knew. And I dumped my stash of sleeping pills, because I began to fear they might not hold the release from this life's complexities that I had hoped. I felt incredibly humiliated, realizing that I'd been looking at everything in life upside down and inside out.

Exams were sheer torment. In the past, I'd relied on an agile mind to take tests. Creative answers relieved my boredom and generally confused teachers into rewarding grades. Professor Jourdain, on the other hand, simply expected one to regurgitate facts. She was very uncompromising, and, as the facts so often contradicted my creative impulses, they caused no end of anxiety. I had never learned to *reason*.

One semester turned into another. Fascinated, I took every course Alice Jourdain von Hildebrand offered. Which brought me to new problems. If there *were* absolute Truths and we human beings had the capacity to know and respond to them, what else might I have misunderstood? Was God real? Was Jesus Christ more than a myth hatched during the Passover Plot? Were there moral absolutes demanding my submission? I no longer wanted to ask Professor Jourdain anything in class, afraid that she would use the question to expose my imbecility. Why didn't I already know these things?

I timidly sounded out the other students. We did what students have done since there have been colleges—passed around books we found inspirational and stayed up late in the coffee shop discussing them. A number of those books turned out to have been written by Dr. Jourdain's husband,

Dietrich von Hildebrand. I was told that he was what Pope Pius XII had called "a twentieth-century doctor of the Church". That meant nothing to me, and my fellow students clearly found the indifference irritating. I'd have to meet the man, they challenged. He was usually at Hunter College, working in Professor Jourdain's office while she taught. In fact, it wasn't uncommon for him to speak with students who had "special" questions.

I mulled this over. The more I hesitated, the more they extolled Dr. von Hildebrand's merits. He began to swell in my mind's eye from a mere mortal into a demigod. He wrote, I was told, books on his knees. Perhaps he was also able to read minds and would see through the counterfeit of mine. *No*, I thought, *I'd just keep a respectful distance.*

But the day came anyway. As I stood in a small knot of students one evening, deep in discussion, Alice Jourdain came sweeping out of class and ushered us into her office. This was unexpected. I positioned myself as far to the rear of the room as I could.

Perhaps I was introduced. I don't recall. I, who was considered brash and aggressive in high school, was overwhelmed with shyness. Dietrich von Hildebrand was a good deal older than his wife but had an alarming degree of vitality that exploded into every corner of the office. The conversation, which I do recall, concerned the beauty of love, and Dietrich von Hildebrand bent over his wife's hand to kiss it. The gesture was at once inexpressibly tender and gallant. Those damned fluorescent lights were overcome by something softer, warmer, and much brighter.

I persuaded my father to take Alice Jourdain's graduate course in aesthetics with me during the spring semester of my sophomore year. As we rode home on the subway, late one night, I tried to explain to my talented father the

difficulty I had in granting to art either purpose or meaning sufficient to sustain life. The most moving Beethoven
sonata, the most exquisite da Vinci painting, even the most
brilliant human love affairs were ultimately perishables.

My father was livid. He, who loved me as the apple of
his eye, used a tone I had never heard before, hissing that
he despised such ideas. It was as if a chasm had opened,
and I was shocked by how rapidly this spiritual earthquake
altered the landscape of our relationship. Even more dev-
astatingly, a few months later he died.

*   *   *

Muttle's birthday came in July. Muttle was my Protestant
godfather's mother, and we often went to a party on or
near the day to celebrate.

It was a grand party this year—1971: good friends, fine food.
Driving home, my dad and I discussed the Dr. Jourdain course
we would take together the coming semester. He was excited
about it—as enthusiastic as I had seen him for a while. He
and his dad had taken college courses together.

In the middle of the night, I awoke from a sound sleep.
The presence was there again, standing in the same place.
"What will you do if your father is no more?" it asked.

What sort of question was that? I sat up in the dark. I
understood that we were speaking about death ... what
would I do if my father *died*? What would be the personal
cost to me if one who meant so much should be taken
out of the world? I went over my memories of the man.
There he was, carrying me in his arms up five flights of
stairs to our apartment. There he was, uncomplain-
ingly wakened in the middle of the night to write down
thoughts I was too small to write for myself but which

consumed me until they were fixed on a page. There he was with our big anthology of English verse, dramatically reading poems that were years beyond my understanding but whose music was delicious. There he was at my bedside, keeping me company during a fever, reading hour after hour. There we were, driving alone and mapless through upstate New York, hunting for adventure. There he was, pounding out a piano sonata, or rolling down a grassy hill, or teasing because I was afraid to climb a tree or jump down a cliff. What would I do if he were no more?

Mom rushed into the room. My father was having a heart attack, and I was to travel with him in the ambulance while she followed behind with the car. In the few moments it took to pull on clothes, police and paramedics arrived, wrapped my father's naked body in a sheet, and carried his racked body down those five flights of stairs.

Strapped to a gurney, he was alone with me in the dark rear compartment of the ambulance as it screamed through the city. Today, paramedics would be working over the heart during the long, momentous ride to the hospital, but this was then. In that dark lonesomeness, I knelt and thought of the *Other*, whom I no longer had any right to petition . . . and watched in horror as my father's soul peeled from the body and went away.

* * *

The consequences to me of my father's death were enormous.

The first day was spent in great shock. The institutional fluorescent glow of a hospital at night gave way to an incongruously beautiful summer morning. Friends and family gathered at the apartment, surrounding my mother. When I could stand it no longer, I left and walked over to the Presbyterian church.

I rang twice at the minister's house and waited. No one came. Later, I learned that the minister was home but had been unable to get to the door quickly.

I walked across the street to a tiny Episcopalian church. I wondered if it could hold a hundred people. It was very beautiful, empty, and filled with light through its magnificent stained glass windows. I sat for a long time, alone.

There was an enormous Bible on the pulpit, and it occurred to me that a Bible might hold some comfort for a mourner. I felt reluctant to enter the sanctuary but was drawn to that huge, leather-bound book.

I opened it. I put my finger down on a random passage and read: "Our fathers sinned and are no more."

It was stunning. In such a big book—filled with begattings and bloody battles and pious warnings—what were the odds of stumbling across an applicable bit? It was a wonderful coincidence, and I thanked the universe for providing it. I went back to the pew, watching sunlight play through the stained glass.

What if it were not a coincidence? What if something— Someone—chose those very words for me?

Ridiculous. Perhaps a million years ago, when men were more monkey than human, one might have thought something cared when death struck. But in a modern, scientific age, we know better.

Prove it.

Prove what?

That it was coincidence. Open the book again.

This is stupid. Suppose someone comes in and sees me trespassing in the sanctuary?

So, you don't really think it was a coincidence, do you?

Of course I do.

Prove it.

I walked quickly to the pulpit and opened the Bible, almost angrily. Here was the next random passage: "Naked I came forth from my mother's womb and naked I shall go back again. The Lord giveth and the Lord taketh away. Blessed be the Name of the Lord."

I sat back down in the pew and was still for a long while. I saw my father, carried from the apartment, wrapped only in a sheet. When the odds are small enough, it takes a greater act of faith to believe in coincidence than to believe ... something else.

If there really was a God who saw everything and knew everything and could do anything, He could make a book open to a page and permit my eye to fall on a verse that would say whatever He pleased. Not to be superstitious about it, or try to abuse the possibility, but God *could* speak to a person through the Bible.

And if God spoke, through whatever vehicle, clear, pertinent words, He must surely Be.

I went up into the sanctuary a third time and opened the Bible slowly, deliberately. I closed my eyes and held an index finger in the air for a moment, over the open page, unsure of what I hoped to read. This was the passage: "We have become orphans, fatherless; widowed are our mothers."

I believed and wept.

*   *   *

The next three months were unspeakably difficult. On the first-month anniversary of my father's death, a friend to whom I hadn't spoken for a year wrote that he had seen my father in an amazingly vivid dream. Was everything all right?

On the second-month anniversary of my father's death, I was staying at my parents' home—now only my mother's home. She had gone to bed, and I was reading. Suddenly, there was distant music, and I roamed around the house, looking for a radio that had perhaps been left playing. There was no radio that I could locate, but on the hunt, I came against an invisible wall from which there peered or poured an overwhelming maliciousness. Terrified, I rejected it, and the experience ended.

Later that night, I was awakened from sleep to see the crucified Jesus, there in the dark, watching and waiting. "I call Heaven and earth as witnesses today against you; I have set before you life and death, a blessing and a curse. Therefore, choose life." That night, I became a Christian.

* * *

I was not happy about these "experiences". I worried that emotional distress had made me unstable. Unstable people "saw" things. Normal people didn't.

I went into the Catholic bookstore around the corner from my apartment building and found a book by Teresa of Avila. She wrote about "religious experiences" as though they were quite common but suggested one discourage them. If they were from God, they would continue. If they were from an overwrought imagination, they would stop. I wanted them to stop.

* * *

I was doing homework—trying to write a bit of counterpoint for a music theory class. It was going badly. It was a puzzle in which every element had to agree with all the others. One might work painstakingly to the end of a phrase only to discover one note had broken one of the hundreds of rules that might not be broken, and one had to begin all over again. I got up to walk around the room and clear my mind.

It takes more time to tell than it took to happen, but the ceiling split and a tunnel—infinite and filled with light—stretched above me into the heavens. It went on forever, past the end of the universe and into the beyond. There was the *Other One*, glorious and infinite and overwhelming. I was afraid, and He left . . . and I was very, very sorry.

* * *

On the third-month anniversary of my father's death, student friends from among the von Hildebrand circle invited me to a Sunday Mass at a Lithuanian national Catholic parish in lower Manhattan. Despite the liturgical revolution that was shaking the Church, this little church went quietly about its business with a simple Missa de Angelis *Novus Ordo* Latin Mass, whose words I already knew from the finer music I had sung in the Presbyterian children's choir. There, I recognized the presence of the *Other*—normal and matter-of-fact to all the worshippers. It was home.

It was awful. I was a Presbyterian elder with responsibilities. I had promised service to my congregation, to people I had known all my life.

I approached Oscar.[1] Oscar was also an elder. He was unique on the board of elders in that he seemed actually to pray, intense about the spiritual life in an environment that was intense about the business of running a church.

[1] Not his real name.

Oscar walked me home. He had been especially kind when my father died and now let me talk to him for a long time. I told him everything about the von Hildebrands and the Lithuanian church and the "experiences". He bought me a hamburger and listened. I wanted him to tell me the reasons one couldn't be Catholic.

He shuffled his feet and looked uncomfortable. He nibbled the burger.

"Tell me!" I exclaimed.

"I don't know if I can be much help."

"Why not?"

"I've been going to daily Mass myself . . ."

*   *   *

Oscar was the one who told me that Catholics believed Communion is really Jesus.

"You mean symbolically, right?"

"No, literally—flesh and blood."

"You're not serious. That would be—cannibalistic!"

Oscar showed me Bible verses that seemed to say Jesus really meant bread and wine were to become flesh and blood. "Presbyterians use grape juice for communion in a memorial meal and assume that Jesus was speaking metaphorically, but the Jews hearing Jesus certainly didn't assume that."

"This is insane! Do you believe this?"

"I'm not sure . . . but Catholics do. If you're going to be a Catholic, you have to believe this too."

So I did.

*   *   *

Religious instruction was accomplished under a priest living near Hunter. It consisted of working through the questions of the *Baltimore Catechism*, questions I read and considered and for which I sought explanations. I'm astounded when I hear that people bear such animosity toward this book.

Question: "Why did God make you?"

Answer: "God made me to know Him, to love Him, and to serve Him in this world, and to be happy with Him forever in the next."

What a wonderful, beautiful answer! We are created for love and eternity ... so simple and so true.

What's next?

Question: "How shall we know the things which we are to believe?"

Answer: "We shall know the things which we are to believe from the Catholic Church, through which God speaks to us."

Now, wait just a minute. What little I thought I knew of God hadn't come from anything the Catholic Church had taught me. This was too much.

I was seriously considering becoming a Presbyterian minister but was ultimately deterred by the Presbyterian structure: a Presbyterian minister who opposes the death penalty, say, might preach against capital punishment only to find himself without a pulpit. He serves at the pleasure of the board of elders. They, in turn, are elected by the congregation. If the congregation doesn't want to hear what the minister has to say, he can be muzzled.

Practically speaking, this has pros and cons. There's no guarantee that a minister will be conscionable, and the congregation is fortunate to have a mechanism to weed out fools and scoundrels.

But the flip side is that unless a minister knows his congregation already agrees with him, trying to speak his conscience is risky—perhaps impossible.

Something wasn't right about a system in which "morality" could be determined by a majority vote.

So, where did a person—minister and congregation and elder—go to know what was moral and what was not?

My religious instructor smiled.

"The *Bible*", I said. "It's all in the Bible."

"And from where does the Bible come?"

"From God!"

"He handed mankind a book, written and bound?"

I was confused. Was there a passage in the Bible that explained how it came to be? Thinking of Moses, I wondered aloud if it had been dictated. But how would one know when a book was genuinely dictated by God and when by imagination or maliciousness?

"Ah, *how* indeed."

"Well, *how*, then?"

"Jesus founded a Church."

I knew that. I'd read that in the ... Bible ... umm ... *hmm* ...

A *Church*?

*   *   *

If only one could convert quietly, but there are so many people who need to know. The eldership had to be resigned, and an entire congregation it seemed wanted a chance to save me from papistry.

My mother's response was, of course, the hardest. Her first objection was a tactical mistake: "You do know

that most Catholics are uneducated immigrants and poor
people ..."

Well, in the first place, that wasn't true. But in the second place, to whatever extent it *was* true, it was more of
an attraction than not. My neighborhood was filled with
undereducated, poor Catholic immigrants, and I *liked* them.
So did she, when it came down to it.

She tried again: We knew some very unpleasant Catholics, she and I. If *they* were indicative of Catholicism ...

Oh, please. We knew some very unpleasant Protestants
too. Of whom are *they* indicative?

The final shot, however, reached its mark: "You know
your father would have been very disappointed."

I knew.

*   *   *

I was baptized when I was three, but as there was no adult
Catholic to witness it, the Church asked that I be conditionally baptized. Had I been a pagan or a Jew, baptism
would have been a rebirth, completely wiping away the original and actual sin of a lifetime. As a baptized Protestant,
however, conditional baptism was simply an insurance policy and accomplished nothing. In order to become a daughter of the Church, I had to make a first confession—
covering my entire, sorry life.

I felt like a runner who had to hurdle obstacles, one after
another. The first few seemed comparatively easy beside
what was yet to come. As the goal neared, the greatest obstacle, it turned out, would be this first confession.

A Protestant confesses his sins to God privately, but a
Catholic abases himself before a fellow sinner, shamefacedly
speaking the thing and asking forgiveness—which God

bestows through this same fellow sinner. Having spent most of my life pretending that there was no God to know what I thought, I not only had to admit aloud that God did know but let another person into the secret as well. I'm not easily intimidated, but this was too much.

The day grew near, and I broke out into horrible, painful hives, all over my body. Of course I couldn't become a Catholic—the very thought was making me sick! I would call the parish office and explain to Father that I wasn't well, and then I'd . . . well, I couldn't go back to the Presbyterians, but I could move to the Midwest and become a . . . Lutheran? No, of course not. An Episcopalian, maybe, unless they have confession too. Being a Quaker might work . . . except, to be honest, I was already a Catholic.

My mother came to accompany me to church, smelled fear, and was elated. She was bold enough to wonder aloud if I might have changed my mind. For once the stubborn perversity of my nature proved a blessing. "Not at all! How could you say such a thing? Let's go!"

*   *   *

I was received into the Roman Catholic Church on Holy Wednesday 1972, with Dietrich and Alice von Hildebrand as my godparents.

Stephanie Block is a noted investigative reporter whose best known work focuses on Catholic social teaching and theological dissent. The Wanderer Forum Foundation has published her studies of the annual Campaign for Human Development collection, through which the United States Conference of Catholic Bishops (USCB) has, over some forty years, donated millions of dollars to the notorious ACORN political action organization.

She writes for various other Catholic publications as well, edits the Catholic Media Coalition Web site, and edits Los Pequenos Pepper, *the newsletter of New Mexico's Los Pequenos de Cristo.*

Stephanie lives in New Mexico with her husband, Steven, a convert from Judaism whose own conversion story appears in both Rhonda Chervin's Bread from Heaven *and Roy Schoeman's* Honey from the Rock. *They have seven adult children and a growing contingent of grandchildren.*

Chapter 15

The Trappists, the Traditionalists, and the UN

Austin Ruse

I think everybody falls from the horse. Some fall fast, like Saint Paul. Others fall more slowly, like I did, over years. And not just converts fall—cradle Catholics do too. They have to. In a sense all of us are converts, and if we are lucky we experience more than one conversion. Life lived properly is a life of conversions. I have experienced three, and I pray there are more to come.

My story starts with an invitation called prevenient grace. Long discussed in the Church, it is the invitation from God to join the Catholic Church. All men not in the Church get it on a regular basis. It comes in many ways but essentially says the same thing: "Come closer."

When you get these invitations, you may not know them for what they really are. Years later you may be blessed to see them as an unbroken line leading toward conversion, though not inevitably; the outcome is far from certain. I do not know the first time I got the invitation, but I believe I know the first time I heard it.

It was the summer of 1972 as I sat reading a book in the basement of the First United Methodist Church in Saint

Charles, Missouri. I was sixteen years old. Reverend Folkins came into the basement and walked toward me, leaned down, and said, "Have you ever thought about becoming a minister?"

What prompted him to say that? That I was reading? That I was in church a lot, Sundays and Wednesdays? I don't remember what I said. I am certain I mumbled something appropriately adolescent.

He couldn't know that I was not a terribly serious Methodist, coming to church mostly to be with my friends and to chase Laura Norwine. Still, that scene remains vivid to me, even down to the book that I was reading, a biography of Adlai Stevenson. For years I have thought that this mysterious exchange was, certainly, God's invitation for me to become a Catholic.

The next invitation I heard came not long after, on the Saint Charles municipal golf course. It was typical summer weather for Missouri—heavy, muggy air, blistering sun. I got hold of a good one on the ninth tee and landed it within ninety yards of the elevated green that stood right in front of the clubhouse. As I assessed my next shot, I noticed a very old man slumped against a tree, his pitiful old golf bag lying beside him. He was in obvious distress. I shouted to him. "You OK?"

"Little hot today." He wore priest clothes—all black, long pants, long sleeves, high collar. Grateful that I could quit my round, I offered to help him to the clubhouse. I got him up and across the remaining 125 yards and plopped him on a bench in the shade. "My ride will be here in an hour or so", he said.

"You can't wait that long. I can take you home. Where do you live?"

"At the Carmelite Home on First Capital."

"That's right next to my church. I can give you a lift."

So I drove him back to the Carmelite Home, a place for retired priests and nuns that was a constant source of wonderment to us adolescents across the street at the Methodist church. I think we might have looked at *Playboy* and smoked cigarettes in their basement when it was under construction.

I don't remember what we talked about on the ride or even after I got him back to his room. He wanted to talk more, but I made excuses and left. I never saw him again. But I have never forgotten Father John and subsequently have thought he was another messenger of God calling me into the Catholic Church.

Reverend Folkins and Father John both planted something in me that stayed. It was a curiosity. It was an invitation. I came to know it much later as prevenient grace.

This impulse to answer the call of prevenient grace showed itself again when I felt compelled to swipe a book from a friend's house, a biography of Saul of Tarsus. I don't remember reading it, and I don't remember what I did with it, but what's important is that I have never forgotten it, and that is the funny way with prevenient grace.

A few years later, at the University of Missouri, I found myself annoyed at a graduate assistant in political science who began to denigrate religious faith. I wondered how this pipsqueak dared so easily to dismiss the thing that has occupied the greatest minds of all time. It is likely here that my conscious search began, but the first book I read was on Judaism. Go figure that. I thought my white-bread Christianity couldn't possibly be the Thing. The Thing had to be something exotic, and Judaism was about as exotic as I could fathom. No Eastern mysticism for me. Plus, I was dating Jewish girls at the time.

I was in the journalism school, one of the best in the country, and it attracted all sorts of wonderful and exotic creatures, including a lot of beautiful and funny Jewish girls from as far away as Memphis. That single book about Judaism was my last, however. I was a Christian; I just didn't know what kind. But the tiniest idea did begin to germinate: If one is to be serious about religious faith, there is only one place to go, and that is the Catholic Church. So I wrote a paper about Cardinal Richelieu. And I read the novels of Anthony Burgess.

I must admit that both Richelieu and Burgess appealed to my vanity. Richelieu was an ordained clergyman—a cardinal—who crafted the idea of modern France. I couldn't help but appreciate that it was the Church and churchmen that seemed to be the warp and woof of history, at the very center of things always. These are truths one does not learn in public school, and certainly not at the Methodist church. Burgess wrote a lot about free will and the debate between Pelagius and Saint Augustine. Though fallen away, Burgess was obsessed with the Church and with theology. I had never heard of free will and was captivated. Because of Burgess, I understood that the Catholic Thing was very intellectual. Yes, my nascent conversion was one of the head rather than the heart, something that would prove to be a shortcoming of mine.

In all of this reading and writing and stumbling toward the faith during my college years, I never once thought about finding a priest or going to the Newman Center. I assumed that they, like my own church, were busy singing hootenanny songs about Jesus, and though I was not at all certain what I wanted, I knew it was more Augustine than G chords.

On the other hand, it was the crazy seventies, and my search was thrown off by other interests, the Jewish girls and other girls, and leftist student politics. There wasn't time to really listen to the voice of God calling out to me.

Graduation came, and the very next day I packed up my 1972 Mercury Montego Brougham. A fetching Jewess slipped into the passenger seat beside me, and we drove fifteen hours straight to Washington, D.C.

My first stop was to knock on the door of a guy named Ralph Murphine, who worked for another guy named Matt Rees. They were old-time political consultants. Rees ran West Virginia for John Kennedy during the 1960 primary and still operated a part of the Kennedy political franchise. Murphine had asked me to look him up when I came to town.

I had done some advance work for Teddy Kennedy when he took a run at unseating Jimmy Carter during the time I was vice president of the student body at the University of Missouri. I was a liberal Democrat, president of the Young Democrats of Saint Charles County, Missouri, and was involved in national student politics that were decidedly left of center. We lefties owned the National Student Association (NSA). We ran it. It was our toy.

Then, one sunny day in 1980, we watched as busloads of Southern evangelicals arrived at the annual NSA convention in Boulder. Taking us totally by surprise, these Southern bumpkins flooded the meeting and without so much as a tip of the hat took it all away from us. This was my first glimpse of the politics to come, both the nation's and my own. As it was, we literally stood and wept.

But a year later, in Murphine's office, I was offered a job to run a phone bank in some congressional election way out west, a move from the minor leagues to the majors. There was no more important project for someone like me than the Kennedy restoration. Still, I told the Kennedy folks no. I hadn't driven all the way from small-town Missouri just to turn around and drive back to small-town Idaho.

This could not have been a broader road not taken. Had I gone down the Kennedy road, could I have made the changes that God would later ask of me? Instead, I went down a road into magazine publishing, a road that would also prove dangerous to my soul.

I began selling advertising for *American Film* magazine, which had offices at the Watergate complex and the Kennedy Center. Still in touch with lefty friends, I attended small dinner parties with grandees from the National Abortion Rights Action League, the National Organization for Women, and others. And still in touch with lefty ideas, I regularly read the *New Republic*, which oddly provided the next opportunity for grace in my life.

The *New Republic* was and is a remarkably unfunny magazine. But one day a tiny ad no bigger than a thumbnail made me laugh out loud. It was a single sentence about some political issue, and underneath was written, "From the current issue of *National Review*". Yikes—the only laugh in the whole issue was from a political adversary. I saw different versions of the ad week after week, laughing each time, and in the end their campaign worked: finally I bought a copy for myself.

The first time I read *National Review* was like the first time I heard the Beatles: "Does anyone else know about this? Is this made just for me?" Domestic issues were not important to me in those days. What I cared most about was foreign policy, having been heavily influenced by Daniel Patrick Moynihan's memoir about his time as ambassador to the United Nations, and *National Review* was ground zero for a muscular foreign policy during what we know now was the beginning of the end of the cold war. I devoured every issue of *National Review* like a hungry man, albeit with the cover bent back so no one could see what I was reading.

I soon noticed that William F. Buckley was Catholic, as were many of his writers and editors. What's more, they were politically conservative Catholics, which told me they would not go in for the current zeitgeist of ecclesial silliness. Their "witness" to me was likely unintended, but nevertheless profound. God spoke to me there in the pages of *National Review*.

He spoke to me also in the Rosary that one of my Capitol Hill roommates, Joe Drake, kept on his dresser. I recall looking at this mysterious device with fascination and wonder. There was power even in its appearance. Joe also went to Mass on Sunday, even if we were hung over from our night before at the Tune Inn. It had been years since I had been to the Methodist church. Joe never knew it, but his matter-of-fact, unostentatious practice of the faith impressed me deeply.

I spent most of my weekends roaming around the mall, sitting and reading under trees, and wandering into the free museums. It was here that I had what I think was a mystical experience. One Saturday I was lying on the grass in front of the Smithsonian Castle, listening to the carousel play "Lara's Theme" from *Dr. Zhivago*. It was a hot and quiet morning, and I could hear the grasshoppers sing. As I looked in the sky at the scudding clouds, I was possessed of an interior vision. It was of myself in old age looking at the young me lying on the grass, with the young me looking back—a barbershop mirror effect, but through time. What I thought then and what I still think is that this was a vision of eternity, given to me to get serious about God, because eternity was where I was living and where I would always live.

It was about this time that I began to want to learn about the Catholic Church. But I didn't have a teacher and didn't know how to get one. How does one get inside this thing called the Church? You can walk through her doors and look at her statues, but how do you learn what they mean? I asked friends who were Catholic to tell me which books I should read, but none of them had the slightest idea. They were of the first great uncatechized generation. I thumbed through Catholic books at the bookstore, but how could I know if they were any good?

I could have gone to a priest, but I knew that this could be an iffy proposition since the Church was in a doctrinal roil. What I was looking for was the straight stuff, not some liberal hoo-hah and absolutely no "Kumbaya". So mostly I yearned. And moved to New York.

After years of traveling to New York to sell advertising, *American Film* asked me to move there and open an office. I flew to New York on July 5, 1982, and immediately began a twenty-year love affair with Manhattan, that small yet immense and finally unknowable island. I tramped up and down and back and forth and believe I touched on almost every street, and as I walked I saw Catholic churches everywhere, dozens of them. Each and every one whispered to me, but I did not go into a single one, not right away.

This could have been a time for great progress. I was new in town and mostly alone. But as prevenient grace tugs you one way, so does the world tug you the other. After another year at *American Film*, I jumped to *Rolling Stone* and into the big-time magazine business. And it was here that the world came calling and I answered—yes, I answered.

My tiny twenty-sixth-floor office at *Rolling Stone* looked out over Fifth Avenue, Bergdorf's, the Plaza Hotel, and Central Park. I happily fell in with a very hip crowd at *Rolling Stone*: a fact checker who would become top editor, an assistant art director who would later head his own design firm, the magazine's photo editor, and the magazine owner's personal assistant. For a low-ranking ad salesman, this was heady company indeed, especially given the strict separation between church (editorial) and state (business) in the magazine world.

Never a fan of beer or wine, I had taught myself to like scotch back in college and was no stranger to the New York bar scene. But I was an amateur. These guys were pros. Out every night, sometimes all night. We would meet at a dumpy restaurant on Fifty-sixth Street just off of Fifth Avenue called the Arirang House—red and Asian and remarkably unhip, where you could imagine CIA guys meeting or guys cheating on their wives—and commandeer the bar. It became known, at least to us, as the *Rolling Stone* hangout. (They had a nasty little drink there called the Ginseng Cocktail, and Peter Wolf of the J. Geils Band drank nineteen of them in one sitting, setting a record.) As places closed or fell out of favor with us, our nightly drink-and-talk fest would gravitate to other venues: Kee-Wah Yang, an equally unhip place up the street; Jean Lafitte, a fancy French restaurant near Sixth Avenue; the Saloon Grill on the Upper West Side.

Ironically, this was both my darkest decade and the time of my most fruitful search for the Church.

Manhattan Island is full of Catholic churches, in those days something like 104 of them. And Manhattan Island is small, a few miles wide and maybe twelve miles long. That is a lot of churches packed into a relatively small area. My weekend days were spent endlessly walking those great uptown and downtown boulevards and those narrow cross streets, every eye blink a movie tableau. And as I walked, I came upon dozens of churches, and this time I went into every one that was unlocked. I recall stopping into a deli and asking about the location of a nearby church and the guy said, "Lookin' for a Mass?" No, but what a marvelous question. I cannot describe the marvel I felt in those days for this great mysterious thing called the Catholic Church.

The churches were dark and quiet and smelled vaguely of . . . was that incense tickling my Methodist nose? Ladies knelt in prayer saying their Rosaries. Sometimes I saw someone standing and facing the wall, saying prayers. What was she doing? I would stand and watch Masses and wonder what was going on. This was a far cry from the Methodist church of my youth. And what were those clothes the priest was wearing? I spent time in the tiny relic shop at Saint Patrick's Cathedral eyeing and fingering the Rosaries, never having the nerve to buy one or to ask anyone what they were about.

It was at this time that I made a decisive move to the right politically, due almost exclusively to Bill Buckley and his magazine. The Strand Bookstore was a Mecca in lower Manhattan for book lovers, with tens of thousands of used books and new review copies. There I discovered a complete collection of Buckley books that someone had unloaded—I mean every book he ever wrote. I bought them all and devoured them in succession, not stopping for a breath between each greedy gulp.

Then it hit me. Who better to ask for reliable reading on Catholicism than Mr. Buckley? I had read somewhere that he answered all his mail, so I took a chance and wrote him a letter. I recall the opening: "Dear Mr. Buckley, you helped save my political life. Now I need help with my afterlife." Not a bad opening, and it worked. Within a few weeks, a package arrived from *National Review*. Inside was a note thanking me for my charming letter, and more importantly, several books, among them *Orthodoxy* by G. K. Chesterton.

Here was what I had been looking for—a book I had never heard of by an author unknown to me, written long before the current troubles. An author untainted by the spirit of the current age and, dare I say, by Vatican II, which in my callow heart was the reason I couldn't knock on a rectory door to unlock the mysteries of the Church but had to shuffle around in the dark, knocking over furniture.

I began with Chesterton and then discovered Hilaire Belloc. I read C. S. Lewis with enthusiasm, though he was not Catholic, preferring his fiction to that of any others. These great Christian writers were so smart they made my head spin. And their writing was wonderfully free of that dominant ethos in religion today that seemed soft and squishy and not at all what I wanted. Reading the real stuff was a revelation to me.

Buckley eventually turned me over to two of his guys, Jim McFadden, at that time the editor of *Catholic Eye* and founder of the National Committee of Catholic Laymen, and Ed Capano, the advertising director and later publisher of *National Review*. Jim and Ed took me out to many boozy lunches at a restaurant on Lexington Avenue not far from *National Review*'s offices where we would talk politics and Catholicism. McFadden also had a nice way of dropping typewritten notecards in the mail with advice about some book about the faith. I still have some of them. He encouraged me to read the lives of the saints, Church history, and the *Catechism of the Catholic Church*.

It was the *Catechism* that most focused my mind and heart. For some Protestants, the notion of the Magisterium is a stumbling block, but not for all and not for me. It struck me as a great consolation that there was a place where you can get your questions answered—and *really* answered too. My friend Bill Saunders of the Family Research Council was a hard case when he converted. He took the universal *Catechism* and argued over every page with a priest. Not me. My mind was like a moving van that drives up to a warehouse and says, "Give me all you got." I wanted to know everything the Church taught. Praying to Mary? Not a problem. Primacy of the pope? Love it. I treasured the multivolume catechism by Father Ken Baker, S.J., and was stunned by things like the hypostatic union. Hypostatic union? The Church figured that out. I also loved Father John Hardon's one-volume catechism and loved reading about heresies like Donatism. The Church knew heresies and called them by name. There were no stumbling blocks for me. I was insatiable.

My life at the time was disjointed, to say the least: making ad sales by day, carousing with the *Rolling Stone* crew until the wee hours at night, and delving ever deeper into the mystery of the Catholic Church on the weekends.

For many years, the *Rolling Stone* gang rented a summer house together on Long Island, a place called the Duck Farm, a musty little farmhouse on a small plot of land out near the Hamptons. Not the fancy Hamptons, though some of my friends later got houses out there. For now, this was *our* Hamptons; we called it the Other Hamptons, the Hamptons-That-Dare-Not-Speak-Its-Name. We didn't need the real Hamptons or the popular restaurants or, for that matter, anyone outside of our closed little group. And it was at the Duck Farm that I experienced another important moment of prevenient grace, one that would determine the course of my interior life for a decade or more.

One Saturday morning Fred Allen and Erica DeMane sat on the floor of the Duck Farm reading the *New York Times*. I sat nearby. Fred and Erica were our only married friends. He was an editor at *American Heritage*, the history magazine owned by Malcolm Forbes, and she was a food writer, later a cookbook writer. They were the brainiest couple among us, authentic intellectuals, substantially living a life of the mind. Erica was reading the book review section, and she mentioned to Fred that there was a new biography of a guy named Thomas Merton. What I gleaned from their conversation was that he was a Columbia student who wrote poetry for the *New Yorker* and later became a Trappist monk, whatever that was. This tiny thing, this bit of overheard conversation, was a turning point and even now is a lodestar in my life.

Back in town, I bought Michael Mott's biography of Merton, still the most authoritative book on the subject, and I read it cover to cover. From that day late in 1984 and for the next fifteen years, I spent a part of every waking day dreaming of Merton's Abbey of Gethsemani. It seemed to me to be a piece of Heaven right here on this earth, a place where men have given up everything to spend long and even leisurely days for the single purpose of coming face-to-face with God. This spoke to me more strongly than anything I had read to date, stronger than Church history, stronger than the lives of saints, stronger than the *Catechism*. This was the story of a modern man, not unlike me, who had struck out into the strange unknown, giving up all earthly consolations for the purpose of seeing God alone. That is what I wanted.

I was ready. I wrote Buckley a letter and asked him for a priest. I waited over Christmas and then waited longer. Buckley did not write. I waited and waited. A friend told me I should meet with her priest. She said he was young and brilliant, orthodox and holy. I said I was waiting for Mr. Buckley.

March came, and I took a two-week trip to France, my first trip outside the United States. I took two friends, and I forced my vision of France on them: churches and butcher shops. I couldn't get enough of either. Look at this church. Look at this meat. They dutifully followed. My friends went home after a week, and I stayed in Paris for another week.

One day toward the end of my stay, I was sitting in a café along the Seine, on the right bank right behind the Louvre, smoking a Cuban cigar and reading Thomas Merton's *Seven Storey Mountain*. I was so moved by Merton's own words that I decided right then to return to New York, find a priest with or without Buckley, and join the Trappists.

I rather hoped that there would be a letter from Buckley awaiting my return, but there was not. One day, though, as I was watching Buckley's interview program *Firing Line* on PBS, I saw two Catholic priests talking about liberation theology. One was Monsignor William Smith, a professor of moral theology from Dunwoodie, the New York archdiocesan seminary, and the other was a parish priest living in Manhattan named Father George Rutler. I knew almost immediately that this latter priest was the one to "bring me in". He was young, brilliant, orthodox, and exuded holiness. He was, in fact, the very priest my friend had earlier recommended.

It was a Sunday. I hastily wrote a letter, mailed it the next morning, and waited. I did not have to wait for long. Father Rutler called me on the morning of the very next day (one-day mail service in Manhattan being itself a bit of a miracle) and invited me to meet with him.

I arrived at Our Lady of Victory and was ushered into his study, a gorgeous room filled with fine furniture and books. We sat knee to knee, and he began to talk. He talked and talked—we were together for close to an hour—and the thing is this: I did not understand a single word he said, including *and* and *the*. It was all completely over my head. We shook hands and parted. Later we became good friends, and I even served on his parish council, but I left that day with no intention of returning.

I called Jim McFadden and told him what had happened. I said I needed someone simple, a fat Irish priest, a real ham-and-egger. He asked around, and eventually I was given the name of Monsignor George Murphy of Holy Trinity Church up on Eighty-second Street near Broadway. He was perfect.

Monsignor Murphy asked me to sit down and tell him everything I knew about the Church, and I proceeded to go through all that I had read over the years. I told him about the life of Christ, the history of the Church, the seven sacraments; I even told him about the hypostatic union. I told him how profoundly grateful I was that an institution had thought so long and deeply about these issues and had come to conclusions so that I too could know, really know. I told him I felt called into the Church and had been preparing for this moment for many years.

I finished talking, and he said, "I have never met anyone who has read his way into the Church. I can bring you in right now, if you wish."

Not so fast, Monsignor! I thought. "I think I need further instruction. For instance, I don't know anything about the Mass."

So we met, Monsignor Murphy and I, every week for several months, and all we really talked about was the Mass. We went through the missalette page by page. Like a stranger in a strange land, I was intimidated by the customs of the people. Frankly, the thought of genuflecting was embarrassing, as was kneeling. Answering the prayers was a stumbling block for me. What if someone noticed I didn't know the prayers? What if someone noticed that I needed the missalette? No one else seemed to need it. And the Creed—no way would I ever memorize that. Steadily we plugged away through all of my doubts and fears. He said, "Whenever you are ready, let me know." Finally, I was.

We scheduled a private ceremony for December 7, 1985, Pearl Harbor Day. I was twenty-nine. I invited a few friends, including some friends from *Rolling Stone*, my girlfriend, my bartender, and a few others. I made my first confession. During my confession, we went through the Ten Commandments, and he would say, "Have you done that?"

"Yes."

"Don't do it again."

I was provisionally baptized and confirmed and made my First Communion. I was in.

You might think this was the happy ending I was working toward all these years. You would be wrong. Almost immediately I became a fallen-away Catholic. I was young. It was the crazy eighties. I was not ready to practice the faith with any kind of faithfulness. You might say I wanted to be in the house but was not willing to clean up my room.

I tried going to Mass and refraining from Communion. I found it embarrassing since I was the only one not receiving. I was not willing to confess my sins, since I was not willing to avoid them, but at the same time I did not question the teachings of the Church. My solution was to stop going to Mass altogether. And thus began the most dangerous period for my soul. I was a confirmed Catholic refusing to go to Mass and sinning with impunity. And this lasted for years.

The *Rolling Stone* gang had begun to disintegrate. Some went into Alcoholics Anonymous. Others just drifted to other things. There was still Bobby Love and me, and now there were others: investment banker David Lamb, financial writer Evan McGlynn, and various girls. I left *Rolling Stone*

and moved to the *Atlantic Monthly*, and in the next half
dozen years would ascend to even greater heights in the
magazine publishing world, including *Fortune* magazine and
Forbes. My tastes had gone further upscale too. We now
hung out almost exclusively at Elaine's, frequented by Woody
Allen and other luminaries. We convened something called
the Thursday Night Club, where we and our friends would
jam the bar. Elaine and her crew took great care of us. She
was very democratic. As long as you were a regular and not
too obnoxious, you were as welcome as any literary grandee.
During one spell of unemployment, she let me drink for
free, and when I got a job I cleared the bill. One of our
crew pawed actor Dabney Coleman's girlfriend; he wasn't
booted out but only told to stop.

A typical night from those days would begin with a dinner cruise with clients on Malcolm Forbes' yacht, followed
by a trip in chauffeured cars up to the Carlyle Hotel for
jazz singer Bobby Short's ten o'clock show, then over to
Elaine's until it closed, then maybe home, maybe not. We
were often out all night, fueled not just by youth and booze
but also by substances designed to cause an almost immediate loss of judgment and morals. I was no longer fresh off
the turnip truck. I had become a seasoned habitué of the
Manhattan night.

This went on for years and years, and I never went to
Mass, though I thought about the faith enough. My girlfriend at the time used to joke that she was the only girl in
New York whose boyfriend had books about monks on his
nightstand.

When not drinking with my friends, I would grab a
book after work and head to a neighborhood place called
Memphis. There I would drink scotches, smoke a million
cigarettes, and read books about the faith, mostly about

monasticism, mostly about the Cistercians. I read Merton— lots of Merton; Saint Bernard of Clairvaux; the Rule of Saint Benedict; histories of the Trappists; the *Institutes* and *Conferences* of John Cassian; William of Saint Thierry; Aelred of Rivaulx; John of Ford; and on and on. I would sit at the bar, getting slowly tight, and dream about the Abbey of Gethsemani, the monks and what they were doing right then, the buildings, the geography around it. I dreamed of that little room where I would live, the narrow bed where I would sleep, my robes, the psalms, the search for a mystical union with God.

"I want to be a monk", I would drunkenly tell my friends. "One day I am going to be a daily communicant", I said on unsteady feet. I carried a Rosary in my pocket and even tried to learn how to use it, kneeling by my bed with the Rosary booklet open before me.

My professional life seemed to an outside observer to be quite good. Every few years I would move to an increasingly impressive magazine, gaining more and more prestige. But the moving around really masked the fact that I hated selling advertising, and had hated almost every minute of it from the beginning. On one of my first sales trips to New York with *American Film*, I recall sitting on a bench in Bryant Park behind the New York Public Library between sales calls, staring at the buildings and wondering, *How did I get myself into this mess? How do I get out?* Yet I stayed in for another twelve years, held fast by a nice salary, a big expense account, fear, and a weak will. But the truth was, I wasn't working very hard. Eventually, that would always show, and I would have to leave, sometimes voluntarily, sometimes not.

My time at *Forbes* ended as the eighties ended, and I left with an idea to start a magazine. To pay my bills, I accepted a job offer from magazine legend Clay Felker to publish a

newspaper in lower Manhattan that he owned with World
Bank president James Wolfensohn. But due to the recession,
local advertising dried up, and I got the boot after six months.
Then I accepted a job from Sir Harold Evans, president of
Random House, to help him launch a magazine. This lasted
a few months. Next the Discovery Channel asked me to turn
their monthly viewer's guide into a real magazine. I did this
for a year and got fired. My career was spiraling to its end.

I decided I needed to take time off and regroup, maybe
find out what I wanted to do with my life.

Six months of loafing turned into a year, and thanks to
Congress, my unemployment benefits were extended again
for another six months. I spent my days reading and lawn
bowling. I was the lawn bowling champion of Central Park
for many years. I had a rent-controlled apartment, so all I
needed was scotch and book money, and unemployment
took care of that.

I lived a life of utter leisure, but I was not content. The reality was, I was thirty-six, mostly alone, unemployed, with a
nearly ruined career. I vividly recall lying in bed one night,
utterly lost, weeping. I had a girlfriend, but I knew I didn't
want to marry her. I had dated a lot of women, was even serious with a few, but I never seriously contemplated marrying
any of them. I thought myself incapable of marriage and of
taking care of another person. For me, this was further evidence that my vocation was elsewhere, in the monastery.

Quite sensibly I eventually determined that I needed to
start going to Mass if I was going to be a monk. So I broke
up with my girlfriend and went immediately to Saint Agnes
Church near Grand Central Station. I had not been to confession since my first one back in 1985 and had not been to
Mass in years. Saint Agnes had hours of confession every
day, eight Masses on Sunday, and sixteen Masses on feast

days. I walked around the block a few times, screwing up my courage to get into that dark box. I went in and told all of it, all that I had done in the previous eight years away from the Church. And I discovered Chesterton was right; I felt seven years old when I walked out. I went to Mass that day and took Communion and pledged to assiduously avoid the company of women from then on so I could test my vocation to Gethsemani. This was May 1993.

Not long after this, two things happened. I decided to go back to work and to look for a spiritual director. For work I went to a broken-down magazine called *Financial World*, something of a joke in the publishing industry, a third- or fourth-tier magazine for the new salesman, the old, or the lost. I was the lost.

I placed two calls for spiritual direction: one to Opus Dei that went unreturned, the other to a young firebrand traditionalist at Saint Agnes Church named John Perricone, who called me back immediately. Father Perricone put me on a military regimen that I took to like an eager recruit: morning offering, morning prayer, daily Mass, daily Rosary, daily reading, afternoon prayer, examination of conscience. I attended weekly confession and spiritual direction sessions with Father Perricone, and he directed my now-voluminous reading. He also asked me to attend the weekly Tridentine Mass featured at Saint Agnes Church. This was a High Mass with full schola and with mantillas everywhere, and it was jammed to the rafters. I was in Heaven.

Perricone ran a small and very energetic apostolate called Christi Fidelis, the purpose of which was to catechize a young generation of orthodox Catholics who would take over the Church from the modernists. I fell in with a wonderful crowd of very smart young Catholics, younger than I was, who were also rediscovering their faith and were on fire to be what Father Perricone called, in a prayer he wrote and that we recited, a "small band of resisters". We were proud traditionalists who hated most of the bishops, were dismissive of Vatican II, and blithely ignored the Holy Father.

In time I became Father's right-hand man. Besides regular retreats and monthly evenings of reflection, we created a weekly study group where twenty of us met to study the *Summa Theologica* for two hours and then the *Baltimore Catechism* for one. Over the years, we learned almost half of the *Baltimore Catechism* by heart. At the end of class every Monday night, we would end with a loud and lusty *Salve Regina*, kneel for Father's blessing, and then retire nearby for burgers and beers.

I created a program for Father called the Torquemada Project, where we would study the work of some heterodox speaker who was coming to town, go to the talk separately so as not to arouse suspicion, and then descend on the microphone at question time to ask very informed but highly critical questions. We were on a crusade.

This was my second conversion, and worlds apart from my first. The first was to the Church; this was to the practice—indeed, a full-body conversion to the practice of the faith.

A few years passed, and my time at *Financial World* came to an end. I wasn't producing much, and the magazine itself was about to go out of business, so I was fired. I went on unemployment again and went to work for Father Perricone full time. This time I was determined not to go back to advertising ever again.

The high point of my work with Father Perricone came when he announced a colloquium on the Latin Mass, the highlight of which was a celebration of the Tridentine Mass led by Cardinal Stickler, former head of the Vatican Library, at Saint Patrick's Cathedral—the first since the old Mass was "banned" by Paul VI.

"Are you going to send out any press releases?" I asked Father one day as we walked along Park Avenue.

"Why don't you do that, Austin?"

So I did. The headline of my press release read, "Once-Banned Mass Returns to Saint Patrick's Cathedral". I sent the releases everywhere and got hardly a nibble. Then, a few days before the event, I received a call from Peter Steinfels, a liberal Catholic writer at the *New York Times* who said he would like to cover the colloquium and the Mass. The *Times* put his story on the front page of the Sunday edition, which comes out early Saturday night, and when the paper hit the racks, my telephone rang off the hook with calls from papers and radio stations and television stations and the networks. The story breaking all over the East Coast and nationally was that the Tridentine Mass was coming to Saint Patrick's Cathedral. When the doors opened, a few dozen news crews crowded in, and throughout the Mass I gave a kind of play-by-play to help the reporters who had never seen such a strange Mass: "Instead of standing and receiving in the hand, the faithful will kneel and receive on the tongue."

And the people came too, about forty-five hundred of them, many of whom had heard about the Mass on the radio and jumped in their cars and driven all night to get there. It was perhaps the largest crowd in the cathedral's history. What they saw was a fairy tale: a few hundred priests processing behind Cardinal Stickler, who wore a *cappa magna* ("big cape") with a fifty-foot train. The *Times* ran another story about the Mass on the front page of their Metro section on Monday.

After the Mass I was approached by Roger McCaffrey, who owned *Latin Mass* and *Sursum Corda*, two Catholic magazines. He was impressed by the way I had managed the press and asked me to write for one of his magazines. How did he know that I wanted to write? And thus began my new, if hardly lucrative, employment as a feature writer on American Catholic communities.

In marked contrast to how I approached my advertising jobs, here I worked like a dog and loved it. I cared deeply about what I was doing. For a story about Star of the Sea Village in Arkansas, I hired a plane to fly me over the village so I could describe it from the air. I wrote a seventeen-thousand-word piece about Steubenville and Franciscan University and all the apostolates there. I did not own a computer at the time, so I would ride my bike to Bobby Love's palatial Upper West Side apartment, spend the early morning writing, then go to Mass at Columbia, then to Central Park for an afternoon of lawn bowling, then to Memphis for dinner, scotches, and reading about monasticism. Though poor and on the dole, these were among the happiest days of my life. *If only I could figure out how to make a living like this*, I thought.

This time unemployment ran out after six months, and I had to find work. I was deep in debt and had no real source of income. All of my friends had been tapped already. Still, I was happy. The only thing I feared was losing my nerve and going back to magazine publishing. I determined that I would do anything to pay the bills just so I could keep this Catholic work going. I had faith that some gainful employment would come along that would allow me to work on the issues I loved, the Church and politics. All I had to do was keep paying the bills—and wait.

So I applied to a staffing agency for temporary office work. I passed the typing test and told them I would work anywhere as long as it was not in publishing. My first assignment led to an offer of full-time employment at a nonprofit firm that developed low-income housing. I made about ten bucks an hour and was deliriously happy. I had learned that I could get along without a big salary, and because of this, the whole world opened up to me.

I was still able to go to Mass every day a few blocks away at Saint Agnes and to work for Father Perricone and for Roger McCaffrey. And then Roger sent me to Front Royal to do a story on Human Life International, Christendom College, Guardian Angel, and all the other elements in that vibrant Catholic community. I vividly recall standing in that majestic building that Father Paul Marx built, wondering why I couldn't work in a place like this. I soon discovered that even casual unspoken thoughts can be prayers.

A few months later, a young woman from Canada joined us for breakfast after Sunday Mass. She had met Father Perricone when he had spoken recently in Ottawa, and he invited her to look us up if she was ever in Manhattan. I asked why was she in town.

Her answer changed my life.

She said that she worked for Human Life International in Canada, that they had raised money for a pro-life lobbying office at the United Nations, and that they needed someone to run it. I swear I heard bells ringing. Here it was: religion, politics, and foreign policy to boot.

I said, "Maybe we should talk. I may be the one you are looking for."

I had never been to the UN, never done any pro-life work. Yet six weeks later I was running the Catholic Family and Human Rights Institute, the first and still the only full-time social conservative lobbying group at UN headquarters, and I was uniquely qualified for the job. Why? Because God had prepared me. Those awful years in the magazine business taught me how to speak in public, how to write with a purpose, how to make a sale, how to run a business. Had God tricked me? Had he led me to my hated career so that I would be prepared for my life's work? How marvelous if it were so.

And thus my third conversion came. It came though the convergence of the three major streams in my life: the Trappists, the traditionalists, and the UN.

I had formally applied to join the Trappists, something I had dreamed about since I read Merton in that Parisian café years before. And I began going on long vocational retreats with them. But try as I might, all I ever really did was bounce off the walls. I was struck by the tyranny of the bells that call you every few hours to stand and chant the psalms for hours every day. The long open afternoons did not give me peace but made me uneasy and unsettled as I wandered from bench to bench and from book to book. When the local community came for Sunday Mass, I felt a great desire to leave with them. And though eventually I realized the Trappists were not for me, still I blanched at how much my traditionalist friends disliked them. They disliked most religious orders, believing most of them had gone off the deep end after Vatican II.

What I increasingly saw in myself and my friends was that we were not traditional Catholics, because traditional Catholics would embrace all the Church councils, even Vatican II. No, I concluded, we were *traditionalists*, a kind of political party within the Church, a Magisterium unto ourselves. What's more, working at the UN—though in opposition to its radical social policy—made me see that there was a great big world out there, much larger than the little traditionalist world I was in, especially since it seemed to me that traditionalists thought the apostolate was little more than sitting around griping about the bishops. And if the traditionalists thought the Trappists were heterodox for bowing rather than genuflecting, then I countered with the thought that this must be a minor thing and what must matter more was the Trappists rising every day at 3 A.M. and singing psalms to God all day.

At the same time, I had begun to discover John Paul II for the first time. Keith Fournier, who was president of the Catholic Alliance, pushed John Paul's encyclicals on me. If it weren't for Keith, I might have missed that grand pontificate altogether. And by pushing the documents of Vatican II on me, my dear friend Bill Saunders helped me to see that council as God's gift to the Church in our time. Bit by bit I was walking back from anger to docility.

The UN showed me the larger world and drove in me a desire to reconnect to the universal Church. The Trappists showed me what was lacking in my traditionalist life, and that was love. So there it is. Love. The final conversion. No longer would I excommunicate. I would try to love.

*   *   *

God speaks to all men at all times, and He always says the same thing: Come closer. He works so hard to bring us closer to Him, and we resist Him mightily. This is the God who condescended to live among us, to die on the Cross, and to offer Himself to us helplessly in the Blessed Sacrament. He is also the God who led me to my hated advertising career in order to prepare me for my life's work in His service. This is the God who put the desire for the Trappists in my heart so that I would eventually become a regular pew-sitting Catholic. He knew I needed an unattainable goal just to become normal.

Prevenient grace can lead to actual grace, and that can lead to love. It is not enough to join the Church, as I did, and it is not enough to practice the faith, as I did. One must also love. Faith and hope will fall away, and all that will be left is love. I had heard this countless times before, but I had never made it my own. And though it has now registered in my consciousness, how do I make it my own? That is the work of a lifetime and the work of countless little moments when we say, "Yes, *serviam*; I will serve." This is what I finally know.

Austin Ruse is president of the Catholic Family and Human Rights Institute (C-Fam), a social policy research and advocacy group that focuses on the activities of the United Nations. C-Fam has offices in New York; Washington, D.C.; and Brussels, Belgium.

Chapter 16

How I Found My Tongue and Why I Needed It

William L. Toffler, MD

Like most American Catholics of the past fifty years, I was educated when the doctrines and moral principles of the faith were tentatively and ambiguously taught, while the assumptions of secular culture were instilled with rigorous authority. I learned that I had no right to make judgments or to impose my own moral views on others by asserting them. So, even though I was raised a Catholic and never openly rejected my religious heritage, I was a product of the times, and I profoundly needed conversion. Our churches today are full of just such Catholics as I was: poorly taught about the doctrines and obligations of the faith, and all too ready to compromise with the world.

As a Catholic, I knew that taking innocent life was forbidden. Specifically, I knew that abortion was wrong. Yet as a medical student in the early 1970s, I had not really thought much about how my own beliefs would interface with actual medical practice. Thus I was not prepared for a dilemma I faced in my third year, while on an obstetrics rotation. One day, along with a classmate (whom I shall pseudonymously call Marian), I was assigned to the East Hospital, where

303

indigents received care. Lined up like airplanes waiting on a runway for takeoff clearance, women in their second trimesters lay on gurneys, awaiting the ministrations of our resident, who had been given the task of performing their saline abortions. Marian and I watched the resident intently, as neither of us had ever witnessed the procedure before.

It looked pretty simple. First cleanse the skin on the mother's abdomen with betadine, insert a long needle into the uterus and withdraw amniotic fluid. Then inject the large volume of salt solution contained in two syringes into the fluid sac surrounding the baby. Withdrawing the needle completed the procedure. The mother could now return to the floor, where labor would subsequently ensue and the dead baby would be passed vaginally.

The whole process took less than three minutes. I stood in silence as an attendant took the mother away. Marian, who was always eager to learn new procedures, asked the resident, "Can I do one?"

He paused a moment, then nodded in affirmation. Under his watchful eye, Marian cautiously repeated the simple steps. Everything went smoothly. When she was done, Marian seemed energized. She was smiling, and after a brief moment, she turned to me.

"Bill, why don't you do one?"

The question took me off guard. While I knew where I stood personally, I didn't want to appear judgmental. After all, wasn't the woman going to have the abortion anyway? What difference would it make who actually did the procedure? What would these colleagues of mine think if I declined? Without further delay, I replied, "Sure, why not?"

Over the next few minutes, I completed the same steps as deftly as had the resident and my classmate. At the time, I was not much troubled about what I had done. If I felt any guilt about my actions, I must have buried it well. I don't remember even talking about it. No one else seemed bothered, so why would I? I simply blended in.

As uncertain as my thinking about abortion was at the time, I was even more bemused about contraception. Despite my Catholic roots, I was blind to any connection between artificial birth control and abortion. I had a vague sense that the Church frowned on birth control, but I thought it was really a matter for the individual conscience, not a serious moral problem. In fact, shortly after Marlene and I married, I thought we should avoid children until I was out of medical school, when I judged we could better afford being parents. Marlene and I both liked the idea of an intrauterine device (IUD). It seemed like a carefree approach for both of us and yet a responsible way to act. When her doctor refused to insert an IUD because of his concerns about the risks of using such devices in women who had not yet had a baby, I was taken aback, even a bit angry. After all, what right did he have to impose his beliefs on Marlene and me if we were both willing to accept the risks? Yet, while we were perturbed, we did not persist with our request, nor did we seek another opinion or a different care provider.

Although I did not realize it then, this incident taught an important lesson that I now share with students, residents, and practicing colleagues: clearly, physicians' own ethical standards have a profound impact on their patients. Their willingness, or unwillingness, to share those standards greatly influences their patients' decisions. When the IUD was subsequently taken off the market because of significant morbidity (and even mortality) in thousands of women, I was thankful that Marlene's physician had not simply "acted like a vending machine". But that is a later story, and I do not want to get ahead of myself.

At the time, I had no difficulty practicing in a contraceptive culture. I quickly learned how to prescribe the Pill and insert IUDs. In fact, in my second year of residency, I regularly staffed a family planning clinic for the county health department. Just as long as my patients knew the risks, I avoided imposing my judgment, even about putting IUDs in teens who had never been pregnant. Prescribing the contraceptive pill was not a problem for me either, even with higher-risk individuals such as older women who smoked. Again, I just explained the risks. In fact, I prided myself on my openness to all options. Obviously, at that time in my residency, I had not yet come to appreciate the wisdom of my wife's doctor. Instead, I let patients make some bad choices as I strove to demonstrate my value neutrality.

As a result, contraception became a big part of what I did. I was good at the procedures; I inserted hundreds of IUDs, and I learned to deftly perform vasectomies. Naturally, one of my first questions before discharging a new mother after her delivery was, "What kind of contraceptive do you want?" If she chose a tubal ligation, I willingly assisted. If a mother wanted an abortion, I would try to offer other options, even by encouraging her to choose adoption or connecting her with helping agencies such as crisis pregnancy centers or Birthright. Yet, if she persisted in her desire for termination, I would refer her to an abortionist. I was following the logic I had internalized in that awkward moment during my third year of medical school: "After all, she's going to do it anyway, so I may as well help."

Looking back, I realize that I was a regular practitioner of situational ethics. The compromises I made were common and perhaps for that reason understandable, but they were wrong. Nevertheless, I considered myself a pro-lifer and a Catholic; I was comfortable with myself and my practice. Attitudinal change would not come quickly to me.

* * *

After I entered full-time practice, I remember a troubling question posed by a resident, Tom, who was working with me on an elective for a month. He was a fellow Christian who was also opposed to abortion. Just as I was about to see a patient who was considering having an IUD, Tom asked, "Bill, what do you do about IUDs, given the probability that they cause abortion?"

Before he had finished the question, I knew what he was really asking: *How could I claim to be pro-life and yet insert abortifacient devices?*

I responded hesitantly, groping for a firm foundational principle on which to base my explanation. "You've got to draw the line somewhere.... I guess it (the conception) is too small.... Besides, I'm not intending to interrupt an already-implanted pregnancy."

I remember that I was not entirely satisfied with my answers; in fact, my response seemed pretty weak, even to me. I did not immediately change anything I was doing, but in retrospect, I can see that his question planted a seed within me.

Years later, at a lecture on contraception, I learned of the emerging concerns about IUDs and their potential for serious complications. The speaker thought that potential for harm so great that he had stopped inserting them in anyone. While he did not oppose IUDs on moral grounds, he provided a strong rationale for me to stop. Under cover of medical concerns for the mother, I did so at once. My burden of guilt over my role as a "passive" abortionist lifted, in part, at least, though my willingness to refer for abortions still nagged.

Soon, another small awakening occurred. One morning in 1990, I was working at an urgent care facility. A thirty-six-year-old female patient suspected that she was again pregnant. An alcohol and narcotic abuser, she had previously been pregnant a total of six times. Three of her pregnancies were ended by abortions. The three children she carried to term had been taken from her by the state because of her neglect and continuing drug addiction. Her pregnancy test confirmed that she was pregnant for a seventh time, and she wanted an abortion. I encouraged her to look at other options; I mentioned support systems and agencies; I offered her free care for the pregnancy, and beyond. She rejected all those options, persisting in her desire to terminate her baby. She asked for a referral. Reluctantly, I agreed to help and left the room.

In the hallway, I asked one of the nurses to assist me in connecting her with an abortion facility. Before I could finish the sentence, the nurse responded, "I don't deal with that."

I started another sentence, and again, she interrupted. "I'm sorry. I don't deal with that at all." Her response startled me, yet I respected her for her stand. In fact, I agreed with it. As she walked away, I stood in silence, wondering why *I* was involving myself in an act I believed to be wrong.

I decided to change.

I reentered the room and gently restated my willingness to help my patient in every way possible, but this time I firmly stated that I was unable to help her obtain an abortion. The nurse's courage in living her beliefs had given me a model to follow, thus helping me to behave more consistently myself. Once again, in retrospect, I felt a sense of relief. At last I had rejected my propensity to compromise my own principles.

However, my practice continued to include contraceptives and sterilization procedures. In fact, I became one of the first physicians in our university practice to learn how to insert progestin implants. If there were problems with those choices, I did not permit the conflict to rise to a conscious level.

But even as I continued to dispense contraceptives in my medical practice, I was growing increasingly aware of the problems with birth control pills, on a personal level. My wife and I had stopped using contraceptives in our own marriage. We had also joined a more orthodox Catholic parish, where the norm among most couples with children was to avoid the use of contraceptives.

Then, in 1993, an epiphany occurred. Marlene and I attended a three-day conference presented by Human Life International in our own parish hall. It was entirely devoted to an in-depth look at *Humanae Vitae*, the encyclical written by Pope Paul VI more than two decades earlier. Experts from around the country explained theological, philosophical, and medical concerns related to all forms of artificial birth control, and most specifically to birth control pills.

Within the first half day of the conference, I understood that I would need to change my professional behavior. At least in some cases, birth control pills induced chemical abortions. Clearly, I could no longer ignore that reality in my practice. Furthermore, I came to see that the whole practice of artificial birth control was a violation of God's plan for married couples.

I knew that I had a decision to make. Having been given these new insights, I would be inconsistent at best and a hypocrite at worst if I went on prescribing the Pill.

Alternatively, I could dissociate myself from all involvement in artificial contraceptives. *Was this feasible? After all, I taught residents and medical students. What would they think? What would my colleagues think? Could I continue to teach?*

I worried too about the financial implications of such a decision on my large family. Prescribing contraceptives and performing vasectomies and tubal ligations had become a big part of my practice.

Nervously, I wrestled with my decision through the remaining two and a half days of the conference. Fearing that even to discuss the issue might limit my options, I was reluctant to talk with Marlene about it. I might be pressured to embrace a new way of practicing that I would not be able to maintain or that would not be able to sustain us as a family.

Despite my fears, and my reluctance even to discuss the issue, I finally made a silent commitment: I would stop using hormonal contraceptives that I recognized to be abortifacient. What is more, I committed myself not to engage in any medical practice that conflicted with the clear and consistent teachings of the Roman Catholic Church. I saw that, morally, I could not help another person to do something inconsistent with God's plan for married couples. This meant I must stop performing vasectomies and assisting with tubal ligations, and I must even refrain from referring for either of those procedures. I was still nervous, but I was determined to keep the resolutions.

*   *   *

To my surprise, the first patient who asked me for birth control pills actually appreciated learning of my perspective. She did not want to take anything that had even a remote risk of acting as an abortifacient. Furthermore, she was excited about the concept of natural family planning and thought her husband would be too. Responding eagerly to her interest, I supplied her with information, community resources, and a follow-up appointment, thinking that maybe the new approach was not going to be as difficult as I had feared.

Not so. Over the subsequent month, I found that not all my patients were equally responsive, and some were frankly annoyed. In such cases, after recognizing their frustration, I would ask for their understanding, apologize that their appointment had been scheduled with me, and assure them that there would be no charge for the visit. Then, fully explaining my personal and religious convictions, I would gently but firmly tell them that while I respected their freedom not to conform to my beliefs, I could not assist them. To this day, I have never encountered a patient who did not respect my position.

While I have lost a few patients, I have gained more who seek me out because of the change in my practice. Despite my fears about the financial situation, my income that year, and in subsequent years, was actually higher than it was when I was prescribing artificial birth control. More important, a weight that I had not even recognized has been completely lifted from my conscience. I believe I am more effective and certainly more consistent with my patients. I believe my advice has helped many couples in my practice to have stronger marriages.

As an academic physician, I have even taken the risk of teaching natural family planning (NFP) to residents and students. The title of my talk to them is "Natural Family Planning: The Forgotten Family Planning Option". Residents, students, and even fellow faculty members are generally astonished to learn that family planning can be done as reliably with natural means as with hormones, and without any risk of side effects.

My journey toward a fully Catholic pro-life position and medical practice has been long, yet I have never looked back. Reflecting now on the path I traveled, I can clearly see God's fingerprints: at each branch in the road, one of God's agents helped me see how to be consistent in applying my faith to my practice. Once it was a resident's provocative question; at other times it was a nurse or a colleague who modeled a different way to practice. Finally, it was the profound witness for the Truth expressed in *Humanae Vitae* and communicated by Human Life International. As a result, I strive to share this life-giving new paradigm with all who will listen. I am grateful to God and to each of the guides He sent to help point the way for me.

*   *   *

The positive impact of my conversion on my conscience, my practice, and the way I teach has been clear. What I did not immediately appreciate was the impact that my striving to live the Church's magisterial teaching might have outside of my practice.

In 1994, promoters of assisted suicide introduced a ballot measure to legalize that practice in the state of Oregon. Years earlier, when we discussed the issue, my wife had argued that legal abortion would lead to assisted suicide and other forms of euthanasia.

Blind to the parallels in logic between the two acts, I had responded, "No way, Marlene. That's too big a leap."

But soon I began to hear assisted suicide defended with the same arguments I had heard used in defense of abortion.

In the abortion campaign, we had been subjected to a steady drumbeat of rhetoric about women's right to reproductive autonomy. Because their pregnancies occur within their bodies, we were told repeatedly, they have an ultimate right to choose whether to end the lives of their unborn children. Now the people of Oregon were being told that in the matter of death too, choice was the paramount concern. At the end of life, we have a "right to die", said propagandists for assisted suicide. Even in dying, we have a right to autonomous choice. Everyone must be legally free to decide to die "with dignity".

Now I realized beyond doubt that Marlene's prediction had been correct. In essence, the advocates for assisted suicide proposed to change the way we value life at its end, just as the Supreme Court, by legalizing abortion, changed the value of life at its earliest stages. My newfound respect for my wife's prophetic insight was intensified by the imminent threat to the traditional practice of medicine. Yet many colleagues and fellow citizens seemed as blind to this ominous paradigm shift as I had long been to the immorality of collaboration with contraception and abortion. Impatiently I wondered how they could fail to see the connection that now appeared so obvious to me.

Understanding this connection depends on believing with conviction that every human life is inherently sacred. God is the author of all life. We are all His children, made in His image and likeness, given the blessing of life. He gave us freedom to use our gifts fully until the natural end of our lives. This is the consistent magisterial teaching of the Catholic Church: we do not have a right to end any innocent human life—our own or another's—at any stage.

In November 1994, Oregon voters rejected those fundamental truths and embraced the situational killing of patients as enacted under the so-called Death with Dignity Act, known as Measure 16.

Many pro-life doctors in Oregon had dropped their membership in the Oregon Medical Association because of the OMA's stance on abortion. When the threat of assisted suicide first arose, a few of us saw it as vital to stay involved in our state medical society even if some of the positions it adopted were contrary to our beliefs. Our voices need to be heard on life-and-death issues even when it seems that we are "crying in the wilderness".

Before the Oregon Death with Dignity Act could be enacted as law, a successful legal challenge blocked its implementation for nearly three years. Finally, the Oregon Supreme Court dismissed the case for "lack of standing". In the interim, several of us launched a new professional group to oppose the assisted suicide movement. We called it the Physicians for Compassionate Care Education Foundation (PCCEF).

Since its founding, the PCCEF has defended the inherent value of human life and has worked to maintain the time-honored principles of the medical profession. We hold all human life inherently valuable and maintain that the role of physicians is to heal illness, alleviate suffering, and provide comfort for the sick and dying. The PCCEF points out that physician-assisted suicide is abhorrent because it changes the role of the physician from that of healer to that of executioner.

In cooperation with Oregon Right to Life, the PCCEF began educating the legislature on the need to repeal Measure 16. PCCEF members became active in their state medical societies, and as a result, we were able to get the OMA to reverse its previous neutral position and adopt a resolution officially opposing the newly enacted law. At 121–1, the vote was nearly unanimous. Individual testimony by PCCEF members played a key role in persuading members of the Oregon House and Senate of the serious flaws in the Oregon Death with Dignity Act. The result was a legislative recommendation for repeal, which was presented to voters in 1997 as Measure 51.

The battle for the recall measure became an uphill struggle. Oregon is one of the least churched states in the nation, a chief reason the assisted suicide movement is headquartered there. Major funding for repeal came from the Catholic Church. Our opponents called themselves the "Don't Let Them Shove Their Religion Down Your Throat Political Action Committee". They played on the euphemisms of "death with dignity", "the right to die", "peaceful death", and "choice in dying" like a well-tuned violin. Ultimately, the repeal effort, Measure 51, failed by 60–40 percent, a larger margin than had opposed passage of the original Death with Dignity Act. Within a month, the legalized killing began.

Since Oregon voters embraced assisted suicide in 1994, there has been a profound shift in attitude toward the aged, the infirm, and those who are labeled "terminal". That shift, I believe, has been detrimental to our patients, degraded the quality of medical care, and compromised the integrity of the medical profession.

Most problematic for me has been the change in attitude within the health care system itself. People with serious illnesses sometimes fear the motives of doctors or consultants, with good reason. Many studies show that assisted suicide requests are almost always made for psychological or social reasons. In Oregon there has never been any documented case of assisted suicide being used because there was actual untreatable pain. But there is evidence that financial considerations can be significant. For example, I regularly receive notices from the state that important services and drugs for my patients—even some pain medications—will not be paid for by the state health plan. At the same time, assisted suicide is fully covered and sanctioned by the state of Oregon and by our collective tax dollars.

In legalizing assisted suicide, Oregon remained a solitary anomaly for eleven years. Voter referenda and legislative bills similar to Oregon's assisted suicide law failed in Alaska, Arizona, California, Hawaii, Vermont, Maine, Michigan, Wisconsin, and Washington. The refusal to embrace assisted suicide extended across the Atlantic, where an Oregon-type assisted suicide bill was rejected in the British House of Lords in 2006. Twice within the year 2007, the Washington State Medical Association rejected a proposal to be neutral in this area and actually strengthened its policy of opposition to physician-assisted suicide. Still, the threat continues: promoters of assisted suicide are hard at work across the United States. And in November, 2008, Washington State voters approved Initiative 1000, despite strong pro-life opposition.

Because of this ongoing threat, in the years since the killing began, I have been asked repeatedly to share my perspective in public debates, on panels, on television, on radio, and in writing. I did not seek the role, but I believe God has called me to speak the Truth and share my lived experience. Where I once was blind, God's grace gave me the gift of sight. Where I once compromised my integrity both directly and indirectly, I was blessed to learn how imperative it is for us to live by the magisterial teaching of our Church. God led me to understand my obligation, and now it appears that He was calling me to share that understanding in the major war of this age, the struggle against the proliferation of a culture of death.

Dr. William Toffler is a practicing physician in Oregon, a professor at the University of Oregon Medical School, and the national director of the Physicians for Compassionate Care Education Foundation (PCCEF). He and his wife, Marlene, are the parents of seven children, and grandparents of five.

Chapter 17

My Three Conversions

Father Sebastian Walshe, O. Praem.

There were really three conversions in my life: first, a conversion to the Catholic faith; second, a conversion to traditional Catholic beliefs and practices; and finally, a conversion to religious life. It is hard for me to pinpoint a certain moment in time for each one, as they were not dramatic and sudden like the conversions of Saint Paul and Saint Augustine. Readers will note an overarching theme of education and formation of the mind and heart in this story. In many ways, I see my conversions as reformations, leading me out of the deformed intellectual custom of the time in which I was born and raised.

* * *

Myles Walshe, my father, was born in 1936, the second of eight children of an Irish Catholic family, in the midst of the Great Depression. The Second World War took place in his preteen years, and ever after he was an avid reader of war stories and novels. He went off to study at the University of Notre Dame in the mid-1950s. While he was there, his own father died. His years at Notre Dame proved to be a time of radical revision of the faith he had received and believed as a child. Subsequent events in the Church, especially in the United States, during and after the Second Vatican Council, appeared to confirm that alteration of his faith. By the time he met my mother, in the mid-1960s, he was no longer a practicing Catholic.

Although he abandoned a number of essential Catholic doctrines (notably the existence of Hell, the universal salvific mission of the Church, and a number of moral teachings), my father always retained a deep love for the poor and was very generous to them throughout his life. His love for the poor was so remarkable that whenever he saw a street person, he always gave him something, even without being asked. I remember many occasions, riding in the car, when my father saw a poor man pushing a shopping cart on the other side of the road. My dad would make the next available U-turn and hand us some money to give to the poor man. On holidays he would make about seventy sack lunches (each complete with an image of Jesus and a plastic Rosary, with instructions) and bring my brother and me with him down to a park in a poor neighborhood to distribute them to transients and drug addicts. Once, when I was a teenager, we visited Tijuana. On the bridge leading from the United States to Mexico, there were hundreds of beggars sitting with paper cups, asking for alms. My father had come prepared. Earlier in the day, he had cashed a hundred-dollar bill for coins and filled his pockets. He stopped and gave something to every beggar on that bridge. I remember being irked that day about the time it took for Dad to give away all those coins. It was only much later in my life that I realized with great compunction that in all the years that Jesus sat begging in the persons of those hundreds of beggars, He never met a man more generous than my father.

My dad's generosity and detachment from money proved to be a source of great grace for me later on, when I embraced religious poverty. Largely due to his example, I can honestly say that the vow of poverty has always been easy for me to practice.

My mother was born into a middle-class Jewish family in Massachusetts on January 28, 1943. The second of three daughters, she lived a very normal life until her early teens. At that point, she began to experience lapses of muscular control, beginning in her feet and eventually causing spasticity and cramping throughout her whole body. She was diagnosed with a very rare disease of the nervous system called dystonia musculorum deformans, a disease that even today remains without a cure. Eventually she was confined to a wheelchair, in such excruciating pain from cramping that pulled her toes from their sockets that she had to have her toes amputated. My aunt told me that she remembers often waking in the middle of the night to cries of pain issuing from my mother's room. At the age of sixteen, she underwent a series of experimental brain surgeries. The last surgery stopped the spasticity and cramps but also deprived her of the power of speech; nor was she ever able to walk again. Yet the years of suffering had forged her will. Throughout Mom's life, I never remember her complaining about her suffering, though I know that it must have been more terrible than I could comprehend.

So strong willed was she that, even in this condition, my mother decided to attend school across the country at UCLA, one of two universities in the country that at the time had facilities for handicapped people. In spite of her physical condition, which made it difficult even to take notes, she graduated with high honors. She majored in psychology in the mid-1960s, something that greatly influenced the way that she raised my brother and me.

At UCLA, she met my father, who was doing graduate work in psychology at the time. As the story goes, my mother was unsuccessfully trying to get her electric wheelchair up one of the steep hills of Westwood. My father thought he would show off by picking her up, wheelchair and all, and carrying her up the hill. Bearing a toy mouse as a gift, my mother went to visit him in the hospital after he had surgery on the resulting hernia. My father proposed on the spot, and they were married shortly thereafter.

My older brother, Raymond, was born in 1967, and I followed a year and a half later, in early 1969. At that time, we were the only known cases of children born to a woman with dystonia. I remember both my parents as loving and affectionate. However, both of them had imbibed a very laissez-faire philosophy of child rearing that exaggerated freedom and self-determination. Influenced by her education in psychology, Mom always held my brother and me facing outward when we were infants in order to encourage independence. She believed so strongly in encouraging and developing our self-reliance that when my brother and I were eleven and nine, she sent us by ourselves to visit relatives in Maine. Supplied with ample funding by our father, who grudgingly acceded to our mother's insistence, we arrived safely in Maine after a four-day trip via Greyhound and returned three weeks later by the same mode of transportation. Raymond, always fiscally astute, carefully saved most of his portion of the money, only to have the remainder confiscated at the end of the trip by my relieved father. I, on the other hand, spent all my extra money on gifts for my mother. (There is an allegory to the spiritual life hidden somewhere in there.)

While our upbringing was marked by this excessive permissiveness in regard to self-determination, my parents were nevertheless very quick to punish such vices as lying or stealing. Once Raymond and I decided that we wanted to go to a little league game at the grade school down the street. Not having any money for hot dogs or sodas, we decided to take a few quarters each out of a big jar of bicentennial quarters that my mom had been saving. Shortly thereafter my brother felt remorse and confessed everything to my mom. For his punishment, he was grounded for a day. I, on the other hand, when confronted directly by my mother, lied and told her that I did not take any coins. I was confined to my room for a week. I do not think that I ever lied to my mother again in my life.

Difficulties between my parents surfaced fairly early on in their marriage, and one of my earliest memories was of my parents telling us that they were separating. This happened when I was three years old. After their separation, we stayed with our mother, but my father came faithfully to spend every weekend with us. He was always involved in our lives, and we never felt unwanted by either of our parents. In fact, on weekends we always did things together as a family, including our mother. This did a lot to make the best of a bad situation. We never experienced or witnessed anger or bitterness in either of our parents toward one another or toward us, and neither of our parents ever remarried.

Neither my father nor mother was particularly religious. Perhaps once a year, Dad would bring my brother and me to see a Catholic Mass. Mom did not seem to mind this, though she never attended herself. But our mother was at least in the habit of attending synagogue services on Saturdays.

I do not know what brand of Judaism my mother adhered to, but I am reasonably sure that it was not orthodox Judaism. She enrolled us in the Jewish equivalent of Sunday school, and thus I passed the first seven years of my life as a Jew, educated in that religion as much as any typical, middle-of-the-road American Jew would have been. I remember wearing a *yamacha* (skullcap) for religious events and that we would celebrate the major religious feasts yearly. My father was even happy to participate in the Passover seder meal with us. As a child, I remember celebrating both Chanukah and Christmas; I suppose every child would be happy to do so, as Chanukah included eight days of gift giving.

My religious experience at that time was superficial, due to my tender age. I peered over the back of the pews in the synagogue to see the rabbi speaking, but I distinctly remember not being able to understand anything of what he said. I was, however, fascinated with the tabernacle (often called an "ark") in which the scroll of the Torah was kept. I remember being rapt with attention as the rabbi took the scroll, sheathed in purple velvet, from the tabernacle and opened it upon the altar to read from a particular passage. I was awed too by the sanctuary light next to the tabernacle, which someone assured me never went out. At the time I thought this was a miracle, but later I learned that it was an electric lamp, kept on all the time by having the bulb regularly changed.

When I was seven years old, two remarkable events happened to my mother that led to her conversion to Christianity, and so to ours. The ravages of dystonia so contorted her body that her spine had a 180-degree scoliosis. Her internal organs were beginning to malfunction as a result of being displaced. At the time, she was taking more than seventy different pills and medications to compensate for her bodily infirmities. Only a radical surgery to straighten her spine would save her life, her doctors informed her. The surgery involved crushing her spine, stretching it straight and inserting two metal rods to keep her spine straight as it healed. She was to be in the hospital for over two months, and because my father worked as a traveling salesman, the decision was made to send Raymond and me to live with my aunt and uncle in Hawaii for those months.

When we came home, we found our mother encased in a torso cast, a metal halo about her head with four screws entering her skull to keep her spine stable. It never occurred to me to ask her if she was in pain, but many years later I realized that her ability to maintain her patience with two young boys during that time was a sign of tremendous virtue. I can only imagine how miserable she must have felt, living a life overwhelmed with pain, and yet she never stopped being our mother.

After we returned, I learned that the surgery had been so traumatic that my mother had actually died for a few minutes on the operating table. After four minutes or so, the doctors were able to revive her. During that interval, she told me, she had experienced her soul separating from her body. I was so fascinated that I asked her many specific questions about the experience, wanting to understand as clearly as possible what happened to her while she was dead. She said that after she felt her soul separating from her body, all the pain went away. She saw herself in a long, dark tunnel with a bright light at the end. She thought that she was going to see God or Heaven at the end, but instead, when she emerged, she found herself looking down upon her body while all the medical staff scurried about trying to revive her. She remembered feeling exceedingly happy and wondering why the doctors and nurses seemed so worried, when she was fine. She also said that she experienced a tremendous sense of freedom. I asked her if she could have gone anywhere she wanted. She said that she knew that she could go wherever she wanted in an instant, though she chose to remain there where her body was lying. Soon she experienced the presence of God, an experience of unspeakable love. He gave her a choice of going back to her body or not. She knew that He wanted her to go back to her body, and since she found His love irresistible, she decided to do that. As she entered into her body, she felt the pain return. This was the first remarkable experience, and it was something that greatly altered my mother's religious convictions. It also had a deep effect on me, though I do not remember making any practical change in my religious practices.

The second remarkable experience came through the hands of a charismatic Lutheran pastor who visited our home a few months after Mom had recovered from her surgery. As my father related later, Mom had had some kind of falling out with the rabbi of the local synagogue. I do not know whether her "near-death" experience was a factor in her new interest in Christianity. What I do know is that the Lutheran pastor came to our house and prayed over our mother. After this prayer she regained use of her left hand, which had been left partially paralyzed by one of her brain surgeries as a teenager. This was enough to convince her to join the Lutheran church, and in February 1977 my mother and brother and I were all baptized in the Lutheran church. Years later, I found out that that baptism was probably ineffectual; my father confessed that he had baptized both my brother and me in the bathtub as infants, a measure he took furtively because our mother was unwilling to have us baptized or raised as Catholics.

One of the first things I remember about my new religion was having a Bible in the house for the first time. It was a gold-covered version of the "Good News" Bible, and

I was fascinated by it. In my first sitting I read for several hours, straight through Genesis and Exodus. Ironically, I did not even realize that these were books that Jews also recognized as Scripture: I had never read them before nor, to the best of my recollection, even heard of them. Already an avid reader, I really loved to read the Bible stories. In Sunday school we received prizes for memorizing Scripture quotes and finding the books in the Bible, and I took my new faith seriously. Once, as a Sunday school project, we were to collect thirty pieces of silver to donate to the poor. Most of the other children gave nickels or dimes, but I tried to give silver dollars and half dollars, as much as I could save. This seriousness about helping the poor was probably due to my father's influence, and I think that Mom was proud of me for being generous.

What drew me most strongly about Lutheran worship services was the reception of communion. Still a year too young to be admitted to communion, I begged my parents and the pastor to let me receive earlier. I attended all the lessons for the first communicants and so was permitted to receive communion that year. Both bread and wine were distributed for communion. The bread was a large loaf of shepherd's bread, cut open at the top. The pastor would take a pinch and give it to each communicant. The wine was distributed in tiny individual cups that a server carried on a tray especially made to hold them. Even the communion rail had small round receptacles for depositing the tiny cups after the wine had been consumed. An elderly lady would go around and collect the glasses after the service. One day I asked her what she did with the leftover communion wine. When she said that she poured it out in the bushes after the service, I was instinctively offended. I understood that as the Lutherans professed it, communion was

symbolic of Our Lord's Body and Blood, but I had understood this symbolism in such a strong sense that I thought
it should be really treated like His Body and Blood after
the consecration. The knowledge that the leftover communion wine was disposed of so casually left a deep disappointment and dissatisfaction in my heart, though I did not
yet fully understand why.

When 1979 arrived, I had no idea how much sorrow it
would bring. Things were going from bad to worse in our
neighborhood, which was no longer the place to raise a
healthy family. Those who lived there were representative
of that segment of American society corrupted not so much
by poverty as by the effects of the sexual revolution and the
drug culture. Pot use was already common among sixth-
graders, including many of our childhood friends. Sexual
immorality was becoming widespread even among quite
young adolescents. Our mother decided that we had to move.

We found a house in a better neighborhood and moved
there in the spring of 1979. The move to the new neighborhood and school was difficult for me, especially leaving
old friends behind, but the greatest trial was soon to follow.

One October afternoon when I came home from school,
I found my mother dead, half in and half out of her wheelchair. I called 911 and sat in the living room pounding my
fist on the ground and, through my tears, asking God
why. When the paramedics arrived, they had me wait in
the ambulance for a while. As I sat there, I made a prayer
to God that could only have been inspired by the pure grace
of the Holy Spirit: *It's all right that you took my mother; you
can even take my father; but don't let me ever lose You.* To this
day that prayer surprises me. I do not remember being so
devout that it would have been natural for me to say such
a prayer, yet at the time I made it I was completely sincere

and serious. I believe it was that prayer that merited for me the grace of conversion to the Catholic faith.

Subsequent months would prove God faithful to that prayer, in spite of my own infidelity. My father moved in to take care of us, but the shock of my mother's death, coupled with the strain of raising two boys on his own and having to find a new job, broke his health. He also became addicted to pain and anxiety medication and finally was so incapacitated that he was no longer able to drive. My twelve-year-old brother started driving to the supermarket and when running necessary errands. Fortunately, Raymond was so big for his age that he passed for sixteen.

Our father's condition grew worse. By a certain point, we had to wake him up in the mornings by dabbing his face with a cold towel. Eventually, he had a heart attack. When he was taken to the emergency room, they were able to stabilize his condition. He remained in the hospital for some time but afterward he was not able to care for us on his own. My brother and I were placed in a foster home.

During this time of family instability, we ceased going to church. I even took a certain pride in my free-thinking approach to religion, beginning to reason within myself, *Why go to church if God is everywhere?* Of course, I did not follow the logical consequences of my position by acting everywhere as if I were in church. On the contrary, I seldom if ever thought of God; I became a practical agnostic and eventually a professed ten-year-old atheist. A social misfit at school, I was very unhappy, and my grades dropped dramatically. I fell into many other sins besides.

Reflecting back upon these things, it is easy to see how even my atheism was a result of the dissolution of my family life. I did not fully understand then how closely linked the life of the family is to our life with God. The family is really the normal instrument of divine grace and was so from the beginning. Perhaps in the same way that there is no salvation outside the Church, it can also be said that there is no salvation outside the natural human family. It is not necessary for all those who are saved to be raised in a normal, natural family environment; yet even for such people, it seems to me that a natural human family is somehow instrumental in their salvation.

Shortly after we were placed in the foster home, my father's mother, Thora Walshe, widowed for nearly twenty-five years, came to our rescue. Unbeknown to us, she and my mother's sister, Susan, had been negotiating behind the scenes about who would take us in. My grandmother finally won out and, at the age of sixty-five, took two preteen boys to raise in her home. My aunt Susan promised her financial assistance in subsequent years and helped us immensely when it came time for college. Once again the family served as an instrument of divine grace. I cannot adequately express my gratitude to either of them.

The decision to have us live with my grandmother proved to be the first of a series of interventions by Divine Providence. In fact, if we had been asked at the time whom we would prefer to have raise us, we probably would have said our aunt Susan. My grandmother was a practicing Catholic, while my aunt was at that time an agnostic Jew. If Aunt Susan had raised us, I have little doubt that neither Raymond nor I would have become Catholics.

I do not know how many times in my life it has happened that God chose for me contrary to what I would have chosen. Yet, looking back on my life, I realize that it was just through those forks in the road that God led me to know and love Him as He is. Sometimes it seems that God is determined to save me in spite of myself.

Life with my grandmother proved to be a difficult adjustment, probably even more for her than for us. Because I had acquired the selfish habit of thinking only of my own problems, I felt little gratitude for the heroic sacrifices she was making. I do not even remember thanking her until years later. One of those harsh changes was learning to live under strict supervision. From the way we had been raised, we had become so accustomed to freedom that living under our grandmother's rules proved nearly unbearable. To compound matters, the six months in which we lived with our sick father had proved to be a time of virtually no supervision. Imagine our shock when our grandmother insisted that we could go only to G-rated movies, when before we had been able to sneak into R-rated movies. But we began the difficult road back to a morally healthy, structured family life, a road that I am sure cost my grandmother dearly.

Because my grandmother was a religious woman, a Catholic who had converted from Presbyterianism when she married my grandfather, she insisted that we go to church every Sunday. At first, we insisted on going to the Lutheran church, but this became unmanageable. She would have to attend both her Catholic Mass and our Lutheran service each Sunday, which was really too much for a woman her age to fulfill. Despite our resistance, she insisted that we all go to the Catholic church together, as a family. At first we were resentful, but soon she arranged for us to get involved in the parish youth group, where we met many good and enthusiastic young Catholics. As we formed friendships with these young people, the barriers that we had raised against the Catholic Church began to disappear.

The little we knew about the Catholic faith was seriously distorted. Our mother had never known a seriously practicing Catholic, and she seemed to consider Catholicism fixated on mechanical external rituals, all form and no substance. Somehow I had inherited this view of the Church. Firsthand experience with kind, loving, and generous Catholics who truly loved God soon dispelled many of my misconceptions. Because of the friendships I formed with the young people in the parish youth group, I began to rethink my position on God and on the Catholic Church. Here again, I was largely unaware of the hidden role being played by the newfound love and stability in my life to heal the wounds that had resulted from the disintegration of my previous family life. Nevertheless, it would be false to characterize my interest in the Catholic Church as merely emotional or based only upon personal friendships. The reintegration of my family life served only to remove the impediments to God's grace that had arisen in my emotional and spiritual life.

I began to read the Scriptures again with an eye to examining the teachings of the Catholic Church. The teaching that interested me the most was that on the Real Presence of Jesus' Body and Blood in the sacrament of the Eucharist. I realized that this teaching somehow corresponded to the belief I had wanted to have even as a Lutheran first communicant, when I had been taught that this presence was fundamentally symbolic and not real. Upon reading the relevant Scripture passages, and reading a number of commentaries, including an analysis of the Greek texts, I came to the conviction that it was much more reasonable, based upon the scriptural evidence, to accept the Catholic position than the Protestant position. The fact that the Real Presence was so clearly and consistently believed by early Christians served only to confirm the hypothesis that it was the Protestants who had changed Christ's teaching, not the

Catholics. The evidence was before me; all that remained was the act of faith, something that God readily granted me.

Though I still had difficulties about the teaching of the Catholic Church on other issues, chiefly the Marian dogmas, I reasoned that if the Catholic Church had been right on such a fundamental teaching as the Eucharist, she could be trusted on the others as well. I believed that my other difficulties would in time be resolved, as in fact they were. Since the time I gave assent to the teaching of the Real Presence, I have never once experienced a serious doubt about Christ's substantial presence in the Eucharist. This, I believe, is a gift from God because of my unhesitating acceptance of this truth of faith and my willingness to come into the Church on the basis of my belief. There is really a sense in which it is true to say that he who rightly believes in the Real Presence has the whole faith. The Eucharist is the mystery of faith, containing within itself all the other mysteries of our faith.

I was received into the Church in the spring of 1983, just shy of my fourteenth birthday, during my first year of high school.

* * *

By this time our father was back working, staying with us on weekends and some weeknights. Living with my grandmother was becoming easier, and thanks to the parish youth group, I had a very active social life, including sports and activities two or three nights a week. The youth group was charismatic in inclination. Many of the members of the adult youth group prayed in tongues, though this was not the practice in the high school youth group. The Sunday evening youth mass was very enthusiastic and included guitar and drum music as accompaniment to songs that were standard fare for a mid-1980s American parish. At the time I liked the charismatic element in the youth group: it appealed to my need for emotional engagement in my faith. Although I was convinced of the need to remain faithful to the Magisterium, I was not very attentive at that time to the differences between Protestant and Catholic forms of worship. As the years passed, some members of that youth group ended up in charismatic Protestant churches, but most of the others moved toward more traditional Catholic practices.

It happened that James Grimm, a friend from my high school class, lived only a couple of blocks down the street from us, closer than any other schoolmate, so I started spending time at his home. James' father, Bill Grimm, always treated me very kindly and seemed happy when I came by. I suspect he took a liking to me because I was good at math and technology, things dear to his heart.

Knowing the Grimm family gave me my first real exposure to traditional Catholicism. Their approach to the faith did not immediately appeal to me; James and I used to jibe each other about our different views on how the Mass should be said or on what the Church taught about particular matters. Still, I was deeply impressed by their family life. First, I was amazed that they had so many kids; James was the fourteenth of seventeen. Second, I was also impressed by the fact that they had a completely Catholic identity as a family.

Through my association with the Grimms, I became aware for the first time of different currents of thought in Catholicism, some of which were not mutually compatible, even about essential principles. In fact, the arguments that I heard at the Grimm home were so often at odds with what I heard during parish homilies that at first I dismissed some of the Grimms' statements as fringe ideas about the Church and about the Mass. But whenever I would raise an objection, they could always point me to an official Church document that taught exactly what they had said. I found out that quite a developed body of Church teaching existed before the Second Vatican Council and that much of the purportedly "official" Catholicism I had been hearing in recent years was not based upon that teaching. Moreover, I realized that some of the things I had been used to hearing in homilies and classes were not reconcilable with the teachings of the council itself. I began to reexamine my faith.

Among the doctrinal matters I had to reconsider were the Church's teaching on worship, the role of Mary in salvation, the role of the sacraments in salvation, marriage and family life, sexual morality, and purgatory. It was not so much that I had denied any of these, though perhaps I did deny some before I knew that the Church taught them; it was more that I failed to see the importance and centrality of a number of these truths in relation to the whole body of the Church's doctrine. For example, I had thought of the Marian dogmas as incidental accents of the faith, beliefs that would not be of that essence of the faith that C. S. Lewis called "mere Christianity". Or again, I had been under the impression that only things like murder and fornication were mortal sins. The idea that Catholics were encouraged to have big families was also foreign to me, and I had thought of contraception as venially sinful at worst. I had not known that music needed more than religious lyrics to make it suitable for the liturgy. The very melody, and even the instruments themselves, had to be sacred. In short, my intellectual and moral formation had left me in a dangerously confused state about a number of fundamental truths and practices of our faith, truths and practices upon which my salvation might depend. The Catholic formation I had received through instruction in the parish and in Catholic high school was dangerous precisely because it was vague. It could easily be adapted to the secular culture; it could be interpreted in a way directly contrary to the Church's perennial teaching. Yet in its origins, it was sufficiently vague to claim the name Catholic and to induce the assent of young persons of goodwill or newcomers to the faith.

About this time, I enrolled as an electrical engineering student at a nearby public university. Like most young people, my main considerations in choosing a college and a major were practical ones. I wanted a good, upper-middle-class income and a "college experience" complete with the beach, coeds, and major sports teams. The university I chose fit the bill. It never occurred to me to ask myself what the reason is for an education in the first place.

The same year that I entered college, James went off to a small liberal arts college in Ventura County, Thomas Aquinas College (TAC). We kept in touch sporadically. During my freshman year, 1985, I even went up to visit him at TAC. I was surprised to find a small campus, consisting of a single permanent building and a cluster of modular trailers. It was not the sort of place I could imagine going myself. James was an idealist, but I had the rest of my life to live. Over the summers, however, we still spent a good deal of time together.

My four years at public university were not employed very well as regards growth in virtue, yet the merciful God supplied me with the grace to at least remain a faithful Catholic. I went to Mass every Sunday, and I avoided situations that I thought were incompatible with being a Christian. At first, I would go to parties in the dorms with friends, but after a while I began to see the darker side of the college party scene. By the time my sophomore year came around, most of my social time was centered on basketball and volleyball and on lounging around in the commons. Those activities wasted a lot of time, but through God's grace they preserved me from worse things. Since so much of my social life was centered on sports, I got to know a lot of guys in the fraternities. Most of the fraternity men I knew did a lot of drinking and often were sexually immoral. In His compassion, God gave me enough insight so that I was never seriously interested in joining one.

By the time my senior year rolled around, I was looking for work and occasionally taking interest in the more speculative aspects of an education. When James would give me a hard time about ignoring the most important things in life, the "big picture" or the broader questions, I would respond that I could attend to all that on my own in my spare time. Browsing through the library one day, looking for some good book on philosophy or theology, I found a book by Saint Thomas Aquinas called *On Being and Essence*. Fifteen minutes later I put it back on the shelf, having understood little or nothing of what I had read.

During a break from school, I stopped by the home of my old friends the Grimms. The topic of philosophy came up in conversation, and Mr. Grimm strongly recommended that I start with a book by Boethius called *The Consolation of Philosophy*. That summer, between my junior and senior years, when my brother and I went to southern Saskatchewan, I brought along the copy of *The Consolation of Philosophy* that Mr. Grimm had lent me. Each morning I would rise early and take a walk down to Kenosee Lake, and as I sat on the small dock, dangling my feet in the water, I would slowly and carefully read about the problems of God's existence, of evil, of time and eternity, and so on. I found that in my own wrestling with some of these questions, I had come to solutions rather like those Boethius offered yet not as refined or carefully thought out. This little book served as a mirror of my own thoughts and experiences, thus helping me to sort through them more faithfully and distinctly. I could see that Boethius' own resolutions of such essential difficulties were not peculiar to his culture or place or time but were of universal import and gave an account of reality, wherever it happens to be found. Normally, when people sit on a dock, they eventually catch some fish, but that summer, I was the one who was hooked!

The following summer, I found work at an intellectual property law firm. It was not a typical job for an electrical engineering graduate, but they were looking for an engineer who could write, and I was interested in the exposure I would get to cutting-edge technology in the patent field. I loved my job. The people I worked with were first-rate professionals and also genuinely kind and concerned about my well-being. The things I was learning and writing were highly interesting: I never remember waking up in the morning not wanting to go to work. Besides these, the perks were great. I had a good salary, a secretary, and my own spacious office with a window overlooking the Pacific Ocean. It was really the ideal job. Within a few months after my graduation from public university, I had already reached my life goals, all the things that I had thought would make for an ideal life, and yet deep within my soul, I was unsatisfied. The things I had thought would finally fulfill me ended up being mere instruments for something else.

I was like a man with money but with nothing available to buy. Perhaps if I had been married, I would have found more satisfaction in my work and in my life. At least I would have been living for someone other than myself. But as things stood, I knew that I would have to look elsewhere if I wanted to be truly happy.

Thoughts of the previous summer and the things the Grimms had told me about Thomas Aquinas College began to come back into my mind. After working for just over a year, I decided to apply for admission to TAC. When I told my grandmother, she cried. My father was more support-ive. In any case, in the fall of 1990 I found myself driving up serpentine Highway 150 and turning right at the Fern-dale Ranch driveway onto the college property, a scene that would soon become familiar.

The four years I spent at TAC were among the happiest of my life. For the first time, I lived in a truly Catholic environment. The faith pervaded every aspect of life at the college. Better still, my mind was being formed by the great-est and most noble truths, truths that were bringing me closer to the First Truth. The examined life, lived in the context of the Catholic faith, forms and orders the soul in a way that begets a deep peace: an awareness that this is what man was made for. There I also made many dear friends, with whom I shared the most important and last-ing goods.

Sometime in my first year there, I met and began dating a good and beautiful young woman. It was she who first persuaded me to attend daily Mass, which was conve-niently offered three times a day at the college. She told me: "Every time someone receives Holy Communion devoutly, his throne in Heaven is raised to a higher place." This was another case in which God determined my path contrary to what I would have chosen: we dated for a little more than a year. Although God had other plans for me, I have been a better man because of that relationship. Since then, I appreciate more profoundly the good effect that a virtuous woman can have upon a man.

By the time graduation came, my soul, both mind and heart, had been deeply transformed through the things I learned and experienced, as well as the friendships I had made at the college. I had been inserted into a living tradition both philosophical and apostolic, which provided a foundation and reference point for everything else that would happen later in my life. One could say that, by this time, my conversion to traditional Catholicism was complete.

By "traditional Catholic", I do not mean one who merely has an attachment to the Latin Mass as said before the Second Vatican Council. Rather, by "traditional Catholic", I mean one who views the Church through her own lens. My view of the Church was not some distortion of the Church coming from outside. When a traditional Catholic reads the Gospels, or Saint Augustine, or Saint Thomas, or the documents of Trent or Vatican II, he is like a fish in water; the traditional Catholic is at home in the Church of any age. He perceives an inner consistency and harmony running through the whole of Scripture and the writings expressive of Catholic Tradition. The traditional Catholic is not perplexed by any of the Church's teachings, no matter how long ago they were issued, no matter how diverse the culture in which they came to be. Nothing of the authoritative writings of the Church seems out of place or wrong.

After graduation, I returned to my old law firm to pay some debts and to save up money for graduate school. I worked for two more years, and though I truly enjoyed my work, I was convinced that I was called to teach philosophy. Some people give up lucrative jobs for a vocation to the priesthood or religious life; I gave up my job for love of wisdom. I applied and was accepted into the doctoral program for philosophy at the Catholic University of America (CUA).

Just a few months before I was to begin studies at CUA, my father passed away. In many ways his death was more difficult for me than my mother's death. When he died, I remembered the words of the prayer I had said in the ambulance the day my mother died, and as much as I was able, I renewed my resignation to God's will. My only consolation, and this was in no way sensible, was the knowledge that God permits evil only to bring some greater, more universal good out of it. Having experienced the magnitude of the evil of my father's death, I rejoiced interiorly at the tremendous, yet hidden, good that God had accomplished. The very night my father died, I read the beginning of the book of Job and Saint Thomas' commentary, and this brought me some relief. In the months following, my prayer was dry and dark, and where I had previously taken great joy at praying before Our Lord in the Blessed Sacrament, now there was nothing but silence and darkness. I could just as well have been another statue in the church, since it seemed to me that nothing issued from my soul toward God. Yet during this time God was working invisibly in my soul, preparing me for a life better than the one I had envisioned for myself.

In August of 1998, I packed all my worldly belongings into a U-Haul trailer and drove across the country to Washington, D.C. My first stop was in Falls Church, Virginia, to see friends from TAC who were living in a townhouse not far from CUA. There happened to be two or three other townhouses in the same complex occupied by young Catholics, and providentially, I saw a sign advertising another vacant townhouse in the same complex. Two days later I moved in, along with two friends from TAC. To find a built-in social life with other Catholics as soon as I came was a great grace. At school I met many good young Catholics, including several young men studying for the priesthood. It was the first time in my life that I had been in close contact with seminarians, and after a while I became close friends with a few of them, notably Tim Meares, a seminarian from the diocese of Raleigh, North Carolina.

Never in my life had I been a personal friend of someone who was going to be a priest. Aristotle observed that a friend is like another self, one soul dwelling in two bodies. Seeing Tim, I was able for the first time to imagine myself pursuing the priesthood. Before, I had thought about the priesthood abstractly, as a rather neat idea, but when I considered my real life, I always just thought that I would get married and have a family. Now priesthood became a real option for me. Tim encouraged me to take concrete steps toward discerning whether God was calling me to the priesthood. In my second year at CUA, I was coming to the end of my studies, and I was not dating anyone. I found myself at a point where I actually had no immediate plans for the next stage in my life. Tim persuaded me to visit a seminary and make a vocational discernment retreat.

For the two weeks before Christmas 1997, I made a "come and see" visit to Saint Michael's Abbey in Southern California. I chose Saint Michael's because the priests I had met from there were all faithful to the Magisterium and were serious about holiness. But I was not very generous in my response to God's grace: I was willing to give it only one shot, having decided that if Saint Michael's was not the place for me, my discernment period would be over.

I really disliked my first week there. The time spent in prayer was more than I was used to, and I felt lonely. But after the first week, I noticed that things got easier. By the time the two weeks were over, I did not feel a strong desire to apply for admission, but I did have some evidence that it might be possible for me to live a life of that kind. Concerning consecrated celibacy, Our Lord had said, "Let he who is able to accept this teaching accept it." He did not say, "Let he who finds this life pleasant accept it." I decided that I should go ahead and apply, to see if God would give me the further grace I would need. I applied and was accepted, and I began religious life on the vigil of the Feast of Saint Augustine, August 27, 1998.

I never had a sense that I could not have been happy if I had not decided to make perpetual vows as a religious. Unlike many other seminarians, I can honestly say that there was no deep dissatisfaction with my life that I felt was fulfilled in religious life. During formation, I could imagine myself as a family man teaching philosophy somewhere. Yet I saw objectively that this life was better, much better, and that the Church needed priests and religious. The only real decision I had to make was whether God had given me the grace to live that life or not. As the months and the years passed, I found more and more that God was giving me this grace. I had doubts up until I made my first profession (that is, temporary vows for three years), but after that time, I never had any doubt that God wanted me to be a religious and a priest. In many ways, my religious life was like an arranged marriage: I fell in love with it after I chose it.

I was ordained to the priesthood on September 24, 2005, in the Year of the Eucharist. It was appropriate that I was ordained in the Year of the Eucharist, for throughout my whole life the Eucharist was the single Good that constantly attracted me, transforming me in both my mind and heart, leading me out of darkness into ever brighter light. More than ever, as a priest, I see my entire life—not only my reason for being a priest but even for being at all—in relation to the Eucharist. In the Eucharist, God exists in His entirety: it makes no difference that it is not apparent to us except by faith, just as the world around us is no less real whether our eyes are open or closed. May the merciful God in His goodness continually convert my heart and the hearts of all men toward Him in the Eucharist so that one day we may feast upon the sight of His face in blessed eternity. Please remember me in your prayers.

Father Sebastian has been a canon of Saint Michael's Norbertine Abbey in Orange County, California, for ten years. After five years of study at the Angelicum in Rome, he is currently assigned to teach philosophy to seminarians at the abbey and to high school students at the abbey preparatory school. On Sundays he celebrates Mass at Saint Mary's in Fullerton.

Chapter 18

To Chaos and Back Again

Anne Brown Agni

God blessed me with loving parents who lived their faith and sacrificed mightily to give me an idyllic childhood in the Midwest. The oldest of ten, I attended Catholic schools, romped in the woods behind our cozy house, and ran along the shores of Lake Michigan almost every day. My passions for books, thunderstorms, and animals of all sorts were encouraged, though my parents sometimes grew alarmed at the intensity I brought to everything I did.

Our faith sustained and surrounded our lives. Family traditions were scrupulously followed: the Christmas tree, for example, always went up on Christmas Eve. Celebrated with reverence and excitement, the sacraments marked defining moments of my childish faith. When I was confirmed, I wrote a melodramatic "letter to myself in the future" inside the cover of the white leather Bible my parents gave me, cascading flowery declarations of my love for God.

Because of my family's deep faith, we were very active in the pro-life movement. From the day we children could hold a sign, they brought us to every picketing, prayer group, rally, and protest we could attend. These experiences, and the fact that my parents had different ethnic backgrounds, blended into two core beliefs: that we are all God's children, no matter what race or creed, and that all life is infinitely precious. These foundational beliefs never wavered, staying with me through the dark times, and ultimately bringing me back to the Lord.

The dark times began during my freshman year of high school, with an announcement: my father, who had commuted for years, had taken a new job on the East Coast. He would begin work there almost immediately, while my mother, who was in the midst of a difficult pregnancy, would stay behind to pack and sell the house.

I had never had many friends. Yet, friendless or not, I was devastated by the idea of moving. What about my cats? What about Lake Michigan? Midwestern thunderstorms? My blue-painted room? All of them had to be left behind. Despite any shortcomings in my Midwest life, I flew into a selfish rage. Until that moment, I had asked God to guide my passionate nature to seek what was good and true. Now that same intense nature led me to embrace what was evil and false.

I threw myself into seeking new friendships with unsavory people. Temper tantrums at home progressed into sneaking around. My poor parents, understandably focused on the forthcoming move and the dangerous pregnancy, were no match for my lies and manipulation.

The move came at last. We had to live in a hotel room for two months, and we all got whooping cough. I rang up huge long-distance bills to those dubious new "friends" back "home". When my baby brother was born, I was not smitten with sisterly love, as I always had been before. Filled with angst, I wanted to make my parents suffer for what they had done to me. Our old intimacy became my most piercing weapon; their once-sweet, introspective daughter knew and exploited their every weakness.

The deadening of my conscience took time. Somehow, during my years of self-destructive behavior, I never turned to alcohol or drugs. But after growing up with the same classmates year after year in a little parochial school, I was now bewildered in the sprawling, ugly, metropolitan public high school. Cowed and miserable, I lost my self-assurance and tagged along with a wayward crowd, who took me in as if delighted to sully the character of a naïve Catholic girl. Passively I let the debauchery flow over me.

A few deliberate lies at home, and I was able to attend parties thrown by drug dealers. One night, a strange man pushed me into an empty room and assaulted me. Luckily, he was too intoxicated to do much damage, but afterward I stumbled down the street to a pay phone and called my mother.

Thinking I was at a friend's house, she asked what was wrong. Another lie came out of my mouth: "I'm fine, Mommy. Just wanted to check in. I'm fine."

From that moment on, my life became a living lie. A few weeks later, I sneaked out to a hotel room to meet Sergio, a much older man. We had become pen pals when I participated in a school-initiated "Dear Soldier" campaign. When he returned from the first Gulf War, he told me he loved me. Once again, I found myself frozen and passive beneath a strong man. But this time he was not a stranger, and it was much harder not to blame myself. Because of this, I decided the next day to love and marry him. I was barely fifteen.

The next few months, Sergio drove down often from his base. My parents knew I was drifting farther and farther away but were at a loss to understand why. Only after he moved to our town did they realize what had happened. They threatened him with prosecution, and he hastily moved back to his family on the West Coast. I tried to kill myself.

No words could ever capture the consuming hate and despair that defined my life during that time nor the sorrow and anxiety of my parents and the unconditional love they showed for me. They had to virtually drag me to Mass. They brought me to confession, but I told the priest I had nothing to say. They compelled me to see a therapist, and I told him it was my parents who needed help. If they would just let me be with Sergio, I would have no problems. Why couldn't everyone see this?

I was diagnosed with bipolar disorder. My mental and physical health suffered. Incessant migraines peppered the creeping weeks, and my menstrual cycles all but ceased. I would punch walls, take too much cold medication. My dreams were full of demonic faces and dark suggestions. I felt crazed and reeling, out of control.

Dangerous men continued to be attracted to me, usually when I was at work at a restaurant. One began stalking me, and when he turned up outside a graduation party for a family friend, I was shocked to see my mother confronting him. As he drove away like a chastised dog, my mother explained in a shaking voice that she had been praying intensely for me when the Blessed Mother told her I was in danger. Secretly scared, I outwardly scoffed at the idea. God had abandoned me, I believed, and I was furious at Him for doing so.

My anger smoldered far below layers of rationalization. If there was a God at all, He had checked out after creating this big mess called the universe, earth, humans, me. Maybe he had laid down some guidelines a while back, but clearly they were way out of reach, just as He was out of touch with the nitty-gritty of my life. Mesmerized by ritual and dogma as a child, I had fallen victim to an elaborate hoax, created to thwart my desires, my will. No more! I would fight for freedom, for love!

Having so decided, and still clinging to hope for an eventual reunion with the supposed love of my life, I muddled through torturous days that became weeks and months. Halfway through my junior year, I began to casually date the senior class valedictorian, but he dumped me on Valentine's Day. When tryouts began for the spring play, I began to notice a slender, handsome, funny senior who was auditioning for the first time. We knew each other from the debate team, but now we were together every day. Even though I initially told him that someday I had to be with another man, we became inseparable.

Besides being gifted, charming, and kind, my new friend, Rao Agni, was South Asian and nominally Hindu. When I asked my mother if she minded our dating, she said, "Of course not. You just can never marry him, because he is not Catholic."

Certain our relationship was doomed, I smiled sadly and assured her that would never happen. But when Rao left to begin college at an Ivy League school in the fall, we were still close.

Just after Rao left, Sergio returned, and I met with him. Somehow, I was saved from myself; wrong as it was for me to meet him at all, I did manage to leave without giving in to his demands. If I had fallen under his spell again, Rao would surely have lost all patience with me, and it was his love for me that was keeping me from complete self-destruction.

Determined to follow Rao, I applied early to his college, and to my parents' horror, I was accepted. Soberly, they warned me that I would get no financial support. I went anyway, working unreasonable hours at a variety of jobs to pay tuition. Once again, I sought to bend reality to conform with my will, whatever the cost.

Though my academic accomplishments remained excellent through all the turmoil, selfishness and deception still defined my character. Far from my family, I abandoned the sacraments entirely. I even turned on Rao, treating him to the same obnoxious displays my parents had endured. He remained calm and gentle, somehow loving me despite my capriciousness. But my restlessness seemed limitless. Consumed by emotions I could not control, I lashed out with little provocation.

Following Rao's lead, I began writing conservative political columns in the campus paper. Our notoriety grew, and we found ourselves reviled and isolated. Working long hours in the cafeteria furthered our disdain for spoiled classmates. My grades remained high, but Rao struggled mightily to find his way toward medical school. Though we clung to each other for solace, our relationship was stormy. We became engaged but found no true peace or joy in each other. Neither of us could understand why life seemed so hard.

One night, while I was waiting in line in a campus snack bar at closing time, a drunken football player groped me clumsily, and a rush of suppressed memories overwhelmed me. When I told Rao what had happened, he urged me to press charges through the university disciplinary system. Reluctantly, I did so, only to have the player acquitted at the university hearing. This reduced me to a new emotional low, and again I reached for too many pills.

Exhausted with life, Rao tried to begin preparing for law school, but his parents lost all patience and demanded that he become a doctor instead. Exasperated, he decided to drop out of school entirely and enlist in the Marine Corps as soon as possible. To do so, he said, would be to participate in something pure, something larger than himself, something entirely different from everything college had turned out to be.

Then I learned I was pregnant.

Having to tell my parents terrified me. My mother, who was expecting her ninth, realized I was due virtually the same day she was. Rather than indulge in well-deserved recriminations, my parents again spoke with love and (worriedly) blessed my decision to get married as soon as possible. A month later, Rao and I were married, first in a Hindu ceremony, and then during a Catholic Mass.

To prepare for supporting his new family, Rao decided to finish school. Our daughter arrived the day after Christmas in my junior year, and we were back in class when she was three weeks old. Oblivious to classmates' stares, I surreptitiously nursed her as I took notes. In the privacy of our little apartment off campus, I struggled with postpartum depression.

Halfway through my senior year, while my husband was applying to law schools, I learned I was pregnant again. Sick and worn, I plowed through a massive senior thesis, my pride goading me to prove that I had not missed a beat. Though I managed to graduate on time and with high honors, my inner life remained burdensome, and my nightmares continued.

Accepted to several excellent law schools, Rao decided to attend a Catholic school in the Midwest, partly because I wanted to return to that region and partly because he was tired of the vapid Ivy League lifestyle.

As yet, neither of us had seriously considered faith as something we needed ourselves. Indeed, we avoided discussing our different faith traditions. After all, we were smart, hard-working scholars. We had endured difficult times, not perfectly, but on our own. God was for the weak, the slow, the superstitious.

Nevertheless, out of a vague sense of obligation, I arranged for our children to be baptized and still occasionally attended Mass. With some vigor, I convinced my husband to be open to life with me, though I had no well-articulated reasons for doing so. The certainty that children in the womb deserve legal protection affirmed my position that the reproductive process should not be artificially curtailed. In His great wisdom, God repeatedly used this belief as an avenue of grace.

Our second daughter was born a couple weeks after my husband began law classes at his new school. The contrast of our law school friends to the people we had known as undergrads was startling: even though they were poor and their futures uncertain, they seemed radiantly happy. Puzzled, we watched as their marriages blossomed and their babies were welcomed with open arms. Conversations inevitably emphasized their excitement with their faith, their true devotion to God. Knowing how intelligent and driven these students were, we could no longer dismiss faith in God out of hand. I even began to attend a weekly Rosary group of young mothers. But too many obstacles were still in our way to open ourselves to genuine exploration.

For if there was indeed an infinite and loving Creator who ordered the universe with His immutable natural law, we had run afoul of that law for years. We would have to own up to our actions as very wrong, and that would still not be enough: we would have to change our actions to conform to His law.

Additionally, after a lifetime of being excluded and teased for not being Christian, Rao was obdurate that he would never consider the Christian faith. To do so would be an intolerable rejection of his cultural heritage.

Finally in his element, my husband excelled in every area of his law school career. He graded onto law review, worked for a professor, and received offers of employment from top law firms. During his second year, he earned a federal clerkship. By then, I was pregnant with our third daughter and sicker than in my previous pregnancies. Ever quiet and supportive, Rao devoted himself to all his responsibilities. By the time his second year drew to a close, I was feeling better, and he was earning his best grades yet.

The spring of his second year, my husband took a class from a well-known Catholic professor, Professor A, who taught him about the idea of natural law. Hearing for the first time that faith and reason can coexist, he began to immerse himself in books and conversations about the Catholic faith. Intellectually, we became excited at the glorious order of creation and the perfect consistency of opinion found in the *Catechism of the Catholic Church*. Pope John Paul II's "Letter to Families" infused us with admiration for the mystical meaning behind the family, and many of my childhood teachings became attractive once again. Truth, no longer threatening and oppressive, beckoned to our minds and hearts.

On a spring night, at a campus shrine to the Blessed Mother, I murmured a kind of skeptic's prayer: *I don't know if you are there, Lord, but if you are, I think I need your help.* Suddenly, my vision blurred, and my heart was filled with a peace and love so exquisite and foreign that I knew I had an answer. The experience led to several intimate conversations between Rao and me. We acknowledged all the wrongs we had committed in the past, forgave each other, and promised to do better in the future. We started to attend Mass as a family.

As summer began, we walked as a family one glorious day to check Rao's final grades. Splashed in sunlight, the campus had never looked so beautiful. Our daughters rambled about, sniffing at flowers and chattering, while I waddled under the weight of their new little sister. After confirming the perfect grades, we walked as a family to the Marian shrine, knelt, and prayed together as a family for the first time. As we turned home, I whispered, "What did you pray for?" to my husband.

His voice low and serious, Rao replied, "I asked God to take the talents He gave me and use them for His purposes."

Nodding happily, I took his hand. Obviously, I thought, God would want us to live in our newly purchased Victorian home, which we would fill with babies. Rao would do ethical, high-quality work at his firm after his clerkship ended, and I would devote myself to pro-life charity work while raising our little ones in the faith. We would be universally admired as a beautiful, giving family, and in due time, my husband would be baptized Catholic. God had spoken.

Or perhaps God had listened.

A few days later, we received a strange phone call from the law school. A Professor X was accusing my husband of academic dishonesty, of violating the school honor code. My husband was horrified, sickened by the very idea. Indignant and shocked, I knew there was just a misunderstanding. I had seen every aspect of Rao's work on his paper for that class. I knew beyond any possibility of an alternative that it was all his own work. There was no further explanation from the school, no timetable given as to when we would know what was happening. We were lost.

In an effort to cheer my husband up, I made a batch of his favorite Rice Krispies Treats. After turning off the stove and smoothing out the mixture in a pan, I watched in absolute disbelief as our twenty-one-month-old daughter fell forward onto the stove from her stepstool. Her arms literally melted from the lingering heat.

The next few hours passed in a blur of screams and an anguish I had never imagined. I hovered by her side as she was rushed to a burn unit two hours away; Rao stayed behind with our three-year-old to finish up some of the firm's office work before joining me.

There was no sleep for me that night. I stared out the window as thunderstorms raged hour after hour, taking no delight in the display as I once had. My daughter lay scarred and sedated in a metal crib behind me. Her pain wracked my soul. I hated myself so much for letting this happen to her. I turned to God in utter dismay: *Why, God? Hadn't you heard? Weren't you listening? We were going to be your humble servants. And this is what we get? This is our reward?*

Our daughter was soon released to our care so she would not need to endure an extended stay in the burn unit, but this meant I had to give her twice-daily bandage changes and drive her back for her appointments and surgeries. Her bandage changes were so painful that she began shaking when she saw me take out the fresh strips.

"Please no, Mommy, please no", she would say in her baby voice. But after another time of scraping her wounds until they bled and tying new bandages on, she always thanked me as I cried for her.

Through all this, my husband was a ghost. Letters began to arrive from the law school, letters changing A's to F's, letters making accusations with no invitation for him to defend himself. Essentially, Professor X believed the paper was "too good" for him to have written it himself, and with this conclusion, he failed Rao and ordered a search for the "real" author. I tried to assure Rao that when no other author was found, all would be cleared up, his record restored. He just nodded listlessly and faded away.

The weeks of that miserable summer passed somehow, and finally, at wits' end, I spoke to the priest at the parish we had begun to attend. He sprang into action and had a dear friend of his call us. The friend happened to be the very Professor A who had inspired my husband about natural law and the Catholic faith. From that night onward, he became our advocate. Without him, we surely would have lost even more than we were about to lose.

Of course, the lengthy search for a "real" author turned up nothing. But the accusing professor pressed forward with a hearing, alleging incorrect formatting for some of the citations. I attended the hearing with our newborn daughter in my arms. Despite our best efforts to explain the errors in the inexorable chain of events, after a hearing that lasted until dawn, the panel came back with a "guilty" finding for one charge. They suspended Rao for a semester.

Until the finding was made official, Rao still had to attend classes. His federal clerkship was revoked. The law firm he worked for grew distant. Several classmates sneered, even as our friends began an insistent letter-writing campaign in his defense. Finally, official word came down: my husband's law school career, once so brilliant and successful, was in ruins.

The devastation wrought by this travesty of justice is indescribable. Our despair was palpable. But Rao made a firm decision. He would enlist as a reservist in the Marine Corps before he returned to finish his final year. Though disillusioned, he still sought something clean, ideal. He chose to see the situation as an opportunity, a chance to be part of a brotherhood—and a way to finish law school on his own terms.

Powerless to deny him anything at this point, I let him go and moved back in with my family while he was gone. After years of our being together constantly, my husband disappeared into the fog of boot camp, while I wrestled with the emotional fallout of our ordeal. The wounds of humiliation, false accusation, and anger at fate seared the core of my being during all those long weeks of separation. As always, my parents' love sustained me. They encouraged me to pray in front of the Blessed Sacrament every day, and I began to attend daily Mass. While this opened me up to the graces necessary to endure, I still had no answers.

Rao faced his dark night of the soul alone. His persecutors—the vindictive Professor X, the panel, and the administrators—were all purportedly "good Catholics". How could he submit to a God who allowed such injustice to go unpunished? How could he live the rest of his life under the cloud they had unfairly given him?

But one Sunday, as he attended Mass at the base chapel, he both felt and understood the Real Presence. As the priest elevated the Host at the consecration, Rao could no longer deny his faith, a faith meant for all nations, through all of history. He wrote a rare letter to me, asking me to arrange for his baptism when he came home on leave.

When we met again on the parade ground on graduation day, we were not the young adults we had been before. A week later, as he received Communion for the first time, after his baptism in his formal Marine uniform, the priest beckoned me to the altar to receive Our Lord at the same time. In that moment, I felt we were married anew, in the light of Christ.

If only this were the end of our story, it would be a more cheerful tale. But the truth of every conversion is that it continues, day by day, until we rest in Jesus at the end of our earthly life. Though we were finally united in an understanding for and appreciation of the one Truth, we still had to live out the life God asked us to live for Him.

The immediate challenge was my husband's conviction that he should serve in the Marine Corps as an active duty attorney, not as a reservist. While he completed his reservist training, he applied to attend officer candidate school that very summer. His application would never have been accepted without the efforts of Professor A, who had tried so hard to save us at the honor code hearing. By vouching for my husband's good character, he gave him the opportunity to prove his mettle as an officer candidate.

Only three weeks into the grueling summer, Rao fractured his ankle. Normally, he would have been dropped for medical reasons, but he begged to stay, and with nothing but a brace, he managed to survive the summer, unlike almost 50 percent of his class. Professor A attended his commissioning ceremony and helped pin on the gold bars of a second lieutenant.

An even greater challenge awaited us back at the law school. Most of our friends had left after what should also have been Rao's graduation. What we perceived as barely veiled hostility or grudging acceptance of our presence wore us down, and my husband seemed crushed under the weight of feelings he had tried to avoid. Our newborn faith sometimes seemed a curse to him, and I feared he would succumb to this festering depression. Only the many prayers of our loyal family and dear friends sustained us through those months of temptation to despair. During winter break, when we learned I was pregnant again, Rao seemed to find new strength. Despite everything, he managed to graduate with honors.

The next immediate obstacle was admittance to the bar. Before he was even allowed to sit for the exam, Rao had to appear before a committee to defend his integrity, and the entire humiliating exercise took place again as Professor X doggedly tried to prevent him from ever practicing law. God be praised, the accusing professor did not succeed. Rao passed the bar exam in time to return to active duty in the fall.

Along with the stresses of infantry training, financial problems plagued our family life. Our Victorian home was not selling, and carrying the mortgage while supporting a family of six on a second lieutenant's salary was nearly impossible. As our debt piled up with no deliverance in sight, our interactions took on a prickly edge we could not control. Without shared faith and a decent prayer life, our marriage would have been in serious trouble. But we prayed and tried to be patient.

After all of Rao's training was complete, he was awarded a prosecutor's billet, a job he relished. Just before we moved to our first official duty station, I learned I was pregnant with our fifth child. We still had not sold our old house, but we began to feel a bit of optimism: new job, new baby, new home, maybe new friends. Surely things were looking up now!

But after putting the four kids to bed in our new home on base, I felt a wetness, and with utter terror, drew back from the blood I saw. As hours passed in the emergency room, I clutched my Rosary and begged God for mercy, but the baby, our little baby, was gone. I bled for the next three months, once landing back in the emergency room as blood soaked through my clothes. I had thought our experiences had taught me some restraint, some trust, some self-control. But in the anguish of loss, I threw it all away and wallowed in the deepest, blackest depression of my life. The loathing I felt for God was fearsome, and my husband's patience wore thin. Only when I became pregnant again did some of the pain begin to recede. The pain of loss was soon replaced by the pain of daily reality.

This time my morning sickness was unrelenting, and the kids were laid low by a series of stomach viruses. Our house still lingered on the market, and our finances were a puzzle impossible to solve. I never felt at home on base and never found a true friend the entire time I lived there. My husband's best friend was killed in Iraq, and he mourned silently for months. When my son was born, the staff at the hospital seemed callous and cold, leaving me feeling worthless and sad. And my husband's all-consuming job was keeping us apart until I wondered if I could stay sane.

Then, two weeks after the birth, my husband told me he would be deploying to Iraq soon and would be gone for seven months.

Yet again, my tenuous faith in a loving God was exposed. For weeks, I stormed and raged and shook my fists at the sky. *Still not enough? We have not yet suffered enough? This is what comes from trying to do Your will?*

Just before he deployed, our old house finally sold, for less than we had paid for it. Rao had no time off before he walked away from us to go to war. Letting him get on that bus was the hardest thing I had yet endured. If we had not had a few fleeting moments before the children woke that morning, enough time to hold each other and pray together, I would have broken down entirely.

Soon after he left, our four-year-old burned herself with some scalding tea and spent the night in the hospital. She brought influenza home with her, and a week later, after not sleeping for days because of the sick kids, I stopped breathing and was taken to the hospital in an ambulance. The doctor said drily, "We don't often see colds in the ER", and he sent me packing with my prescriptions in a paper bag.

Actually, it was well that these crises happened so quickly, because they kept me from understanding for a little while longer that for all practical purposes, I was a single mother of five children. Once that reality set in, my grip on sanity slipped again. Every moment of every day, I waited for news, shattering news. When I went to sleep alone every night, fear kept me from praying too hard. *What if I asked God's will be done? What if His will was intolerable?*

Thankfully, Rao communicated with me frequently, and he always assured me his base was relatively safe. But the access I had to him turned on me about halfway through his deployment, when I accidentally saw some e-mails intended for his superiors. He was not sitting behind a desk on base. He was "outside the wire" constantly, and this time, he was going on a particularly dangerous mission.

For almost three days, I lived on the edge of human existence. I fully expected to see uniformed Marines at the door at any moment. Was the ultimate sorrow about to be mine? We had lost our old home, the life of our dreams. We had lost a baby, and our daughter's scars would never fully heal. But we had always had each other. *Surely no, but O God, what if yes?*

Then the phone rang, and I heard the familiar echo of a transcontinental connection. He was alive, and he would survive many more operations to step off the bus and into my arms seven months after leaving us to wait in fear.

Some time after his return, I saw a letter in the mailbox, awkwardly addressed to me. Opening it, I realized it was "the Letter", the one all Marines write when they arrive in a war zone, to be given to their loved ones if something happens. Somehow, my husband's letter had been left behind, and someone had simply placed it in the mail when it was found, thinking it was just a regular letter needing to be mailed. Holding my breath, I read what would have been his last words to me. He asked me to love the children and to turn to my faith. He spoke of suffering, and redemption, and salvation. It is not for us to decide what we can and cannot bear. It is for us to trust God and ask Him for the graces necessary to endure. As I folded the paper back into place, I swore I would never forget these lessons, so dearly learned.

Now we knew a happiness that had seemed elusive before. We used his deployment pay to erase our remaining debts. We attended the Marine Corps ball, and our smiles shone in the formal pictures. Grateful for our family's reunion, we found it easier to trust God and His Providence.

Even so, the transition back to family life proceeded slowly. Our oldest, who had been so steady during the deployment, regressed into sulky moods. Our next daughter had frequent night terrors, from which she would not wake, even if we shouted. Our third daughter had to start wearing diapers overnight again. And the boys seemed more rambunctious than ever. Hardest of all was my husband's move back to life stateside. Months of living in mortal danger, seeing the terrible sights of war, left their mark on him. As always, however, he shouldered his burden without complaint.

As for me, my cheerful expectation to find myself pregnant immediately did not come to pass. Eventually, a series of tests showed I had polycystic ovarian syndrome, and just as I began taking medication, I learned I was again pregnant. At the same time, my husband's new billet was changed to an entirely different base, in Washington, D.C., and we had to find housing quickly. After an exhausting, whirlwind house-hunting trip, we signed lease papers for a large home in Fairfax and planned our move.

A couple of weeks before moving day, our new landlord called and regretfully informed us we could not rent the house after all, as their moving plans had changed dramatically. Gently dropping the phone, I laughed a little. *What did God have in store for us this time? Homelessness?* Finding a place to rent months in advance had been near impossible. What would be available just a few days in the future?

Checking a military housing resource, I found a new listing, just posted, for a house half an hour away from D.C. The description stated that a Catholic church stood a few houses away and that the local homeschooling community was excellent. Incredulous, I called and spoke to the owner, a member of the military who had been unable to sell in a cooling market and hoped to find a nice family as renters immediately. We had five children—but so did they. They homeschooled—so did we. Suddenly we had a new lease for a huge, sunny home right next to the commuter train.

And that was only the beginning. Now we could walk to Mass. Our once-lonely family found itself wrapped in the embrace of the local homeschooling network. Our children, who for years had been crammed into dark government-issue houses, suddenly had airy rooms in which to play and sweet-natured friends knocking on the door all the time. With no hesitation, I threw myself into the many clubs and activities offered by the church's homeschool group, amazed at the intelligence and kindness of each new mom I met. My husband found the commute by train bearable, his work stimulating. And a few months after we moved, our new little daughter was born, to everyone's utter delight.

Every day, we wake up and shake off the cobwebby feeling of impending doom. Even now, as we live a life of relative ease and comfort, with no deployment looming, no financial or professional ruin ongoing, no major crisis of any sort, we cannot forget what it was like to live under a cloud of sorrow and uncertainty. Our greatest spiritual challenge now is to offer our worries up to God. The temptation is to keep a low profile, try to strike a bargain: *We don't bother You, You don't bother us, OK, God?*

But after all, God disciplines those He loves. However my story ends, it is, and always was, a love story. God's love has found me at every stage of my life, through my parents' love first, then through my husband's love, and through the intercession of the Blessed Mother. Even as I stormed and screamed, twisting and fighting off His embrace, He waited with infinite patience for my tantrum to subside.

With a bit of perspective, it is easy to see how I lost my way. Ever willful, I indulged in rebellion with all the power of my strongly impulsive nature when I lost my childhood home. This placed me in situations that could have only bad endings. Rather than admit the enormity of my mistakes at the time, I tried to conform the world to the fantasy I needed to believe: if only everyone would respect that I was in love, everything would be fine! Sustaining this illusion took so much effort, I broke under the strain. The Master of Lies was only too happy to offer a web of deceit in which I floundered, even as he assured me it was too late: God could never love me now. Only when I humbled myself enough to admit I had been grievously wrong did I begin to find my way to peace.

God created me with an intense temperament: strong willed, perfectionist, driven, melancholic. This does not excuse my actions, but it does explain how someone who was given so much as a child—a loving, faith-filled home, security, and an extraordinary family—could have fallen so far from God. Now, as an adult who knows what is right and good, I still struggle with the vices I cultivated all those years. But God, in His great mercy, never lets me break beyond repair.

And all that happened before He led me to this place, at this time, where I have the friends I always yearned to have, the support I craved so earnestly, the life I sought in vain. Whatever the future holds, this reprieve is God's gift to me.

Truly, God is the master Sculptor; while the chisel may sometimes hurt abominably, each strike is surgical, inspired by pure Love and joy in His creation.

Anne Brown Agni and her husband, Rao, live with their seven children in northern Virginia, where she homeschools those of school age.

Chapter 19

Three Miracles

Kari Beckman

In His unimaginable mercy, God sent three miracles into my life to rescue me from a life of almost certain misery and bring me into the full light of the Catholic Church. They were such overwhelming demonstrations of His love and power that, once I could recognize them, they moved me through direct experience to deep faith. Of course they were more than I deserved. In my ignorance and foolishness, I did not *deserve* anything. He did it out of pure love, and I can never love Him as much as He deserves in return. I can try only to serve Him always, and love Him, and thank Him with all my heart.

*   *   *

At fifteen, I was floundering in high school. After an unstable childhood troubled by parental divorce and remarriage, chronic poverty, and a painful and frightening medical condition, I had just discovered high school social life and was headed into danger. I decided that as soon as I was sixteen and legally able to do so, I would escape my troubles by dropping out of school. My plan was to move out on my own, get my General Educational Development (GED) certificate, and start college early.

I did not even think of God in those days, but during my sophomore year, His providential hand began moving in my life in an unmistakable way. He led me to the nursing program, where I thought I could earn an associate degree in nursing, then put myself the rest of the way through college by working as a nurse.

In the high school's nursing program, there were three amazing instructors. Each of them managed to get to know every student, not only on a professional level but on a personal level as well. They quickly pegged me as having leadership potential, but they knew that I needed a great deal of formation.

It was Mrs. Aston, the chair of the nursing program, who was the most significant figure in the department. All her students would describe her as a unique model of love, dedication, and determination. Several times she won the outstanding teacher of the year award, and later she became the assistant principal. Somehow she saw a beauty in me that no one had ever noticed before.

She changed my life forever.

*   *   *

As what I thought were my final days in high school approached, I took the required dropout slip to each of my teachers. Each one signed it without any question, until I got to the last. She was one of the nursing instructors, and she said that she was unable to sign the form, that I had to take it to Mrs. Aston, the department chair.

As soon as I stepped into her office, Mrs. Aston told me that she could not sign the dropout form because she and I had to put everything else on hold and write my campaign speech right then. To my amazement, I learned that she had signed me up to run for state president of the Vocational Industry Club of America (VICA), a huge national organization that teaches leadership and job skills to students preparing for careers in trade, industry, technology, and the health field. I was scheduled to deliver the speech just two days later. Thrilled, I set aside my dropout plans, wrote the speech, and to my further astonishment, won the election.

With that new responsibility, and the unaccustomed support and guidance of people who believed in my abilities, I stayed in school. Through the many opportunities and activities VICA provided, I received top-notch administrative training, eventually becoming a national officer, an honor bestowed on only fifteen of some three hundred thousand student members.

As an officer, attending many VIP functions, I met a few celebrities like pro football star Terry Bradshaw and Olympic gold medal gymnast Mary Lou Retton, as well as powerful senators and congressmen. I spoke at conferences with audiences as large as twenty-five thousand people. Once I was privileged to lay a wreath at the Tomb of the Unknown Soldier.

During those two years, Mrs. Aston became my virtual foster mother. On weekends, I would stay at her house, and she would make sure my schoolwork was done. Many times she stayed up late into the night helping me to write papers and finish projects.

Mrs. Aston was a Catholic, and part of being her live-in guest was going to Mass with her on Sundays. We also had many discussions about the sacredness of life and why abortion is evil. Often she would talk to me about my own life too. It was she who first taught me that what is important about any person is not where he comes from but where he is going. She would always tell me how proud she was of me and how much she loved me. The gifts she gave me, of attention, encouragement, respect, and love, are greater than I can ever repay. Her entrance into my life was my first miracle.

*   *   *

Further dramatic changes marked my eighteenth year. First, Mrs. Aston brought me into the Catholic Church and became my godmother. Sadly but not uncommonly for the time, my catechesis could only be described as "Catholic Light". In my Rite of Christian Initiation of Adults (RCIA) class, I learned that as "American Catholics" we were free to use birth control and that we would have to go to confession only if we killed someone. This was a relief to hear, as those were the very aspects of being Catholic that I was most reluctant about.

During that same year, I met, fell in love with, and married my husband. Richard was twenty-nine then, and an ardent agnostic. It was hardly surprising that the adults in my life were alarmed about our decision. Mom was appalled, and Mrs. Aston too was concerned that I was so young. In the end, though, she became highly supportive.

We married under a shadow of fear that we might never be able to have children because of the congenital reproductive anomaly that had caused me physical pain since puberty. I was born with a medical condition called uterine didelphys, which means that I had two complete uteri and cervixes. At the time, my gynecologist said it would be nearly impossible for me to conceive, but he advised us to try for a couple of years before looking into more drastic fertility assistance measures. To our surprise, I became pregnant a mere six months into our marriage.

This pregnancy proved to be an extremely difficult one, and I spent much time in the hospital. The day of my cesarean section, the delivery room looked like a classroom for medical students, as everyone wanted to see my unusual abnormality—a son in one uterus, the other one empty.

While I was thankful for the gift of our son, Joshua, I had little real comprehension of the marvelous blessing God gives us in a child. The memory of my difficult pregnancy, combined with my husband's recent loss of his job and the false assurance that the Catholic Church would approve of our behavior, led us to begin to do what society said was the responsible thing: that is, to contracept.

* * *

My Catholicity played a very small part in my marriage and personal life. We attended Mass when we felt inclined and said prayers only in emergencies. Eventually, however, my husband's work took us to Atlanta, Georgia, where by God's grace, both our lives came to be transformed.

We settled in a small town outside Atlanta, where we knew no one. The first day we attended Mass, we saw a notice in the bulletin announcing a weekend seminar known as "Life in the Eucharist".

Exactly what I need! A seminar where I can meet a bunch of people, I thought. *Surely church is the best place to meet nice people!* What I did not know is that this is where I would meet Jesus Christ in a new and utterly fulfilling way. That meeting was my second miracle.

Full of excitement, I arrived at the seminar early. People were milling about talking when I walked into the hall. Suddenly, silence fell over the crowd and a man in a white cape walked through the center of the crowd, carrying in his raised hands a beautiful gold object shaped like a sunburst. Everyone followed him into the main church. I was confused. What had happened to my seminar? But I simply followed, doing what everyone did. When they walked, I walked; when they knelt, I knelt. They started to sing in a language I had never heard before. Now I was really perplexed. The next thing I knew, my gaze focused on that splendid gold object, now enshrined upon the altar, and silent tears began to stream down my face.

Sure that I must have something in my eye, or that my contacts were irritating them, I went to the restroom, cleaned my lenses, and reinserted them. Then I went back into the Church, and as I knelt down, still weeping, an old woman leaned over and said, "Honey, I think you have the gift of Holy Tears."

The congregation began to sing "He Is Truly Present". As I reflected on the words of the song, the realization stirred in my bewildered mind that I was actually sitting before my Lord. In my sketchy RCIA instruction, I had not been taught that we were supposed to believe literally in the Real Presence. I began to tremble. No matter what I did, the tears kept on falling. (In fact, they continued to fall for two whole days after I went home, even while I slept.)

When the ceremony ended, I could barely speak. My knees felt weak as I walked back to the hall, where the seminar was to begin. There, in a mere two hours, I learned what the Catholic Church really teaches regarding the Eucharist, confession—and contraception.

Three people told their personal stories of conversion at the seminar that day. Their witness marked the start of my new life, because they led me to offer my life entirely to Christ as well. During the weekend, I made my first confession.

I also recognized that when I got home, I would face the intimidating task of talking to my agnostic husband about the Church's teaching on contraception. Driving home, I realized that he would be in the middle of watching his beloved Braves play game 6 of the World Series. How was I to tell him that we had to surrender the planning of our thoroughly planned life to God?

As with everything I do, I just did it. I walked in and said, "Honey, it's really important I talk to you."

"What's up?" Richard said, his eyes still locked on the television screen.

"Honey," I said, "I just learned that if we're going to be Catholic we cannot use birth control."

"Okay", he replied, his attention swiveling back to the game.

I reached over, grabbed the remote control, and shut off the TV. "I know you didn't hear me."

"Yes, I did", he said. "If we're going to be Catholic, we can't use birth control."

I was stunned. My agnostic husband, who wanted to control everything in his life, was going to allow God to plan our family! That this marvel established the presence of the Holy Spirit was confirmed a little more than a year later when Richard, too, joined the Church.

* * *

During the following months our marriage remained open to life for the first time. Yet we saw no results. It seemed that my reproductive abnormality and residual problems from my youth were rearing their ugly heads again. Much pain, and fear of the possibility of my endometriosis returning, led us to a renowned fertility specialist in Atlanta. He recommended surgery to clean up my uterine scar tissue and improve our chances of conceiving.

Of course, I was sleeping in the recovery room following surgery, but Richard was there, and he loves to tell about his exchange with the doctor as he emerged from the operating room. Here is how he tells the story:

"The doctor came into the waiting room with a perplexed look on his face. My immediate reaction was fear that something had gone wrong. When I asked him what was wrong, he said, 'Nothing. Everything is fine.'

"His tone still indicated that something was wrong, so I pressed the question again. This time he said, 'You don't understand. *Everything* is fine. Your wife has only one uterus and one cervix.'

"My incredulity was equaled only by his own, as he had seen the videos, the X-ray films, and past surgery notes, and he had no explanation."

That was my third miracle.

*   *   *

A mere six weeks later, I was pregnant with our second son. When this same doctor confirmed it, he proclaimed, "I'm good, but I'm not *that* good."

Our initial reaction to this obvious miracle was not to accept it as a clear sign that God was validating the purpose of our marriage but to doubt all my previous doctors. At that stage in our faith journey, we still wanted to look for plausible natural explanations for the wonderful things God did for us.

Now we see obvious confirmation of God's helping hand in Zachary's conception in his regular declaration—since the age of two—that he is called to be a priest.

No doubt, God does have something special in mind for him, just as certainly as He does for Joshua, our oldest son, and for the five brothers and sisters who followed after Zachary's birth: Kathryn, John Paul, Siena, Juliana, and Joseph.

* * *

My own subsequent faith journey has been filled with gratitude for a deeper understanding of the truth. God sent an extraordinarily holy priest into my life, who has guided me gently through the ongoing challenge of filling the gaps in my knowledge of doctrine and learning to trust and love the very God who saved me from a life that could have been filled with sorrow.

A growing desire to love as Christ loves us has impelled me over the years to look for more and more ways to express this love in every aspect of my life. Today I am blessed by graces too abundant to count. The way I first came to learn about God's love was entirely experiential, but I recognize that such experiences will always be extraordinary, so I know that students need the basic cognitive foundation that fits with ordinary experience. That is why the founding of a classical homeschool academy—now enjoying its eighth year of success—holds first place among various apostolates I am privileged to be involved in.

The true spiritual birth I experienced through baptism and the people God has placed in my path have brought me a life rich with good examples of patience, fidelity, and sacrifice and have made it possible for me to write this story with an ending so happy that it could have originated only in the love of Christ.

Kari Ann Beckman lives with her husband and eight children in Atlanta, where she directs a classical Catholic satellite academy for homeschoolers and coordinates various other programs to promote the importance of marriage, family, and the dignity of life.

Chapter 20

Looking for Truth in the Wrong Places

Robin Landon Pudewa

Eight years ago I was received into full communion with the Catholic Church. Looking back on the journey that brought me here, I recall Saint Augustine's famous statement that "our hearts are restless until they rest in Thee." My wandering led me through Eastern mysticism, the New Age movement, evangelical Christianity, and Reformed Christianity before Christ, in His astonishing grace, brought me to His Holy Catholic Church.

As the Lord was gradually leading me toward Catholicism, I found it helpful to read of others who had walked the path of conversion. Most were famed converts; many had previous theological training. I am neither famous nor a theologian; I have neither towering intellect nor remarkable natural virtue. I live an ordinary life as a wife and mother of seven. Yet God put a passionate desire for Truth in my heart, and that was my lodestar even as I made wrong turns. It was not until He brought me home to His Church that I knew I had found the fullness of Truth. Now that my restless heart has found peace in the Lord, I can reflect with some objectivity on the dangerous detours I took along my way.

Born in the late 1950s, the elder of two children, I grew up in a loving home in the San Francisco suburbs. My parents were "born-again" Christians, active in their church and in various Christian ministries. My childhood was pleasant. At nine, I "accepted Christ as my Savior", and often I read the Bible on my own. Wholesome summer experiences at a Christian camp in the Santa Cruz Mountains supported my faith. With my family, I also backpacked to a mountain cabin my father had helped build when he was a teen. There, in the solitude of the High Sierras, with God's reality so evident in His creation, an awareness of His transcendence stirred in me, kindling my longing to know Him at a deeper level. Until the age of eleven, I never questioned the faith my parents had passed on to me.

But like most of their generation, my parents were ill equipped to respond to the paradigm shift that shook the 1960s. They trusted the public schools and believed that the faith they taught me at home, along with the support of the Christian community, would see me though the challenges of my teen years. They were mistaken. Like the seed that fell among thorns (Mark 4:5–6), my faith was choked out by the increasingly radical anti-Christian character of secular society.

Unfortunately, subversive secular humanism was rampant in the public schools. From fifth grade through eighth, I was subjected to frequent "values clarification" drills, like the notorious exercise that asked, "If you found yourself in an overcrowded lifeboat, whom would you eliminate?" In junior high I was required to read books and watch films that challenged my traditional Judeo-Christian belief system at its core. One disturbing example etched in my mind is a film version of Shirley Jackson's short story "The Lottery". We watched it in an English class, with no prior warning and no discussion afterward. In the film's final scene, after one of the main characters, a woman, is chosen by lottery, her son is given a rock to throw at his mother. It is then you discover that the person chosen by this yearly lottery is the town's sacrificial victim, to be stoned to death by the rest of the community, including his own family, in order to ensure a good harvest. One can debate the value of reading the story in college (which is when I actually read it), but to show such a film to younger children serves only to shock them and destabilize their beliefs.

By the time I reached high school, I had concluded that Christianity was a flawed and inadequate attempt to address the world's evils. It was not Jesus I condemned but His followers, at least those I had met. To my adolescent eyes, the contrast between the wealth of the society around me and the gospel command to care for the sick and poor exposed the Christians as hypocrites. How could they justify their Cadillacs, Mercedes, and Jaguars while so many people were suffering from poverty? Were not Christians supposed to sell all they had and give it to the poor?

In 1972 I went from my small neighborhood junior high school to one of the large high schools in the Bay Area. The Vietnam War was raging, the counterculture was growing, and a feeling of intoxicating change was everywhere. There were protest marches, free rock concerts, drugs, and a pervasive call to jettison all vestiges of the past, especially its "oppressive" mores. Living next door to Stanford University, I was in the thick of it. At fourteen, I considered myself part of the counterculture, the people who were trying to transform the world with a new culture of "peace, love, and brotherhood". I was ready to go forth and conquer with them.

Unfortunately, I had to get through high school first. This meant navigating a dysfunctional school system where education was mediocre at best. School had always been easy for me, and I became adept at manipulating the system. I saw high school as something to be endured with as little attention as possible and to be escaped as quickly as possible. In order to do so, I knew I had to meet certain requirements and complete a designated number of credits. By taking extra classes after school and in the evenings, I could graduate by the time I was sixteen and get on with real life. But even as I plugged away at graduation requirements I considered irrelevant, I yearned for answers to my own burning questions. Seeking direction but with no real guide, I tried to educate myself, haunting the library, local bookstores, and adult education classes; I went to museums, attended lectures, and read lots of books. Because my Christian roots had been dislocated, I was easily sucked into alternate views of life and reality.

By the time I hit my sophomore year in high school, the endless routine of parties, hanging out, and superficial conversations was growing tiresome. One acquaintance seemed to transcend this petty culture. The adopted daughter of a wealthy family who entertained the rich and famous, she seemed quite extraordinary. She dressed simply and radiated a tranquility I found refreshing and attractive. She looked so much like Caroline Kennedy that the rest of us used to speculate that she might actually be an illegitimate relative. She showed me a book called *An Autobiography of a Yogi* by Paramahansa Yogananda and told me she wanted to become a Self-Realization Fellowship nun after high school. I read it hungrily. It was my first significant exposure to Eastern mysticism, and I was hooked.

When I compared Yogananda's spiritual beliefs and experiences with what I understood of Christianity, his Eastern mysticism seemed deep, rich, and new; Christianity appeared superficial, materialistic, and trite. Besides, I thought Yogananda did not reject Jesus; he seemed to have great respect for Him. In retrospect, I see that he did not acknowledge Jesus as God's only begotten Son, the unique incarnation of God. Rather, he lauded Him as a channel of cosmic wisdom, one in a long line of avatars, adepts, and yogis who had achieved "Christ Consciousness" through the process of self-mastery. Unfortunately, my basic Christian upbringing had not prepared me to counter that claim. Already annoyed by what I considered superficial observance of Christianity, and wrenched with longing for deeper spiritual experiences and greater understanding of reality, I concluded that what I had learned in the past was only a dim part of the picture. There must exist a vast realm of spirituality of which I had been deprived. In his book *The Divine Romance*, Yogananda describes succinctly the alternate view of Jesus that he and many other Eastern and New Age devotees hold:

> Jesus the son of man lifted himself to the state of being a son of God. That is, he rose above the ordinary human consciousness and entered the cosmic Christ Consciousness, the pure reflection of God present in all creation. When St. John said that "as many as received him, to them gave he power to become the sons of God", he meant that anyone who could receive that Christ Consciousness, who could increase the capacity of his consciousness to hold that infinite ocean of truth, would become, as did Jesus, a son of God—one with the Father.[1]

Yogananda's writings led me to reject the Christianity of my childhood for what I saw as a more enlightened form of "Christianity".

[1] Paramahansa Yogananda, *The Divine Romance* (Los Angeles, Calif.: Self-Realization Fellowship, 1986), 335–36.

Around the same time that I read Yogananda's book, I also read a book condemning the effects of eating meat. I decided to adopt an organic vegetarian diet. Persuaded that our Judeo-Christian heritage was responsible for the pollution, rampant materialism, and consumerism that surrounded us, I was intrigued by the idea of living off the land in an intentional community and sought out books on homesteading, organic gardening, herbs, and natural healing.

Once I turned sixteen, I had free use of our old family station wagon. At that time, my dad was frequently traveling for his company. My mom, an only child, was preoccupied with caring for my grandmother, who had developed dementia after suffering many small strokes. Out of respect for her, Mother did not reveal the seriousness of the situation to my brother and me. Rather than asking our help with what must have been an overwhelming burden, she dealt with her mother's condition by herself. Thus, for all practical purposes, I was free to come and go as I pleased. Quite content with my new freedom, I cut school to go to museums, bookstores, or libraries or simply to soak in the world of nature, hiking in the Redwoods, camping, or hanging out at the beach.

In my Stanford University neighborhood, I was drawn to the many people in their late teens and twenties who shared my dissatisfaction with the social status quo. With them I could throw around my ideas and not meet a blank stare. Some were experimenting with communal households, developing community gardens, starting natural food cooperatives, going to protest rallies, getting involved in grassroots politics, or practicing different forms of spirituality. To me they seemed to be people making a difference, offering solutions to the problems I saw around me. They became my role models.

At sixteen, I graduated from high school. I wanted to head off to Berkeley but learned to my chagrin that, although I had completed all of the high school graduation requirements, I lacked some classes needed for acceptance into the University of California system. So the following fall I enrolled in a community college. Unlike the high school atmosphere, I found the college environment exciting. Many people shared my point of view, and I could take classes that interested me. My fascination with Eastern spirituality continued to grow, and in my spare time I read and studied the beliefs of different religions, taught myself astrology, and took classes in Eastern healing techniques. My beliefs had so shifted that I saw the "law of reincarnation" as on a par with the law of gravity: an absolute law upon which the entire structure of things depended.

As I entered more completely into the countercultural lifestyle, however, some cracks in its system started to become apparent. All was not peace, light, and goodness. There was a dark side to this alternative spirituality and the lifestyle that accompanied it. Absolute Truth was replaced by relative truth, based on the needs and desires of each person. In this world view sin was no longer part of the equation, so there was no real judgment or Hell. Bad choices produced bad karma; good choices brought good karma. Each individual soul had its own karma to balance. In practice, this meant that sex outside of marriage was perfectly acceptable if it was done with "love" and mutual consent. Drugs could be positive if used to heighten "spiritual awareness" or foster love and friendship.

This relativism created division in our lives. We talked about expanding our consciousness and getting closer to God, even as we fell into destructive behavior patterns. While I avoided the worst excesses of recreational drug use, I saw

its effect on many lives around me. Similar self-delusion
was employed to justify the "sexual revolution". It seemed
progressive not to be "uptight" about sexuality. But in reality, God created our sexuality as a means of expressing committed, fruitful, faithful love, within the security of marriage.
By violating the very safeguard God established for our protection, many people were hurt. My own embrace of this
tempting lie made me one of its victims.

When I turned eighteen and had been in college for two
years, I decided to take time off to travel before transfer-
ring to a university. With my college weaving class I took
a summer trip to the Hopi and Navajo Indian reservations
to study their weaving and dyeing techniques. From there I
went on with two friends to the "Rainbow Gathering" in
New Mexico. This quintessential hippie gathering attracted
New Agers from an eclectic assortment of spiritual persua-
sions who formed a temporary "intentional community"
on national forest land. Such Rainbow Gatherings still go
on; some have drawn upwards of thirty thousand people.
At the time, I thought it was a utopian experience.

It was there that I met Rick. After the gathering, he and
I joined with several other friends to travel across the country. One had a car, so we piled in and set off in search of
adventure. In Alabama, we were ordered out of a county
when the sheriff thought the herbs hanging from the rear-
view mirror were marijuana. In another state we attracted
unfriendly attention by swimming in a lovely warm rural
lake, which the sheriff informed us was warm because it
had cooled the nuclear reactor at the local power plant.
Eventually we made our way to New England.

By fall our travel companions went on to other adventures, while Rick and I stopped off in Vermont. With another
couple and their two-year-old child, we moved into a

turn-of-the-century farmhouse with an outhouse and only wood stoves for heat. Rick and I got jobs at a local ski resort. In the spring, however, I discovered I was pregnant. Facing life-altering decisions, I knew with crystal clarity that abortion was not an option. I also knew that I did not want to marry Rick, and I did not want to stay in New England. This meant a future of single parenthood.

Trying to figure out what to do, I headed back west and went with friends to Oregon for the next Rainbow Gathering. There I encountered my old friend Diane, then known as "Flying Cloud". We decided to find a community where we could stay until I had my baby. We spent a few weeks in a commune near Ashland, Oregon, and then moved on to another in northern California. This commune had been started by folks from San Francisco, who offered us a vacant house where we could live. At first the situation seemed ideal. But some of the communards were quite strange. One older man, a Berkeley radical who had trained in revolutionary tactics in Cuba, made me uneasy by displaying a particular attraction to me. Then, one night, in a profoundly frightening experience, I ate some cookies from the community kitchen, unaware that a large quantity of THC (the active ingredient in marijuana) had been added to "spice them up". The effect on my body was dramatic and alarming. The THC brought on terrifying hallucinations. I started having contractions, which made me fear that I would lose my baby. In the midst of all this, I had to fight off the advances of Mr. Berkeley Radical, who had decided to visit me in the middle of the night. By the time the THC finally passed through my system, I knew that I must make a major change in my life.

The night had been harrowing for my friend Diane too. We decided to consult the *I-Ching* for advice. The *I-Ching* is an ancient Chinese tool for divining the future. The reading we cast talked about "crossing the great waters". Based on this "insight" and some discussion, we decided to move to Hawaii.

Before our move, I visited my parents. During that visit, two events occurred that significantly affected my future. First, I encountered Terence, with whom I had begun a friendship several years earlier at an ecumenical conference on world hunger. I appreciated his gentle spirit, as well as his commitment to the principles he believed in, and we had had many pleasant times together. Terence had been raised in a nominally Catholic home, but his family lapsed with the changes that came after Vatican II. He did, however, come away from his upbringing with a love of Franciscan spirituality, which he combined with a love of Buddhism. Although he was part of the counterculture, he had never allowed himself to get involved in either drugs or casual sexuality. Compared to most men in the world where I had spent the last few years, he seemed a paragon of virtue. Evidently he had cared deeply for me when we first knew one another and had continued to do so even though we had not seen each other for so long. Seeing him again sparked an answering interest in me. We spent a lot of time together, and at last he decided that after setting some necessary matters in order, he would join me in Hawaii.

The second significant event during my visit home was running into my old friend Callie, whose spirituality had so impressed me in high school. As we caught up on each other's lives, I asked whether she was still planning to become a Self-Realization Fellowship nun.

"No", she said. She had found something even better. Eagerly, she told me about the Summit Lighthouse, which published the teachings of the "ascended masters", "the mystics and sages of East and West who had graduated from earth's schoolroom and attained union with God."[2]

Once when visiting Mount Shasta, I had met a distinguished elderly woman who told me about the "ascended masters" and showed me pictures of them. That memory came back to me now and, combined with my respect for my friend, aroused a desire to learn more. Callie told me as much as she could about the group's spirituality in our short time together. The technique that struck me most was called the "science of the spoken word" or "decreeing", through which we could "transmute" our past karma and effect real change in the world around us. We had only a few hours together, but what Callie said planted a seed of interest in me that would take root in Hawaii.

Diane and I flew to Kailua-Kona in Hawaii. From there we hitchhiked toward the Kona coast. A friendly hippie couple picked us up, and as we traveled, I asked whether they knew any midwives on the island, because I had decided to have a home birth. They did not, they said, but they knew another pregnant woman who might. We gratefully accepted when they offered to take us to her home.

We were dropped off at the bottom of a long dirt driveway, and they pointed toward a house at the top of a hill. As we approached the house, I heard some unusual chanting. I had only heard one short demonstration by my friend Callie, but I had an intuitive sense that what I was hearing was the same thing. Turning to Diane, I said, "Those people are decreeing."

We were welcomed to the house by a warm, radiant, pregnant woman named Bernadette and her husband, Paul.

---

[2] Summit Lighthouse, "Teachings of the Ascended Masters", Summit Lighthouse official Web site, http://www.tsl.org/AboutUs/.

The house was humble but exceptionally clean and impressively peaceful. On the walls hung pictures of various ascended masters. When I told them about Callie and my interest in the Summit Lighthouse, they said they were sure some cosmic destiny had brought us together. They became my mentors. Bernadette's family had been involved in the organization for years. Her parents and some of her siblings were also active members. She was a good teacher. Feeling that I had finally found a spiritual home, I too became a member of the Summit Lighthouse's Keepers of the Flame Fraternity.

The Summit Lighthouse was founded in 1958 by Mark L. Prophet (his real name). He was later joined in his mission by his wife, Elizabeth Clare Prophet. These two said they were messengers in the tradition of the ancient prophets whose mission was to deliver the teachings of the ascended masters. On a regular basis, Mark and later Elizabeth Clare Prophet channeled messages—called "dictations"—from these masters directly to their listeners. Messages were recorded and later published in written form as *The Pearls of Wisdom*. By the time I joined the organization in 1978, Mark Prophet had died, and Elizabeth Clare Prophet was at the helm. She channeled a pantheon of well-known "masters", including Gautama Buddha, El Morya, Saint Germain, Kuthumi, Jesus, Mary, the Archangel Michael, and others not so well known outside theosophical circles, like Sanat Kumara. For those who sought a deeper relationship with the ascended masters, Elizabeth Claire Prophet started a formal church in 1974, calling it the Church Universal and Triumphant (CUT). Quotes from the church's Web site describe its syncretist beliefs and practices:

> Today many people are looking for the essential truths that are at the core of all of the world's major religions. They

ask, "Is there a church for the age of Aquarius that unites the world's religions?"

The answer is "Yes!" Church Universal and Triumphant is that church. Sponsored by the ascended masters Jesus Christ and Gautama Buddha, the church embodies principles, practices and rituals that are based on the essential truths found at the heart of all faiths. . . .

It is a church where Eastern and Western spirituality converge. The mystical paths of Hinduism, Buddhism, Judaism, Christianity, Zoroastrianism, Taoism and Confucianism are infused with new revelations from the ascended masters. Devotees combine these traditions in the practice of the Science of the Spoken Word by intoning the AUM [the sacred syllable of creation], praying the Our Father, giving devotions to the Divine Mother and joining in prayers for world conditions.[3]

According to CUT theology, the goal of life is "the path of the ascension":

It is the goal of life. But there are a number of tests and a number of challenges that you must meet before you can say you are actually on the path of the overcomer. Those who are on that path are daily pursuing the balancing of their karma and the fulfilling of their dharma—the duty to be oneself, to fulfill one's reason for being.

The ascension ritual, whereby the soul reunites with the Spirit of the living God, the I AM Presence, is through the acceleration by the sacred fire at the natural conclusion of one's final lifetime on earth. It is the process whereby the soul, having balanced her karma and fulfilled her divine plan, merges first with the Christ consciousness and then with the living Presence of the I AM THAT I AM. Once the

[3] Summit Lighthouse, "Church Universal and Triumphant", ibid., http://www.tsl.org/AboutUs/TheMysticalPath.asp.

ascension has taken place, the soul—the corruptible aspect
of being—becomes the incorruptible one, a permanent atom
in the body of God, free from the round of karma and
rebirth.[4]

My searching soul felt that I had found a church that combined the best of Eastern and Western spirituality and that
I was now back on track in my search for Truth. Also, unlike
the amorphous New Age spirituality of which I had been
a part, with its lack of moral absolutes, Summit Lighthouse
was morally quite conservative. Sex outside marriage was
considered wrong, abortion was condemned, drugs and alcohol were forbidden. After my experiences over the past several years, I could see the value and importance of living a
moral life. However, the place where one would normally
think to look for a strong moral ethos, traditional Christianity in its different forms, was not even a blip on the
radar screen of my mind. That was for "young souls", not
for "evolved" truth seekers like me.

Diane and I found a house to rent on a hui (a collec-
tively held piece of property where everyone had his own
house). Very soon after that, when I was six months pregnant, I developed appendicitis. This necessitated my being
rushed to the hospital to have my appendix removed. My
mom came over to help, and when Terence heard what
had happened, he dropped everything and came immediately. My pregnancy slowed my recovery, but I was well in
time for my daughter's birth. Terence and I were now living together, but chastely. Our love grew, and we came to
the conclusion that we wanted to marry after the birth. On
New Year's Eve day, when my daughter was three weeks

[4] Summit Lighthouse, "The Path of the Ascension", ibid., http:
//www.tsl.org/AboutUs/PathOfTheAscension.asp.

old, Terence and I were married. My family flew in, we found a local minister, and on the rocks overlooking the ocean, we exchanged vows we wrote ourselves. I felt blessed to have met a wonderful man who was enthusiastic about raising my daughter as his own. After the wedding festivities were over, we headed back home.

Bernadette and Paul, our friends and mentors, had their baby too but lost their home. We invited them to live with us, and as a result I was further immersed in CUT mysticism. Soon I decided to attend a summer conference at Camelot, the church's headquarters in California. Although Terence had no real desire to join CUT, he was respectful of my interests and supported my decision to go. I flew to California with my daughter, now seven months old, to attend the summer conference and stayed on for a two-week "World Teacher's Seminar".

It is hard to explain the effect those three weeks had on me. Camelot, on the picturesque grounds of a former Catholic seminary in the hills above Malibu, was unlike anything I had ever experienced. Everyone was welcoming. The main church was a traditional mission-style building, its altar resplendent with flowers, with statues of Buddha and Kuan Yin arranged around an ornate gold monstrance. Above the altar hung large representational paintings of Jesus and Saint Germain. In the center was a painting of a man with a figure of Christ above him (his "Christ Self") and, above that, a glowing figure surrounded by rings of color symbolizing his "I AM Presence". Everything seemed to combine into an overall effect of otherworldliness.

In addition to the beauty that enveloped my senses, I was amazed by everything that was taught. All the threads of my interests in various religions and spiritualities seemed woven together into a beautiful tapestry of "truth": that there were many paths to God and that each of the world's religions, including Christianity, was but part of the whole and was teaching essentially the same thing.

Perhaps the most gripping part of the experience was being present for live "dictations" channeled by various ascended masters through Elizabeth Clare Prophet. She took on an almost supernatural presence during these "dictations", and what was being said seemed so profound that I could not imagine that anyone could just make it up on the spot. This, I concluded, must be the real thing. Jesus, Mary, Sanat Kumara, Gautama Buddha, and other great beings were really speaking through their messenger, Elizabeth Clare Prophet.

This was not simply a clever cult leader manipulating gullible followers, as many readers might suppose. An ancient and real battle rages still for the hearts and souls of God's people. The Bible clearly states that their enemy, Satan, appears as an angel of light (2 Corinthians 11:13–15). I am persuaded that the preternatural phenomena I witnessed firsthand in CUT were prime examples. No mere human being could have produced them even if he were a great charlatan.

One example: I was sitting near the front of the church during a dictation of "Archangel Michael". When Elizabeth spoke, there was often an intensely bright field of light and energy surrounding her. This day, I noticed that her body was becoming more and more transparent, until I could actually see the altar through it. Afterward, I first thought it must have been my imagination, but others had seen it too, and someone photographed the phenomenon. I kept the picture for many years.

Satan, the Great Deceiver, is more effective when he mixes his lies with truth than when he shows himself as he truly is. Adam and Eve were deceived through their desire to become like God, but on their own terms. That desire persists in our present age. It takes different forms, but at its heart is the sin of pride, the desire for hidden knowledge—*gnosis*—that only privileged initiates may know. CUT and other New Age cults are drawing souls away from Jesus Christ, "the Way, the Truth, and the Life", to a gnostic distortion of Christ, who is seen as only one in a line of many avatars or masters who have come to show mankind how to become Christs and masters themselves. Notice all the allusions to Scripture and the odd mixture of truth and subtle error in these passages from a dictation I heard the first time I went to a CUT conference:

> When ... Jesus Christ gave his discourse on the Good Shepherd, he spoke of the role of personal Christhood, the office he had assumed and would assume to set the example for the true shepherds of the sheep who are called by the World Teachers to come forth in this era to deliver the sheep of my pasture from the false pastors who scatter and destroy them.... Tarry with the Son of God and the sons to whom he has granted the status of full and coequal Sonship that they might hold the flame of the Good Shepherd (the Beloved Christ Self, the Lord Our Righteousness) for and on behalf of the disciples of Christ on earth. Submit to the initiations of the Son of God for the balancing of karma and the transmutation of energy misqualified, through the perfection of the mind of God in Christ.... "Let this mind be in you, which was also in Christ Jesus." Learn the way of the dharma of surrender and learn its virtue in the moral discipline of self and society.... The discourse of Jesus Christ on the Good Shepherd outlines the distinct differences in the paths of the true Christs and the false Christs whom the Savior Jesus prophesied would come in his name. Those who would master the mind of God in Christ must enter by the door of the heart.... The true shepherd enters in

by the door of the one who holds the office of the Son of
God, the Lord Jesus Christ, and of the one, the Christ Self
within, who is indeed the selfsame manifestation of that
Son of God.[5]

According to CUT teaching and New Age thought, it is
this "Christ Self" within each person that enables us to
become like God. Jesus Christ is ultimately no different from
us except that He has already become united with His
"Christ Self" and become a Christ, thus earning the right
to hold the "office" of Christ, an exemplar for us to follow.
He is not the only begotten Son of God, the second Person of the Blessed Trinity who died on the Cross for our
sins so that we, by God's supernatural grace, can become
adopted sons and daughters of God. In CUT's belief we are
not sinners redeemed by Jesus Christ but coequals with Him.
The emphasis is on this "Christ Self" or "Christ consciousness" within each person, which we must develop on our
own, instead of on the saving grace of Jesus Christ, which
transforms us supernaturally. Most in the New Age movement make a distinction between Jesus the man and the
impersonal Christ consciousness, which we are all supposed to attain. In *The Lost Teachings of Jesus*, Elizabeth Clare
Prophet wrote:

> Jesus was both the actual and symbolical representative of
> this Christ Self. Jesus was the example, the one who self-
> realized the Christ Mind and was at one with it at all times.
> Jesus himself was not the only begotten Son of the Father.
> The Christ of him was and is the only begotten Son of the
> Father; and Jesus was the pure vessel of that Universal One.
> He was the One Sent, chosen from among the Sons of

[5] Dictation by Sanat Kumara, July 1, 1979.

heaven to embody the Christ on earth as the avatar, the
exemplar for all to follow.[6]

For those already predisposed to New Age thinking, all of
this makes sense. But in order to hold this world view, one
must discount clear scriptural evidence of Jesus Christ's
unique claims to divinity. New Age adherents tend to do
so by claiming that the Bible was altered, that the teachings
about reincarnation and our own divinity were removed or
veiled. They assert that there was a conspiracy of sorts during the first three or four centuries of the Church to keep
Jesus' true teachings from the masses. To support this view,
ample use is made of statements from other writings extant
at that time in support of what was then called Gnosticism
but is now known as New Age thought. Some alternate
"gospels" from this time period do exist. The problem with
accepting these writings as true and accurate reflections of
the teachings of Jesus Christ is that those who walked and
talked with Jesus, and who were eyewitnesses of His Resurrection, proclaimed a very different gospel. From the
Church's earliest years, heresies arose that Church leaders
challenged definitively, precisely because these heresies introduced erroneous views of Christ, His divinity, and the means
by which we are saved. They recognized their sacred duty
to preserve the deposit of the faith that had been entrusted
to them by the apostles and clearly discerned which doctrines in such Gnostic writings were not taught by Christ
or the apostles. Perhaps the best-known challenge to Gnosticism came from Irenaeus of Lyons (A.D. 140–202), in his
famous treatise *Against Heresies*. Irenaeus, the second bishop
of Lyons, in Gaul, was a student of the early Christian bishop

---

[6] Elizabeth Clare Prophet, *The Lost Teachings of Jesus* (Livingston, Mont.:
Summit University Press), 241.

and martyr Polycarp, who was himself taught by Saint John, Christ's "beloved disciple". Irenaeus' treatise powerfully affirms the truths of traditional Christianity:

> It is within the power of all, therefore, in every Church, who may wish to see the truth, to contemplate clearly the tradition of the apostles manifested throughout the whole world; and we are in a position to reckon up those who were by the apostles instituted bishops in the Churches, and [to demonstrate] the succession of these men to our own times; those who neither taught nor knew of anything like what these [heretics] rave about. For if the apostles had known hidden mysteries, which they were in the habit of imparting to the perfect apart and privily from the rest, they would have delivered them especially to those to whom they were also committing the Churches themselves. For they were desirous that these men should be very perfect and blameless in all things, whom also they were leaving behind as their successors, delivering up their own place of government to these men....
>
> The Church, though dispersed through the whole world, even to the ends of the earth, has received from the apostles and their disciples this faith: [She believes] in one God, the Father Almighty, Maker of Heaven, and earth, and the sea, and all things that are in them; and in one Christ Jesus, the Son of God, who became incarnate for our salvation; and in the Holy Spirit, who proclaimed through the prophets the dispensations of God, and the advents, and the birth from a virgin, and the passion, and the resurrection from the dead, and the ascension into Heaven in the flesh of the beloved Christ Jesus, our Lord, and His [future] manifestation from Heaven in the glory of the Father "to gather all things in one" [Ephesians 1:10], and to raise up anew all flesh of the whole human race, in order that to Christ Jesus, our Lord, and God, and Savior, and King, according to the will of the invisible Father, "every knee should bow, of things

in heaven, and things in earth, and things under the earth, and that every tongue should confess" Him [Philippians 2:10–11], and that He should execute just judgment towards all. . . .

As I have already observed, the Church, having received this preaching and this faith, although scattered throughout the whole world, yet, as if occupying but one house, carefully preserves it. She also believes these points [of doctrine] just as if she had but one soul, and one and the same heart, and she proclaims them, and teaches them, and hands them down, with perfect harmony, as if she possessed only one mouth. For, although the languages of the world are dissimilar, yet the import of the tradition is one and the same.[7]

Unfortunately, I was unaware of this clear refutation of the New Age world view until much later in my spiritual journey, and so I fully embraced the form of modern-day Gnosticism taught by CUT.

Back in Hawaii after my summer experiences, I prepared to return to Camelot for a three-month session of Summit University courses in the fall of 1979. After finishing that course, I returned to Hawaii with a longing to commit myself full time to the work of the church. Terence, with his strong dislike of any organized religion, was still not interested in joining. It became a source of tension between us. In the spring of 1980, I discovered I was pregnant. During several months of caring for Terence's terminally ill mother, the friction between us grew, and by December, two weeks

[7] *Adversus Haereses*, trans. Alexander Roberts and William Rambaut, in *Ante-Nicene Fathers*, vol. 1, ed. Alexander Roberts, James Donaldson, and A. Cleveland Coxe (Buffalo, N.Y.: Christian Literature Publishing Co., 1885), bk. 3, chap. 3, and bk. 1, chap. 10. Revised and edited for New Advent by Kevin Knight, http://www.newadvent.org/fathers/0103303.htm, http://www.newadvent.org/fathers/0103110.htm.

before my due date, we separated. I felt my whole life crumbling around me and sought solace within my church community.

When my new daughter was about six weeks old, I moved to Camelot with my two children and became a staff member, working as a secretary for Summit University. After about six months, I realized that I wanted to finish my own college education. I applied to live at one of the church's Teaching Centers in Minneapolis, Minnesota, so I could attend the University of Minnesota. I was accepted and moved there with my small daughters. The schedule at the Teaching Center was rigorous, and combined with single parenthood and school, it proved too much for me. When I developed pneumonia, I decided to move out on my own until I finished my education. Running a business and taking classes as I could, I managed to get by. After my junior year, I decided to spend the summer volunteering at CUT's new property, a huge ranch in Paradise Valley north of Yellowstone Park in Montana. It was a beautiful area, and I was thrilled to be part of the founding of the community there. As the summer drew to a close, I could not bear to leave. I felt I was achieving the fulfillment of all of my earlier longings to live in a spiritually centered, intentional community in the wilderness. Since there was not enough housing yet, I bought a trailer behind the Ranch Kitchen, a restaurant on the church's property, and moved in. For me, this was an idyllic time. Life on the ranch was like living in a convent or monastery. We awoke early for prayer, worked hard, ate together, studied our faith together, had fun together, and ended our day with more prayer. There was a church-run Montessori school on the property, so my children, now four and six, had a place to go to school and shared in the life of the community. At the time, I had no real doubts about the church. Anything that did not quite make sense I put on a "back burner", figuring that it would make sense to me later.

After Elizabeth Clare Prophet sold Camelot, she and the remaining staff members from California moved to the ranch. This caused some growing pains and adjustments as the small, intimate, community atmosphere changed. One of the "permanent staff", an elite group with close access to Elizabeth Claire Prophet, created an awkward dynamic when he took an interest in me. Deciding to leave for a time and complete my degree, I transferred to Montana State University and moved to Bozeman. My children and I remained active in the church. In addition to attending local prayer services during the week, we drove sixty miles every weekend to hear the latest dictation from the mouth of Elizabeth Clare Prophet.[8]

Also living in Bozeman was Constance, a close friend from Santa Cruz, with her husband, a professor at Montana State University. As there was no real alternative, we both

---

[8] Because I see so many people embracing components of this belief system today, I have covered New Age spirituality in some depth. I hope readers will learn to recognize its errors.

Those who have never veered from orthodox Christianity may find it hard to understand the seductive power of New Age beliefs. As elements of ancient Gnosticism and other heresies creep into mainstream Christian circles, even well-meaning Christians may fail to recognize the errors of the New Age mind-set. Sometimes in the guise of charity or tolerance, souls are drawn away from the Truth that can be found only in Jesus Christ and His Church.

Parents especially need to teach their children to recognize heresy when they meet it. We need to read the writings of the early Church Fathers, who had to combat many of the same heresies that have reemerged in our own time. St. Irenaeus, in his second-century work *Against Heresies*, expertly refutes the claims of the early Gnostics, the spiritual forerunners of today's New Age leaders. His work is still relevant.

enrolled our children in public schools. However, I grew increasingly dissatisfied with the quality of education my children were receiving there, as well as the social influences to which they were being exposed. I had long been interested in homeschooling, but as a single parent I believed I could not do it successfully. However, when my oldest daughter's teacher began swearing at the students in her third-grade class, and her classmates took to discussing sex on the playground, I pulled both children out of school, brought them to college with me, and taught them myself. Meanwhile, Constance also withdrew her daughter after she had a traumatic experience at school. We decided that a practical solution was to start our own school. Constance met a former nun with teaching experience, we found another interested family, and together we opened Thomas More School in Constance's family room the following fall. It was an exciting time for me; my major was education, so this project was right up my alley. Other families began to express interest. The next year we expanded into a house offered by a member of our local church community and hired additional teachers.

Back at the CUT ranch, the church bought adjacent property to develop as a community for members who were not up to the rigorous commitment of staff life on the ranch. In this new town, called Glastonbury, church members could buy or build their own homes and start their own businesses. I wanted to live there. Constance and her husband also decided buy land there. We felt called to move Thomas More School to Glastonbury, since children living there then had to attend the local public school. With money inherited from my grandmother, I bought an old house, transported it to the property, remodeled it, and moved in. That summer we organized a camping trip for families who planned to be part of the school. It was there that I met my future husband, Andrew.

Andrew had just moved to Montana from Philadelphia, where he had been teaching for three years. He was joining our staff of teachers in the fall. Andrew was the son of my children's voice and piano teacher, who introduced us. Our mutual interests in children and education sparked an immediate friendship between us. I was impressed by his keen intellect, his generous heart, and his wonderful sense of humor. Through our work together at the school, our friendship blossomed into something more serious, and eventually we married. After years as a single parent, I was thrilled to have finally met a man I believed would be not only a wonderful husband for me and father for my children but a soul mate as well.

I did not guess that my life was about to take a turn in a radically different direction. About two months after our marriage, I discovered I was pregnant. We were overjoyed, but soon I found myself in the grips of horrible morning sickness. It was so severe that I had to stop working. Then I threatened to miscarry. This meant that I had to rest in bed for several weeks. During that quiet time, I picked up my Bible and started to read in the New Testament. It is not that I had not read the Bible at all since joining CUT, but as I lay in bed feeling dreadful, it seemed as though a kind of veil lifted from my eyes and I started to see inconsistencies between what I was reading in Scripture and what I had believed for so long. All the questions and problems with CUT theology that I had put on the "back burner" over the years shifted to the forefront. A crack seemed to form in my previously impenetrable wall of spiritual pride. Was there more to biblical Christianity than I had allowed myself to see? The very idea was repugnant to me, but I wanted to know the Truth no matter what the cost. For the first time I allowed myself to consider the possibility that my whole world view might be wrong. Earnestly, I begged Jesus to make the truth about Himself clear to me.

As I read, several Scripture passages captured my attention and dealt serious blows to my New Age defenses. The first was in Paul's First Letter to the Corinthians, where he writes:

> For Christ sent me not to baptize, but to preach the gospel: not with wisdom of words, lest the cross of Christ should be made of none effect. For the preaching of the cross is to them that perish foolishness; but unto us which are saved it is the power of God. For it is written, "I will destroy the wisdom of the wise, and will bring to nothing the understanding of the prudent." ... For after that in the wisdom of God the world by wisdom knew not God, it pleased God by the foolishness of preaching to save them that believe. For the Jews require a sign, and the Greeks seek after wisdom: But we preach Christ crucified, unto the Jews a stumbling block, and unto the Greeks foolishness. (1 Corinthians 1:17–19, 21–23)

To most New Age believers, and certainly to followers of the ascended masters, a belief in Christ crucified and the efficacy of His death on the Cross for our salvation is complete foolishness. Higher "wisdom" is sought and embraced. In this view Christ's death and Resurrection are not the pivotal events in salvation history; we thought we had no real need for a Savior who willingly took our sins upon Himself so that we might have eternal life. Rather, we thought we could become one with our "Christ Self" through our own efforts and so become a "Christ" like Jesus.

As I lay in bed reading the Bible with fresh eyes, I was seeing passages of Scripture that were diametrically opposed to what was being taught in CUT. In his book *Science of the Spoken Word*, Mark Prophet, Elizabeth's late husband, wrote: "God the Father did not require the sacrifice of his son Christ Jesus, or of any other incarnation of the Christ, as an atonement for the sins of the world; nor is it possible according to cosmic law for any man's sacrifice to balance either the original sin or the subsequent sins—the karma—of the one or the many." [9] This statement by a "messenger of the ascended masters" seemed to stand in stark contrast to this passage of Scripture:

> Therefore, if anyone is in Christ, he is a new creation; old things have passed away; behold, all things have become new. Now all things are of God, who has reconciled us to Himself through Jesus Christ, and has given us the ministry of reconciliation, that is, that God was in Christ reconciling the world to Himself, not imputing their trespasses to them, and has committed to us the word of reconciliation. For He made Him who knew no sin to be sin for us, that we might become the righteousness of God in Him. (2 Corinthians 5:17–19, 21)

Later, in 2 Corinthians, Paul states:

> I fear, lest by any means, as the serpent beguiled Eve through his subtlety, so your minds should be corrupted from the simplicity that is in Christ. For if he that cometh preacheth another Jesus, whom we have not preached, or if ye receive another spirit, which ye have not received, or another gospel, which ye have not accepted, ye might well bear with him. . . . For such are false apostles, deceitful workers, transforming themselves into the apostles of Christ, and no marvel; for Satan himself is transformed into an angel of light. Therefore it is no

---

[9] Mark L. Prophet, *Science of the Spoken Word* (Malibu, Calif.: Summit University Press, 1984), 87.

> great thing if his ministers also be transformed as the minis-
> ters of righteousness. (2 Corinthians 11:3–4, 13–15)

With grace-given clarity I saw that if CUT was actually so
wrong on something so essential, then I might have been
deceived by a "false apostle". I might have joined the wrong
church. But what should I do? Here I was, newly married,
pregnant, and living in a CUT community. This church
had been at the center of my life for twelve years. I had
many beloved friends here. I knew that if I left, I would be
viewed in the worst possible light. It was bad enough if
people left the church for another New Age belief system;
to leave the church for traditional Christianity would be
unthinkable. Who would want to align himself with a primitive, outmoded form of belief? Yet I knew I had no other
choice. If I were not at least willing to explore traditional
Christianity, I would be nothing but a hypocrite.

During this initial questioning of my beliefs, I decided
that I needed to read some Christian books prayerfully and
with an open mind. My faithful mother had long been concerned about my involvement in CUT. Out of a desire to
understand my beliefs and to be ready to challenge them,
she had turned for information to the Spiritual Counterfeits
Project, a group of Christians who do scholarly research
and write about the distortions of truth in religious sects.
She had sent me information on CUT, but I had never
looked at it. Now, at last, I knew it was time to dust it off
and read it. It contained disturbing information about the
history of CUT, especially its roots in Madame Helena Blavatsky's Theosophical Society. Although she lived most of
her life in the 1800s, Madame Blavatsky is still widely hailed
as the "mother" of the modern New Age movement. In
her writings, all CUT's foundational beliefs, as well as the

core beliefs of the entire the New Age movement, could be clearly seen. But the most deeply unsettling was how openly she praised Lucifer as the initiator of the "new age": "Lucifer is divine and terrestrial light, the 'Holy Ghost' and 'Satan', at one and the same time.... Satan will now be shown, in the teaching of the Secret Doctrine, allegorized as Good, and Sacrifice, a God of Wisdom, under different names." [10]

As we searched for a way to leave the church, God provided a providential answer. In order to support our family, Andrew needed additional work. We sold our home in Glastonbury and bought one in Bozeman, where there was a larger population base. I began homeschooling my children there and continued reading Christian books. Andrew was bewildered to see his committed CUT wife becoming a "fundie" (CUT's derogatory term for Christians). It was a difficult time for our marriage, but because I was pregnant, we chose to stick it out.

Eventually I decided to start attending a Christian church. When I came to Grace Bible Church after almost two decades in New Age circles, I experienced a complete culture shock. The church was austere: just a basic Christian church, with no smells and bells, no profound cosmic experiences, not even any real outward beauty. The gracious pastor welcomed me and answered my many questions. Among the homeschooling mothers at the church I began to form new friendships. Even my speech patterns had to be changed, I discovered, lest my New Age terminology slip into conversations. However, God in His great mercy enabled me to humble myself, to learn from "the foolishness of preaching" and accept by faith the "simplicity that

[10] Helena Petrovna Blavatsky, *The Secret Doctrine*, vol. 2 (Theosophical University Press, 1888), 513, 237.

is in Christ". It was a season my soul needed in order to be
stripped of layers of spiritual pride and error. Rededicated
to Christ and newly baptized, I experienced inner peace
and profound gratitude to the Lord for freeing me from my
New Age delusions.

After three years in Bozeman and in the midst of another
pregnancy, we moved on to California. During our time
there, no longer surrounded by the CUT members we had
known for years, Andrew was finally willing to consider
the claims of Christianity. We began attending a Calvary
Chapel filled with young families, where I developed a deeper
understanding of and love for the Bible. Before two years
had passed, however, we moved again, to Moscow, Idaho,
where my husband was offered a teaching position.

Friends from our Bozeman church had also moved to
Moscow and were attending a Community Evangelical Fellowship (CEF) church. We visited one Sunday and decided
to make it our church home. By then, Andrew and I had
progressed in faith to the point where we were hungry for
spiritual "meat". We wanted a faith that not only nurtured
our hearts but also challenged our minds. The CEF seemed
perfect for us. The pastor, Doug Wilson, came from a decidedly Reformed persuasion and had a thorough understanding of covenant theology. We found ourselves challenged
by his intellect to think more deeply in our faith. We especially appreciated his theologically rich yet practical instruction on how to live out our faith amid the challenges of
the world.

Over time, however, Andrew and I began to notice inconsistencies between what we were hearing in church and what
we were reading for ourselves in Scripture. This raised a
troublesome question for us: How can we know for sure
that a particular interpretation of Scripture is correct? At

first this was just a niggling concern, but it emerged as a growing issue when we faced the question of infant baptism. This is a surprisingly divisive issue in the Protestant world. Some churches believe that infants should be baptized, while others subscribe to baptism of "believers" only: those old enough to make a conscious profession of faith. To them, infant baptism is viewed as futile, unscriptural, or downright sinful. In our previous evangelical churches, baptism was viewed as a declaration before the Christian community of one's decision to follow Christ and as a sign of obedience to His command. Doug Wilson's view was that baptism was the covenantal sign in the New Testament, which replaced the covenantal sign of circumcision in the Old Testament. Since in the Old Testament, infants were circumcised, it would follow that in the Christian Church, infants should be baptized. Both sides used Scripture to support their position. The problem was how to know which view was right. Each side used Scripture to justify its stands on the many contentious theological issues dividing different denominations. We wanted Truth, not opinion. By what authority could we be sure that a particular interpretation of Scripture was truly correct? We started to wonder if reading some of the earliest postbiblical writings of the Church might help us to see which interpretation of Scripture most closely mirrored that of the early Christians.

At the time, along with teaching, my husband was beginning to develop a new project. After a seminar in Seattle, a homeschooling father with a videotaping business had approached Andrew with an offer to videotape his seminars so they could reach more people. When their discussion drifted to the topic of religion, Andrew mentioned his quandary about baptism and was surprised to learn that the man was a Catholic. During the next week he mailed us a set of books containing writings from the early Church Fathers. Their arrival was so timely that we felt it must be providential. We started to read the first volume eagerly but were completely unprepared for what we found.

The last thing on our minds was any possibility of becoming Catholics. In a charitable moment, I might have thought it possible that there were "real" Christians in the Catholic Church, but to seriously consider the claims of the Catholic Church would have been out of the question. Yet, as we read the writings of Clement of Rome, Ignatius of Antioch, Polycarp, Irenaeus, and others, many of whom either knew the apostles directly or knew men taught by the apostles, what utterly shocked us was how Catholic their teachings were. We expected to find reflected in their writings a Church that looked and believed the way modern nondenominational churches do. After all, were not these churches trying to get back to the basics of Christianity, to what it was before being corrupted by the Catholic Church? What we were reading completely dispelled that notion.

How were we to respond to this discovery? Again, I found myself at a crossroads. If I was honestly seeking Truth, I had to be willing at least to consider the claims of the Catholic Church. Again, as I had done when God opened my eyes to the flaws in CUT's theology, I begged Jesus to make His Truth known to us, to show us which way to go. I pleaded with Him not to let us stray, not to let us be seduced into error again, but rather to make it clear to us where His true Church was to be found. And again, it became clear to me that He was asking me to follow Him, no matter what the personal cost. I loved the CEF community; I had learned and grown so much there. But I knew I must leave that behind if Christ willed me to do so.

We asked our Catholic friend to send us more books, and then, on a trip to Seattle, we decided to visit his church. He and his family attended Saint John Chrysostom Byzantine Catholic Church. When we entered, I felt as if I had stepped back in time. Inside, the walls were painted with beautiful icons, and the sanctuary and altar were resplendent. In the center of the ceiling was a large dome, and painted within it an icon of Jesus. Around the dome were smaller icons of the twelve apostles. As the Divine Liturgy[11] began, my eyes filled with tears. When I left CUT, I had surrendered my desire for spiritual experiences filled with beauty in order to embrace the simplicity of Christ. But now I was experiencing an ancient liturgy, parts of which dated back almost to the time of Christ and to the apostle Saint James, the bishop of Jerusalem. My soul had been starving for such beauty and reverence. It was deeply Christocentric, spiritually rich, and filled with beauty and transcendence. I was profoundly moved.

We began driving to Spokane several Sundays a month, an hour and a half each way, to worship at a Byzantine Catholic church. For a time we remained involved in the CEF, as we went through a process of study, prayer, and discernment. There were so many doctrinal sources of conflict among the different nondenominational churches. Even in the mainline Protestant churches, key doctrinal issues were a source of division. How could we determine which church possessed the correct understanding of a given issue? During this time we also studied the most controversial issues dividing Catholics and Protestants. Over and over we found that the Catholic interpretation was the most scripturally faithful. It became obvious that without the protective

---

[11] This is what the Mass in the Byzantine rite is called.

guidance of the Holy Spirit to preserve the Church from error, each church and each individual would be left to invent their own theology based on their own reading of God's Word. We concluded that our ultimate decision about whether or not to become Catholic hinged on the issue of Church authority. Did any church have the authority to definitively interpret what the Bible taught?

We became convinced that both Scripture and the witness of the early Church were clear on this point: Christ established the Catholic Church and upheld her as "the pillar and foundation of the truth" (1 Timothy 3:15). He entrusted to Peter the Keys of the Kingdom, and to His apostles the deposit of the faith. They in turn faithfully passed this on to their successors. This apostolic succession has continued in an unbroken line to the present time. In the structure of the Church, Our Lord provided a way to preserve the faith and to correct error. We knew that the Catholic Church throughout the ages had faced many challenges, and in our studies it was painfully clear that the Church today still must confront problems and combat errors. That the Church remains standing despite her past problems and despite the flaws and failures of many churchmen was proof to us of Our Lord's promise that the gates of Hell will not prevail against her.

At last, after several years of intensive prayer and study, we realized we were ready to join the Catholic Church. We wrote to our respected pastor, Doug Wilson; to the elders of the CEF church; and to our friends in the parish and told them of our decision. People were shocked, but most were gracious. Finally, on September 12, 1999, and with immense happiness and inner peace, we were received into the arms of the Catholic Church. Andrew was baptized, and we both were confirmed. We also had the great joy of getting married again, this time in the eyes of God and His Church.

More than eight years have passed since that blessed day. I have honestly never had any regrets. My soul is no longer restless. As each year passes I realize more fervently that I have found not only a home but a Kingdom, filled with great beauty and treasures of inestimable value, a foretaste of my eternal home. I will be grateful to the Lord forever for His mercy in redeeming me, a sinner in no way deserving of His grace. With unfathomable mercy He chose to free me from the errors that deluded me and to guide me at last into the safe haven of His Church. "Thou hast made us for Thyself, O Lord, and our hearts are restless until they rest in Thee" (Saint Augustine).

Robin Pudewa lives with her husband, Andrew, near Atascadero, California, where they raise children, cattle, camellias, and hymns of praise to God.

Chapter 21

Snatched from the Burning

Shannon Counihan

Candles were the only source of light in the room. Eight witches in black robes gathered around a leather-bound book of spells. One by one, each made a small incision on the wrist or finger, drawing out just enough blood to sign a name with it in the book. They were swearing an ancient oath that evening, one that would bind them forever to the horned god Bacchus as either a bride or a devoted son. As my turn drew closer I felt mounting nervous excitement. I had come so far, and now the world of magic was about to open wide to me.

In the Darkness

At twenty, I was the youngest member of my coven. We were twelve witches—nine of us women, the other three men, including the priest—who had formed a close, familial bond. For three and a half years, I had been taking classes in witchcraft, which we knew as the Druidic Cult of the Wise. I had learned a great deal, passed through four initiations, and was well on my way to becoming a priestess with my own coven to lead. My whole life was centered on the use of white magic, also known as Wicca.

It was my loftiest dream to become high priestess of the Los Angeles area. I used spells for everything from buying a new car to getting a better job; I practiced cleansing rituals to discourage unwelcome or too-persistent suitors, and I cast love spells to gain the affection of people I admired. My experiences with the preternatural realm were very real, but instead of frightening me away from witchcraft, they intrigued me and drew me further in. I had found a power I could wield that was greater than anything I had ever known.

Initially I was drawn to Wicca for understandable and subjectively blameless reasons. As a young adolescent with no religious formation, from a profoundly broken family, I had many psychic hurts that cried out for healing. No one seemed able to address them until one charming young man entered my life. When I asked him the questions that burned in my heart, he answered every one with apparent depth and clarity, and a self-assurance I craved. To him I confided my sorrows, fears, weaknesses, and dreams. He told me I could turn my sorrow to joy, conquer my fears, become so powerful that no one would ever hurt me again and all my dreams could come true. This glittering promise sounded almost too good to believe, but he assured me that witchcraft classes would unlock the door to my destiny. For a long time, I had felt weak and vulnerable, so when I was shown the power of witchcraft in my first ritual, I was hooked. It offered me a glimpse of a life where I could control my past, present, and future. No longer would I be the victim, the helpless one; I would be master of my own destiny. With the intensity of a born-again Christian, I immersed myself in the secrets of magic.

On the December night when I signed my name in blood as the bride of the horned god, I felt a power surge through me. I knew that my life would never be the same again, and I was ready for whatever would come next. Until then we had learned only about the light side of magic. After this ritual we were going to start learning about the dark side.

And we did. That was when the priest warlock of our coven revealed a secret "truth" of witchcraft. Until then, we had been told that in the spiritual realm there are energies that are good and evil, white and black, positive and negative, but now that we were advanced witches, he said, we were mature enough to understand that there really is no right or wrong, no good or bad. Everything simply *is*; there are only shades of gray. Therefore, there is no such thing as white or black magic: they are the same. In exposing this "truth", he laid the groundwork for nude rituals, animal sacrifice, and other kinds of diabolical spells.

The priest spoke to us with authority. Our practice of Wicca was not a frivolous prank. We were entirely serious about it and believed it to be the true religion. There were rules about everything, not only for instruction, initiation, and practice, but also for how to handle any misguided witch who might want to withdraw from the coven, the act of which required a lengthy exit procedure.

Light in the Darkness

New Year's Eve 1991 marked an unforeseen but critical turning point in my life. I had ended a stormy personal relationship with a fellow witch who refused to accept the breakup with resignation. He began stalking me. After weeks of dodging him and engaging in spiritual wars, I was desperate for an escape. In my intense anxiety, I uttered a prayer, asking God, whom I did not know, to help me. Within hours my telephone rang. My parents and some of their friends were inviting me to a week-long ski vacation at Lake Tahoe. As I accepted their invitation, I did not guess that it was part of a secret plan to match me up with Patrick, one of the bachelors in the party, who had been a friend of my stepdad's for four years.

When Patrick arrived at my house to drive me to Tahoe, I found his innocent manner appealing. During the long drive north I tried to find out if he would be an easy convert to Wicca. He, however, had a belief in the One God that I could not shake. He could not answer any of my questions about metaphysics, but he would not deny his faith. It was this simple strength that got us through the next few months.

During the ski vacation in Tahoe, we "fell in love". Back home, we spent two months commuting between our different apartments, until, in March, he moved in with me. Then I could no longer hide all my paraphernalia, and so I had to tell him that I was a witch. Patrick took the shock rather well; at least he did not run away. But he was not about to abandon his faith, though it was as unformed as that of an untutored child. At the time, he did not even realize that he was living in mortal sin.

A Mother's Gifts

The Christmas before we met, Patrick's mother had given him three special gifts: a small porcelain statue of the Madonna and Child, a Bible, and a Rosary. Patrick had never prayed the Rosary before, but in the following months he began to teach himself. As I went off to my coven meetings at night, he would sit on the back porch and pray for me.

In March, when his birthday came, I wanted to do a special ritual for him. I made all of the required preparations and then, at the apex of the ritual, I asked him what he wanted to do, explaining to him that he could take advantage of the power that had been raised in my spell by doing anything he wanted.

"I'd like to pray the Rosary", he replied.

With no idea what a Rosary was, I agreed. Afterward I thought, *What a boring thing to do; what a waste of time and energy.* But much later I came to realize what enormous power the Rosary holds.

Not long after this spell, Patrick wanted to buy a piece of jewelry to give to me as a token of his affections. With a Catholic friend, he went to a jewelry store and found a small gold medal with an image of Mary, the Mother of God, on it. Around the edge of the medal there were words inscribed, but neither he nor his friend knew what they said. After weeks of asking around, he finally discovered that the words were in French, and they said: "O Mary, conceived without sin, pray for us who have recourse to thee." It was a sacramental, called a Miraculous Medal. We knew nothing about such things at the time, but she must truly have prayed for us.

When I accepted the medal as a token of his love, I had no intention of wearing it in honor of Mary. To me, it symbolized instead the "goddess energies" in mother form. I showed the medal to my coven members, but they did not share my detachment toward the image on it. My coven priest refused even to touch it. At this point, he became openly concerned about my spiritual condition. He tried to persuade me that Patrick was dangerous for me and would destroy me.

Patrick asked if he could put his little wooden statue of Mary on my home altar, on which I did daily spells. Since I saw her as the perfect representation of the mother goddess, I agreed. From then on, Mary stayed in the center of the altar.

In May, witches observe a special spring fertility rite called Beltaine. During this festival, witches may marry in a ritual known as handfasting. Such a marriage is not recognized as valid in civil law, so it is more for fun than for serious commitment. When I asked if he would like us to get handfasted, Patrick was a little nervous, but he agreed. For the ritual, he was required to make a wand from wood that he had found and decorate it with stones and symbols. He did this with such attention to detail that I was sure I had found a powerful mate who would be accepted into my Wiccan family as soon as they met him. But when the time came for Patrick and the other non-Wiccan members to enter into our circle of power, our priest stopped and silently studied him, while Patrick nervously fingered the Rosary in his pocket. Our priest was not going to let him in! I could not believe it.

As You Stand before the Powers of Hell

My coven priest kept Patrick hostage at the entrance of our circle, studying him with great care. Minutes crawled by as we waited, wondering what we would do if Patrick was not admitted. Undoubtedly the priest was trying to read his mind as he stood staring at him, trying to understand this person who seemed to him to threaten one of his coven members. All of us held our breath, I most of all. At last the priest signaled the guards, and they reluctantly lowered their athamaes—their witch's swords—and allowed Patrick to enter. But the subsequent celebration was rushed through, with many parts cut short. My pride in finding a powerful mate soon became my shame that Patrick was seen more as a threat than as a prospective member. Later I learned that my priest had seen a man dressed in white standing protectively by Patrick. He told us that this man was not a human but a spiritual being who had not been invited to the handfasting but insisted on being present anyway.

Greatly troubled, all of the members of the coven let Patrick know that he would not be invited to participate in any more rituals until he gave up his Catholic faith. We also became the focus of many spells and spiritual wars. I would retaliate with my own spells, while Patrick would pray the Rosary. I thought my methods were more effective, but in reality it was Patrick's prayers that worked miracles.

Realizing finally that I was caught between two worlds, I knew that I had an enormously important decision to make. If I remained in Patrick's world, my coven members could no longer be the center of my life. This world would take me into an uncertain future; I knew only that the man I loved would be there to care for me. By contrast, the world of Wicca offered me unlimited power and success. I was well on my way to becoming a Wiccan priestess. My career as an executive secretary and vault teller at a bank was thriving, and my ambition to become a model was beginning to materialize. As I tried to discern what the future held for me, I got so confused that I asked my coven priest to help me. He studied our astrological charts and divined the future.

"Patrick will be the death of you", he said. "You cannot continue to see this man. He is a triple fire sign, and you are triple water. You will always be at war until one of you is destroyed."

The Path That Leads to God Is the Narrow Path

In my own meditation, I saw before me two different gates, each with a dirt path leading off into a forest. One path was visibly smaller and seemed to lead upward into darkness, while the other path was broader and seemed to lead toward a field of many flowers. Because I always love a challenge, I chose the darker, narrower path, and I saw myself starting out on a journey. Suddenly Patrick arrived in my meditation. I saw him stand beside me ready for a journey. Together we started up the steep, dark incline and disappeared into the forest. Even though my meditation left many secrets to be revealed, I no longer felt alone. Loneliness had been the only thing Wicca could not cure for me. The sting of loneliness still filled my heart, aching daily. My Wiccan family did not fill the empty space; neither did any of my successes. What I longed for was love: not physical *eros* love, but selfless *agape* love. Patrick seemed to offer me an insight into the nature of such a love.

Every Sunday Patrick would go off to his Catholic church and be with hundreds of people he did not know for about an hour. He invited me to go with him every time.

"You can come with me if you want to, but don't make me late!" he would say.

Intrigued, I decided one day to go with him. When we walked in, I felt as if every eye was upon me. Surely the roof would collapse, and they would see that a witch was among them. My skin crawled, and my head felt dizzy. Perhaps they would turn their Christian eyes toward me as if I should be tied to a stake and burned. To my surprise, no one seemed to care that I was there. Even Patrick was oblivious to my discomfort. All of them seemed wrapped up in the words being spoken at the altar. Turmoil and panic filled my mind with such noise that I could not hear anything else. When it was time for Communion, Patrick told me I could not go up to receive, so I closed my eyes and leaned back in the pew while he, and what seemed the whole congregation, went up front to eat something. As I listened I seemed to hear thousands of feet walking upward on creaking steps. Higher and higher they climbed, yet no one came down. I opened my eyes and looked for the stairs that carried everyone off, but there were none to be seen. I wondered what mystical power could seem to carry so many people off, and yet they still remained behind.

After the service was over, the people were visibly happier than they had looked when we arrived. Instead of feeling like they wanted to stone me because they could see that I was a witch, I felt like they were so joyful about what they had just received that they were extending love toward each other and even to me. I had never experienced this kind of love before, and I felt its finger touch my heart. I longed for more. I wanted to understand the secret that was bound up in this thing they all shared.

As Mothers' Day came nearer I spent less time with my coven family and more time with Patrick. This meant that I went to Mass with him a few more times, and each time I felt a sense of something great and mysterious but full of love. Patrick had asked the priest at the church he attended in Seal Beach if he would marry us, but the priest said no. He called several other Catholic churches, asking if we could be married there, but each priest said the same thing: "You do not belong to this parish; she is too young; you have not known her long enough; she is not a Christian." This so frustrated Patrick that we eloped back to Tahoe and were married in a civil ceremony. Now, we thought, we could begin a new adventure together.

Our new adventure came in completely unexpected form, both for me and for Patrick. In July he took a job in Palmdale, and I left my entire life behind to begin a new one with him. We moved to a small home in Tehachapi. I looked around for a new coven to join, but I could not find even one witch. This is strange because I discovered later that there are many witches in Tehachapi. But God was preparing us for something else: for conversion. He sent us the first step in a book a colleague of Pat's gave him.

One blistering hot day when we were driving home through the barren desert from Lancaster back up to the Tehachapi Mountains, Patrick suddenly pulled the car over to the side of the road, so eager to show me a book he had borrowed from a friend at work that he could not wait until we got home. It was called *Medjugorje: The Message*.[1] I recall leaning back in my seat listening as he read aloud, as excited as a little boy at Christmastime. I rolled down the window to let the hot wind dry the sweat off my face. He continued to read to me until we could not bear the heat anymore, and then we went home and read some more. I could not believe what I was hearing.

After a few days of this, I became so absorbed that I took the book from him and read it cover to cover myself. Afterward, I was faced with the hardest question I ever had to answer. How could this be true? How could the "Mother of God" come to several little children and tell them truths that were contrary to everything I had been taught? If witchcraft was the true religion, then everything in this book had to be a lie. Or else everything I believed in was a lie, and truth was to be found with the Mother of God and her Son, Jesus Christ.

Once in my witchcraft class someone had asked about the reported visitations of the Blessed Virgin Mary. I had no idea what he was talking about so I did not pay attention to the claims at the time, but now I remembered the coven priest explaining that they were merely manifestations of the goddess in mother form. He said people were getting her message confused, that she was really trying to

[1] Wayne Weible, *Medjugorje: The Message* (Brewster: Paraclete Press, 1989).

tell them to become better caretakers of the earth. But when I read her Medjugorje message, I discovered that it was neither about witchcraft nor about taking better care of the earth. It was about repentance.

Repentance from what?

Repentance from sin.

The thing that hit me the hardest was that the lady of the visions called herself Mary the Mother of Jesus. She talked about her Son, Jesus—not the god Bacchus or Pan but about Jesus Christ. In my little witchcraft world there was no room for such a claim. Jesus was seen as a historical figure but not a deity. The goddess of my religion would never limit herself to such a claim. Yet this woman spoke with authority. She talked about Hell. She spoke of sin and what sins were punishable by Hell. She told the children to sacrifice for souls so that souls might be converted. Suddenly the blinders were removed from my eyes, and I found myself stripped of my illusions. I felt the scales fall from my heart. It was as though I had been stabbing around in the dark chasing after fairy tales and suddenly someone had turned on the lights and I could see clearly.

I was headed to Hell.

I was an unbaptized pagan who regularly practiced idolatry and sorcery and fornication. A holy fear gripped my heart, and with every fiber of my being I believed in the One God. I believed in His Mother. I knew that I was wrong and that I must immediately change my ways.

Though the initial shock of conversion was instantaneous, I did not come to full repentance until I heard a priest talk about confession and the punishment reserved for those who do not confess. My conversion grew deeper and more informed over the following months as the Lord prepared me for a more thorough cleansing.

As I was going through my conversion, I left the Seal Beach coven without going through the multistep process required. The rule said that you must inform the priest and coven members of your intentions to leave, tell them why you were leaving, and then make three more visits at two-week intervals so they could do a kind of "debriefing". I just left, cold turkey, without trying to get permission and without even offering any reasons.

God sent several people into our lives just at this time to help us prepare for our formal conversions. Saint Malachy's parish priest, Monsignor Seamus McMullan (of blessed memory), made sure that Patrick promptly received the opportunity to confess his mortal sins in the sacrament of penance. He also arranged for me to start taking a Rite of Christian Initiation of Adults (RCIA) class, which he taught himself. Like a loving shepherd tending his flock, Monsignor McMullan took special care to bless our marriage before I was baptized so that we would no longer be living in a state of mortal sin. And he introduced us to several people in the community who led us by the hand down the road of faithful conversion.

It had been just one year since the ski trip to Tahoe where we had fallen in love, and we had been in a spiritual whirlwind the whole time. We had been married three times: first in the handfasting in my Wicca coven, then in a civil ceremony when we eloped to Tahoe, and finally when we had our marriage blessed in the Catholic Church. We had moved to Tehachapi, conceived and lost a child, and started taking RCIA instruction. The next year promised to be even more dazzling. As Lent approached I felt more and more anxious about my baptism. I was afraid that the Devil, who had revealed himself to us several times, would not allow me to taste the sweetness of redemption. There is no glory in diabolical attack. It produces an unholy fear that is an open door for evil to work in the imagination. I was sure that somehow I would die before I could be baptized.

One cold, dark morning after Patrick left for work, I lay in bed but felt restless and afraid. It was too early for me to get up and start the day, so I pulled the covers more tightly around me. The house was quiet, but the coyotes outside began the eerie yipping that echoed like laughter across the hills. The sound always sent shivers up my spine, but this morning I was especially uncomfortable. I felt the familiar alertness that I would get when a fellow coven member was doing a spell against me. *No*, I told myself. *I am not going to surrender to the temptation to get up and fight with a spell of my own.* So I turned my thoughts to my upcoming baptismal day and closed my eyes.

No sooner had I done so than the side of my face grew warm, as if someone had leaned close to me and I could feel his breath on my hair and ear. In a whisper filled with loathing, he murmured, "Shannon, you don't understand."

Hearing this, I jumped up and turned on the lights. *How do I fight this evil thing?* There was only one way. Not with spells and incantations, not with candles and incense, not by my power, but with the name of Jesus. So I rebuked the evil spirit by calling incessantly upon the Lord. When I grew calm enough to talk to someone, I called Patrick and asked him to pray for me. Then I called my prospective godparents, told them about the attack, and asked them to pray for me. Next, I snatched up a Rosary and began to pray until daylight filled the room and my dread of another attack passed. Fear became my companion as my baptismal day grew nearer. I felt that my life was on the line, that I would never live to see my sins be forgiven and my soul reborn.

Patrick decided to fast on bread and water for forty days before my baptism. God must have given him the strength, for he remained true to his commitment even when it was most difficult. I could not fast because Our Lord had blessed us with another baby, and I did not want to lose this one. At last the most beautiful day in my life arrived. The longing I had to receive Jesus in the Most Blessed Sacrament burned in my heart. I was shaking uncontrollably when Monsignor McMullan said the holy words that I can still hear to this very day: "I baptize you, in the name of the Father and the Son and the Holy Spirit."

Over the fifteen years since that first Easter, the narrow, mysterious road we chose has taken us on the most wonderful journey possible. We have had seven sons and one daughter. We have been involved in many aspects of the Catholic Church, from the Charismatic Movement to Marian piety to traditional practice, settling at last in the Norbertine Third Order, in which our lives are enriched by focus on the Eucharist, Mary, penance, zeal for souls, praying the Liturgy of the Hours, and becoming a domestic church for the Glory of God. We homeschool our children, teaching them about the treasures we have found in the Catholic Church. Most of the time I am learning right along with them.

What beautiful gifts God has given to us! He has shown us His astonishing love and mercy, freely given us His forgiveness, and brought us to this bountifully abundant life. He has given us Himself.

Shannon Counihan lives with her husband, their seven sons, and their one daughter in Tehachapi, California, where she rejoices in the truth, feeds and tends all her children, and homeschools those of suitable ages.

Chapter 22

Prisoner Without Chains

Russell L. Ford

All my life, I have heard people talk about searching for God. Yet it seems to me that man rarely does search for God. Most of the time, he runs from Him. Throughout our lives it is God who searches for us. All we have to do to meet Him face-to-face is to stand still. If we let God catch up to us, He embraces us with overwhelming love. His love for us is infinitely greater than our curiosity about Him.

God reached into my life dramatically several times before I stayed around to accept His love. When He finally caught up with me, it was not because I was searching for Him but because a court forced me to stop running by sentencing me to twenty-five years in prison. Yet these last twenty years since God embraced me with His love and freed me from my old self have been the best part of my life. The important work I found in prison has made those years the most exciting and interesting I could possibly imagine living.

* * *

Born in 1957, I was a child of the 1970s. As an early teen, I attended a huge Illinois high school just outside Saint Louis.

My music of choice was acid rock, by Grand Funk Railroad and Uriah Heep, and my drug of choice was LSD. I smoked weed and took any sort of pill offered but found nothing more satisfying than a good acid trip. Of course, being cool was important to me. I played bass in a rock band and looked older than my age, so my rocking and partying began when I was in seventh grade. But all that soon changed.

My parents originally came from a little town in the beautiful Ozark foothills. They liked the life they had built in the city, where the money and jobs were, but high living was costing them their son. In an attempt to save me from myself they moved back to their hometown while I was a high school sophomore.

Suddenly I was transplanted from the fast lane in the city to a village like Mayberry R.F.D.,[1] where the town marshal was actually named Slim. In the city, I had enjoyed anonymity, with no worry that what I did or said would get back to my parents. My new high school had only six hundred students. Everybody knew everybody, and they were quick to tell Mom and Dad what I was up to.

My mother said I would get along better if I got my elbow-length hair cut, so I got it cut to shoulder length. Even that was too long. I was the only long-haired boy at school, viewed by most people as a big-city hippie who had come to town to spread drugs, violate the girls, influence the minds of teenagers, and help the Communists win the war in Vietnam. Adults would not give me the time of day, and I could make no friends because the boys resented me.

There was also the problem of adjusting to the life of a rural community. Drugs were not easily accessible here, yet

[1] Mayberry was the fictional site of the Andy Griffith television series popular through the 1960s.

I seldom did without. Stung by my status as a social outcast and driven by the pain of my father's brutality, my drug problem reached the level of addiction by spring. At its peak I was eating one hundred pills a day in an amphetamine-barbiturate cycle. I would swallow a handful of downers after school, then a handful of uppers in the morning. About midmorning I would eat another handful of uppers to make it through the day. At midafternoon I would start eating downers to curb the effect of the uppers, with more downers between then and bedtime so I could sleep.

During the last week of the school year, all my problems came to a head, and I became suicidal.

I could not see it then, but I can see now that God was working in my life. Our lives usually look to us like the back of a piece of embroidery. Only when the Artist is finished can we turn the embroidery over and witness the immense beauty He has worked in our lives. Looking back now, I see where God was beginning to work the embroidery that would be my life. One teacher recognized that I was in trouble, and God bless him, he wanted to help me. He invited me to church with him that night. I did not really want to go, but his kindness made me feel obligated, so I said yes.

After school, my father and I had another conflict. I had had enough. About an hour before I was due to meet the teacher at church, I went into my parents' medicine chest and ate every pill they had. Then I ate all of my drug stash. I did not know what I was taking, and I did not care. I was just tired of waking up.

My ancestors were among the founding families of this small community, and the church to which I had been invited was their "family" church. Within half an hour the teacher who brought me realized that I must be drug intoxicated.

He took me outside and sat with me on the curb until he got me to admit what I had done. I told him the truth only because I thought it was too late to save me. The teacher rushed into the church and got my aunt and uncle, and they loaded me into the car. Then he called my folks to let them know I was being sped home. In front of the house my dad got into the car, then we shot off to the hospital.

At the hospital, the emergency room team pumped my stomach until they thought they got all of the drugs that had not yet been digested. They wanted to keep me in the hospital for observation, but my father would not hear of it. Furthermore, he did not want anyone outside that room ever to know his son attempted suicide, so he threatened each person there. His manner made them believe him.

*   *   *

My parents needed a break from me, so they sent me to stay with an Indiana cousin for two weeks. I returned on June 15, 1973. In a town as small as mine you cannot spit on the sidewalk without everyone knowing it, so everyone knew I was back. On June 16, a kid I knew from school called and invited me to church with him. I told him I would go, though I had no intention whatever of doing so.

The next morning, he called again after the church service. Ignoring the fact that I had lied to him, he invited me to the evening's services. I was out of dope and in such bad shape that I was looking for any distraction. So I decided to go to church after all.

The church was Southern Baptist, the second-largest church in town, and only a block and a half away, so I walked down in time for the evening service. That short walk turned out to be a major turning point in my life.

Several things struck me at the church. The first thing I noticed was that there were thirty other teenagers. As it turned out, they were about 15 percent of the congregation, and many of them were kids considered "cool" at school.

As I have said, I was a pariah. Everybody in that town believed the worst about me, mostly with good reason. But though all the adults there knew who I was, these folks welcomed me like I was someone special and made me feel welcome.

The singing stood out to me too. This was not just a group singing from a hymnal. They were into their singing, and they meant what they sang. Smiling, they almost shouted:

> Oh, victory in Jesus! My Savior forever.
> He sought me and He bought me with His
> redeeming Blood.
> He loved me ere I knew Him, and all my love is
> due Him.
> He plunged me to victory beneath His cleansing
> flood.

The third thing that struck me was the preacher. Only twenty-six years old, he was pastor of the church and had a master's degree in divinity. Clearly this man was highly intelligent. More important, he was deeply in love with his Creator.

At the altar call, the congregation sang an old Protestant invitational hymn called "I Surrender All". I felt an irresistible urge to surrender everything to this Jesus guy those folks seemed to love. So on June 17, 1973, at approximately 7:45 P.M., I walked to the front of the church auditorium and collapsed onto my knees. Before the pastor came to pray with me, I prayed on my own, telling God all I wanted was to live a normal life apart from chaos, confusion, hatred, and fear.

*   *   *

During that summer of 1973 I decided I wanted to become an evangelist. Most people were skeptical that I could make such a complete about-face. The first thing I did was to put down my bass and quit playing in the bars. The second thing was to get a haircut all the way above my ears. Next, I started to look for good, hard, honest work. Opinions about me began to change almost as fast as the changes I had made in my own life.

We went to church camp near the end of June, and that was where I got my first opportunity to preach. Before I preached that first time, I told God I was afraid. Certainly I was afraid to stand before a group of people to do something I had never done before, but I was also afraid of actually doing more harm than good. In many ways the human species is very fragile. I understood that well because of my own life. I also understood what it was to begin building a new life, and I feared harming others' lives by doing something to others that might be outside the will of God. So I asked God to show me that I was doing His will by moving just one person to make a decision for Him when I finished speaking.

Well, that is exactly what happened. I asked for one, and I got one. That convinced me that I was called to preach. So I spent the rest of the summer being mentored by the pastor. I also got heavily involved with our church youth group and the regional Baptist youth association.

I was not the only wanna-be preacher at our church. Along with the men who acted as associate pastors, we also had a young man home from his studies at college. It was decided to use this pool of preachers to hold a youth revival near summer's end. For several weeks prior to it, the pastor announced who would preach at the weekend youth revival. He assigned the college student to preach Friday night, one associate pastor to speak Saturday night, and the other to preach Sunday morning. The pastor said he had not yet decided what to do about Sunday night.

I had hoped to be chosen to preach Sunday night, but I gave up that hope by the first service on Friday. The entire youth revival seemed a disaster. The auditorium was less than half full when the college student preached the first night. I quickly understood why. It was the most boring, disjointed sermon I had ever heard.

Saturday night was a little better. The associate pastor preaching that night was a meek and humble man, and certainly one who studied well, but he had no gift for preaching. Only a little over half the church was filled.

Sunday morning's congregation was our regular attendees. The *other* associate pastor did a fine job of preaching, but he seemed to have little impact. What did have impact, though, was the pastor's announcement at the end of service. He told the people I would be preaching the last service of the youth revival. Everybody was surprised—especially me!

After we were dismissed, I went to the pastor to verify the announcement. The pastor said, "Russ, I don't want to put you out there. I've got a lot of reservations about it, but I believe God wants you to preach." Then he gave me the keys to his study and told me to get ready.

The text I chose was the third chapter of Daniel, about the faith of the three young men who were thrown into the furnace rather than obey the king and worship a false god. I chose to preach on faith, more for myself than for the people. After the pastor telling me his doubts, I really began having doubts of my own. I prepared all day but still had only about ten to fifteen minutes of material.

That night I met with the pastor in his study, where we prayed until it was time to go into the auditorium. I was nervous enough already, but when we entered the auditorium and I saw the place packed beyond capacity, I was stricken with terror. As I looked at and identified the faces, I was able to discern three specific groups: those who wished me well, those who wanted to see me fall flat on my face, and those who just wanted to see if it was true that the ex-druggie would preach. Even my parents had shown up, which was a shock to me.

When I was introduced, I merely stood there like an idiot. I was terrified. After a moment that seemed an eternity, I asked, "Don't you all feel just a little bit sorry for me?" There was a little laughter. At last, I began to preach.

What began as a ten-minute sermonette became a thirty-three-minute sermon (according to the pastor), and I put my heart into it. The harder I preached, the more "Amens" were roared back at me. When I finished, I turned the altar call over to the pastor. While he spoke and the people sang, I prayed. I asked God for just one soul so I would know I was doing what He wanted. Sure enough, I got one soul at the altar call.

After the service, every person there shook my hand. Everyone seemed pleased with what I had done. My mother hugged me and broke into tears. I did not understand why everyone was so pleased, as I thought I had not done very well, but that service was a turning point.

When everyone had gone, I told the pastor about asking God for one soul each of the two times I had preached. He looked at me like I was an idiot and said, "Well, you're going to have to start asking for more than that."

I took his advice to heart. I seemed to get everything I asked for after that. I asked for the opportunities to preach and got so many invitations to fill pulpits for vacationing pastors and youth revivals that I finally had to form the R. L. Ford Evangelistic Association.

I quit asking for just one soul too. I asked for all God could send, and the results were amazing. Sometimes the altar calls were longer than my half- to three-quarter-hour sermons. The front would fill with people and then empty. As I was about to close the invitation, the front would fill up again.

Opportunity led to opportunity. Some of my youth revivals were broadcast over local radio, and one was televised. I preached in high school auditoriums across Missouri, northern Arkansas, southern Iowa, and southern Illinois. I preached in rural churches with congregations as small as thirty, and metropolitan churches with memberships in the thousands. It seemed God had blessed me with an ability to convey with passion what I believed to be His message.

Members of my home church were planning my career for me. It was decided I would earn my bachelor's degree at Southwest Baptist University and then go to Fort Worth for a master of divinity at Southwestern Baptist Theological Seminary. Following school I would serve as a pastor for several years to gain practical experience, then go into full-time evangelization and hold crusades all across the country.

Everything looked great from the outside. I was only a teenager, and it looked like I had nowhere to go but up. However, I was beginning to experience a whole new misery that was getting harder and harder to justify in my conscience. I took my mentor and other adults in my church at their word when they told me to read and study the Scriptures. That produced an insurmountable problem, as what I was being taught about Baptist theology simply did not agree with the Bible.

As a Baptist, I was taught that baptism was not necessary for salvation but was merely an ordinance that should be obeyed. My take from the Bible, though, was not only that baptism is necessary but also that it has a supernatural effect on the soul.

As Baptists, to be forgiven, all we had to do was ask God to pardon us, but that seemed to nullify John 20:23. Throughout His ministry Jesus told us to forgive, forgive, forgive. This passage in John is different. He tells His apostles after His Resurrection that they have the choice to forgive or not forgive. I had to ask myself several questions behind this passage: Why give only the apostles the choice to forgive or not forgive? Why use the word *retain*? Was He giving them a power not given to others? If so, who are those taking the place of the apostles today? Since Jesus is God and He is the same yesterday, today, and forever, and if He is giving the apostles a new power, it is impossible for that power to cease with the passing of the apostles. I could not figure this out.

The Lord's Supper was special to Baptists. We observed it only on the last Sunday of those months with five Sundays, but it was an important and moving event for us. Then I stumbled across something Paul wrote: "Whoever, therefore, eats the bread or drinks the cup of the Lord in an unworthy manner will be guilty of profaning the body and blood of the Lord. Let a man examine himself, and so eat of the bread and drink of the cup. For any one who eats and drinks without discerning the body eats and drinks judgment upon himself" (1 Corinthians 11:27–29).

That passage stopped me in my tracks. The only thing I could understand about what Paul had written was that there would be condemnation for anyone unworthy to participate in the Lord's Supper. I never felt worthy, but I could not see how I could be condemned for memorializing Jesus' Last Supper by being unworthy to eat an oyster cracker and drink a swallow of grape juice. I could not understand this at all, but it worried me.

I began to address those questions to my pastor, who had a master's degree in divinity from the same seminary I planned to attend. Whether because he was too busy, or too uncomfortable with my questions, he put me off. He told me to wait until I got to college, when all my questions would be answered.

My pastor's prediction was not fulfilled. At college I had a mentor, a learned professor who was the epitome of charity. He and I met once or twice each week to address my questions, but that turned out to be an exercise in futility. I would pose a question, and he would form an answer. The problem was, his answers merely caused more questions. We would pursue my difficulties like a dog chasing his tail. Finally, in frustration, the professor would end our sessions the same way every time. He would say, "Mr. Ford, there are some things about the Christian life we are simply not meant to understand."

Baloney, was my unspoken response. Nature itself taught me that God is a logical Creator. All of creation on the natural plane is logical, and Christianity is given to us on that plane. Certainly Christianity is supernatural, because the Supernature founded it, but He presents it to us on the natural plane. So the life the Creator expects us to live must be knowable. After all, Jesus said, "He who *believes* and is baptized will be saved; but he who *does not believe* will be condemned" (Mark 16:16). If my salvation is contingent upon my belief, then what I believe must be knowable. Even mysteries such as the Trinity and the Eucharist are knowable, though not fully understandable.

Near the end of my first semester, I reached a crisis in faith. I could no longer preach in good conscience what I could no longer believe. The professor and I would have to reach closure one way or the other, I decided. At our final meeting, we debated furiously. I think the professor recognized my urgency, understanding that this was my crossroads, so he threw himself into our discussion with a passion. This time, though, our conversation ended differently. After telling me that some things are not knowable, he said, "Perhaps, Mr. Ford, you should reconsider your call to the ministry."

I replied, "Doctor, perhaps you are right."

I left school that day, with only one semester completed. Since the nation was in a recession and jobs were scarce, I joined the army. After training at Fort Leonard Wood and Fort McClellan, I was sent to Fort Wainwright in Alaska. I began investigating all the major Christian religions, except Catholicism. When I ran into a contradiction that could not be adequately explained, I would walk on to the next denomination.

For all my talk of logic in religion, my own logic was selective. I had been taught that Catholicism is pagan, so I never checked it out. Yet the people who taught me that were the same folks who taught me Baptist theology, and because I found what they taught me about it illogical, I should have found their bias against Catholicism illogical too. But I was completely closed to Catholicism. Many times in those years, when I was alone, I would fall to my knees and cry out to God, "If You are real—if You are who You say You are—show Yourself to me so I can worship You!"

Always I was left in silence. Before long I became an agnostic, never guessing that, in 1988, God would show me how He had already answered that prayer.

*　*　*

After the army, I became a private investigator and bounty hunter. Eventually, having lost everything I owned in Missouri, and tired of being beaten and shot at, I moved to Alabama for a fresh start. I was a first-rate sales professional, good at business and ambitious in the extreme, so I figured I could own a substantial portion of Alabama in five years. I chose the Anniston area because I had fond memories of it from my army days at Fort McClellan. But the Alabama I found as a civilian was not the same state I had known as a soldier. The folks did not like aggressive, slick-talking Yankees, and that made earning a living nearly impossible.

My situation deteriorated rapidly from bad to worse to desperate. Psychologically, I was a mess, suffering from some sort of psychological and emotional breakdown. When the stress got to be too much, I would blank out everything. Once I came to my senses while driving my car, lost and forty miles from home, with no idea of where I had been or what I had done.

I experienced such an episode the same night a person was brutalized by a man who matched my general description. When I was arrested, the police told me they had a solid case against me. In those days, before I knew anything about prosecutorial misconduct, I thought if the cops said you were guilty, then you were guilty. So I thought I must have been guilty, despite the fact that I recalled nothing.

The court assigned me a lawyer. I will never forget his first words to me: "Mr. Ford, my name is Billy Hardegree.

I've been appointed to represent you. I don't like you, and I believe you belong in prison, but I've been appointed to do the best I can for you." At the time, I was ignorant of the law, like most laymen, and I did not know I could have fired Mr. Hardegree, who had been a member of the bar less than a year.

Several months later, Hardegree came to see me again and told me the district attorney was offering me a one-time deal of twenty-five years. He said that if I went to trial I would get a life sentence, so Hardegree advised me to accept the offer. Taking him at his word, I agreed. I did not see my lawyer again until the day I was sentenced.

In the courtroom, we stood before Judge Quattlebaum. Hardegree handed me some papers, saying I did not have time to read them before signing them. Then he told me that when the judge asked if anyone had promised me any sort of deal I was to say no. He also told me I would have to tell the judge what happened that night.

"How can I do that, since I don't remember anything?" I asked. He told me to repeat what I had read in the police report.

We stood shoulder to shoulder before the bench. The district attorney and the assistant district attorney were both standing behind us, to my left. The judge asked how I pled, and I said guilty. He asked if anyone had promised me any deals, and I said no. Then he told me to tell the court what happened that night. I dutifully recited the police report as best as I could remember it, which seemed to satisfy His Honor. The judge then sentenced me to twenty-five years in the state penitentiary.

Immediately after the judge pronounced the sentence, I heard the assistant district attorney say to the district attorney, "Whew! We couldn't have convicted him!"

I looked over my shoulder and saw the district attorney and assistant district attorney smiling at me. As I turned back around, I felt a hard slap on my shoulder and heard my lawyer mumble, "Good luck." By the time I turned to face him, Hardegree was heading out the door.

Hardegree's quick exit saved his life. When I realized I had been sold out, I had every intention of killing him where he stood. The only reason I did not bolt to catch him was that I was bound by chains.

* * *

While sitting in county jail awaiting sentence, I thought a lot about the twenty-five years I had agreed to serve. It was equivalent to a death sentence for me. I would be fifty-four when the sentence was complete, and Ford males all die at fifty or younger, always from heart disease. My father is the only Ford male to have lived past fifty. He had a major heart attack at forty-eight, followed by a quadruple bypass. With the best medical care money could buy, he lived on only until he was fifty-two.

By that time in my life, I was bordering on atheism. The more I thought about that twenty-five-year sentence, the more it simply did not make sense to me to keep living. After all, if there is no God, why worry about an afterlife? Why live twenty-five years in prison if I could end it quickly?

While contemplating suicide, I decided to try God one more time. I sat down and reread the Bible in three or four days. Then, late one night and alone in my cell, I got on my knees and prayed. I said, *God, if You're real, show me. Jesus, if You are who You say You are, prove it to me. Otherwise, there is nothing.*

Suddenly, in the silence, something happened. As to its origin, as with other extraordinary phenomena I have experienced, I rely on the authority of the Roman Catholic Church to make such judgments. But I take a solemn oath that what I am about to relate happened just as I am telling it.

I heard an audible voice, neither male nor female. The voice came from nowhere, yet it came from everywhere. The voice said, "Wait. Be patient. I have great plans for you." What followed was a silence so thick that it seemed I could feel it literally.

A few days later, I decided my "voice" must have been a figment of my imagination, so I tried suicide after all. A county doctor had prescribed a medication to help me sleep. Security on medications was lax; they gave inmates an entire day's dosage in a tiny envelope at dinner. I decided that any medication that would make me sleep would kill me if taken in large enough doses. So I saved thirty days' worth of pills, which amounted to ninety pills. One night, I ate all ninety pills, fully expecting to die. All that happened was that I slept for two days.

Some months later, in prison, I told a psychologist what I had done. He looked at the record to see what I had been prescribed, then told me ninety of those pills would have killed a horse. Plainly, he did not believe me.

A couple of weeks after my overdose attempt, I tried something else. In need of some new shoestrings, I had written to Dad, asking him to send me a set. He thought he was sending me a pair of shoestrings, but what he actually sent was one long boot string. The string was a quarter to three-eighths of an inch wide and was made of woven nylon. I tied one end of the string around the corner bar of my bunk and tried to break it. The string was a lot stronger than I. So I tied one end around my neck and the other end onto the iron air-vent grate over the toilet. Then I simply stepped off the toilet.

The choking was uncomfortable at first, but I recall the peace I felt as I began to lose consciousness. I recall thinking, *This isn't bad. Death is good.*

The next thing I knew, I woke up on the floor by the toilet with a huge bump on my head. I was angry, thinking the string had either come untied at the grate or the grate had cut the nylon string. Imagine my surprise when I stood up and saw that the nylon string had broken about halfway between the grate and my neck. Suddenly I remembered, "Wait. Be patient. I have great plans for you."

Did God send an angel to break my death cord? I do not know, but I honestly believe that if I had had a gun, God would not have let its bullet penetrate my skull. I think God was saving me, for myself and for others.

At any rate, that incident got my attention. I decided to just be a passive observer in my own life for a while to see what would happen. I did not have long to wait.

* * *

In March 1988, I was sent to Bullock Prison, forty miles from Montgomery. It was a new facility, but no Alabama State prison was a pleasant place to be in the late 1980s. I could say a lot about the harsh, crowded environment, the widespread degradation and despair, the brutality of many guards, and the culturally ingrained anti-Catholicism of the staff—then and now—but this account is limited to experiences relating directly to my conversion.

In June, an old convict was moved onto the bunk next to mine. He was Michael Anthony Mayola, and he looked seventy, though he was only fifty-five. He had been in prison for twenty-five years, which makes a man old before his time. At the time that I write this, he has spent forty-two years in prison.

A cradle Catholic who lapsed from the faith as a teenager, Mike returned to the practice of the faith after going to prison in the early 1960s. He spent many years trying to evangelize, with little or no success. Finally, in the early eighties at Kilby Prison, the Holy Spirit began to move, using Mike to reach perhaps a dozen prisoners.

When Mike showed up at Bullock Prison in 1988, he was ready to start all over again. He spent a couple of days observing me before deciding to approach me. Mike has said that what attracted him was my vocabulary and apparently strong intellect. But writing of our first meeting several years later, he said he was afraid to approach me, because I was "the most evil man [he] had ever met in twenty-five years of prison."

I am eternally grateful that the graces of the sacrament of confirmation defeated Mike's fear. He began by inviting himself to sit on my bunk and talk. That rubbed me the wrong way, but I tend to be tolerant of elderly people. After a few exchanges, Mike began talking religion. I told him I was not interested, but he was ready for that.

With an old *Baltimore Catechism, No. 2*, in his hand, Mike challenged my ego. He said it was a seventh-grade religion book, with tests at the end of each chapter. He bet I could not pass the first test, but he promised that if I did pass it, he would leave me alone and never bring up religion again. How could I resist that? I could kill two birds with one stone: prove I was smarter than he thought, and stop him from annoying me later.

To Mike's shocked surprise, I passed his test. Though I got all the answers right, the experience left me troubled.

The answers I gave Mike were not those I was taught as a Baptist but rather those I had figured out for myself years earlier. This disturbed me by raising the possibility that the Catholic Church might have answers to all my questions.

True to his word, Mike told me not to worry, he would not bother me again. To his amazement, I told him I was willing to study. And study we did! So overcrowded was the prison that there were not enough jobs to go around, and as neither Mike nor I had one, we were free to study all we wanted. We studied together seven days a week, a minimum of eight hours a day, for nine months. I could not get enough, and Mike was just the walking Catholic encyclopedia I needed.

I never told Mike I had questions and doubts, because I was afraid he would tailor his answers with that in mind. I decided that if Catholicism were genuine Christianity, it would answer my questions on its own merit. I was right. Within a few weeks all my questions had been answered, scores of new ones raised, and all of them answered. Mike has said I was the best student he ever had and that he knew intuitively that God had some big job in store for me.

By the time we finished studying the ninth article of the Creed ("I believe in the Holy Catholic Church, the communion of saints . . ."), I was persuaded that the Catholic Church was the one authentic Christian Church founded by Jesus Christ, true God and true man. On the Feast of Saint Bartholomew, August 24, 1988, I made the intellectual decision to become a Roman Catholic. My emotional commitment came later.

After lapsing into agnosticism some years earlier, I had found that my torment about religious questions was unending. When I was most distressed, I would cry out to the God I doubted, *Jesus, if You are who You claim to be, show*

Yourself to me! I will worship You and devote myself to You, if You will only show Yourself!

On that hot August afternoon, Mike began teaching me about the Real Presence of Christ in the Holy Eucharist. As the truth of the Eucharistic reality began to seep into my consciousness, I recalled all those times I had presumptuously demanded that the Alpha and Omega appear to me. Now I realized that He had been there all along, reposed in every Catholic Church in the world, awaiting my adoration. The realization stabbed through my heart into the depths of my soul. I wept in shame for my arrogance, for joy at my discovery, and for regret at the irony of learning these sacred truths in a place where I would be forever deprived of His Presence in a tabernacle or monstrance. That was when I made my emotional commitment to Jesus Christ and His Church.

For the first time in my life, I could look to His Majesty with no doubt remaining at all and cry, "My Lord and my God! Have pity on this worthless convict!"

*   *   *

Despite this landmark moment in my conversion, God was not yet through converting me. Next, He made me face a challenge that would test my mettle and commitment.

While studying with Mike, I had kept my father informed of the things I was learning and thinking. We wrote to each other several times a week and spoke on the phone a couple of times a month. When Dad realized I was getting serious about becoming a Catholic, I began to encounter a lot of resistance from him, which quickly became an open break between father and son. A few days after I learned about the Eucharist, we began to argue on the phone about my desire to become a Catholic. As always, it was Dad who put an end to the conflict. He said, "No son of mine is a Roman Catholic!" He then hung up.

For several minutes I sat and stared at the phone, crushed. All my life the thing I had most wanted was my father's approval, but it had always been withheld from me. Now, by telling me that no son of his was a Catholic, he had disowned me.

I could have reversed the situation by telling Dad I would not convert, but painful as it was, I had made up my mind that my Father had to be the one in Heaven, not the one who sired me.

Although my parents had been divorced for eight years, my mother and sister joined Dad in breaking with me. I received no more letters from anyone. Feeling the full impact of my loneliness, I responded by praying several Rosaries each day for Dad, who was in poor health. I prayed for his conversion, offering up the pain of my loss of his affection.

Less than two months later, my mother and grandmother made a surprise visit to me. Mom said she wanted to give me her news in person: Dad had died on October 19, and his funeral was taking place as we visited. I was devastated, until I talked to my grandmother.

Dad was home alone when he had another heart attack, Grandma said. He was found dead on the kitchen floor, with a smile on his face. Even after he had been embalmed, the smile was still on his face. I believe that Our Blessed Mother answered my prayers, that either she or his guardian angel appeared to him at the moment of his death, inspiring him to perfect contrition.

Of course, Dad's death did not lift my excommunication from the family. I have not seen Mom in sixteen years; we exchange letters about twice a year. I cannot remember when I last heard from my sister.

Jesus never promised us a bed of roses on earth. Those who try to live the Catholic faith understand and accept thorns in life. My family's rejection is just one of my thorns. Our duty as Catholics is to accept the thorns and offer them back to God in reparation for our sins and the sins of the world.

* * *

At the same time that I was experiencing my father's final rejection, God sent one of the greatest gifts possible into my life: a holy, humble eighty-year-old priest named Killian Mooney, of the Missionary Servants of the Most Holy Trinity. Never has anyone changed my life so radically as he did.

I had grown up with a distorted notion of fatherhood. As Father Killian began to understand my soul, he realized that my malformed concept of fatherhood was keeping me from loving and trusting my Heavenly Father. He knew I would have to acquire a more authentic conception of fatherhood if I was to persevere in the faith. As a result, over the three and a half years we knew each other, Father Killian became my true father in every sense of the word except the biological. He loved me as a son; I loved him as the only real father I had ever had, and as my confessor, teacher, spiritual director, and friend. I have the honor of being the first state prisoner Father Killian ever baptized. He came to call me a "co-worker", and even his "right hand".

Bullock Prison had been open only nine months when I got there. From the very beginning, Father Killian had been coming every other Saturday at his appointed time. But until Mike Mayola arrived at Bullock, Father had sat all alone in the small classroom reserved for him. Week after week, month after month, Father would show up and sit for an hour and a half, praying for souls he could reconcile to God, souls he could celebrate Mass for, souls he could love into Heaven. Father never wasted a moment, and his patience and prayers were first rewarded through Mike Mayola and, later, through me.

The first eight months I knew Father Killian, I had attended Mass only as a catechumen, so I did not get to go to confession or receive Communion. But as I continued to learn, my zeal for our faith continued to grow. Ever the missionary, Father Killian decided to cash in on it. One day after Mass, he handed me a little catechism.

"Here, Russ", he said. "I want you to teach the catechism to the other prisoners."

"No, Father, I'm not really interested in teaching the catechism", I replied. "All I want is to be left alone to learn and enjoy my new faith."

Father never missed a beat. Thumbing through the book, he said, "Okay, but make sure they learn the theological virtues."

"No, Father. I don't think you understand. I don't want to teach the catechism."

With a twinkle in his blue eyes and a leprechaun's grin, he said, "Sure, I understand. Now, be certain they understand fully the ninth article of the Creed."

Growing impatient, I asked, "Father, what part of *no* don't you understand? I told you I don't want to teach the catechism."

"Of course I understand", he said, undaunted. "Be quite thorough when teaching about the Eucharist ..."

Arrrrrgh! I was frustrated, but I did not want to hurt the priest's feelings, so I held my tongue. Instead, I wrote a letter to Archbishop Oscar Lipscomb. Its gist was, "Will you please get this holy old priest off my back?"

His response surprised me so much that I shall never forget it. "Russell," he wrote, "obey your pastor. I think you will make a wonderful catechism instructor."

What could I do? Disobedience to my bishop would seem to be, in effect, disobedience to God. I began teaching the catechism.

*   *   *

Eventually God showed His approval by sending a stream of conversions, but they did not come immediately. Though I went after souls with enthusiasm, my efforts at first produced no fruit.

Getting men interested in learning about the faith was easy because enthusiasm is contagious. I began by scheduling individual lessons, an hour each, going from one cellblock to another for fourteen hours a day. But by the time I got to the fifth or sixth article of the Creed, the students would say they did not want to study anymore.

Why could I not hold their interest through the whole catechism? When I was not teaching, I was studying, so it was not that my material was incomplete. No, the reason for my failure lay not with the teachings but with the teacher. Christ Himself showed me the answer.

One rainy morning, instead of going out to the yard, we were all packed into the gym for our required hour and a half of recreation. The noise from a thousand convicts made prayerful meditation impossible, so I just watched what was going on around me. On one side a group was boasting about the crimes that had put them in prison, the crimes they got away with, and those they planned to pull on release.

On another side, men were boasting—and probably lying—about sexual exploits. Homosexuals were trying to avoid the attention of the guards while prostituting themselves. Another huddle of prisoners was gambling with contraband dice. What I saw distressed me, because it was so contrary to my own efforts to become the sort of man Christ expects me to be.

Suddenly, all the noise ceased. I could see mouths moving, but I heard nothing. At first I thought something was happening to my ears. Then I heard a voice in my mind, saying, "Look at them, Russell. These are my children, walking blindly into the abyss. You are the only tool I have here to bring them to me, yet you sit here and do nothing. Love them."

At once the noise returned, but I hardly noticed. Tears of shame rolled down my cheeks, because the accusation was true. I had failed to love these sons of God. That was the central reason for my failure as a catechist.

I promised Christ that with His help, I would learn to love His incarcerated children. It is a promise I have never broken. I have loved all the men who came into the Church through Father Killian's and my apostolate as if they were my own sons.

*   *   *

After that experience in the gym, actual graces began to pour from Heaven like a spiritual rainstorm.

I had written to an Ignatius Press publication and asked for a gift subscription, explaining that I was a prison catechist who needed to prepare students for eventual release. After my letter was printed, a Catholic layman from Chicago replied, offering to pay for the subscription and to send anything else we needed. He is John Finnegan.

I know John would prefer to serve Jesus anonymously, but I feel compelled to name him in gratitude. Our prison apostolate could not have accomplished what it has without John's help. He has donated more than twenty thousand dollars' worth of books, tapes, and videos and has initiated a global network of other Catholics who pray for us. Thanks to his efforts, thousands of Masses have been celebrated for our work. Anyone who wants to curb crime and help bring about lasting change in his imprisoned brothers can take John as a model of how to live out Christ's counsel that "as you did it to one of the least of these my brethren, you did it to me" (Matthew 25:40).

With the materials John sent us, we established a new program that managed to engage and hold the interest of more men. First came thirteen videos by Father Robert J. Fox, the internationally known "Fatima priest". The series, called *Sharing the Faith*, was originally recorded for the Eternal Word Television Network (EWTN). Mike and I reviewed it together, and as we watched, I noticed that Mike kept wiping tears from his eyes. I asked what was wrong. Mike said the tapes were a balm on the gaping wound in his heart caused by twenty years of mushy or heretical catechesis. He said, "Russ, we gotta use these."

As soon as we arranged a place to meet each week, it was nonstop evangelization. Over the next year, we developed a class routine. We began with a prayer: "Holy Spirit, Soul of our souls, we ask that You open our hearts and minds to truth and help us imbibe those truths, then learn to live by them. Grant this through Christ Our Lord. Amen."

Next, I would choose two team captains, who took turns choosing team members. Then each team got a pencil and half a sheet of paper. All was set, and the video player was turned on.

Father Fox is an excellent teacher, and the scripts for the tapes are printed in a companion book. At the end of each lesson is a series of discussion questions, which we used later.

While the video played, I would pour a pack of instant coffee into a big one-hundred-cup coffee maker, open a couple of fifty-cent packs of cookies purchased from the canteen, and figure how many each student could have. Our supplies were mighty lean in those early years. The state did not pay us, and my family did not send me money. I began writing articles in *Fatima Family Messenger* and *Immaculata* magazines, and mail came pouring in from good Catholics all over the country, an average of three hundred letters a month for almost two years. Mike and I began writing letters to possible benefactors, explaining the needs of the prison apostolate. Eventually enough money came in to cover the program's necessities.

So, after sitting for half an hour in uncomfortable metal chairs watching the video, the men could take a welcome ten-minute coffee-and-cookie break. Then came a contest between the two teams. In the early days, all the winners won were bragging rights. Later, thanks to donors, we could give them prizes of five or six extra cookies. I always chose competitive people as team captains. The competitive atmosphere may seem childish, but it works. Men who showed up only for coffee and cookies found they were learning, and most of them eventually converted.

As good as Father Fox' series was, no competent priest would accept exposure to those twenty-six lessons as sufficient instruction for reception into the Church. Men who came to me after class saying they wanted to become Catholics had to receive personal instruction. So my days were still filled with teaching, but my time was better spent because these students were no longer just inquirers but catechumens.

I have never asked anyone to join the Church. After all, she is not a club. When we invite someone to attend class, we make it clear up front that no one will ever urge him to join. When he is ready to make the move from enquirer to catechumen, he will tell us.

I have started men in group classes who asked for individual instruction without saying they wanted to become Catholic. The free coffee and cookies at the meetings would often motivate them to keep coming, and many eventually became Catholic. Others I took through the entire catechism, only to have them thank me and say good-bye. Someday the man who walks away may receive the graces of conversion. If he never does, though, at least he will be a friend of the Church.

As the apostolate grew and conditions affecting our work improved, we began to get Catholic movies. We also received an abundance of excellent Catholic books. In fact, by the time I left Bullock Prison, we had over 1,000 books, more than 150 videos, and more than 200 audiotapes. A local layman built us a huge, serviceable portable library cabinet.

One night each week we would show a Catholic movie. Although the men enjoyed them, I had a different agenda than mere recreation in mind. We showed *The Miracle of Our Lady of Fatima* to inspire Marian devotion; *Henry V* to demonstrate Catholic history; *The Song of Bernadette* to familiarize the men with saints; and *Going My Way* to instill pride with an image of a Catholic culture. Always, at the close of the movie, I would offer a selection of related books from the library. The men all became avid readers.

* * *

For several years, we had a deputy warden named Chuck Greer, who was a Catholic convert and a good man.

Although not even his authority could overcome the anti-Catholic discrimination we faced daily, he did help us in other ways. One big way was allowing the Saint Louis province of the Carmelite Sisters of the Divine Heart of Jesus to send our Catholic group six or seven boxes at the maximum UPS weight each Christmas season.

The sisters sent us huge sausages, hams, dried fruit, shelled nuts, imported chocolates, and just about any other treat you could imagine. When the boxes arrived, I would gather several of our community and two gigantic weight lifters to go to the chaplain's office with me. To avoid being robbed on our way back, we would form a convoy, led by one weight lifter and closed up in the rear by another. Once we arrived at my cellblock, we would divide the booty evenly into grocery sacks, one for each member, while the weight lifters stood guard. Since the laborer is worthy of his hire, the two weight lifters got an equal share for helping, although they were not Catholic.

During the first Christmas when the sisters helped us, I discovered how poverty-stricken some of our men were. Alabama convicts are just plain poor. A lot of men have no one to send them money or packages at Christmas. So we started our Christmas Box program under the inspiration of Saint John Bosco, who believed in caring for the temporal and spiritual needs of his boys in a way that made them feel they earned whatever he gave them. We promised any man who wanted one a Christmas box in December, but to qualify for the box, each man had to attend all catechism classes and all Masses from the end of August through December. If he missed anything without a valid, verifiable excuse, he could not receive the package.

Some critics charged us with buying converts with our treats. Of course, none of us is capable of converting anyone.

I am merely a seed planter. Only the Holy Spirit makes converts. All the rest of us can do is provide an environment in which men can hear the truth, and then actually present that truth. What any individual soul does with that truth is strictly between him and the Holy Spirit, and it takes place in the deepest core of the human intellect.

One of many possible examples is my godson, Carl James Monroe, a legend in this penal system. Feared by convicts and guards alike, he was so violent that I heard stories about him while I was still in county jail awaiting transfer to prison. His early years were a study in the formation of a criminal. Born the illegitimate child of a West Virginia barmaid in 1945, Carl grew up in the places where his mother worked, often subsisting on meals of bar nuts and pickled eggs. By fourth grade, Carl was a chronic truant. When he was eighteen, a judge let him choose between prison and the military. Carl chose the Marine Corps and went to Vietnam, where he distinguished himself by killing two Viet Cong who bayoneted him while he was drunk on guard duty. Torn between giving him a decoration or a court martial, the Corps opted to decorate him. His first sergeant told him, "Monroe, you're a damn fine soldier ... but a sorry Marine."

Carl continued his criminal career on returning to the United States, serving two years in a West Virginia prison before beating an Alabama man to death in a drunken rage. When he went to Alabama's death row in 1970, he was twenty-five years old and functionally illiterate. He taught himself to read before the Supreme Court outlawed the death penalty across the United States in 1972. At that point his sentence was commuted to life in prison. Carl became the man to talk to if you wanted liquor, drugs, sex—anything illicit. Because he was deadly, few men ever crossed him.

Yet he had great respect for education. We met when he transferred to Bullock Prison to attend a Faulkner University extension program while there were still Pell Grants for convicts. We became friends while working toward our degrees, but Carl would never discuss religion with me.

One day in August 1994 Carl came to me and said, "Look here, Ford, I hear you Catholics are giving away a Christmas package to anyone who goes to your classes. Is that right?"

I told him it was and explained our requirements.

Carl laid down some rules of his own. "Well, I'm gonna come just to get that package, because I've got nobody out there to send me one. But I don't want no one trying to convert me to that Catholic stuff, and I don't wanna hear none of that rah-rah, praise the Lord s—— either." I laughed and told him there was no hidden agenda, that all he had to do was attend and we would see to it he got a box.

By mid-October, Carl was asking some pretty serious questions about Catholicism. My tactic was to answer his questions, then change the subject. Sometime in December he said, "Russ, I want to be a Catholic, but I'm going to wait until after the first of the year. I don't want to do it now, 'cause I don't want nobody accusing me of doing it for the package." That did not make sense to me, but I agreed to keep his decision between us and the priest until after the new year.

Carl dug into Church history like a scholar. Today he is a courageous lay evangelist, a catechism instructor, a virtual Church historian, and a competent apologist.

To me, Carl's story proves several things. First, it demonstrates that no soul is beyond God's reach. Most people had written off Carl James Monroe, but Providence had not written him off. Without our Christmas Box program,

Carl would never have been in a position to learn the truths of the faith, but I did not purchase his soul with our Christmas box. His soul was purchased with Blood by a Lamb on a Cross two thousand years ago. All I did was provide a means for Carl to learn about that purchase.

Finally, his story convinces me that we should put an end to the death penalty. Had Carl been executed as scheduled, he would never have become a Catholic, and since he went on to share the faith with countless others, they might also have been cheated out of the sheer joy of knowing God.

Conversion is possible only through grace. We cannot begin to know or understand the infinite mind of God. He gives the actual graces for conversion when *He* chooses, not when we want it to happen. In Carl's case those graces appeared a quarter of century after he landed on death row.

* * *

Suddenly we were making one convert after another. The apostolate grew so explosively that soon I had to train others to teach. Conversions became so frequent that Father Killian summed up our system as, "You catechize 'em, I'll baptize 'em."

Father came to celebrate Holy Mass for his prison sons twice a month. The rest of his time was devoted to Holy Redeemer parish in historic Eufala, where he served as pastor. Despite his age, he seemed tireless. His love for the Blessed Sacrament fired his energy. Before sunrise every day, he walked into the sacristy, pulled his chair up next to the tabernacle, and conversed with Jesus. The more hours he prayed, the more God let him accomplish.

The parish included some of the poorest parts of Alabama. One day a week, people who could not pay their rent or their utility bill or buy medication or food for their families would line up at Father's rectory door, out to the sidewalk, down past the front of the church, and around the corner. Father would pray with them, counsel them, and then write vouchers to the electric company, the supermarket, the landlord, or the drug store. Those vouchers were always honored, because all the merchants knew that the words "Father Killian sent me" meant that Father Killian would make them good.

Nobody knew who funded Father's vouchers, which amounted to several thousand dollars a year. How he did it remained a mystery even after his death, when parish records were scrutinized. No receipts, no canceled checks, no donor list, no trace of anything offered a clue as to where the money came from. Having known Father Killian well enough to witness other unexplainable events, I am convinced that He who multiplied loaves and fishes simply multiplied dollars as Father Killian needed them.

Father Killian's confessional was another extraordinary place. He meant for it to be a place where the penitent came face-to-face with God's Fatherly love, both in its mercy and its justice. While the penitent confessed, Father Killian would squint his eyes shut and bow his head. After the penitent had accused himself, Father would counsel him much as a father does his child. The penances he typically assigned were light and almost always Marian in nature, unless he was your spiritual director. When it was time to make an act of contrition, Father would say, "Now, tell God you're sorry." This made me feel like a little boy sitting on Daddy's lap, apologizing, and it helped to change my concept of God the Father from that of a supernatural tyrant waiting to punish me to that of God as a loving Father who wanted only the best for me.

Finally, Father Killian would give absolution, ending the sign of the cross with a fatherly tap on the penitent's head. His method was to work on one particular sin until it became a thing of the past. If he was your spiritual director, as he was mine, penances were seldom light, and his fatherly tap at absolution was not always a mere gesture. When I had to admit that I had failed to act on the counsel he had given me, or had not adequately completed my previous penance, Father would surprise me with a solid thump on the head. I always left the confessional knowing I was loved, and feeling that all was right in my world.

Deputy Warden Chuck Greer was a member of Father Killian's parish. He constantly tried to make things easier for Father at Bullock, but not even his authority could overcome the anti-Catholicism that was so ingrained in his subordinates' minds that they firmly believed the Catholic Church was the Whore of Babylon, and the pope the Antichrist.

Father was routinely mistreated by prison authorities, though he never complained about it. He did not mention it even to us, but we knew because we could see the abuse from where we waited for him. Chuck Greer found out about it because we told him.

The abuses were absurd. When Father came to the prison, guards would search everything he had. Many times we watched Protestant ministers arrive and walk right around Father, greeting the guards as they went by. They were never searched or questioned, but poor Father Killian was regularly harassed. Sometimes, in the hundred-degree heat of an Alabama summer day, the guards would make him stand for two hours in direct sunlight, wearing his heat-absorbing black clothing and carrying his Mass kit and vestments, before they let him into the prison.

Once, after standing in that heat for nearly an hour, Father Killian realized he had forgotten the wine. He asked the guard admitting him to call Chuck Greer and ask him to bring over a little wine.

Curtly the guard replied, "If you want anything from the warden, go see him yourself." Wardens in Alabama live on state property near the prison. So Father Killian had to gather up all his things, walk another hundred yards in the heat to Warden Greer's house, get the wine, walk back to the prison, and go through the entire admission process all over again as if he had not done it already.

Father was the first man I had ever known with absolutely no guile in him. Soft-spoken but fearless, he fully understood the authority his priesthood carried. As a rare treat, the Christmas before he died, he managed to arrange a Christmas Vigil Mass for us. But just as he pulled into the parking lot, there was a stabbing in one of the cellblocks, and immediately the prison was locked down tight. The guards told Father to go home, that all activities had been canceled.

Father refused to be deterred. He went to Warden Greer's house. Greer told him it was standard procedure to lock down after a stabbing.

"I will not let my boys go another Christmas without Mass", Father Killian replied.

Chuck knew that once Father's mind was made up, there would be no changing it, so he escorted him back to the prison. While Father got ready for Mass, Warden Greer personally went to each cellblock to gather us for Mass. We heard that Christmas Vigil Mass after all.

This is the man who taught me, nurtured me, and loved me for three and a half of the very best years of my life.

* * *

Perhaps the saddest time in my Catholic life came in late January 1992. The prison chaplain, Steve Walker, a kind Assembly of God minister who had only recently come to Bullock, called me to his office to tell me Father Killian had suffered a massive stroke and was not expected to live.

I was stunned. Somehow it never occurred to me that I might one day lose my spiritual father. Devastated, I went to look for Mike Mayola, my godfather, who was in the yard, praying as he walked. Choking with sobs, I told Mike what had happened.

Never have I prayed so intensely as I did then. I begged God for a miracle to restore Father Killian's health. I begged Him to take me instead, telling God the men needed Father.

On January 25, the Feast of the Conversion of Saint Paul, Father had been due to celebrate Mass for us. We all met in the room where Mass was heard, and prayed the Rosary for Father. At the exact moment when Father would normally arrive, I got an overwhelming sense of his presence—so much so that I looked up to see if he had come into the room, though I understood that was impossible. Then I looked at my watch and knew in my heart that Father Killian was dead. I believe he asked Our Lady to take him by the prison to say good-bye to us before she took him to Heaven.

In this world I will never stop missing him. What I had not yet realized was that Father Killian was about to become even more helpful to us than he had been before.

*   *   *

Father Killian was gone, but he sent me a special gift while I grieved. Father had taught me about the great benefits of meditation, and I used to practice it each day, usually after lights out, when I could count on relative silence. This particular night I meditated on the Passion of Christ, but what happened was different from any other meditation I ever made, before or since. I seemed to participate in what my mind saw. I seemed to take the place of Christ. I felt the plucking of His beard. I felt my flesh being peeled off by the scourge. I felt the weight of the Cross on my shoulders. I felt the nails being driven through my wrists and feet. I felt the force of gravity cause the nails to rip my flesh as the Cross was dropped into place.

Then suddenly I was no longer in Christ's place but next to Him, in the place of Dismas. When I looked over at His Majesty, his head was bowed. Slowly He raised it to look at me, His expression so sad that it wrenched my heart. A solitary tear ran down His divine face. He seemed to be telling me He was thirsting for souls, reminding me of my duty to remain on the cross, through which I would give Him souls.

Suddenly my meditation ended. It had been so real to me that I actually looked myself over for injuries. At first I was baffled by the entire event. Then it dawned on me that Father Killian had sent me this extraordinary meditation. It was time to stop grieving and start working. Once again, I obeyed my spiritual director.

* * *

The day after Father Killian's funeral, I called Archbishop Oscar Lipscomb to ask him who would be our priest now. His Excellency said the Trinitarians were giving the parish to the archdiocese, but they would staff it until a new priest took over five months later, in June. Then he asked how many catechumens we had ready to be received into the

Church, and I told him we had seven men ready for baptism and First Communion.

His voice brightened, and he said, "I think it's time I come up there to see what you're doing. Would it be all right if I came to give them confirmation?"

My heart and soul soared! "Oh yes, Excellency! Please come", I replied. The archbishop promised to be with us May 7, 1992.

In the intervening months, it became obvious that Father Killian's prayers for us were carrying a lot of weight. First, I was inspired to make an act of consecration to the Sacred Heart of Jesus. Then, I went through the same thing for consecration to the Holy Spirit. Finally, I studied to make an act of consecration to the Immaculate Heart of Mary.

What was most fascinating was what happened to some of my boys. I never said a word to anyone about the consecrations I had made, yet men were suddenly coming to me individually with vague ideas of giving themselves to Our Blessed Mother. Although they did not understand what they were asking, I knew they wanted to make an act of consecration to her Immaculate Heart.

At this time, we had twenty to twenty-five men in our group. All of them took the faith very seriously. I called the group together to explain what an act of consecration to the Immaculate Heart of Mary is, what it means, and what obligations it entails. They all listened attentively as I explained, and all of them were honest about what they felt they could do. Thirteen of them decided to prepare for the act of consecration.

I realized that if we started the next day, using Saint Louis de Montfort's formula, our consecration day would coincide with the archbishop's visit. The exigencies of prison life being what they are, the only time we could all meet daily would be early in the morning, outside on the recreation yard, before any of us had to be at work. Faithfully, every day, in rain, snow, sleet, or burning sun, the fourteen of us met, and I led them through the preparation exercises. Other convicts threw things at us and called us horrible things while uttering terrible blasphemies. It is hard to tame pride after a lifetime of criminality, so several times I had to save our tormentors from the wrath of our group.

As the great day approached, the boys decided they wanted to modify the act of consecration to fit more particularly our situation. We rewrote the consecration to include our commitment to evangelize all prisoners, guards, and administration personnel, and their families, with the graces Mary would win for us.

Mike asked a priest who would be coming with the archbishop to bring a statue of Our Lady. I paid the convict gardener to clip thirteen flowers for us, so my boys could lay them at her feet. I paid another convict to draw Our Lady as the Immaculate Conception on a sheet of poster board in colored pencil and to copy the consecration on the back.

Father Jude McCaully, the Trinitarian filling in until we got our new priest, made a special trip to the prison the night before the archbishop was due, to baptize the seven men who needed that sacrament. Then he took all the men through a dry run of the planned events.

The archbishop arrived with an entourage that included a deacon and two priests. With Father Jude was a parish layman. Deputy Warden Greer was also present.

No man there could possibly forget his confirmation. Archbishop Lipscomb put his face close to each one so he could peer into the man's eyes. Then, pressing hard enough to stretch the skin white, His Excellency slowly traced the sign of the cross on each forehead as he said, "Be sealed . . . with . . . the gift . . . of the . . . Holy Spirit."

When Mass ended, thirteen men, converts, convicts, and sinners all, processed to the altar where Our Lady stood. Each one laid a flower at her royal feet and then knelt before her sacred image. As I led the reading of the consecration, each man followed along devoutly on his own copy. The consecration was made.

That day's Mass and act of consecration constituted a dramatic turning point for our little community. Afterward, our numbers simply exploded.

Alabama's free population is only 3.5 percent Catholic. Statistically, that same percentage is reflected in the prison population. The Catholic Church is hated, feared, and held in suspicion by a great majority of Alabamians. Most believe that we are evil and Hell-bound for being Catholic. Yet despite this, at the pinnacle of our success, Catholics made up 10 percent of our prison population.

I began to think the Holy Spirit was preparing His people to reach out to prisoners, their families, and their victims. The nation's prison population was just over one million, the highest per capita prison population in the world. At the same time, the Catholic laity had responded with such warmth and generosity to our pleas for assistance in that mission field that, with the help of several free-world people, I founded a new organization for the express purpose of carrying Christ's Catholic message into every prison in America. We called it First Century Christian Ministries (FCCM).

I wrote to the Alabama secretary of state for the forms necessary to make it a nonprofit corporation. Sitting on my bunk in the cellblock, with my godfather, Mike Mayola, and my first godson, Phil Hanna, I chartered FCCM with a board of directors and a chairman. The chairman was and is Dr. Joseph Strada of Virginia. As honorary board members we had Dr. Peter Kreeft of Boston College and Father Robert J. Fox.

Using addresses from all the letters I had received, and some shoestring funding, we began an FCCM newsletter, calling it *Prisoners of the Perfect Prisoner*. The future looked hopeful.

* * *

Then, just ten months after Father Killian's death, Chuck Greer died of a massive stroke, at the age of thirty-eight. Soon we had a new warden and a new deputy warden, who viewed everything Catholic with suspicion and resented our successful and growing programs. When these authorities discovered that I had established a national apostolate as an Alabama nonprofit corporation, right under their noses, they could not believe I had done it. They were furious. The new warden told me right up front to close FCCM down or he would have me killed. Then he threw me out of his office.

The next day the warden called me to his office again. He told me to break ties with FCCM or he would ask the attorney general to investigate and indict all those involved for running a con game. He admitted that ultimately no one would be convicted, but he suggested that several people involved would be bankrupted trying to defend themselves. I was unwilling to risk that possibility, so I promised to break all ties with FCCM while I was in prison.

We had all assumed that I would be granted parole soon. Many supporters had written letters urging my parole, and things looked promising. Nobody expected that I would still be in prison after all these years, and I planned to take over as president upon my release. But when the hearing came, one woman on the parole board, Judith O'Conner, demanded that I grant my confessors permission to tell them every sin I had ever confessed. Of course I could not do so, nor could Father Michael Sreboth have testified even if I had begged him to. As a result, parole was denied in 1995, and subsequent parole hearings were denied for the same cause. Fourteen years later, I am still a prisoner.

Today, Phil Hanna is president of FCCM, and he runs it under the supervision of Dr. Joseph Strada, the chairman. But it is teetering on the brink of oblivion. I hope it survives until the day I am free.

One morning shortly after that experience, I was called into the guard's office in the wee hours. Half a dozen guards were there. I started praying some Hail Marys, and before I had finished the first one, a guard hit me with his riot baton. From there on it was a free-for-all. I vaguely remember being dragged down the hall to the segregation unit by my wrists. I recall choking on my blood. I was kept in the single-man cell until I had healed enough to be seen.

It may shock the average reader to hear it, but the reform of prisoners by conversion to Catholicism was not welcomed by Alabama's penal system, not only because of the way its authorities were taught in their formative years, but for pragmatic reasons as well.

Like slaves in the Old South, inmates are considered less than human. Guards and other authorities go out of their way to deprive us of dignity. Power and violence are used to keep us cowed. We live in a constant state of fear. Beatings are quite common, as are bizarre punishments. Frequently we are told to do things that are otherwise considered illegal and immoral. To help keep us in line, we are often threatened with actions that will keep us from making parole or going to work release.

What prison authorities had discovered about practicing Catholics is that we cannot be controlled the way others are controlled. Faced with a choice between giving up human dignity or losing a chance for freedom, we choose to lose freedom. Given a choice between committing an immoral act or taking a beating, we take the beating. Because we know that Christ loves us, we will not be intimidated. We will not prostitute our human dignity to entertain or please our keepers.

It is ironic that Catholic evangelization has not been welcomed in the Alabama prison system, because it does so effectively what prison is supposed to do. On the whole, 70 to 80 percent of convicts return to prison within two years of release. Over the last sixteen years, most of our converts have been freed, but only 1.6 percent of them were later returned to prison. Evangelizing criminals to the Holy Roman Catholic Church, the one true Church Christ established for sinners, is the only proven method for reducing crime.

*   *   *

The hostility of prison authorities prevented FCCM from flourishing as I hoped. But God's Divine Providence sent us a different way to bring the light of the faith to convicts in other Alabama prisons. When the authorities finally had to admit to themselves that they could not stop the men from becoming Catholics, they reacted by splitting us up and sending us to prisons all over the state. It was traumatic to have our family split up, but in many ways our diaspora was a boon for God's ultimate plan, just as it had been in

Jerusalem two millennia ago. No two of the lay evangelists I had trained were sent to the same prison. Today, my godsons are competent, well-trained catechists and apologists actively teaching the faith at eleven of Alabama's thirteen prisons.

New evidence has surfaced in my case, and a legal team has my case before the court. Due to the possibility of a gag order, I cannot discuss any particulars here. Still, whether or not I ever get a new legal verdict, I am not bitter. From a physical perspective, these years have been hard on me. Yet this harsh journey has been worth far more than it has cost. God, who always brings good out of the bad things in our lives, has made prison one of the best things that ever happened to me. From a spiritual standpoint, I acquired a new life in prison. I am freer than most of the people I know in the outside world. My body is behind iron bars, stonewalls, and razor wire, but my spirit and soul are unchained.

If I had not come to prison I would probably have remained a bitter agnostic, denying God's gifts. Most likely I would never have become a Catholic. That means I would have missed the greatest blessing He can give, of sanctifying grace and the hope of eternal life with Him in Heaven. And had I not been converted to Catholicism in prison, a lot of other men might also have missed that same blessing. This, I believe, is where God wanted me to serve Him.

Early in his imprisonment, Russell Ford became a Catholic and entered on his lifelong conversion experience. After launching his Catholic evangelism program, he was officially installed as a lector and catechist by Archbishop Oscar Lipscomb, by authority of the 1984 Catholic Code of Canon Law. Under the supervision of Archbishop Raymond Burke of Saint Louis, he earned the status of Marian Catechist. The evangelism program he established has made some three hundred inmate converts, seventy-six of them Ford's own godsons.

Ford's articles have been published in popular Catholic publications, including This Rock, Communio, Homiletic and Pastoral Review, Catholic World Report, the Wanderer, Immaculate Heart Messenger, and Militia Immaculata. He is the author of The Missionary's Catechism (*Magnificat Institute Press, 1998*), currently in use as a text in Catholic parish religious education in the United States, Great Britain, Australia, and South Africa.

During his years of incarceration, Ford also earned a business degree from Faulkner University, a degree in computer science from J. F. Ingram State Technical College, and certification as a cabinet maker from J. F. Ingram. He also earned certification as a Laubach literacy tutor and, with inmate Phil Hanna, cofounded the first inmate-tutored GED (General Educational Development) program in the Alabama Department of Corrections. Later, Governor Guy Hunt ordered the program duplicated in all Alabama prisons.

Currently, Russ is petitioning the Alabama court for disclosure of evidence, which could overturn his conviction and release him from his prison sentence. He asks that readers, in their charity, include his intention in their prayers.

Chapter 23

How Many Ways Are There to God?

Vivian Dudro

"How many ways are there to God?" a journalist once asked Joseph Cardinal Ratzinger, now Pope Benedict XVI.

"As many as there are individuals", answered the cardinal, who was then head of the Congregation for the Doctrine of the Faith.

The statement might seem inconsistent with the Church's assertion that none other than Jesus can reconcile us to God, that Jesus alone died and rose again so that all may have communion with the Father through Him, but it is not inconsistent. Whenever we find ourselves in the arms of our Father, it is Christ, however invisible, who has carried us there.

My own path to God began in my early childhood, when I was so sick that my parents thought I would soon die. From infancy, I had been a frail, unhealthy child, and when I was two years old doctors discovered that a tumor was to blame. After surgery and chemotherapy, my prognosis was poor, and my mother began preparing me for death. Though she had been raised in a haphazard mix of Southern-style Protestantism, Christian Science, and Freemasonry, Mother had entered the Episcopal church at some point. I do not know when or why she made that step toward Catholic Christianity, but as a result, I was baptized in 1962, at the age of three.

Mother told me about the good God who creates everything. He lives in a beautiful place called Heaven, she said, and He invites every person, even children like me, to live there with Him in perfect happiness forever. She told me about children who suffered difficulties even greater than my own. Would I not part with some of my toys for their sakes? she asked me. Well, not cheerfully, for I was not one of those sickly but saintly children one reads about in books. I cried when she gave some of my things away.

Mother introduced me not only to God but also to beauty, the intense beauty that still brings tears to my eyes and convinces me there is more to reality than randomly moving molecules. A classical pianist who practiced almost every day, she let me lie beneath her piano while she played lovely pieces by her favorite composers: Grieg, Liszt, and Chopin.

Like some other artistic people, Mother suffered from mental illness and went in and out of psychiatric wards. Our affectionate and loyal live-in housekeeper took such good care of my two brothers and me that we hardly noticed when our mother was not well. That is, until she jumped out a window in our downtown Chicago apartment.

Even then, my older brother, Don, was the only one of us children who knew the reason we were abruptly packed up and sent to live with our maternal grandparents. It was days or perhaps even weeks before I knew that my mother had died, and years before I learned the whole story. Burdened with shame and grief that was borne stoically, at least in front of my brothers and me, neither my father nor my grandparents took us to our mother's funeral, or to her burial in an unmarked grave. I do not recall anyone telling me that I must not cry or speak of her, yet I felt as though the grown-ups in my life expected me to soldier on as if she had never existed. So I withdrew into my sad little self and wrote stories about orphaned creatures in search of a home.

Grandmother's faith was a mixture of Christianity and the spiritual fads of her day, but while I lived with her, she knelt and prayed beside my bed each night. She taught me the Our Father, the Hail Mary, the Glory Be, and "Now I lay me down to sleep ..." She told me that I had a guardian angel and that I must always try to be a good girl, even though being naughty usually seemed easier.

Grandmother knew Catholic prayers because when she was about four years old, some kind of misfortune visited her parents, and they sent her and her sisters to a convent boarding school that was also an orphanage. She told me stories of sneaking into bed with her older sisters, stealing persimmons from the convent orchard, and listening for the clicking Rosary beads that always betrayed Mother Superior when she was closing in on some mischief.

After a while, my father settled us in a house about a mile from my grandparents. Over the course of several years, he hired various live-in housekeepers, some of whom worked out better than others, and none of whom stayed for very long. One wrinkled woman watched the vampire show *Dark Shadows* every afternoon and occasionally read me stories from an illustrated children's Bible. My favorite housekeeper was Frances, a young, pretty German woman who tried to make our house into a home. She baked us cakes, sewed me clothes, and gave me a Rosary, though I did not know what it was. Unfortunately, she stayed only about a year, and when she left I felt like I was losing a mother all over again.

To lend my father a hand and give us a more stable environment, Dad's parents took us children for the summers.

They had a large place in a small Wisconsin town near Lake Michigan where we could climb trees, sail boats, and go fishing to our heart's content. Unlike my maternal grand-mother, my father's mother spoke so little to me that I was astonished to learn later she had once been a schoolteacher. She turned me over to the care of a "summer girl", while my brothers were kept in line by my grandfather's hired hands.

In spite of the summer girl, I spent many hours playing alone in my grandfather's Japanese garden, which he had created out of a marshy parcel by constructing a series of waterfalls and ponds. He built a teahouse by one pool, and a curved bridge over another, which he stocked with rainbow trout. He laid stone walks through beds of exotic plants, which he tended on his hands and knees. Throughout the garden were statues of Asian deities—Buddha, of course, in his lotus position, but also lovely goddesses with asymmetrically swaying garments. These mysterious beings awakened in me, a sensitive, griev-ing child, a pagan longing to connect with the divine. Quite spontaneously, I sang and danced and left offerings of flow-ers to them and wrote petitions for this and that, which I tucked underneath their dainty feet. Through them, I tried to communicate with my mother, who I thought surely dwelled in the Heaven she had described.

The daughter of Grandmother's cleaning lady encour-aged me in these practices. Occasionally her mother brought her along to my grandparents', and a few times I went to their house, where a statue of the Blessed Virgin stood enshrined in a backyard arbor. There my playmate took me to pray, and Mary's eyes, unlike those of my goddesses, were open and seemed to look tenderly upon me.

Dad's parents neither prayed nor discussed matters of faith. If such things did come up in conversation, Grandfather would frown. "Religions are just fairy tales", he would say. "Christianity is a fairy tale that happens to be true", I wish I could reply to him now.

Several years after he died, I learned from one of his sisters that Grandfather and all his siblings had been baptized Catholics. My great-grandmother was born to Irish immigrants who homesteaded in the Dakota Territory. When she was eight years old, her mother was kicked by a cow and died of the subsequent infection. The priest failed to arrive in time to give her last rites, and her disappointed and bereaved husband never again went to Mass.

My great-grandmother married a skeptical newspaper man, and they surrounded themselves with intellectuals, authors, and progressive political activists. When their children were young, the live-in Irish maid scolded, "It's bad enough for you to leave the Church, but it's even worse for you to neglect the souls of your children." Great-grandmother must have felt a pang of conscience, for she gave the maid permission to take my grandfather and his brothers and sisters to a priest for instruction.

Some Protestant neighbors did for me what the Irish maid did for my grandfather. Seeing that Dad was indifferent toward religion, they took me to church and Sunday school. One of these evangelically minded families had a daughter about my age. Laura and I became close friends, and she brought me with her to Awana Club, a Baptist organization that teaches children the Scriptures and leads them to Christ.

At many of these Awana meetings the teacher used a felt board with removable felt characters to tell Bible stories or morality tales. Once one of the characters was a cross little girl about my age. "Do you see how unhappy this little girl is?" asked the teacher. "This is because she has placed herself on the throne of her heart. She is selfish and cares nothing at all about anybody else." Then the teacher put up an image of a girl with a sweet and gentle face. "Now this little girl is happy, and do you know why? Because she has made Jesus the king of her heart. Jesus loves her very much, and she loves Him back by being obedient to her parents and kind to others." Then the teacher placed on the board a figure of Jesus with His arms held out to receive me. "Now, children, let us close our eyes and fold our hands and ask Jesus to come into our hearts to be our Savior and Lord."

I was about nine years old, and I did just as she asked, praying silently but intently, *Dear Jesus, please come into my heart and be my Savior and Lord and help me to be a good girl.*

Needless to say, I was not instantly transformed into a young Saint Catherine of Siena. For one thing, my life at home lacked discipline. Dirty dishes and rumpled clothes lay about in every room. Pets of all sorts—rodents, cats, birds, snakes, lizards, fish, and a dog—inhabited untidy niches throughout the house. Dad and my brothers conducted scientific experiments and erected building projects in the basement and backyard. We children quarreled a lot with each other but got along well with our father, who took us to boatyards, museums, and even bars. He gave us very few rules to follow, unless we were sailing with him on Lake Michigan.

All that changed when Dad remarried in 1970. Eleven years old, I very much welcomed the idea of having a new mother. My departed mother had already become a faded memory, and I was ashamed of the way we lived. Nevertheless, the foundation shook beneath my feet when our stepmother began imposing some necessary cleanliness and order. She established a family dinner time and forbade eating in front of the television or in any place other than at the table. She assigned chores that needed to be done before and after school and on Saturdays, and if we failed to complete them well or on time we were punished. Overcoming bad habits and replacing them with good ones was extremely difficult for me and my brothers. The climb toward virtue goes uphill, and the later in life it is begun, the harder it is.

Within a year of her joining the family, our stepmother gave birth to a baby boy, and a new situation emerged. On the Sunday after our second Christmas together, the Feast of the Holy Family, a priest baptized my new half-brother and blessed the marriage vows of my father and stepmother. Sadly, this event did not unite our family. Dad seemed to grow distant from my brothers and me, and we began to feel like unwanted strangers in our own home.

We children were too immature to recognize that Dad had new responsibilities and that our stepmother had her hands full with a baby and three nearly grown, but not very well behaved, older children. In our eyes nothing our stepmother did was quite enough. She got up with us in the morning to cook us breakfast, pack our lunches, and drive us to school when we missed the bus. She washed and mended our clothes and cooked us dinner every night. Yet I had a nagging sense that our family was wounded and that my brothers and I were misfits. Out of self-pity, and in an unspoken pact with my older brother, I started to rebel. I became argumentative and uncooperative both at home and at school and looked for escape among friends with worse problems and vices than my own.

At the age of fourteen I impulsively ran away. I had been grounded for speaking disrespectfully to my stepmother, and without a penny in my pocket or a plan in my head, I climbed out my second-story bedroom window. Dad pulled into the driveway as I was hanging from the sill and called, "Vivian, what are you doing?"

"I'm running away."

"Okay, you do that", he said.

With wounded pride, I decided to head for my grandfather's place in Wisconsin. Dusk had fallen by the time I stood hitch-hiking on I-94. If I had not been so stupidly obstinate, I would have been scared to death. A kindly gentleman who looked and talked like television host Mister Rogers picked me up. When we reached the state line, he pulled into a truck stop "to get us something to eat", and while there, he called the police.

As I was being led by the arm to the patrol car, I was both pained at his "betrayal" and relieved to be going home.

"Do you realize how lucky you were to be picked up by such a good man?" asked the officer who drove me back to my hometown. He gently but firmly explained the terrible things that could have happened to me, and when he asked me why I had acted so rashly, I could only whimper that I had a mean stepmother.

At the police station Dad excoriated me for causing him and my stepmother so much worry. He said I had acted selfishly and thoughtlessly, and I knew he was right, though I was not about to admit it. At some level I understood that his reaction revealed love and concern for me, but I wanted more from him: his attention, understanding, and affection. My stepmother, whom I have since grown to love and appreciate greatly, claims to this day that I was a different child after that incident. I did become meeker and more helpful at home because my childhood grief, which had developed into adolescent anger, turned inward instead.

During those trying teenage years, a good friend entered my life. Audrey lived around the corner, and we had attended the same kindergarten, but she had spent her grammar school years at the parochial school, while I continued at the public school. Now, attending the same municipal high school drew us together again.

Audrey had been born in Germany, and her family observed many customs that I found very attractive. During the Christmas season they lit real candles on their Christmas tree. Holy water fonts hung throughout the house, and in her jewelry box, my friend kept holy cards and tiny relics. On special days they ate special foods, like homemade doughnuts on Shrove Tuesday. At other times they abstained from meat or gave up treats. Their traditions seemed to match and give meaning to the cycles of nature and of life itself.

I enjoyed many happy hours with Audrey, and together we planned a trip to Germany. I signed up for a German course at school and found a part-time job at the public library. Our dreams and plans came to fruition two years later, the summer before our senior year, when we traveled through Germany with Audrey's grandmother, staying with their relatives along the way and making side trips into France and Italy.

We visited many Catholic churches, and they made a tremendous impression on me. The presence of God was palpable in the incense-scented sanctuaries, and I could not help but kneel and pray. Notre Dame in Paris especially filled me with awe. The alcoves peopled by sculpted saints and the cold stony darkness dappled with colored light from stained glass windows lifted my mind to thoughts of God. I felt particularly close to my mother there, and though I had never been taught to pray for the dead, I lit a candle and prayed for her soul.

In Trier, Germany, on the Feast of Corpus Christi, we witnessed a procession as it wove its way through the old narrow streets. Young girls in white dresses with flowers in their hair scattered rose petals on the ground, while altar boys in black cassocks and lace-trimmed white surplices manfully carried large ornate candlesticks. Behind them the bishop walked solemnly under a canopy held up by several men. Wrapped in a kind of shawl that cloaked both his person and his hands, the bishop carried the Host aloft in something that looked like a golden sunburst. Without knowing a thing about the holiday being celebrated, or even the meaning of the words *Corpus Christi*, I perceived God beckoning me, but I did not know how to answer His invitation.

* * *

When we graduated from high school, Audrey and I went our separate ways—she to a private and prestigious university, I to a small Midwestern liberal arts college. Looking for adventure, I signed up for a "wilderness experience" orientation, which involved two weeks of backpacking and canoeing in Canada. Searching for the truth that would make sense of my life, I enrolled in a "Self, Society, and Values" introduction to the liberal arts. From the very first day of trudging through the mountains, I was bombarded with socialism, feminism, and environmentalism. The themes were sustained in the classroom, where I was taught that the egalitarian paradise visualized by the eighteenth- and nineteenth-century revolutionaries had yet to be fully realized because of stubbornly resistant man-made constructs like authority and because of socially conditioned behavior like mothers taking care of infants. My professors combined contempt for Western civilization and the Christianity that is its bedrock with smug confidence that they could transform the world into a better place. Bereft of Audrey's stabilizing influence, and beset by unresolved disappointment with myself and my family, I fell for this leftist view of things. Before long I was a vegetarian radical "in love" with a senior.

I turned my back on Jesus, but He did not turn away from me. My childhood friend Laura, who was attending a nearby evangelical Bible college, began writing me letters exhorting me to keep the faith. An on-campus Christian group hounded me to join them in prayer. I did so a few times, and someone among them gave me a green pocket-sized Psalms and New Testament. This I began to read every day, first a Psalm and then a chapter from the Gospels or Epistles. However, after stumbling over some passages on marriage by Saint Paul, I threw the book aside. *Surely the man was an antiquated chauvinist*, I thought. Christianity, therefore, must be on the wrong side of history, while I was as an agent of progress, free to reject "conventional norms" of behavior and invent my own standards to suit only myself.

After my freshman year, I went to Oregon for an internship in an "eco-utopian community" that had advertised itself at my college. When I arrived I was shown a pile of two-by-fours and a forest and told to build myself a platform six feet above the ground without hammering any nails into the trees. I threw myself joyfully into the task and thought I had at last discovered the way human beings ought to live.

The land was owned in common by an odd group of countercultural types, including two California university professors who had left their families to live with coeds in the woods. We summer interns were assigned projects for which we received college credit. Mine was rebuilding a kiln that had been photographed frequently while being taken apart and now was a heap of bricks. Other students were farming using organic techniques, pasteurizing human waste with solar energy panels in order to make fertilizer, and developing new methods of wastewater treatment. Meanwhile, we defecated in oil drums full of sawdust and bathed in a nearby lake.

Work teams were organized for cooking and washing up, and everyone managed to get along rather well, at least on the surface; but here was no Heaven on earth. A cohabitating couple basing their lives together on nothing more than the Beatles' mantra "Love is all you need" frequently argued and then smoothed things over by smoking hash. A professor's children from his previous marriage came to visit him in the tepee he shared with his girlfriend and their offspring, and it was written on their faces that they felt abandoned by the adults who should be taking care of them. A polyamorous group homesteading nearby showed up in our camp to recruit new members, and their slogan that "everybody belongs to everybody else", inspired by Marx, left me cold. Questions pressed upon my mind: Is marriage between one man and one woman an arbitrary social convention designed to inhibit and enslave? Or does marriage serve to protect spouses and their children from human caprice?

Another thought provoker was a lecture on civil disobedience delivered by a group determined to shut down a nuclear power plant on the Oregon coast. The leaders of this effort were members of the Communist Party, and they explained that all of their propaganda against radioactive waste was beside the point. Closing nuclear power plants was only a means to an end, they said. The long-term goal was to bring the United States' economy to its knees. Unconvinced that this was a reasonable way to bring about positive social change, I did not sign up for further information about how I could help the cause.

Ideologies aside, my childhood paganism awoke from its slumber that summer. Often I would steal away by myself to a picturesque spot in the forest and adore the beauty before me. These moments, however, left me gripped by loneliness and uncertainty, for nature does not love one back. Living outdoors as crudely as I was, I had no illusions that the trees, insects, and animals were friendly toward me, as they were to Walt Disney's Snow White. Quite the reverse, I discovered; the untamed wilderness is harsh and unfit for human habitation. For all I knew, if there was a God, He might be only an impersonal clockmaker, who created the cosmos and all of its amazing mechanics but who is as indifferent to the sufferings of men as He is to a mudslide.

When the summer was over, I headed to Philadelphia for an urban studies internship. I was assigned to a for-credit job with an environmental lawyer who was suing the city over its noncompliance with federal water quality statutes. Two other sophomores and I shared a cheap, semifurnished apartment in an Asian immigrant neighborhood bordering a black ghetto. We tore up the filthy carpeting and threw it out the window, painted the walls, and scrubbed every inch of the place.

Living in this location placed me and my roommates in the way of frightening, but instructive, experiences. Twice I was almost mugged or raped but managed somehow to talk my assailant out of hurting me. One brazen fellow ended up sympathizing with me and my roommates, as we had lost our way home and had ended up in a very rough block. With the help of two companions he walked us back to our apartment because, as he said, "If we don't hurt you, somebody else will." As he spoke these words a brick thrown by a youth across the street crashed on the sidewalk behind me. Though my heart was pounding in a physical reaction to danger, my mind remained uncannily calm, as if some invisible but benevolent force was protecting me.

As we walked side by side, I asked the young man, who could not have been more than sixteen years old, why his hands were bandaged with bandanas. "Are you hurt?"

"You really are stupid", he said. "No, I ain't hurt. I wrapped my hands 'cause I might git me into a fight."

Curiosity got the better of me, and I asked him if he went around bullying people because he saw nothing wrong with that.

"You think I don't know the difference between right and wrong?" he huffed indignantly. "Of course I do, but I gotta become a man somehow. You're just lucky I decided that for right now I'm gonna be nice to you."

In a flash, I saw that the choice of this young man to do me a good turn demolished the environmental determinist argument against free will.

Working at a public interest law firm introduced me to a wide assortment of politically involved people and the ideologies that inspired them. A woman whose boss was suing the police department for brutality invited me to a Marxist book club, where I met some local union leaders. Soon I learned that the American Communists operating inside the East Coast labor unions were not interested in helping working men obtain better pay or benefits but only in ushering in the revolution. Hmm. Where had I heard that before?

Vanguard feminists I met at a party tried to persuade me that in order to advance women's rights, I must become completely emancipated from men, that is, become a lesbian. They asked me to join their group, which was a cross between the Island of Sappho and a witches' coven. Their arguments failed to convince me, though, for they revealed the ugly core of feminism and clarified my nascent desire to marry someday and have children.

To fulfill a class assignment, and the demands of social justice, I signed on to my roommate's scheme to prevent our landlord from collecting any more rent from his tenants, including us, until certain demands for improvements to the building were met. This kind of collective refusal to pay bills is called community organizing, and conveniently, it also saved me money. Long ago my actions had become inexplicable to my father, but when he heard about this move he asked sadly, "How can you say you are just when you are cheating your landlord out of money you agreed to pay him?" I pretended to ignore the question, but it planted a seed of self-doubt.

The seed had grown into a sapling by the time I returned to my college campus and resumed regular classes in the spring of my sophomore year, disillusioned and confused. I needed to declare a major and had no idea what to choose. Toward the end of the quarter, I was so depressed that I had difficulty deciding whether to get up or stay in bed, to eat or not, to go to class or skip it. My behavior became more and more irrational—wandering through the seedy side of town, walking along the middle of train tracks, skateboarding down hilly streets in the middle of the night. What, or Whom, was I seeking? My mother's death began to haunt me, and I feared I was losing my mind. I met with the campus psychologist and told her my life story. She had me write down my "achievements" on a piece of paper and lent me a book on positive thinking. I left her office in a state of despair.

There really is nothing, then, I said to myself. *Everyone makes up his own reality, and therefore everyone's reality is equally unreal.*

One morning when I rose from my bed, I fell to the floor, weeping. "Oh, God, I'm so sorry for making a mess of my life", I cried. "If you are there, please save me."

My tears subsided, and I stood up convinced that Someone had not only heard but answered my prayer. Walking into the common room where my roommates had sat up all night studying for finals, I announced, "Jesus Christ is real!"

They looked up from their notes and books with expressions on their faces that said, "She's cracked."

I too might have thought that I was crazy, except that a couple of days later I answered my dorm room door and there was my brother Don with a Bible under his arm. We had been talking on the phone a lot lately, and he and some other members of my family had become alarmed by my condition. He had flown from Arizona to Michigan, to bring me back with him to his place, he said.

We went to a pizza joint, where he told me the story of his conversion, which until that moment had been unknown to me. Even more angry and rebellious than I, Don had become increasingly self-destructive. He had raised his fist at the heavens in agony and demanded, "God, if You are there, show Yourself to me."

God did show Himself—in the love and mercy of Christ. Now he was going to a Baptist church and living a responsible life with a few other guys who called themselves born-again Christians. He had been praying for me, he said, to have a conversion experience like his. Years later I found out that Laura had also been praying, and even fasting, for me.

I did not leave with Don just then because I wanted to finish my finals. I snapped out of my depression and wrapped up the school year. On my way to Arizona, I stopped in Wisconsin to see if I had any other options besides Jesus. Since my grandmother's death a few years back, Grandfather had sold the old place and had dramatically downsized his living quarters. Sad, lonely, and unoccupied, he could not last long on his own, he admitted, and he talked about moving into an assisted-living apartment next to his sister in Florida. While staying with him I fell back into doubt, depression, and erratic and dangerous behavior. Grandfather was distressed that I seemed headed for some kind of disaster, and so was I. While he put no stock in religion, he counseled me to follow my brother's advice.

I moved in with Don first, and then with my mother's sister. Aunt Lynn and Uncle George, who lived near my retired maternal grandparents, provided me with a very supportive environment. Aunt Lynn said she believed in God and the power of prayer, but she and Uncle George mistrusted "organized religion". She read a daily devotional published by the Unity Society of Practical Christianity, while Uncle George would laugh at both of us, saying, "Churches are nothing but businesses."

In spite of his jabs, which were kindly meant, I regularly attended Sunday service and Wednesday night Bible study at my brother's Baptist church. Reading the Scriptures and coming to terms with the demands of the gospel challenged me, but this was a joyful chapter in my life, for I was convinced I had encountered the living Lord, who had saved me and my brother from the pit of destruction. He had endured His Passion and death out of love for us, and so I loved Him in return.

* * *

Soon I found a job, and after a couple of months, with the help of my relatives, I bought a car. Having achieved this much stability, I enrolled in the local state university to finish some kind of degree. With two other evangelical Christians, I rented a house closer to campus. Then I landed a reporting job on the student newspaper that would cover my tuition and living expenses. For the first time in my life, I felt like a virtually normal person. It was a new year, 1980, and in a few months I would be twenty-one.

I wanted to continue my studies in the liberal arts, and on the recommendations of other Christian students, I signed up for a class on American cultural history. It was taught by a Jew whose keen and often humorous insights made me think and laugh so hard that my head reeled and my sides ached by the time class was over. The professor assigned works of political philosophy by Leo Strauss, Harry Jaffa, and Eric Voegelin, all of whom helped me to understand where my intellectual development had taken a wrong turn. A pivotal book was C. S. Lewis' *The Abolition of Man*, which lays bare the irrationality and even monstrousness of moral relativism. I looked up other titles by Lewis, and soon I was reading his *Mere Christianity*, followed by G. K. Chesterton's *Orthodoxy*, which I found on the same shelf in a nearby Christian bookstore. I replaced my former ideological notions with a more credible explanation for all the heartache in the world: original sin.

My Jewish professor had also experienced a conversion. He had not been raised in a religious home, but at some point he came to know God as Being, as Moses did when God revealed himself as "I AM." He greatly respected the faith of his Christian students, but he made a few comments that led some of us to deduce that he favored Catholicism over Protestantism. "If you are interpreting the Scriptures for yourself, you're writing them", he said in defense of sacred Tradition during a lecture on early American Christian sects. Once he complained that he was under the law, and not under grace, so a student dared to ask him why he did not become a Christian.

"The Incarnation is serious business", he answered. Like many of the other Protestants in the class, I had never heard that term before; when I looked it up, I discovered a thread that would lead me to the Catholic Church.

At this time I also was taking another recommended class on the poet John Milton. The professor, who introduced me to *Paradise Lost*, impressed me immediately as a man of both erudition and faith. I made an appointment to see him and asked him directly whether he believed in God.

Yes, he said, he was a Roman Catholic who had experienced a spiritual awakening. He knew other students on campus with faith and zeal like mine. Would I like to meet them? He introduced me to Nan, a graduate student who became a dear friend, a mentor, and eventually my confirmation sponsor.

As an undergraduate, Nan had been involved in the Catholic charismatic movement at the University of Notre Dame, and she took me to an ecumenical prayer meeting at the nearby Newman Center. The waving of hands, singing in tongues, and prophesying unnerved me a little, but reading from the Scriptures and praying extemporaneously were comfortingly familiar forms of devotion. Most inviting were the other students, who after the meetings talked intelligently about their faith and current issues both on campus and in the world at large. At the student newspaper, I was grappling daily with abortion, homosexuality, and pornography, all of which had proliferated because of a false understanding of human rights, and here I was meeting Christian young people, both Catholics and Protestants, who thought seriously about these topics and yet exuded hope, joy, and brotherly love for one another. In a spirit of common cause

and with the encouragement and advice of my English professor, we met regularly to pray and support each other. As
our numbers grew, great and lasting friendships were formed.
Many couples who later married met each other within
this group, including my husband and I.

One day I happened to enter the Newman Center while
the Mass was being celebrated, and I was surprised to discover a service more worshipful than the one at my church.
The atmosphere was informal, with university students in
shorts and sandals and the musicians playing guitar and piano,
but the words of "Glory to God in the highest ..." and
"Holy, holy, holy ..." moved me to pray with the congregation. The words and gestures of the priest I did not understand, and even mistrusted a little, but they culminated in
the Host, held aloft to the words "This is the Lamb of
God, who takes away the sins of the world. Happy are those
who are called to his supper." As at that Corpus Christi
procession in Germany, I was being summoned.

The next time that I attended the monthly communion
service at my Baptist church, I was stuck by the contrast
between it and the Mass. The pastor read the same words
from the story of the Last Supper that the priest had recited
during the consecration, yet the minister and his congregation believed that the bread and grape juice remained
unchanged and that intimacy with the Lord was not to be
had by consuming them. As the platters of tiny crackers
and cups made the rounds through the pews, I saw no point
in taking my portion.

Coincidentally, at this time our Baptist young adult group
was learning about the Catholic Church. A guest minister,
who fancied himself an expert on this topic, gave several
weekly lectures on the many errors of Catholics: they are
idolaters who worship Mary and the saints; they believe in

dogmas, such as the Assumption of Mary, that are not found in the Scriptures; they try to earn their way to Heaven with their own good works and do not allow Jesus to be their Savior; they go to confession one day and commit the same sin the next, never really repenting because they can simply go to confession over and over again.

My charismatic Catholic friends knew and lived their faith in Christ admirably well, yet I did not know enough about the Catholic Church to defend them from these spurious claims. So I went to the university library in search of Catholic classics and found some works by Saint Thomas Aquinas and *The Confessions* by Saint Augustine. These convinced me that Catholicism deserved more respect than that shown by the minister, so I decided to talk things over with my pastor.

"I am troubled by some of the statements about Catholics that are being made in class", I said. "I do not think they are accurate."

He admitted that not everything Baptists say about Catholics is entirely correct, but he maintained that people must be kept away from the Catholic Church by any means because she is the Whore of Babylon in the book of Revelation.

"Are you telling me that you use error to teach truth?" I asked.

He did not deny it, and I stopped attending his church.

Though no longer a Baptist, I was not ready to become a Catholic. There were still dogmas, like papal infallibility, that I did not yet understand, and the divisions in the Church disturbed me. A seminarian I met at the Newman Center told me that he did not believe in the bodily Resurrection of Jesus but wanted to become a priest in order to build better social structures to help the poor and oppressed. He had been reading works of liberation theology and sounded more like a Marxist than a Christian, and I was through with Marxists. Some of the Dominican preachers at the Newman Center made a terrific amount of sense, but others ranted like leftists, championing the cause of the Communist Sandinistas in Nicaragua, for example. *More of Lenin's "useful idiots"*, I thought. Then I read Thomas Merton's *Seven Storey Mountain* and recognized that these misguided clerics were not representing the Catholic faith but the same modern messianic ideologies that Merton and I had fallen for and then rejected. If Merton had found a home in the Catholic Church, then perhaps I could as well.

Meanwhile, my evangelical housemates were warning me to stay clear of the Catholic Church and exhorting me instead to check out their congregation, which boasted a large group of university students. Aunt Lynn suggested I return to the Episcopal church. "After all, dear, why would you want to join a church that says you must have all the babies you can?"

The statement revealed both her concern for me and her ignorance of Catholic doctrine. Already reading about Catholic sexual morality, I was coming to the conclusion that the Catholic Church, with its appeal to natural law, was the only Christian body consistent on these matters. My Catholic sensibilities toward sex had already begun to be formed by my public high school "health" teacher, who had courageously diverged from the curriculum and shown my class photos of aborted babies, forever etching in my mind the injustice and barbarity of killing a child in his mother's womb. Thanks to my back-to-nature episode, I had already discarded as oxymoronic such notions as "free love" and "safe sex" and considered contraceptives repulsive, if not harmful, to a woman.

Though studying, praying, and even occasionally going to Mass, I still was not sure if I should enter the Church. One night, after having put the student newspaper to bed, I was driving home and praying out loud.

"Jesus, here I am lost again. How can I possibly judge if the Catholic Church is the right one? What should I do?" Just then, out of the corner of my eye, I caught a glimpse of a red light and noticed that I was passing a modern Catholic Church with big glass windows facing the road. I pulled into the parking lot and walked up the steps to peer through the front entrance. All was dark inside except for a golden glow illuminating the sanctuary and a tiny red flame burning beside the tabernacle. *Surely the church is closed for the night*, I thought, but I tried the doors, and they opened. I walked in and knelt in a pew. The modern interior was plain and uninspiring, the plastic crucifix I found ugly; but all that was shrouded in darkness, and my attention was riveted to the tabernacle in front. I bowed my head and prayed again, "Jesus, please tell me what to do."

In the silence I heard a voice, within me but not my own: "Go to daily Mass and you will know."

Years later I had the opportunity to tell this story to the longtime pastor of that parish. His eyes opened wide with surprise, and he said, "It was a miracle that you happened by on a night when I forgot to lock the church."

A Dominican priest from the Newman Center celebrated a weekday noon Mass in a small ecumenical chapel on the university campus, and I began attending regularly. Usually when the priest lifted the Host and said, "This is the Lamb of God ...", my eyes would brim with tears. Somehow I had the grace to believe that the Lord was drawing near to me, and I longed to receive Him in Communion.

After seeing me there at Mass a few times, one of the older priests approached me and said, "I noticed that you cry a fair amount. Are those tears of sorrow or tears of joy?"

"They must be tears of joy, Father, for I do not know why I cry, and I cannot seem to help it."

"Ah, well", he said. "Those tears are a gift of God. Benefit from them while you can."

* * *

After several months of daily Masses, combined with continued study of the history and teachings of the Catholic Church, I asked the pastor of the Newman Center if I might become a Catholic.

"Of course you can", he said. "Have you ever been baptized?"

I explained that I had been christened in the Episcopal church and later immersed by Baptists who told me that I had been too young to be validly baptized.

"Either one of those would have been sufficient", Father said, and with a sigh of tremendous relief, I knew I had at last come to the right place.

The time had arrived to tell my dear brother Don that I had made up my mind to become a Catholic. The news troubled him, and he begged me to talk it over with my former Baptist pastor before making my decision final.

I agreed and met with the man one last time. When he told me that I would go to Hell if I became a Catholic, I said, "But you Baptists say that once a person makes Jesus his personal Lord and Savior, he cannot lose his salvation."

He said that was true: people who *really* accept Jesus do not lose their salvation. How one *really* accepts Jesus, he

did not explain, but he told me about his Catholic grandmother, who, fearful of God's judgment all of her life, had
died without knowing that this kind of faith in Jesus could
have provided "assurance of salvation". He then warned me
that such a fate awaited me and that one day I would regret
my decision.

I have not regretted my decision. From my first Holy
Week, which ended with the Easter Vigil and my confirmation and First Communion, received with trembling hands
and tears of inexpressible joy, the sacraments and seasons of
the Church have been the fount of my life. Hidden in the
mysteries celebrated by the Catholic Church, I have found
the God I had ached for as a child and searched for as a
young adult. Rather, I should say that the Lord has found
me, for it is Christ Himself who goes in search of the lost
lambs and carries them home upon His shoulders.

*Vivian Dudro and her husband live in San Francisco, where both
work for Ignatius Press. They have four children, two in college
and two being educated at home.*